AN AGE OF CONFLICT

READINGS IN TWENTIETH CENTURY EUROPEAN HISTORY

AN AGE OF CONFLICT

READINGS IN TWENTIETH CENTURY EUROPEAN HISTORY

LESLIE DERFLER

Florida Atlantic University

HARCOURT BRACE JOVANOVICH, PUBLISHERS

San Diego New York Chicago Austin Washington, D.C.
London Sydney Tokyo Toronto

PREFACE

This volume comprises a collection of readings taken from the books and articles of forty-six historians writing on thirteen topics in twentieth-century European history. It is intended to supplement, not to replace, a main study textbook. The topics range from the reorientation of social thought and the origins of World War I to the coming single European market and the recent overthrow of communism in many former Eastern bloc countries. Different, and sometimes conflicting, interpretations are presented for each topic. The readings were selected not only for the information they provide but to show how historians writing on the same subject differ, and how once-popular interpretations can give way to other ones. For example — and at the risk of oversimplification — one historian describes the Nazis as the product of the German past; another sees them as criminals relied on by capitalists who had forsaken parliamentary means to preserve their assets; a third sees Nazism as not essentially different from communism; and a fourth regards it as a desperate effort by the middle classes to maintain economic and social respectability. Students can consider how each interpretation may fit a particular period or ideological orientation and ask whether it was only coincidental that the "Nazism as Germanism" school gained prominence during World War II, the "Nazism-as-no-different-from-communism" school during the Cold War, and so on.

The readings also provide some more recent analyses: Roy Medvedev on Stalinism, Jill Stephenson on how German women fared under Nazi rule, Walter Laqueur on why the Allies did nothing about the Holocaust, and Vickers and Wright on the motives of those interested in "privatizing" state-owned industries and utilities. Hence, the anthology provides supplementary readings and a modest introduction to the history of historical writing on twentieth-century Europe. In so doing it informs the student, whether "major" or "nonmajor," about the nature of the discipline.

Are "readers" still appropriate? I would obviously suggest they are. At a time when book costs are soaring, students cannot be expected to purchase the number required even to begin exploring the literature relevant to a particular topic. Admittedly, using an anthology is a poor substitute for going to the reserve room of a library and reading assigned pages in the books where these pages originally appeared. But, for universities and colleges struggling with inadequate library budgets, especially with making available several copies of the same book, and for the growing number of commuting and employed students, a reader can be immensely useful. Even students in well-endowed residential institutions, who out of necessity or convenience tend to run up sizeable photocopying bills, may be spared expense.

Why not source, instead of secondary, readings — that is, why not documents, memoirs, treaties, and the like? This editor certainly has no quarrel with the use of primary material, but will point out that another dimension is added when students are exposed to varied treatments of the same event. Some students may find this frustrating, looking for the certainties they believe they find in the sciences, and some of the more cynical among them may be tempted to reject history as wholly relativistic — which is always a danger. Nevertheless, it is important for them to see that people with different motives, or similar motives writing at different times, do not necessarily see things the same way. A generation brought up to believe that truth is what "the book says" needs to become aware of this.

Why a new reader now? Because while there are several good single-problem books, none of those available tackle a variety of problems, particularly since the highly regarded, but dated, volumes by Gordon Wright and Arthur Mejia have gone out of print. Those who have used those volumes, as I have, will recognize my debt to their editors.

I want to express my appreciation to colleagues and friends who made numerous helpful suggestions — particularly Robert Paxton, John O'Sullivan, Samuel Portnoy, and Irwin Wall, but also others too numerous to identify individually. I am especially grateful to the students on whom these readings were tested. Indeed it was their enthusiasm that encouraged me and their suggestions for improvement that strengthened the book. Drake Bush and Eleanor Garner of Harcourt Brace Jovanovich made the path from proposal to reality a remarkably smooth one, while Katherine Watson provided expert editorial help, Cathy Reynolds contributed the design, and Alison Howell managed the budget and schedule. My thanks to all these people.

CONTENTS

5

THE NAZIS   121

6

APPEASEMENT: THE MUNICH PACT   163

7

RESISTANCE OR COLLABORATION?
THE EXAMPLE OF VICHY FRANCE   193

8

THE HOLOCAUST   223

9

The Outbreak of the Cold War   251

10

The End of European Empire   285

11

The Dismantling of the Welfare State   319

12

THE SINGLE MARKET AND EUROPEAN UNITY   343

13

TOWARD A NEW EUROPEAN ORDER?   365

AN AGE OF CONFLICT

READINGS IN TWENTIETH CENTURY EUROPEAN HISTORY

THE OPENING
OF THE
TWENTIETH
CENTURY:

The Reorientation
of Social Thought

M any older texts on twentieth-century European history provided only a political and economic survey of conditions in the decade prior to World War I. They described and generally applauded Europe's favored position that gave her worldwide economic, technological, and artistic supremacy. Before 1914 Europeans were secure, showed confidence, and set the standards by which the rest of the world was measured. Nineteen fourteen was seen as a dividing line, bringing to an end an equilibrium "so stable as almost to give an illusion of permanence."[1] Then with the publication of H. Stuart Hughes' *Consciousness and Society*

---

[1] Frank P. Chambers, *This Age of Conflict: The Western World. 1914 to the Present* (First published in 1943, New York, 1962), p. 4. In the next sentence, however, the author states that "the illusions concealed the reality."

(1958), Gerhard Masur's *Prophets of Yesterday* (1961), and other works, the awareness emerged of a prewar climate of "cultural revolt," "intellectual disquiet," and movement "toward a new consciousness."[2] These analyses suggested that "Victorian certainties" were no longer appropriate; the "competitive power of the individual" was no longer seen as "a source for progress"; belief in the "superiority of European culture" was shaken. Historians began to wonder whether cultural disharmony played as important a part in bringing on World War I as the discredited alliance system and whether it accounted for the younger generation's enthusiasm for war and willingness to endure the unparalleled horror and destruction that followed.

During the quarter century that preceded the outbreak of the war, advanced sectors of the European climate of opinion indeed underwent tremendous change. Intellectuals no longer offered ultimate answers, and doubted they could be found. Certitudes, absolutes, and established codes of conduct no longer seemed relevant. Einstein's insistence on relativity destroyed forever Newton's mechanistic world view; the belief in an orderly universe governed by predictable laws was shattered. Nietzsche questioned the basis of Judaeo-Christian morality. Ibsen exposed the hypocrisy of that bastion of stability and order, the bourgeoisie. In psychology and sociology Freud and Weber contended that rather than controlling their environment people were products of it. Such innovative thinkers, regardless of their intentions, rejected the positivist tradition that so well complemented Western Europe's march toward industrial progress — a tradition that emphasized rational and objectively verifiable thought. According to the new school, people did things not as a result of rational decision making, but because of unconscious processes they did not even understand.

Existing values were challenged on all sides. In addition to Nietzsche's repudiation of the scriptural bases of morality, Bergson maintained that the impetus of life transcended rationalism. Freud taught that thinking was a circuitous path toward the goal of wish-fulfillment. Sorel believed that myths and not reason accounted for great collective movements. Artists, too, joined in intellectual revolt: the paintings of Fauvists, cubists, and futurists violated all traditional standards; in music the first

---

[2] David Sumler, *A History of Europe in the 20th Century* (Homewood, 1973); Felix Gilbert, *The End of the European Era. 1890 to the Present* (New York, 1984); and Robert Paxton, *Europe in the 20th Century* (New York, 1985). Taken from chapter headings.

atonal work was composed in 1908; in literature, Joyce and Proust developed new forms based on the workings of the subconscious, while Mann and Galsworthy wrote of the decay of great bourgeois families as symbolic of larger European decay.

The three readings that follow address this intellectual revolution in different ways. H. Stuart Hughes defines this "reorientation" of thought, distinguishing it from the romanticism that prevailed near the beginning of the nineteenth century. Robert Wohl looks especially at the generation that accepted the teachings of these cultural rebels, and tries to assess the impact of this acceptance. Zeev Sternhell is more interested in the political consequences; he sees similarities between these avant-garde beliefs and the fascism that emerged between the two world wars. If he is right, the revolution in thought that preceded World War I — specifically the antirationalism and nationalism it engendered — had profound consequences for subsequent twentieth-century history.

Consciousness and Society

꙰

H. STUART HUGHES

H. Stuart Hughes, now professor emeritus at the University of California at San Diego, is perhaps the most influential American intellectual historian of his generation, a reputation he established with the publication in 1958 of *Consciousness and Society*. His grasp of the relationship between ideas and political and social realities issues from varied experiences in public life: he headed the State Department's Division of Research for Europe, was an independent candidate from Massachusetts for the U.S. Senate, and co-chaired the National Committee for a Sane Nuclear Policy. Questions to keep in mind while reading are: How does Hughes characterize the revolution in European thought? Why does he object to describing this movement as "neoromanticism"?

There are certain periods in history in which a number of advanced thinkers, usually working independently one of another, have proposed views on human conduct so different from those commonly accepted at the time — and yet so manifestly interrelated — that together they seem to constitute an intellectual revolution. The decade of the 1890s was one of such periods. In this decade and the one immediately succeeding it, the basic assumptions of eighteenth- and nineteenth-century social thought underwent a critical review from which there emerged the new assumptions characteristic of our own time. "A revolution of such magnitude in the prevailing empirical interpretations of human society is hardly to be found occurring within the short space of a generation, unless one goes back to about the sixteenth century. What is to account for it?"

Nearly all students of the last years of the nineteenth century have sensed in some form or other a profound psychological change. Yet they have differed markedly in the way in which they have expressed their understanding of it. In the older, more aesthetically oriented interpretations (we may think of Henry Adams), the 1890s figured as the *fin de siècle*: it was a period of overripeness, of perverse and mannered decadence — the end of an era. We need not stop to ask ourselves how much of this was simply an artistic and literary pose. For our present purposes, it is irrelevant: the *fin de siècle* is a backdrop, nothing more.

Somewhere between an aesthetic and a more intellectual interpretation, we might be tempted to characterize the new attitude as neo-romanticism or neo-mysticism. This formulation has considerable plausibility. Unquestionably the turn toward the subjective that we find in so much of the imaginative and speculative writing of the quarter-century between 1890 and the First World War recalls the aspirations of the original Romanticists. It is not difficult to think of writers who in the 1890s or early 1900s felt that they were reaching back over a half-century gap to restore to honor those values of the imagination that their immediate predecessors had scorned and neglected. It was writers such as these who established the cult of Dostoyevsky and Nietzsche as the literary heralds of the new era. There is a pathetic paradox in the fact that the year of Nietzsche's madness — 1889 — coincides with the time at which his work, after two decades of public neglect, first began to find wide acceptance. Again and again in the course of the present study we shall find one or another social thinker elaborating more rigorously and systematically the suggestions with regard to unconscious strivings and heroic minorities which Nietzsche had thrown out in fragmentary form.

Yet to call Nietzsche a neo-romantic is surely misleading. Any such characterization does less than justice to the critical and Socratic elements in his thought. And when it is applied to the social thinkers of the early twentieth century, it fits only a very few — and these are minor figures like Péguy and Jung. The truly great either were hostile to what they took to be neo-romantic tendencies or, like Freud and Weber, sought to curb the romanticism they discovered within themselves. Durkheim was perhaps the most categorical of his contemporaries in protesting against what he called a "renascent mysticism," but he was not an isolated case. It was rather the "mystic" Bergson (whom Durkheim may have been aiming at) who was less typical. Indeed, of the major new doctrines of the period, the Bergsonian metaphysics was unique in having frankly mystical aspects — and even this doctrine was couched so far as possible in acceptable philosophic terminology. It was on the "lower" levels of thought, rather — on the level of semipopular agitation — that the neo-romantic tendencies were to have their greatest effect. And it was here that their application to politics eventually produced that "betrayal of the intellectuals" which Julien Benda assailed with such telling effect three decades later.

If not "romanticism," will "irrationalism" serve as a general description? It is neat, it is frequently used, and it at least begins to suggest the real concerns of early twentieth-century social thought. Unquestionably the major intellectual innovators of the 1890s were profoundly interested in the problem of irrational motivation in human conduct. They were obsessed, almost intoxicated, with a rediscovery of the nonlogical, the uncivilized, the inexplicable. But to call them "irrationalists" is to fall into a dangerous ambiguity. It suggests a tolerance or even a preference for the realms of the unconscious. The reverse was actually the case. The social thinkers of the 1890s were concerned with the irrational only to exorcise it. By probing into it, they sought ways to tame it, to canalize it for constructive human purposes. Even Sorel, who has often been held up as the supreme irrationalist, had as his life's goal the enunciation of a political formula that would fit the new world of industrial logic and the machine.

Sorel, Pareto, Durkheim, Freud — all thought of themselves as engineers or technicians, men of science or medicine. It is obviously absurd to call them irrationalists in any but the most restricted sense. As a substitute, the formula "anti-intellectualist" has sometimes been employed. This characterization is both flexible and comprehensive. It suggests the revulsion from ideology and the *a priori*, from the abstract thought of the century and a half preceding, which served to unite writers otherwise so far apart as Durkheim and Sorel. It recalls the influence and prestige of William James — an influence at the same time comparable, opposed, and complementary to that of Nietzsche. "Anti-intellectualism," then, is virtually equivalent to Jamesian pragmatism. It offers a satisfactory common denominator for grouping a large proportion of the intellectual innovations of the 1890s.

Yet it is at the same time too broad and too narrow. It fails to take account of the unrepentant abstraction and intellectualism in the thought of Benedetto Croce — or, to take quite a different example, the later elaboration by Max Weber of social theory in terms of "ideal types." It suggests, moreover, that the turn from the principles of the Enlightenment was more complete and decisive than was actually the case. The main attack against the intellectual heritage of the past was in fact on a narrower front. It was directed primarily against what the writers of the 1890s chose to call "positivism." By this they did not mean simply the rather quaint doctrines associated with the name of Auguste Comte, who had originally coined the term. Nor did they mean the social philosophy of Herbert Spencer, which was the guise in which positivist thinking was most apparent in their own time. They used the word in a looser sense to characterize the whole tendency to discuss human behavior in terms of analogies drawn from natural science. In reacting against it, the innovators of the 1890s felt that they were rejecting the most pervasive intellectual tenet of their time. They believed that they were casting off a spiritual yoke that the preceding quarter-century had laid upon them.

As a preliminary characterization, to speak of the innovations of the 1890s as a revolt against positivism comes closest to what the writers in question actually thought that they were about. Yet even this last formula has its pitfalls. We must be on guard against the tendency of someone like Croce to use positivism as a philosophic catch-all, to embrace under this epithet every doctrine for which he had a dislike. We must not forget the number of influential thinkers of the period — men like Durkheim and Mosca — who remained essentially in the positivist tradition. And, finally, we must take proper account of the others, like Freud, who continued to use mechanistic language drawn from the natural sciences long after their discoveries had burst the framework of their inherited vocabulary.

. . .

So much for the cultural setting. Against this background we may outline in preliminary and schematic form the major ideas that were initially stated in the 1890s, preparatory to their fuller elaboration in the first decade of the twentieth century.

1. Most basic, perhaps, and the key to all the others was the new interest in the problem of consciousness and the role of the unconscious. It was the problem implicit in the title of Bergson's first book, the *Essay on the Immediate Data of Consciousness*. In it he had tried to distinguish between a "superficial psychic life" to which the scientific logic of space and number could properly be applied, and a life in the "depths of consciousness" in which "the deep-seated self" followed a logic of its own: he had come to the conclusion that the world of dreams might offer a clue to this secret and unexplored realm. "In order to recover this fundamental self," he had added, "a vigorous effort of analysis is necessary." A decade later, and proceeding from a philosophic and professional preparation almost totally in contrast to that of Bergson, Freud began to carry out the program that the former had outlined. Freud's first major work, *The Interpretation of Dreams*, built on his own "vigorous effort" of self-analysis a theory of unconscious motivation to which the life of dreams offered the key.

2. Closely related to the problem of consciousness was the question of the meaning of time and duration in psychology, philosophy, literature, and history. It was the problem to which Bergson was to return again and again in an effort to define the nature of subjective existence as opposed to the schematic order that the natural sciences had imposed on the external world. It represented one aspect of the task that Croce had set himself in trying to establish the qualitative and methodological differences between the realm of history and the realm of science. In somewhat different form it was the problem with which the natural scientists were themselves contending in postulating a universe that no longer strictly conformed to the laws of Newtonian physics. Finally it was the dilemma that obsessed the novelists of the first two decades of the new century — Alain-Fournier, Proust, Thomas Mann — the tormenting question of how to recapture the immediacy of past experience in language that in ordinary usage could reproduce no more than the fragmentized reality of an existence that the logical memory had already stored away in neat compartments.

3. Beyond and embracing the questions of consciousness and time, there loomed the further problem of the nature of knowledge in what Wilhelm Dilthey had called the "sciences of the mind." In the early 1880s Dilthey had attempted to establish rules that would separate the areas in which the human mind strove for some kind of internal comprehension from the realm of external and purely conventional symbols devised by

natural science. A decade later Croce had resumed the task, with his first important essay, *"La storia ridotta sotto il concetto generale dell'arte."* Croce soon abandoned the simple solution of including history among the arts. But his conviction of the radical subjectivity of historical knowledge remained. By 1900 it was apparent to the more imaginative of Croce's contemporaries that the nineteenth-century program of building an edifice of historical and sociological knowledge by patient accumulation and painstaking verification no longer sufficed. By such means it would prove forever impossible to penetrate beneath the surface of human experience. One had, rather, a choice between the exercise of the sympathetic intuition postulated in Croce's neo-idealistic theory of history, and the creation of useful fictions, as Max Weber was later to elaborate them, as models for critical understanding.

4. If the knowledge of human affairs, then, rested on such tentative foundations, the whole basis of political discussion had been radically altered. No longer could one remain content with the easy assurances of the rationalistic ideologies inherited from the century and a half preceding — liberal, democratic, or socialist as the case might be. The task was rather to penetrate behind the fictions of political action, behind what Sorel called the "myths," Pareto the "derivations," and Mosca the "political formulas" of the time. Behind these convenient façades, one could postulate the existence of the actual wielders of power, the creative minorities, the political élites. The discussion of politics, then, had been pushed back from the front of the stage to the wings — from the rhetoric of public discussion to the manipulation of half-conscious sentiments.

Such, indeed, is the most general characterization we may give to the new intellectual concerns of the 1890s. They had displaced the axis of social thought from the apparent and objectively verifiable to the only partially conscious area of unexplained motivation. In this sense the new doctrines were manifestly subjective. Psychological process had replaced external reality as the most pressing topic for investigation. It was no longer what actually existed that seemed most important: it was what men thought existed. And what they felt on the unconscious level had become rather more interesting than what they had consciously rationalized. Or — to formulate the change in still more radical terms — since it had apparently been proved impossible to arrive at any sure knowledge of human behavior — if one must rely on flashes of subjective intuition or on the creation of convenient fictions — then the mind had indeed been freed from the bonds of positivist method: it was at liberty to speculate, to imagine, to create. At one stroke, the realm of human understanding had been drastically reduced and immensely broadened. The possibilities of social thought stretched out to infinity. It was perhaps this that Freud had in mind when in 1896 he spoke of "metapsychology"—the definition of the origin and nature of humanity—as his "ideal and problem child," his most challenging task for the future.

.   .   .

In the retrospect of [World War I], the year 1905 most clearly offered the watershed. It marked the first time for a quarter-century that all Europe seemed astir. The revolution in Russia had come as the first major social disturbance since the Paris Commune of 1871—and for a moment the Socialist parties of France and Germany, Austria and Italy, had faced the embarrassing prospect that they might be obliged to give reality to the Marxist professions that had gradually been transformed into little more than a litany for the faithful. The revolutionary danger soon passed. But the effects of the other decisive event of the year—the First Moroccan Crisis—were not to be eradicated so quickly. From 1905 on, one diplomatic crisis followed on another in regular succession. The shock of Tangiers—as Péguy put it—"within the space of . . . two hours" introduced a new epoch in his own life, as it did in the history of his country and of the world. For the next decade the youth of Europe lived and breathed in an atmosphere of impending war.

It was this prospect of war service which most sharply marked off the new generation from those who had reached intellectual maturity in the 1890s. By 1905, men like Freud and Weber, Durkheim and Bergson, Mosca and Croce, were already getting too old for front-line duty. Of them, Weber alone put on a uniform during the war, and even he was not permitted to engage in actual combat. The war, when it came, was not *their* war: it was their sons' war. For them the decisive experience had been the intellectual renewal of the 1890s—or perhaps, in the case of the French, the defense of Captain Dreyfus. For the generation of their sons the great event was obviously the war itself. Here we find a dramatic instance of the contrasting experiences that serve to demarcate one age group from another in intellectual history.

Living as it did in a state of nearly constant war alert, the new generation was more impatient than that of its fathers. It respected its elders: in this it differed from the conventional image of a younger genera-tion. But it was looking for something more arresting and dogmatic than its seniors had provided. It admired the discoveries they had made — but it understood these discoveries in cruder fashion. Where the writers of the 1890s had restricted themselves to a questioning of the potentialities of reason, the young men of 1905 became frank irrationalists or even anti-rationalists. This crucial distinction, which so often remains blurred in the history of ideas in our century, was largely a matter of contrasting age groups. The younger men were no longer satisfied with the urbane detachment of their elders. Everywhere they were in search of an ideal and a faith.

Thus in Germany they began to apply the teachings of Nietzsche in the sense of direct action, and thought of themselves as that "first generation of fighters and dragon-slayers" whom he had called on to establish the "Reich of Youth." One of Nietzsche's self-styled disciples — Stefan George — became their poet: from George they learned to regard themselves as a new spiritual aristocracy, with a lofty if ill-defined mission. The newly formed youth groups gave them an organizational outlet and an intoxicating sense of physical and spiritual liberation. Ten months before the outbreak of the war, in October 1913, representatives of the Free German Youth assembled on the Hohen Meissner hill in central Germany and drew up a melodramatic pledge to "take united action . . . under any and all circumstances . . . for the sake of . . . inner freedom." It was young people of this sort that Weber encountered four years later, when, at a gathering at Burg Lauenstein in Thuringia, he declined to serve as the prophet for whom they longed.

In Italy the years between the turn of the century and the First World War brought into prominence new writers, new reviews, and new political organizations. The reaction from positivism that in Croce's case had expressed itself in rational and measured form, with the younger generation became a kind of spiritual explosion. Nationalism in politics, dynamism and "Futurism" in literature, above all the example — both artistic and personal — of the flamboyant word-magician Gabriele D'Annunzio, marked the changed temper of Italian youth. It was not until the review *La Voce* was founded in Florence in 1908, that some of the new writers were able to collaborate with their elders in reconciling a moderate type of nationalism with the older liberal tradition.

It was in France, however, that the cleavage between generations was most self-consciously delineated, and it is from here that we shall chiefly draw the literary evidences of a changed temper. In France after the turn of the century, as in Germany a decade earlier, the young people began to declare themselves Nietzscheans. André Gide's *The Immoralist*, published in 1902, is an early example. Subsequently, still younger writers like Alain-Fournier were to recognize the influence, either explicit or unconscious, of Nietzsche on their own thought. But in France the Nietzscheans were only a minority. It was Bergson, rather, who ranked as the tutelary deity of the new generation. After 1905 the educated youth of France became militantly "Bergsonian."

The young people seized hold of Bergson with avidity and interpreted him according to their own tastes. They read into his teaching the notion of direct-action politics — usually of the Right — which was distinctly in contrast with his own convictions, and of dogmatic religion, on which his personal position still remained obscure. As so often has happened in the history of ideas, the originator of the doctrine lost control of his own creation: his disciples escaped from his tutelary guidance. For the half-decade before the First World War, "Bergsonism" was living a life of its own, almost independent of its founder.

It was a curious phenomenon, this new generation in which the sons were more conservative than the fathers. The latter had done battle for the innocence of Dreyfus and fought the power of the "reactionaries" and the clergy. Their children were as likely as not to embrace the neoroyalism of Charles Maurras and the *Action Française*, or the milder version of conservative nationalism preached by the novelist Maurice Barrès. At the Ecole Normale Supérieure the influence of Lucien Herr, the librarian, and of Jean Jaurès, the great Socialist alumnus, began to wane: Léon Blum — who three decades later was to be prime minister of France, but who at this period still ranked only as a brilliant lawyer and a rather precious *littérateur* — was one of the last of their great converts. And, to the more critical of the younger minds, Blum seemed rather superficial: he still took Jaurès's rolling periods seriously.

.   .   .

In 1900, in intellectual circles, it had been bad form to be a practicing Catholic. By 1910, while the majority still consisted of unbelievers — philosophical positivists for the most part — a growing minority of the sensitive and discriminating spirits were returning to the faith in which they had been baptized. A few great conversions had served as examples — the poet Paul Claudel from the elders, the philosopher

Jacques Maritain in the younger generation. It was the latter who was to appeal in vain with the anti-clerical wife of Péguy to ease her husband's torments of conscience by letting her children be baptized.

.   .   .

With this contrast, we touch the central ambiguity in the generation of 1905. In France — and the same was true in Germany — during the years just before the outbreak of the war there reigned among the youth a spirit that combined respect for authority with the cult of spontaneous creation. Depending on where they have chosen to lay their emphasis, historians of the epoch have judged it very differently. On the one hand, they have found in it a threatening proto-fascist atmosphere, on the other hand a renaissance of culture and of living brutally cut off at its start. This was the generation of French and Germans of whom the best were to perish in battle — or so, at least, their contemporaries saw it. And the tragic irony of the matter was that they greeted the outbreak of the slaughter with enthusiasm. The more bellicose felt at last within their grasp the life of action for which they had longed. The more reflective welcomed it as a deliverance from unfruitful anticipation: "Better that war should come," they repeated, "than to go on with this perpetual waiting."

The Generation of 1914

࿊

ROBERT WOHL

Robert Wohl, who teaches at the University of California, Los Angeles, has published a comprehensive study of the origins of French Communism. The work from which the following is taken is interesting both for its conceptual approach and for the information it provides. According to Wohl, what constitutes a "historical generation"? Compare Wohl to Hughes in regard to the nature of avant-garde thought at the turn of the century. To what extent does the psychological rebellion of the younger against the older generation explain the former's willingness to accept theories they knew their parents rejected? Finally, why did the "generation of 1914" welcome, rather than draw back from, the prospect of war?

Generational theorists worked hard to devise a reliable and scientifically respectable method of determining the chronological limits of generations. Their goal was a periodic table that would set forth the history of modern Europe in a succession of quantifiably delimited generations. These efforts were in vain because they rested on a misconception of the generational phenomenon. A historical generation is not defined by its chronological limits or its borders. It is not a zone of dates; nor is it an army of contemporaries making its way across a territory of time. It is more like a magnetic field at the center of which lies an experience or a series of experiences. It is a system of references and identifications that gives priority to some kinds of experiences and devalues others — hence it is relatively independent of age. The chronological center of this experiential field need not be stable; it may shift with time. What is essential to the formation of a generational consciousness is some common frame of reference that provides a sense of rupture with the past and that will later distinguish the members of the generation from those who follow them in time. This frame of reference is always derived from great historical events like wars, revolutions, plagues, famines, and economic crises, because it is great historical events like these that supply the markers and signposts with which people impose order on their past and link their individual fates with those of the communities in which they live.

What allowed European intellectuals born between 1880 and 1900 to view themselves as a distinct generation was that their youth coincided with the opening of the twentieth century and their lives were then bifurcated by the Great War. Those who survived into the decade of the 1920s perceived their lives as being neatly divided into a *before*, a *during*, and an *after*, categories most of them equated with the stages of life known as youth, young manhood, and maturity. What bound the generation of 1914 together was not just their experiences during the war, as many of them later came to believe, but the fact that they grew up and formulated their first ideas in the world from which the war issued, a world framed by two dates, 1900 and 1914. This world was the "vital horizon" within which they began conscious historical life.

The primary fact of this world — and the first thing that young people noticed about it — was that it was being rapidly transformed by technology. Europeans were being freed increasingly from the traditional constraints imposed on mankind by nature. Life was becoming safer, cleaner, more comfortable, and longer for most sectors of the population. Death had not been vanquished (though many death-bearing diseases had), but its arrival was now more predictable, and the physician, along with the engineer, had been elevated to the priesthood of the new civilization.

At the same time that life was becoming more secure, its pace quickened and the sense of distance among people shrank. Even rest became recreation. Instead of picnicking *sur l'herbe* or strolling on resort boardwalks, Europeans began to pedal, swim, ski, and scramble up the sides of mountains. The great events of the era, from a technological point of view, were the invention and diffusion of the automobile, the motorcycle, and the airplane. Speed still implied romance and adventure and had yet to be connected with traffic fatalities, tedium, and pollution. It is difficult to determine the precise effects that these changes of velocity had on the sensibility of intellectuals growing up in early twentieth-century Europe. Certainly, though, the acceleration of movement enhanced the feeling of novelty and encouraged the conviction that the twentieth century would be fundamentally different from its predecessor, if only because it would be faster.

The second characteristic of the prewar world, prominently featured on the front page of every daily newspaper, was that it was undergoing a revolutionary change in political and social structures. Old empires were under attack in Central and Eastern Europe. Oppressed peoples were clamoring for statehood. Workers were insisting on higher wages and shorter hours. Peasants were demanding land or more favorable sharecropping arrangements. Everywhere in Europe there was a movement to open political participation to larger groups of people. The old systems of deference were under attack, and the old elites were being pressed to make concessions. Authority, whether exercised by landlords, factory owners, clergymen, or fathers within their own families, was being angrily disputed. As Ortega was later to complain, people were no longer content to occupy the place that destiny had assigned them. And since the number of people in Europe was increasing at a rapid rate, there was much talk about "the masses" and what they were likely to do. The great political and social movement of the day was Socialism. It seemed certain that Socialism would play as important a role in the twentieth century as liberalism had played in the nineteenth. In 1900, though, it was far from clear what that role would be. The still unsatisfied ambitions of the subordinate classes and their organization into groups that challenged the forces of public order on the streets of Europe's capitals meant that the threat of revolution hovered menacingly on the horizon of the middle- and upper-class mind. But the commitment of the most prominent Socialist leaders to democracy and peace and their often professed abhorrence of violence kept alive the hope that the transition to a new society could be made painlessly and with benefit to all.

A third characteristic of this world — one that is especially difficult to grasp today — is that while it stood under the cloud of threatening war, its inhabitants viewed the possibility of this war from the perspective of a century in which warfare in Europe had been kept within such narrowly circumscribed limits that it had never interfered with improvements in the quality of life. War among the major European powers seemed both inevitable (because of Germany's determination to dominate the continent and challenge England's control of the world's seas and markets) and impossible (because of the complex economic interrelationships that bound the great powers to each other and made the prosperity of one dependent on the prosperity of all). This was the paradox that defined European international relations between 1900 and 1914. There was no lack of signs that conflict was coming. Major European crises erupted with regularity almost every year after 1895. The Boer War, Faschoda, the Russo-Japanese War, Agadir, the Balkan wars — these were the events with which the generation of 1914 grew up. But somehow the final breakdown of the system was averted, and war became in people's minds a dangerous sport, like big game hunting, that some particularly adventurous Europeans practiced outside or on the periphery of Europe. These conditions of increasing ease of life, along with increasing sources of domestic and international conflict, explain how among Europeans of the ruling classes optimism about the future could be "allied insanely" with the expectation of Armageddon.

This was the world that young people growing up between 1900 and 1914 encountered; this was the vital horizon within which they had to act. To understand what they thought about that world, we must look at the prevailing state of culture. Toward the end of the nineteenth century, European high culture began to split into two related but mutually antagonistic camps. On the one hand, there was the official bourgeois culture; on the other hand, there was the culture of the trailblazing vanguard. Middle-class intellectuals born during the last two decades of the nineteenth century reacted fiercely and self-consciously against the first and gave their allegiance to the second. It was from the leaders of the avant-garde that young intellectuals learned how to interpret their world; and it was from them that they took their criticism of contemporary society and their visions of the future. These cultural innovators were in the process of redefining and restructuring European culture. Men like Bergson, Poincaré, Sorel, Freud, Weber, James, Blondel, Mosca, Pareto, and Croce had brought about a radical change in the way European intellectuals thought and the way they viewed the products of thought. The very possibility of achieving sure knowledge had been called into question. Philosophers of science and society showed that the laws linking subject and object were fictions, thus not really laws at all, unless legislated into fleeting reality by human will. Time was redefined in subjective terms to free experience from the determinism of sequence. The standard of truth was abandoned in favor of the idea of efficacity. The bridges between the individual consciousness and the outside world were blown up. Even the unity of the self was thrown into doubt. Descartes's *Discourse on Method* became a favored example of faulty thinking, the product of an age now disappeared.

The new culture was, in one of its most important aspects, a "culture of Anti-Necessity." Varieties of neoidealism competed for the allegiance of the European intellectual elite, and the prophets of these systems of belief dedicated the major part of their energies to demonstrating that no self-respecting intellectual could assume a materialistic outlook on the world. Reality, they said, was a perspective and a construction rather than a verifiable fact or a thing. Man was not the executor of natural and historical laws, but a creator of his life with no limits on him but those imposed by lack of imagination and weakness of will. Scientific analysis was considered to be a mental instrument of severely limited validity; intuition into the multiplicity of human realities took its place; and action rather than contemplation was recommended as a source of knowledge. With organized religion in retreat and reason exposed as the greatest of illusions, it became essential to find new bases for life and new systems of morality by which to judge men's actions. No longer was it possible to count on the beneficence of history or to rely on receiving steady dividends handed out by progress. The mind became an instrument with which intellectuals dominated and took possession of the world; civilization, a precarious achievement of the spirit that must constantly be renewed through the process of destruction and re-creation.

These attitudes represented a break with the main tradition of European rationalism. Yet the very intellectuals who prided themselves on being liberated from the illusions of progress and the mystique of science remained strangely indentured to determinisms of various kinds, determinisms, furthermore, that were themselves inspired by scientific theories. For some, it was the determinism of biology; for others, the determinism of geography; for still others, the determinism of history or race. Whatever the determinism chosen, however, it led toward the acknowledgment of a painful contradiction: that man was free to create his own life, as the novelist creates a fiction; and yet was a slave to the material conditions of his existence. Most European intellectuals of the late nineteenth century sought escape from this dilemma by asserting that man could master the determinisms that bound him only by raising them to consciousness, accepting them, and living life with vitality and passion.

Some intellectuals were quick to perceive the political implications of these attitudes and to push them to their most extreme consequences. Democracy and socialism, they noted not unhappily, were based on faulty premises. All societies were dominated by aristocracies and all civilizations were doomed to collapse. Why, then, get concerned about the misery of the masses? Suffering was the price that peoples paid for culture. Progress, insofar as it existed, took place in individual minds. Better, then, the cultivation of one truly successful human being than the futile, life-destroying pursuit of an impossible egalitarian utopia. Since life was struggle, truth was a matter of perspective, and annihilation awaited us at the end, we ought to endeavor, as Unamuno put it, "to stamp others with our seal, to perpetuate ourselves in them and in their children by dominating them, to leave on all things the imperishable impress of our signature." War was the seedbed of culture, the foundation of morality, and the form of social intercourse that brought men closest together. Peace came at a cultural price too high to pay. This was the message that many people derived from Nietzsche's teachings; and if, for some reason, they were put off by the mists of Teutonic terminology that surrounded Nietzsche's aphorisms or the intimations of derangement with which the message was relayed, they could get the same complex of ideas from a dozen other sources, for the notions of an aristocracy of intellect and a tragic sense of life were everywhere in the air.

Naturally, the new culture was not taught in schools. It remained the possession of a small elite: that literary and artistic vanguard living in the great capitals of Europe that Hugo von Hofsmannthal called the "conscience" of the young generation. But it was discovered and disseminated among young intellectuals during the years immediately preceding the war. The spiritual guides and mentors acknowledged by the members of the generation of 1914 — Barrès, Péguy, Sorel, and Romain Rolland in France; Nietzsche, Langbehn, and Moeller van den Bruck in Germany; Shaw, Wells, and Hardy in England; Unamuno, Azorín, and Baroja in Spain; D'Annunzio, Croce, Gentile, and Pareto in Italy; Ibsen and Strindberg in Scandinavia — were all proponents of the new culture. Their syntheses of neoidealism and biological determinism, their elitism, their pessimism about the future of Western culture, and their critiques of democracy and socialism were the ideas that seemed most up-to-date between 1900 and 1914. The existence of this new culture, and the excitement it produced, contributed to the consciousness of a generational rupture among people born between 1880 and 1900; yet, paradoxically, the generational idea concealed the extent to which the new culture was a creation of the intellectuals of the preceding generation. "I could not have defined what all this was about that had laid so strong a spell on me," Carl Zuckmayer (1896) later wrote, "but it was *our* time, *our* world, *our* sense of life that came rushing upon me, falling upon me, and suddenly I awakened to a consciousness of a new generation, a consciousness that even the most intelligent, most aware and unbiased parents could not share." What Zuckmayer and other young intellectuals like him did not realize was that the intellectuals in the generation of their parents had created that new art and those new ideas which his generation experienced as a "revelation" and an "illumination."

Thus it was from intellectuals among the age-group of their fathers that men born between 1880 and 1900 learned to think of themselves as a generation. Massis inherited the idea from Barrès; Ortega took it from Unamuno and Azorín; Prezzolini and Papini found it in Croce and D'Annunzio. Moreover, it was these same intellectuals who taught their disciples what to think about the society in which they lived. Prewar European intellectual youth grew up in revolt against the comfort, coziness, and predictability of modern life. They feared that they had been born into a declining world, and they longed after risk, danger, and brutal contact with the elemental realities of life, as they imagined that life was lived outside of European cities. The first images of the generation of 1914, devised during the decade or so before the outbreak of the war, were nothing but a reversal of the qualities that young intellectuals disliked or feared in the generation of their parents. The previous generation had been thinkers; they would be doers. The previous generation had floundered in moral relativism; they would seek assurance in calm faith. The previous generation had been weak and indecisive; they would be strong and vital. This supposed change in character was rendered superficially plausible by the spread of team sports, the quickening of the pace of life, greater possibilities for travel, and the weakening of the authority of fathers over their sons as society became more complex and opportunities for employment and careers became more varied.

The sentiment of generational unity grows out of and is nourished by an even deeper feeling. What draws young people together and ignites the sparks that join them is a sense of common grievance. This does not happen regularly, as some generational theorists assumed. But when it does, groups of coevals will form to set the world aright. The complaint voiced most often by young intellectuals during the period before 1914 was that they had the misfortune to be born into a dying world that lacked energy, vitality, and moral fiber. It was characteristic of this age-group of European intellectuals that they perceived the problem of decadence in connection with a crisis of the nation. The nation was perceived as being weak, morally flabby, a shaky structure that might at any time collapse into its constituent parts. The desire for a reform of the nation and a renewal of its spiritual resources was ordinarily allied with a profound ignorance of the realities of national life. Young intellectuals generally knew little about the people or their problems. But their longing for regeneration was nonetheless strong, and it was a feeling capable of inspiring action. Hence the prevalence of national revivals and the popularity of nationalist movements during the decade preceding the Great War. The nation, they believed, must somehow be whipped into action; its classes and contending factions must be reconciled; its citizens must learn to subordinate their corporatist and selfish interests to the spiritual interests of the national community conceived as a whole. This was what Ortega meant in 1914 when he said that Spanish society must be nationalized; but his program for backward Spain was an ideal shared by Massis and Prezzolini and others like them all over Europe.

Partisans of national revival perceived two ways by which their goal of national regeneration could be accomplished. One was to implement the Socialist program, which called for the democratization of political institutions, the extension of political participation, the elimination of social inequities, and the defense of international peace. Between 1900 and 1914 most young intellectuals felt some attraction toward this program; many called themselves Socialists and even joined their country's Socialist party. Among these converts to Socialism were Brooke, Ortega, and Gramsci. But most middle-class intellectuals of this generation withheld their adherence from Socialist parties, or withdrew soon after joining, because of their feelings that Socialism was a plebeian movement in which intellectuals had no place and their fear that Socialism's victory would destroy elitist values and undermine the cohesion of the nation. Socialism, Henri Franck confided to a friend in 1908, could be the salvation of life, sensibility, and art. It could create new values and bring about the renewal of civilization. But if the Socialists remained bound to a "sterile Marxism" and a "base materialism," if their movement resulted only in "appetite, envy, and hate," and if they were not willing to give their lives to defend "that ensemble of feelings of veneration that is called France," then everything would be finished. "There is something more important yet than the success of the working class; it's the preservation of France."

The other way the nation could be rejuvenated and civilization saved from decadence was through a sudden trauma or blow of fate. The only deliverance from the languor of bourgeois complacency that most young Europeans could imagine was the outbreak of a general war. Hence some leaped to the treacherous assumption that it was on the field of battle and in the stress of national emergency that a sense of national consciousness would develop and that a new, more ethical, less commercial man would emerge to replace the bourgeois and the proletarian, both products of the hateful and selfish society into which young intellectuals cursed themselves for having been born. This idea may seem strange and even demented; but it will appear less so when we remember that all European wars since 1815 had been short, progressive in their effects, and, in memory at least, heroic. One did not have to be a reactionary like Walter Flex to believe that war offered a means of breaking the impasse of prewar politics, of creating a sense of national unity where none existed, and of nourishing "those virtues of sacrifice, fortitude, and boldness that constitute the essence of the combatant and that make of the fighting man, with all his excesses and brutality, a type infinitely superior to that shrewd sybarite who finds in the cult of peace the best expression of his sensual concept of life."

Attitudes like these explain the feverish enthusiasm with which large sectors of European intellectual youth greeted the outbreak of war in 1914. European youth did not actively want war; but many young European intellectuals desperately wanted change and were willing to risk their lives (and those of others) to achieve it. More than one prewar intellectual had gazed into the future and sensed that something new and wonderful was coming. "It is brooding heavily in the air as a storm does, and soon, oh, very soon, it will thunder upon the world. Flashes of lightning have appeared on the horizon, the echoes of thunder have been heard in the air, but the great reckless storm, the storm that will make us abandon mediocrity and will set us free from pettiness, has not yet come — yet soon it will break over us." When war did break over Europe, it was interpreted by intellectuals as an hour of redemption, a rite of purification, and a chance, perhaps the last, to escape from a sinking and declining civilization. This is why Rupert Brooke could sing "Now, God be thanked Who has matched us with His hour"; why the German poet Bruno Frank could shout "Rejoice, friends! that we are alive"; why the Italian writer Giani Stuparich was so happy that he wept with joy; why Drieu la Rochelle remembered the outbreak of the war as a marvelous surprise and the unexpected fulfillment of his youth; and why Ortega immediately interpreted the news of war on August 5, 1914, as the end of one world and the birth of another. "History," he wrote, "is trembling to its very roots, its flanks are torn apart convulsively, because a new reality is about to be born."

Neither Right nor Left: Fascist Ideology in France

∿⁄⊱

ZEEV STERNHELL

Zeev Sternhell is an Israeli who studied at the University of Paris and has published works on French nationalism and French fascism. He now heads the political science department at Hebrew University in Jerusalem. This excerpt comes from his most recent book on fascism in France. Compare his insistence on the "cult of instinct" and the "subordination" of the role of the individual to Hughes and Wohl's analyses of social thought at the turn of the century. What in Sternhell's view is the relationship between rationalism and political liberalism, or, put another way, how does the belief that man is irrational help undermine the foundations of democracy?

The thirty years that preceded the First World War and the decade that followed it formed a truly revolutionary period in the history of Europe. In the space of less than half a century the condition of society, the form of life, the rate of technological progress, and in many respects people's way of looking at themselves underwent a greater change than at any other time in modern history. The growth of industry and technology transformed manners and morals, radically altered the pace of life, brought into being great metropolitan cities, and had a profound effect on life in the provinces.

In the second and third decades of our century, there was a strong and widespread awareness of living in a world that was changing with unprecedented rapidity. As Henri De Man wrote, "In reality, there are not many qualitative changes in the history of mankind that can be compared, as regards their revolutionary significance for society and culture, with the change from mechanical movement to electrical movement, from the technique of the lever to the technique of waves, from the cogwheel to the electric wire and wireless transmission, from material to energetic work processes, from mechanistic thought to functional thought." De Man felt that the world of that period was a world in gestation, "which differed as much from the world of our grandparents as that differed from the world of their ancestors six thousand years ago." And he concluded, in a manner very characteristic of his generation, "We are living in the midst of the greatest social revolution that history has ever known. There is an old world that is passing away and a new world that is being born."

However, if it was only in the interwar period that this consciousness of the new situation became practically universal, a presentiment of the upheavals that were to overtake an entire civilization already existed at the end of the nineteenth century. Indeed, in the sphere of ideas, that period was already deeply affected by a resurgence of irrational values, by a cult of instinct and sentiment, and by an affirmation of the supremacy of the forces of life and the affections. The rationalist and "mechanistic" explanation of the world that had been dominant in European thought from the sixteenth century onward now gave way to an "organic" explanation, and the new importance given to historical values and various idealistic factors amounted to a condemnation of rationalism and individualism. The role of the individual was made subordinate to that of society and of history. To state the matter differently, for the generation of 1890 — Le Bon, Barrès, Sorel, Georges Vacher de Lapouge, and others — the individual had no value in himself, and therefore society could not be regarded simply as the sum of the individuals who composed it. This new generation of intellectuals was violently opposed to the rationalistic individualism of the liberal order, to the dissolution of social bonds that existed in bourgeois society, and to the "utilitarianism and materialism" that prevailed there. It was precisely in this desire to overturn the prevailing order of values that the most clear-sighted fascist intellectuals of the interwar period perceived the origins of fascism. Gentile defined fascism as a revolt against positivism.

That revolt, which was also an attack on the way of life produced by liberalism, an opposition to the "atomized" society, led to a glorification of the institution that was felt to represent the element of unity — the nation. This glorification of the nation, the emergence of a nationalism involving a whole system of defenses and safeguards intended to assure the integrity of the national body, was a natural outcome of the new conception of the world. The new school of thought, rejecting the system of values bequeathed by the eighteenth century and the French Revolution and assailing the foundations of liberalism and democracy, had a very different image of things: "The selectionist morality gives one's duty toward the species the position of supremacy that Christianity gives one's duty toward God," wrote Vacher de Lapouge.

Here we must insist on something of great importance for an understanding of subsequent developments. The antirationalist reaction that questioned the underlying principles of both Marxism and democracy was not the mere product of a literary neoromanticism that affected only the world of arts and letters. These principles were challenged in the name of science, and this was the real significance of the intellectual revolution of the first quarter of the twentieth century. When one sees them in this context, one can understand the nature and scope of the new directions taken in many fields in this period: the new humanistic and social sciences, Darwinian biology, Bergsonian philosophy, Ernest Renan and Hippolyte Taine's interpretation of history, Le Bon's social psychology, and the so-called Italian school of political sociology — Pareto, Gaetano Mosca, and Michels — all opposed the basic premises of liberalism and democracy. The new social sciences, which inherited many aspects of social Darwinism (this was especially true of anthropology and social psychology), created a new theory of political conduct. They thus contributed to an intellectual climate that helped to undermine the foundations of democracy and to enable fascism to come to power.

The positivist character of their scientific method cannot alter the fact that the objective criticisms of given realities of Mosca, Pareto, and Michels amount, in actuality, to sweeping attacks on democracy. The rational explanation of the irrational provided by the theory of elites constitutes a bridge between social research and fascist practice. This explanation by the Italian school of political sociology contributed to the development of revolutionary syndicalism and nationalism, and in many respects represented the meeting point of these two schools of thought.

A conception of man as being essentially motivated by the forces of the unconscious, a pessimistic idea that human nature is unchangeable, led to a static view of history: human conduct cannot change, since psychological motivations always remain the same. According to this view, in all periods of history, whatever the current ideology, under whatever regime, human behavior is unchanging, and therefore the character of a regime is finally of little importance in itself. Moreover, these three authors, like Max Weber at a later date, were agreed that the social sciences could not provide a basis for value judgments either of political structures or of ideologies. This scientific objectivism, based on a vision of man as an essentially irrational being, thus played an important role in undermining the foundations of democracy, and the theory of elites associated with Mosca, Pareto, and Michels remained until the forties one of the most formidable offensive weapons against both Marxism and democracy. Their writings influenced every form of rebellion against democracy, liberalism, and Marxism; nationalists, syndicalists, and nonconformists of every kind referred to them, but in fact, from the end of the nineteenth century, all the social sciences contributed to the erosion of the spirit of optimism, of faith in the individual and in progress, without which it is difficult to conceive of the survival of democracy.

Here we must mention another important factor. From Mosca and Pareto at the turn of the century and Michels on the eve of the First World War up to De Man and Déat, the social sciences — sociology, anthropology, political science, psychology, and Bergsonian philosophy — were working toward what seems, at least in retrospect, to have been an attempt to create an alternative system to Marxism — a system that could give a total explanation of things comparable to the one given by Marx's. But this long-drawn-out competition with Marx involved not only people like Pareto, Michels, and Mosca but also Weber and even, by implication, Émile Durkheim and Freud. De Man's revision of Marxism was based on psychology, and it was by no means fortuitous that his major work was called, in the best tradition of Gustave Le Bon, *Zur Psychologie des Sozialismus*.

Throughout the interwar period, the influence of these modern disciplines was enormous. They were the only ones with enough authority to be able to speak, along with Marxism, in the name of science, and they were the only ones to provide revisionism with its conceptual foundations.

Thus, at the beginning of the century, these new social sciences, particularly psychology and anthropology, which in turn influenced sociology, political science, and historical research, provided both the anti-liberal and the anti-Marxist reactions with their conceptual framework. They also helped to fuse the ideas of the generation of 1850 (Darwin, Arthur de Gobineau, Wagner) and those of the generation of 1890 into a complete and coherent system. The old romantic outlook, the old historicist tendencies, the old theory of the unconscious origins of the nation, the idea of living forces that make up the soul of the people thus received scientific legitimation. One sees the reappearance, modernized and adapted to the requirements of mass society, of the old principles of the subordination of the individual to the collectivity and the integrity of the national body. These new theories completely rejected the traditional mechanistic conception of man that made human behavior dependent on rational choices. The idea became prevalent that feelings and the unconscious played a far greater role in politics than did reason, and this, by a logical process, engendered a contempt for democracy, its institutions, and its machinery.

The biological and psychological determinism of Le Bon, Vacher de Lapouge, Barrès, Drumont, and even Taine, and of innumerable publications in every field of intellectual endeavor led finally to racism.

According to Le Bon, a people's life, its institutions, its destiny are "simply the reflection of its soul," or, that is to say, the "moral and intellectual characteristics" that "represent a synthesis of its whole past, the heritage of all its ancestors, the motivation of its conduct." "Human conduct," he said, "is inexorably predetermined" because "each people is endowed with a mental constitution that is as fixed as its anatomical characteristics," and these "fundamental, unchanging characteristics" derive from a "special structure of the brain." Here Le Bon introduced the idea of race that, he said, "is becoming increasingly prevalent and tends to dominate all our historical, political and social conceptions." He often returned to this theme, claiming that race "dominates the special characteristics of the soul of crowds," and represents the influence of past generations on the living.

The critical attitude to individualism, democracy and its institutions, parliamentarianism, and universal suffrage owed a great deal to this new view of man as an essentially irrational being, confined by historical and biological limitations and motivated by sentiments, associations, and images, never by ideas.

The belief in the dominance of the unconscious over reason, the stress on deep, mysterious forces led, as a natural and necessary consequence, to an extreme anti-intellectualism. To rationalism, to the critical spirit and its manifestations, the rebels of the end of the nineteenth century opposed intuitive feelings, emotions, enthusiasms, an unthinking spontaneity welling from the depths of the popular subconscious. Thus, for the generation of 1890, as for the generation that emerged from the trenches, the motive force of political conduct was the unconscious will of the people. This anti-intellectualism was paralleled, moreover, by a demogogic populism that decried intelligence and the use of words and glorified action, energy, and force. Barrès, for instance, no longer asked which doctrine was true, but which force would enable one to act and be victorious. This was the basis of the new nationalism that came into being at the end of the last century and hardly altered until the time of Munich.

The new nationalists sang the praises of every source of power, and all its forms: vitality, discipline, social and national cohesion. Convinced that nothing can be accomplished unless one joins the majority, the crowd, Barrès, the committed intellectual par excellence, was able to "savor deeply the instinctive pleasure of being part of a flock." He deliberately sacrificed the values of the individual to collective values: "What gives an individual or a nation its values is that its energies are tensed to a greater or lesser degree," he maintained. Thus, the new nationalism of the turn of the century was a mass ideology par excellence, designed to embrace and to mobilize the new urban strata.

Based on a physiological determinism, a moral relativism, and an extreme irrationalism, nationalism, in the definitive form it assumed at the beginning of this century, well expressed this new intellectual direction. The new ethics that Barrès developed in the last years of the nineteenth century and that he opposed to the Jacobin mystique at the time of the Dreyfus affair was perhaps the most striking expression of the transformation of French nationalism. To be sure, it was Péguy's achievement to have stamped an important fringe of that nationalism with the mark of his universalistic genius, but his voice was scarcely audible among the chorus of such journalists, writers, and agitators as Rochefort, Drumont, Gustave Tridon, Barrès, and Maurras and such scientists as Jules Soury, Le Bon, and Vacher de Lapouge, for it was this form of determinism that provided the conceptual framework for the nationalism of the end of the century, and its underlying racial argument was precisely the main legacy of the generation of 1890 to the generation of 1930.

These two generations had another point of resemblance: like the neonationalists of the 1890s, the fascists of the interwar period rejected the political and social consequences of the industrial revolution and of liberal and bourgeois values. Moreover, just as the turn-of-the-century nationalists could not imagine their revolt without the support of the masses, so the fascist ideology was a mass ideology par excellence. One could multiply these parallels. Was not fascism also an anti-intellectual reaction, a reaction of the feelings against the rationality of democracy? Was it not a kind of reflex of the instincts? Did it not also have a cult of physical force, of violence, of brutality? All this explains the importance attached to the setting, the attention paid to decor, great ceremonies, parades — a new liturgy that substituted songs, torches, and processions for deliberation and discussion. In this respect, fascism seems a direct continuation of the neoromanticism of 1880–90, but the scale of that revolt was determined by the mass society that the generation of 1890 was only beginning to glimpse.

However, the intellectual malaise, the political tensions, the social conflicts that characterize the end of the nineteenth century and the beginning of the twentieth were already manifestations of the enormous difficulties experienced by liberalism in adapting itself to the age of the masses. It was toward the end of the century that one began to feel the full impact of the intellectual revolution effected by Darwinism, of the industrialization and urbanization of the European continent, and, finally, of the long-drawn-out process of the growth of a popular nationalism.

Contemporaries had no doubt that they were entering a new period. "The age we are entering will be truly the ERA OF THE MASSES," wrote Le Bon. "It is no longer in the councils of princes but in the heart of the masses that the destiny of nations is being prepared." The entry of the new urban masses into the political arena posed problems for the liberal regime that had not previously existed. Liberalism is an ideology based on rationalism and individualism; it is the product of a society that was supposed to have stopped undergoing structural changes, and in which political participation was necessarily very limited. At the end of the century, an increasing number of people questioned the usefulness of an ideology in which the new social strata, the millions of workers and wage earners of all categories crowded together in the great industrial centers, could find no place. The crisis of liberalism had its roots in the enormous contradictions that existed between the idea of individualism and the way of life of the urban masses, between the traditional concept of the natural rights of man and the new laws of existence that the generation of 1890 discovered in social Darwinism. The great changes that took place after the First World War are really comprehensible only if one examines them against the background of this first prewar period.

THE
ORIGINS OF
WORLD WAR I

I n spite of repeated international crises and, in some quarters, dissatisfaction with material and cultural conditions, most Europeans wished to preserve peace. Peace organizations thrived; *Lay Down Your Arms*, a pacifist novel by Austrian writer, Bertha von Suttner, became a best-seller. Two peace conferences took place at The Hague in 1899 and 1907 with the aims of bringing about arms reductions and finding ways to settle international affairs. Yet little was accomplished, mutual distrust remained unchecked, and aside from agreements over Germany's railway plans in the Middle East and British and German interests in Portugal's African colonies, few genuine understandings were reached.

If few people actively wanted war, many came to expect it, and prepared accordingly. "I only meet people who assure me that an early war with Germany is certain, in fact, inevitable," the Belgian envoy

reported from Paris in 1913. "People regret it, but they accept it."[1] Their
resignation becomes more understandable if we realize that only a handful
anticipated conflict on the scale that was to come. War in the nineteenth
century had been acknowledged as a legitimate means of pursuing defined
objectives and all conflicts had been short in duration and limited in
scope. The losers were perhaps embarrassed and made to pay in the form
of reparations or territory, or both, but none of these wars escalated beyond their original geographic limits.

When war broke out in the aftermath of the assassination of Archduke Franz Ferdinand, heir to the Austro-Hungarian throne, by a Bosnian nationalist, and what initially had started as a local struggle rapidly
escalated into widespread European conflict, each nation was convinced
it was fighting in defense of vital and legitimate rights. The Entente
powers feared the extension of German hegemony; the Central powers
believed they were struggling for survival. Indeed, the news that war had
come was greeted with some relief; after years of recurring crises the hour
of decision had finally arrived, and inasmuch as almost everyone expected
a short war, the risks did not seem great. In the summer of 1914 few could
imagine the devastation in lives and property that Europeans were bringing upon themselves by accepting a military solution.

Precisely because of the unparalleled dimensions of the cataclysm
that ensued, and because the victors held the losers morally guilty of
having unleashed it, no subject in history has evoked more discussion
and debate than the origins of and the responsibility for the outbreak of
World War I. The Treaty of Versailles blamed Germany and her ally
Austria-Hungary. To counter these accusations the Germans — soon followed by the British, the French, and the Austrians — published volumes
of documents demonstrating the guilt was not theirs alone, thus making
the half-century between the end of the Franco-Prussian War and the
start of World War I the most richly documented period in diplomatic
history.

In the 1920s as the wave of retribution receded and many within
Britain, France, and the United States rejected what they considered
the excesses of a "Carthaginian" peace, some historians sought to revise the treaty's judgment, contending that every country shared at
least some blame. One of the most noted "revisionist" historians was

---

[1] Andreas Dorpalen, *Europe in the 20th Century* (New York, 1968), p. 10.

Sidney B. Fay, whose conclusions are cited below. Also revisionist, but in a wholly different way, was the Communist party of the Soviet Union, whose official history emphasizes the imperialism engendered by the capitalist systems of wartime belligerents — systems which ensured that war was essential to achieve redivision of imperial gains. Also significant in this history is the opinion that capitalist Europe wanted to suppress proletarian revolution by persuading workers to accept nationalist goals.

Responsibility for World War II was attributed to Germany's Nazi government, headed by Adolf Hitler. Consequently, during and after World War II the question of responsibility for World War I was linked to the origins of World War II. Whether through insinuation or demonstration, many historians concluded that German refusal to accept the 1919 settlement made the interwar period a "long armistice" with the foreign policy of Hitler's Germany marking a continuation of the foreign policy of the Kaiser's Germany. Anglo-Saxon and French historians found few difficulties in accepting this interpretation, but conservative German historians, who acknowledged German guilt for the 1939 war, could not accept unilateral German guilt for the 1914 war.[2] Hence when in 1961 German historian Fritz Fischer published his *Griff nach der Weltmacht* (translated in shortened form as *Germany's Aims in the First World War* but more literally meaning "Grab for World Power"), these traditionalists were outraged, because Fischer's book showed not only the extent of German annexationist aims in World War I but also suggested that the German government deliberately went to war in 1914 in order to attain them. To compound matters, Fischer's next book, *Krieg der Illusionen* (translated as *War of Illusions. Germany's Policies from 1911 to 1914*), published in 1975, developed the theme that domestic political and social problems are inextricably linked to and often responsible for a country's foreign policy — a thesis that generated considerable reexamination of the European domestic scene before 1914. This belief in the primacy of *innenpolitik* (domestic policy) in contrast to *aussenpolitik* (foreign policy) was reinforced by the fact that in the 1960s many Americans were examining the origins of the Cold War and the Vietnam War in terms of economic matters, and did the same for pre-World War I Europe. Arno Mayer's essay on the domestic causes of World War I reflects this thinking.

---

[2] James Joll, *The Origins of the First World War* (New York, 1984), pp. 4–5.

Mayer cites the numerous problems faced by the soon-to-be belligerents at home — problems generated not only by the left but by militant conservatives, who in radicalizing moderate elements threatened effective government — as at least partly responsible for their governments' decision to risk war in order to divert attention from internal turbulence.

What then can be concluded from this discussion of the origins of World War I? That there will never be agreement on the question of responsibility? That the underlying causes of the war, such as nationalism, imperialism, the alliance system, the arms race, and coordination of military plans in the event of war, were more significant than the immediate cause, the assassination of the archduke? Such historians as the highly respected Pierre Renouvin have shown that the alliance system effectively preserved peace in a number of prewar crises: for example, the imbroglio that issued from the Austrian annexation of Bosnia-Herzegovina in 1908 and the second Moroccan crisis in 1911. Most divisive imperialist rivalries, Renouvin argues, like British opposition to Germany's proposed Berlin–Baghdad railroad, had been resolved by the summer of 1914.[3] Doesn't an arms build-up create a deterrent and is it not the military's function to make preparations for war? Whether put in political, social, or economic terms, the causes examined by these historians gloss over the antirationalism discussed in the previous chapter. How should we evaluate the importance of ideas in this context? Which are of greater significance in the determination of foreign policy, internal or external matters? How crucial is the role of individual diplomats and statesmen? Finally, how inevitable was World War I?

---

[3] Pierre Renouvin, *De 1871 à 1914. L'apogée de l'Europe*, vol. 6, part 2 of *Histoire des relations internationales*, ed. Pierre Renouvin (8 vols.), (Paris, 1953–1958), pp. 380–84.

The Origins of the World War

࢐

SIDNEY B. FAY

Sidney B. Fay was educated in Germany and wrote on the history of Prussia in the eighteenth century. He has been charged with showing a pro-German bias. Even so, his two-volume history, *The Origins of the World War*, admirably reflects the revisionist view. What follows is his conclusion, in which the responsibility of all the participants is assessed. His account will be more intelligible if the personalities referred to are identified: Pashitch headed the Serbian government; Berchtold was the Austro-Hungarian minister for foreign affairs; Bethmann was the German chancellor; Grey, the British foreign secretary; and Poincaré, the president of France. In contrast to the immediate cause of the war, what importance does Fay attach to underlying causes? Why was Fay's revisionism more acceptable in the 1920s than in subsequent decades?

None of the Powers wanted a European War. Their governing rulers and ministers, with very few exceptions, all foresaw that it must be a frightful struggle, in which the political results were not absolutely certain, but in which the loss of life, suffering, and economic consequences were bound to be terrible. This is true, in a greater or less degree, of

Reprinted with permission of Macmillan Publishing Company from *The Origins of the World War* by Sidney B. Fay. Copyright 1930 The Macmillan Company; copyright renewed 1958 by Sidney Bradshaw Fay.

Pashitch, Berchtold, Bethmann, Sazonov, Poincaré, San Giuliano and Sir Edward Grey. Yet none of them, not even Sir Edward Grey, could have foreseen that the political results were to be so stupendous, and the other consequences so terrible, as was actually the case.

.   .   .

Nevertheless, a European War broke out. Why? Because in each country political and military leaders did certain things which led to mobilizations and declarations of war, or failed to do certain things which might have prevented them. In this sense, all the European countries, in a greater or less degree, were responsible. One must abandon the dictum of the Versailles Treaty that Germany and her allies were solely responsible. It was a dictum exacted by victors from vanquished, under the influence of the blindness, ignorance, hatred, and the propagandist misconceptions to which war had given rise. It was based on evidence which was incomplete and not always sound. It is generally recognized by the best historical scholars in all countries to be no longer tenable or defensible. They are agreed that the responsibility for the War is a divided responsibility. But they still disagree very much as to the relative part of this responsibility that falls on each country and on each individual political or military leader.

Some writers like to fix positively in some precise mathematical fashion the exact responsibility for the war. This was done in one way by the framers of Article 231 of the Treaty of Versailles. It has been done in other ways by those who would fix the responsibility in some relative fashion, as, for instance, Austria first, then Russia, France and Germany and England. But the present writer deprecates such efforts to assess by a precise formula a very complicated question, which is after all more a matter of delicate shading than of definite white and black. Oversimplification, as Napoleon once said in framing his Code, is the enemy of precision. Moreover, even supposing that a general consensus of opinion might be reached as to the relative responsibility of any individual country or man for immediate causes connected with the July crisis of 1914, it is by no means necessarily true that the same relative responsibility would hold for the underlying causes, which for years had been tending toward the creation of a dangerous situation.

One may, however, sum up very briefly the most salient facts in regard to each country.

Serbia felt a natural and justifiable impulse to do what so many other countries had done in the nineteenth century — to bring under one national Government all the discontented Serb people. She had liberated those under Turkish rule; the next step was to liberate those under Hapsburg rule. She looked to Russia for assistance, and had been encouraged to expect that she would receive it. After the assassination, Mr. Pashitch took no steps to discover and bring to justice Serbians in Belgrade who had been implicated in the plot. One of them, Ciganovitch, was even assisted to disappear. Mr. Pashitch waited to see what evidence the Austrian authorities could find. When Austria demanded cooperation of Serbian officials in discovering, though not in trying, implicated Serbians, the Serbian Government made a very conciliatory but negative reply. They expected that the reply would not be regarded as satisfactory, and, even before it was given, ordered the mobilization of the Serbian army. Serbia did not want war, but believed it would be forced upon her. That Mr. Pashitch was aware of the plot three weeks before it was executed, failed to take effective steps to prevent the assassins from crossing over from Serbia to Bosnia, and then failed to give Austria any warning or information which might have averted the fatal crime, were facts unknown to Austria in July, 1914; they cannot therefore be regarded as in any way justifying Austria's conduct; but they are part of Serbia's responsibility, and a very serious part.

Austria was more responsible for the immediate origin of the war than any other Power. Yet from her own point of view she was acting in self-defence — not against an immediate military attack, but against the corroding Greater Serbia and Jugoslav agitation which her leaders believed threatened her very existence. No State can be expected to sit with folded arms and await dismemberment at the hands of its neighbors. Russia was believed to be intriguing with Serbia and Rumania against the Dual Monarchy. The assassination of the heir to the throne, as a result of a plot prepared in Belgrade, demanded severe retribution; otherwise Austria would be regarded as incapable of action, "worm-eaten" as the Serbian Press expressed it, would sink in prestige, and hasten her own downfall. To avert this Berchtold determined to crush Serbia with war. He deliberately framed the ultimatum with the expectation and hope that it would be rejected. He hurriedly declared war against Serbia in order to forestall all efforts at mediation. He refused even to answer his own ally's urgent requests to come to an understanding with Russia, on the basis of a military occupation of Belgrade as a pledge that Serbia would carry out the promises in her reply to the ultimatum. Berchtold gambled on a "local" war with Serbia only, believing that he could rattle the German sword; but rather than abandon his war with Serbia, he was ready to drag the rest of Europe into war.

It is very questionable whether Berchtold's obstinate determination to diminish Serbia and destroy her as a Balkan factor was, after all, the right method, even if he had succeeded in keeping the war "localized" and in temporarily strengthening the Dual Monarchy. Supposing that Russia in 1914, because of military unpreparedness or lack of support, had been ready to tolerate the execution of Berchtold's designs, it is quite certain that she would have aimed within the next two or three years at wiping out this second humiliation, which was so much more damaging to her prestige than that of 1908–09. In two or three years, when her great program of military reform was finally completed, Russia would certainly have found a pretext to reverse the balance in the Balkans in her own favor again. A further consequence of Berchtold's policy, even if successful, would have been the still closer consolidation of the Triple Entente, with the possible addition of Italy. And, finally, a partially dismembered Serbia would have become a still greater source of unrest and danger to the peace of Europe than heretofore. Serbian nationalism, like Polish nationalism, would have been intensified by partition. Austrian power and prestige would not have been so greatly increased as to be able to meet these new dangers. Berchtold's plan was a mere temporary improvement, but could not be a final solution of the Austro-Serbian antagonism. Franz Ferdinand and many others recognized this, and so long as he lived, no step in this fatal direction had been taken. It was the tragic fate of Austria that the only man who might have had the power and ability to develop Austria along sound lines became the innocent victim of the crime which was the occasion of the World War and so of her ultimate disruption.

Germany did not plot a European War, did not want one, and made genuine, though too belated efforts, to avert one. She was the victim of her alliance with Austria and of her own folly. Austria was her only dependable ally, Italy and Rumania having become nothing but allies in name. She could not throw her over, as otherwise she would stand isolated between Russia, where Panslavism and armaments were growing stronger every year, and France, where Alsace-Lorraine, Delcassé's fall, and Agadir were not forgotten. Therefore, Bethmann felt bound to accede to Berchtold's request for support and gave him a free hand to deal with Serbia; he also hoped and expected to "localize" the Austro-Serbian conflict. Germany then gave grounds to the Entente for suspecting the sincerity of her peaceful intentions by her denial of any foreknowledge of the ultimatum, by her support and justification of it when it was published, and by her refusal of Sir Edward Grey's conference proposal. However, Germany by no means had Austria so completely under her thumb as the Entente Powers and many writers have assumed. It is true that Berchtold would hardly have embarked on his gambler's policy unless he had been assured that Germany would fulfil the obligations of the alliance, and to this extent Germany must share the great responsibility of Austria. But when Bethmann realized that Russia was likely to intervene, that England might not remain neutral, and that there was danger of a world war of which Germany and Austria would appear to be the instigators, he tried to call a halt on Austria, but it was too late. He pressed mediation proposals on Vienna, but Berchtold was insensible to the pressure, and the Entente Powers did not believe in the sincerity of his pressure, especially as they produced no results.

Germany's geographical position between France and Russia, and her inferiority in number of troops, had made necessary the plan of crushing the French army quickly at first and then turning against Russia. This was only possible, in the opinion of her strategists, by marching through Belgium, as it was generally anticipated by military men that she would do in case of a European War. On July 29, after Austria had declared war on Serbia, and after the Tsar had assented to general mobilization in Russia (though this was not known in Berlin and was later postponed for a day owing to the Kaiser's telegram to the Tsar), Bethmann took the precaution of sending to the German Minister in Brussels a sealed envelope. The Minister was not to open it except on further instructions. It contained the later demand for the passage of the German army through Belgium. This does not mean, however, that Germany had decided for war. In fact, Bethmann was one of the last of the statesmen to abandon hope of peace and to consent to the mobilization of his country's army. General mobilization of the continental armies took place in the following order: Serbia, Russia, Austria, France and Germany. General mobilization by a Great Power was commonly interpreted by military men in every country, though perhaps not by Sir Edward Grey, the Tsar, and some civilian officials, as meaning that the country was on the point of making war — that the military machine had begun to move and would not be stopped. Hence, when Germany learned of the Russian general mobilization, she sent ultimatums to St. Petersburg and Paris, warning that German mobilization would follow unless Russia suspended hers within twelve hours, and asking what would be the attitude of France. The answers being unsatisfactory, Germany then mobilized and declared war. It was the hasty Russian general mobilization, assented to on July 29 and ordered on July 30, while Germany was still trying to bring Austria to accept mediation proposals, which finally rendered the European War inevitable.

Russia was partly responsible for the Austro-Serbian conflict because of the frequent encouragement which she had given at Belgrade — that Serbian national unity would be ultimately achieved with Russian assistance at Austrian expense. This had led the Belgrade Cabinet to hope for Russian support in case of a war with Austria, and the hope did not prove vain in July, 1914. Before this, to be sure, in the Bosnian Crisis and during the Balkan Wars, Russia had put restraint upon Serbia, because Russia, exhausted by the effects of the Russo-Japanese War, was not yet ready for a European struggle with the Teutonic Powers. But in 1914 her armaments, though not yet completed, had made such progress that the militarists were confident of success, if they had French and British support. In the spring of 1914, the Minister of War, Sukhomlinov, had published an article in a Russian newspaper, though without signing his name, to the effect, "Russia is ready, France must be ready also." Austria was convinced that Russia would ultimately aid Serbia, unless the Serbian danger were dealt with energetically after the Archduke's murder; she knew that Russia was growing stronger every year; but she doubted whether the Tsar's armaments had yet reached the point at which Russia would dare to intervene; she would therefore run less risk of Russian intervention and a European War if she used the Archduke's assassination as an excuse for weakening Serbia, then if she should postpone action until the future.

Russia's responsibility lay also in the secret preparatory military measures which she was making at the same time that she was carrying on diplomatic negotiations. These alarmed Germany and Austria. But it was primarily Russia's general mobilization, made when Germany was trying to bring Austria to a settlement, which precipitated the final catastrophe, causing Germany to mobilize and declare war.

The part of France is less clear than that of the other Great Powers, because she has not yet made a full publication of her documents. To be sure, M. Poincaré, in the fourth volume of his memoirs, has made a skilful and elaborate plea, to prove "*La France innocente.*" But he is not convincing. It is quite clear that on his visit to Russia he assured the

Tsar's Government that France would support her as an ally in preventing Austria from humiliating or crushing Serbia. Paléologue renewed these assurances in a way to encourage Russia to take a strong hand. He did not attempt to restrain Russia from military measures which he knew would call forth German counter-measures and cause war. Nor did he keep his Government promptly and fully informed of the military steps which were being taken at St. Petersburg. President Poincaré, upon his return to France, made efforts for peace, but his great preoccupation was to minimize French and Russian preparatory measures and emphasize those of Germany, in order to secure the certainty of British support in a struggle which he now regarded as inevitable.

Sir Edward Grey made many sincere proposals for preserving peace; they all failed owing partly, but not exclusively, to Germany's attitude. Sir Edward could probably have prevented war if he had done either of two things. If, early in the crisis, he had acceded to the urging of France and Russia and given a strong warning to Germany that, in a European War, England would take the side of the Franco-Russian Alliance, this would probably have led Bethmann to exert an earlier and more effective pressure on Austria; and it would perhaps thereby have prevented the Austrian declaration of war on Serbia, and brought to a successful issue the "direct conversations" between Vienna and St. Petersburg. Or, if Sir Edward Grey had listened to German urging, and warned France and Russia early in the crisis that if they became involved in war, England would remain neutral, probably Russia would have hesitated with her mobilizations, and France would probably have exerted a restraining influence at St. Petersburg. But Sir Edward Grey could not say that England would take the side of France and Russia, because he had a Cabinet nearly evenly divided, and he was not sure, early in the crisis, that public opinion in England would back him up in war against Germany. He could resign, and he says in his memoirs that he would have resigned, but that would have been no comfort or aid to France, who had come confidently to count upon British support. He was determined to say and do nothing which might encourage her with a hope which he could not fulfil. Therefore, in spite of the pleadings of the French, he refused to give them definite assurances until the probable German determination to go through Belgium made it clear that the Cabinet, and Parliament, and British public opinion would follow his lead in war on Germany. On the other hand, he was unwilling to heed the German pleadings that he exercise restraint at Paris and St. Petersburg, because he did not wish to endanger the Anglo-Russian Entente and the solidarity of the Triple Entente, because he felt a moral obligation to France, growing out of the Anglo-French military and naval conversations of the past years, and because he suspected that Germany was backing Austria up in an unjustifiable course and that Prussian militarists had taken the direction of affairs at Berlin out of the hands of Herr von Bethmann-Hollweg and the civilian authorities.

Italy exerted relatively little influence on the crisis in either direction.

Belgium had done nothing in any way to justify the demand which Germany made upon her. With commendable prudence, at the very first news of the ominous Austrian ultimatum, she had foreseen the danger to which she might be exposed. She had accordingly instructed her representatives abroad as to the statements which they were to make in case Belgium should decide very suddenly to mobilize to protect her neutrality. On July 29, she placed her army upon "a strengthened war footing," but did not order complete mobilization until two days later, when Austria, Russia, and Germany had already done so, and war appeared inevitable. Even after being confronted with the terrible German ultimatum, at 7 P.M. on August 2, she did not at once invite the assistance of English and French troops to aid her in the defense of her soil and her neutrality against a certain German assault; it was not until German troops had actually violated her territory, on August 4, that she appealed for the assistance of the Powers which had guaranteed her neutrality. Belgium was the innocent victim of German strategic necessity. Though the German violation of Belgium was of enormous influence in forming public opinion as to the responsibility for the War after hostilities began, it was not a cause of the War, except in so far as it made it easier for Sir Edward Grey to bring England into it.

In the forty years following the Franco-Prussian War, as we have seen, there developed a system of alliances which divided Europe into two hostile groups. This hostility was accentuated by the increase of armaments, economic rivalry, nationalist ambitions and antagonisms, and newspaper incitement. But it is very doubtful whether all these dangerous tendencies would have actually led to war, had it not been for the assassination of Franz Ferdinand. That was the factor which consolidated the elements of hostility and started the rapid and complicated succession of events which culminated in a World War, and for that factor Serbian nationalism was primarily responsible.

But the verdict of the Versailles Treaty that Germany and her allies were responsible for the War, in view of the evidence now available, is historically unsound. It should therefore be revised. However, because of the popular feeling widespread in some of the Entente countries, it is doubtful whether a formal and legal revision is as yet practicable. There must first come a further revision by historical scholars, and through them of public opinion.

History of the Communist Party of the Soviet Union

∿⁄∾

The History of the Communist Party of the Soviet Union, revealing the official Marxist-Leninist version of events, places emphasis on the contradictions contained within capitalism, on the need of advanced (monopoly) capitalism to resort to imperialism, on class conflict in general, and on the role of the Soviet proletariat guided by its party in particular. To what extent is evidence cited in support of the conclusions reached?

The imperialist world war broke out on August 1 (July 19, old style), 1914: It was the cumulative result of sharp imperialist contradictions.

The distinctive feature of imperialism, the highest and last stage of capitalism, is the domination of monopolies — syndicates, trusts and similar organisations of a handful of millionaires controlling vast amounts of capital. Not content with the home market, the capitalists made their way into the colonies and economically underdeveloped countries in search of profit. By the beginning of the century the whole world had already been divided among a small group of leading capitalist powers.

But under capitalism, an even course of development is impossible. Individual enterprises, industries and, indeed, countries overtake and

From the *History of the Communist Party of the Soviet Union*, Moscow, 1963, pp. 181–183. Reprinted by permission of the Soviet Copyright Agency.

outstrip others, which have to give way to their more successful competitors; or the latter themselves yield place. Imperialism, with its domination of giant monopolies, accentuates this unevenness, both in the economic and political fields. The development of capitalism becomes spasmodic, and this uneven development constantly upsets the international equilibrium, changing the relative economic and military strength of the powers. And the greater their strength, the more insistent becomes their demand for more markets and for new colonies, because in a society based on private ownership of the means of production, division of spoils is always in accordance with strength or capital. With the world already divided up among the biggest capitalist states, its redivision could only take place at the expense of one or another of these states, that is, through war.

Lenin pointed out that the emergence of powerful capitalist monopoly associations and their struggle for an economic redivision of the world which was already divided territorially was bound to lead to imperialist wars.

The imperialists had, in fact, long been preparing for a war to redivide the world. The most bellicose in this respect were the German militarists, who considered that they had been cheated out of their share of colonies. By the close of the last century, Germany had overtaken Britain in industrial development and was ousting her from her traditional markets. Germany's aim was a radical redivision of the world in her favour. This contradiction between British and German imperialism was in fact the root cause of the war. However, a big part was also played by the imperialist contradictions between Germany and France, Russia and Germany, etc. Long before the war, in 1879–82, Germany had formed an alliance with Austria-Hungary and Italy against Russia and France. The latter retaliated by forming an alliance of their own, and the British imperialists, fearing Germany's advance to world domination, concluded an agreement (Entente) with France to combat Germany by joint effort. In 1907 Russia concluded a treaty with Britain, as a result of which Russia joined the Entente. The two mutually opposed imperialist blocs in Europe thus took final shape.

Economically dependent, mainly on French and British capital, Russia was drawn into the war on the side of the Entente. But the tsarist government had its own reasons for taking part in the imperialist war. The Russian capitalists strongly resented German competition in the domestic market. The dominant classes of Russia wanted new markets in which there would be no competition. The Russian imperialists were out to gain possession of Constantinople and the straits leading from the Black Sea to the Mediterranean; they wanted to seize Turkish Armenia and thereby bring the whole of Armenia under Russian rule. This clashed with German imperialist plans in the Middle East: Germany was penetrating into Turkey and Iran and had secured a concession for a railway from Berlin to Baghdad. Russo-German contradictions in the Middle East became especially keen in the twentieth century.

Another major cause of the war was the imperialists' desire to suppress the revolutionary movement, which in the past ten years had grown to powerful dimensions. The Russian revolution of 1905–07 had greatly stimulated the working-class struggle in Europe and America and set off a national liberation movement in the East. The governments of the leading powers — and the tsarist government first and foremost — feared a further spread of the revolution, and believed that war would sidetrack the masses from revolutionary struggle. The imperialists hoped that by instigating the workers of different countries against each other they could split the international proletarian movement, poison it with the venom of chauvinism, physically annihilate a big section of the advanced workers and in this way crush, or at any rate weaken, the revolutionary pressure of the masses.

Germany's Aims
in the First World War

ᴺⱽⱽⱽ

FRITZ FISCHER

Fritz Fischer is a professor of history at the University of Hamburg.
He has lectured widely in the United States and was a member of
the Institute for Advanced Studies at Princeton. The excerpts that
follow come from his book, *Germany's Aims in the First World War*.
Described as possibly the most important historical work, certainly
one of the most controversial, to come out of Germany since World
War II, it contains a wealth of documentation from previously un-
used archives. How may Fischer's arguments be compared with those
of Fay? Whose do you find more persuasive? Why?

. . . The fundamental changes in economic conditions, the wide-spread
prosperity, the rapid growth of the population, the swift expansion in
all branches of economic life, combined to create a general conviction,
which was reinforced by nation-wide propaganda, that Germany's frontiers had become too narrow for her, but that the ring of powers round
her would never consent to their extension. The diplomatic campaign to
'split the Entente' by peaceful means cannot be understood without a
glance at these structural changes.

Germany's claim to world power was based on her consciousness of
being a 'young,' growing and rising nation. Her population had risen from

about 41 millions in 1871 to about 68 millions in 1915, while that of France, with a larger area, had remained almost stationary, reaching only 40 millions in 1915. Moreover, more than one-third of the population of Germany was under fifteen years of age, and this gave the national consciousness a dynamic element which further reinforced the demand for *Lebensraum*, markets and industrial expansion. Although emigration had been high (1.3 million persons emigrated between 1881 and 1890), the population figures for 1910 were nevertheless far more favourable than, for example, those of France: an excess of births over deaths of 800,000 (8.9 per 1,000 against 3.4 per 1,000 in France), while the expectation of life was increasing and infant mortality on the decline. With increasing industrialisation, internal migration was beginning to replace migration overseas and immigrants were beginning to come in from Austria, Italy, Russian Poland and other European countries. Germany was developing more and more into a highly industrialised exporting country, and the problem of finding markets and raw materials to support her population was growing increasingly urgent.

. . .

Economic expansion was the basis of Germany's political world diplomacy, which vacillated in its methods between rapprochement and conciliation at one moment, aggressive insistence on Germany's claims the next, but never wavered in its ultimate objective, the expansion of Germany's power.

. . .

In spite of all the surface calm, the feeling, or conviction, that a great European conflict could not be long postponed had become general in Europe. Germany found herself, as Moltke put it, 'in a condition of hopeless isolation which was growing ever more hopeless.' Her confidence in the invincibility of her military strength had been deeply shaken by the increases in the French and Russian armies (of which the latter would in 1917 reach its maximum peacetime strength of 2,200,000 men), and the idea of a 'preventive war' was acquiring an increasing appeal, especially in military circles. 'We are ready, and the sooner it comes, the better for us,' said Moltke on June 1, 1914. At about the same time, Moltke asked Jagow to precipitate a preventive war as soon as possible. Jagow refused, but admitted later that he had never wholly excluded the idea of a preventive war and that Moltke's words had influenced him during the crisis of July–August 1914. Another element of danger was the fact that

Conservative circles had come, especially since the Reichstag elections of 1912, to regard war as a 'tempering of the nation' and calculated to strengthen the Prusso-German state. Bethmann Hollweg, who in December, 1913, had already rejected the suggestion passed on to him by the crown prince, and emanating from the panGermans, that a *coup d'état* should be carried out against the Social Democrats, spoke out again just six months later against these speculations on the internal political consequences of a war. He told Lerchenfield, the Bavarian minister, at the beginning of June, 1914, that:

> There were still circles in the Reich which looked to war to bring about an improvement, in the conservative sense, of internal conditions in Germany. He thought that the effects would be the exact opposite; a world war, with its incalculable consequences, would greatly increase the power of Social Democracy, because it had preached peace, and would bring down many a throne.

A month later the Chancellor agreed on foreign-political and military grounds to take the risk of a great war, while recognising — unlike the Conservatives — that the war could not be carried on without the co-operation of Social Democracy.

.   .   .

There is no question but that the conflict of military and political interests, of resentment and ideas, which found expression in the July crisis, left no government of any of the European powers quite free of some measure of responsibility — greater or smaller — for the outbreak of the war in one respect or another. It is, however, not the purpose of this work to enter into the familiar controversy, on which whole libraries have been written, over the question of war guilt, to discuss exhaustively the responsibility of the individual statesmen and soldiers of all the European powers concerned, or to pass final judgment on them. We are concerned solely with the German leaders' objectives and with the policy actually followed by them in the July crisis, and that only in so far as their policy throws light on the postulates and origins of Germany's war aims.

It must be repeated: given the tenseness of the world situation in 1914 — a condition for which Germany's world policy, which had already led to three dangerous crises (those of 1905, 1908 and 1911), was in no small measure responsible — any limited or local war in Europe directly involving one great power must inevitably carry with it the imminent danger of a general war. As Germany willed and coveted the Austro-Serbian war and, in her confidence in her military superiority, deliberately faced the risk of a conflict with Russia and France, her leaders must bear a substantial share of the historical responsibility for the outbreak of general war in 1914. This responsibility is not diminished by the fact that at the last moment Germany tried to arrest the march of destiny, for her efforts to influence Vienna were due exclusively to the threat of British intervention and, even so, they were half-hearted, belated and immediately revoked.

It is true that German politicians and publicists, and with them the entire German propaganda machine during the war and German historiography after the war — particularly after Versailles — have invariably maintained that the war was forced on Germany, or at least (adopting Lloyd George's dictum, made for political reasons, that 'we all stumbled into the war') that Germany's share of the responsibility was no greater than that of the other participants. But confidential exchanges between Germany and Austria, and between the responsible figures in Germany itself, untinged by any propagandist intent, throw a revealing spotlight on the real responsibility.

A few weeks after the outbreak of war, during the crises on the Marne and in Galicia, the Austrians asked urgently for German help against the superior Russian armies facing them. It was refused. Count Tisza then advised Berchtold to tell the Germans: 'That we took our decision to go to war on the strength of the express statements both of the German Emperor and of the German Imperial Chancellor that they regarded the moment as suitable and would be glad if we showed ourselves in earnest.'

The official documents afford ample proofs that during the July crisis the Emperor, the German military leaders and the Foreign Ministry were pressing Austria-Hungary to strike against Serbia without delay, or alternatively agreed to the dispatch of an ultimatum to Serbia couched in such sharp terms as to make war between the two countries more than probable, and that in doing so they deliberately took the risk of a continental war against Russia and France. But the decisive point is that, as we now know — although for a long time it was not admitted — these groups were not alone. On July 5 and 6 the Imperial Chancellor, Bethmann Hollweg, the man in whom the constitution vested the sole responsibility, decided to take the risk and even over-trumped the Emperor when he threatened to weaken. That this was no 'tragic doom,' no 'ineluctable destiny,' but a deliberate decision of policy emerges beyond doubt from the diary of his private secretary, Kurt Riezler, who recorded in it his conversations with the Chancellor in the critical days (and, indeed, over many years). These diaries have not yet been published, but the extracts from them which have seen the light furnish irrefutable proof that during the July crisis Bethmann Hollweg was ready for war. More than this. Riezler's entry for the evening of July 8, after Bethmann Hollweg's return to Hohenfinow (where Rathenau was also stopping) shows what advance calculations the leaders of Germany were making in respect of the situation produced by the Sarajevo murder. According to his secretary, the Chancellor said: 'If war doesn't come, if the Tsar doesn't want it or France panics and advises peace, we have still achieved this much, that we have manoeuvred the Entente into disintegration over this move.'

In other words, Bethmann Hollweg reckoned with a major general war as the result of Austria's swift punitive action against Serbia. If, however, Russia and France were again to draw back (as in 1909 and 1911) — which he at first regarded as the less probable eventuality — then at least Germany would have achieved a signal diplomatic victory: she would have split Russia from France and isolated both without war. But war was what he expected, and how he expected its course to run we learn from his predecessor in the Chancellorship, Bülow, who had a long discussion with him at the beginning of August. Bethmann Hollweg told Bülow that he was reckoning with 'a war lasting three, or at the most, four months . . . a violent, but short storm.' Then, he went on, revealing his innermost wishes, it would 'in spite of the war, indeed, through it,' be possible to establish a friendly relationship with England, and through England with France. He hoped to bring about 'a grouping of Germany, England and France against the Russia colossus which threatens the civilisation of Europe.'

Bethmann Hollweg himself often hinted darkly during the war how closely Germany had been involved in the beginning of the war. He was less concerned with the 'staging' of it than to register the spirit of the German leaders who had made it possible for the war to be begun even after the premises for it had collapsed. The following bitter words are taken from his address to the Central Committee of the Reichstag at the beginning of October, 1916, during the sharp debate on the initiation of unlimited submarine warfare; they outline Germany's real 'guilt,' her constant over-estimation of her own powers, and her misjudgment of realities:

> Since the outbreak of the war we have not always avoided the danger of underestimating the strength of our enemies. The extraordinary development of the last twenty years seduced wide circles into over-estimating our own forces, mighty as they are, in comparing them with those of the rest of the world . . . in our rejoicing over our own progress (we have) not paid sufficient regard to conditions in other countries.

The July crisis must not be regarded in isolation. It appears in its true light only when seen as a link between Germany's 'world policy,' as followed since the mid-1890s, and her war aims policy after August, 1914.

Domestic Causes
of the First World War

ᔐᢣ

ARNO MAYER

Arno J. Mayer teaches at Princeton University. His books, which
have shown how foreign and domestic policies are necessarily intertwined, reveal an interest in the peacemaking process and in the
diplomacy practiced after World War I. He has also published on
what he calls the persistence of monarchical conservatism well into
the modern period. His most recent book reexamines the Holocaust. This excerpt from an essay on the domestic tensions which
may have affected diplomatic decision making in 1914 comes from
an anthology compiled in honor of the distinguished historian of
Germany, Hajo Holborn. How close to a Marxist view is it to state
that errors are inherent in capitalism and that the internal contradictions of capitalist society in 1914 increased the likelihood of war?
Does this make the argument any less legitimate? Compared to the
Communist party history, does Mayer offer evidence in support of
his conclusions?

When analyzing the origins of the Great War, diplomatic historians
continue to focus on two sets of underlying and precipitant causes: those
rooted in the dysfunctions of the international system and those rooted
in the mistakes, miscalculations, and vagaries of the principal foreign

policy actors. These historians assume that in a multiple-state system the balancing of power is a natural and essential method of control, notwithstanding its inherent uncertainties. In other words, they do not question or criticize the balancing-of-power system or process as such. Instead, they tilt their lances at four developments that complicated, if not obstructed, its smooth operation: 1. the alliance system, which became increasingly polarized and rigidified, thereby threatening to transform any limited, local conflict into an unlimited, general war; 2. the attendant armaments race, which exacerbated mutual hostility, fear, and distrust; 3. the new military metaphysics, which inclined civilian foreign-policy actors to become increasingly responsive to the military leaders and their ironclad timetables; and 4. public opinion, expressed and mobilized through the daily press, notably the yellow and jingoist dailies, which were impatient with accommodation.

In addition to diagnosing these four dysfunctions in the balancing-of-power system or process, diplomatic historians also probe into the personal attitudes, motives, and objectives of the principal foreign-policy actors — heads of state, chief executives, foreign ministers, permanent foreign office officials, ambassadors, and military and naval officers. Not surprisingly, each major historian tends to have his favorite villain. Rather than indict entire nations, scholars tend to return verdicts against individual actors of a given nation or alliance. Three categories of charges are most commonly preferred: 1. that they made grave mistakes in diplomatic tactics; 2. that they miscalculated the responses of potential enemies; and 3. that they pursued objectives that were incompatible with the maintenance of the European equilibrium. But whatever the charge, in the last analysis their actions and judgments are said to have been warped by personal ambition, caprice, pique, or lack of backbone in the face of ruthless warmongers.

Admittedly, this framework of orthodox diplomatic history, tempered by amateur psychology, has been used to good advantage. It has served to uncover a great deal about the origins of the First World War in particular, and about the causes of international conflict in general.

Just the same, this time-honored approach has some rather grave limitations. In particular, it slides over 1. the proclivity of key foreign-policy actors to risk war in general, and preventive war in particular; 2. the degree to which they realized that any localized conflict was likely to develop into a major all-European or even world war; and 3. the extent to which they entertained recourse to external war for internal political purposes.

This third limitation stems very largely from the diplomatic historian's disposition to detach foreign policy hermetically from domestic politics; and to disconnect foreign-policy and diplomatic actors rigorously from the political and social context from which they originate and in which they operate.

Admittedly, this twofold dissociation, for analytic purposes, may not fatally handicap the study of the international politics of the relatively calm and elitist mid-eighteenth century. There seems little doubt, however, that this dual disjunction hinders the examination and understanding of foreign policy and diplomacy in such revolutionary eras as 1789 to 1815 and in such brief revolutionary spasms as 1848–50.

This interconnection of domestic politics and foreign policy is exceptionally intense under prerevolutionary and revolutionary conditions. Characteristically, in the prewar years domestic tensions rose sharply at the same time that the international system became increasingly strained. Moreover, this symbiotic growth of domestic and international tensions occurred in that part of the world in which, for the first time in recorded history, government policies, including foreign policies, were shaped in the crucible of organized party, pressure, and interest politics.

In other words, on the eve of war the major European politics were far from quiescent; and both the making and the conduct of foreign policy had ceased to be the private preserve of an encapsulated élite free of political pressures and neutral in the explosive domestic controversies of their respective societies. Accordingly, the 50 per cent increase in military spending in the five prewar years may not have been exclusively a function of mounting international distrust, insecurity, and hostility. In some measure it may also have been a by-product of the resolve by conservatives and ultraconservatives to foster their political position by rallying the citizenry around the flag; and to reduce the politically unsettling cyclical fluctuations of the capitalist economies by raising armaments expenditures. In this same connection it should be stressed that the chief villains of July–August 1914 — those foreign-policy actors whom diplomatic historians identify as having practiced reckless brinkmanship — were intimately tied in with those social, economic, and political strata that were battling either to maintain the domestic status quo or to steer an outright reactionary course.

To attenuate if not overcome the limitations of diplomatic history's conventional approach to the causes of war its analytic framework should be recast to accommodate three aspects of the historical and immediate crisis that conditioned and precipitated hostilities in July–August 1914:

1. the dysfunctions in the international system; 2. the domestic dysfunctions in the would-be belligerent nations; and 3. the inextricable interplay between these two sets of dysfunctions.

Whereas the dysfunctions in the international system and the diplomatic rivalries among the major powers have been studied exhaustively and are well-known, the same cannot be said about the prewar domestic dysfunctions, notably about their all-European scope.

During the decade, including the weeks immediately preceding July–August 1914, the European nations experienced more than routine political and social disturbances. Even Britain, that paradigm of ordered change and constitutionalism, was approaching the threshold of civil war. Judging by the Curragh incident, Carson and the Ulster volunteers had the sympathy if not outright cooperation of influential civil and military leaders in their defiance of Parliament; and the Triple Alliance of railwaymen, miners, and transport workers, among whom militant syndicalists were ascendant, threatened a paralyzing general strike in case their minimum demands were not met by the fall of 1914. Whereas Ulster became the rallying issue and symbol for an influential conglomeration of conservatives and reactionaries, the strike project of the Triple Alliance roused extensive support throughout the restless Labour movement. The resulting polarization, along with the shift from debate in Westminster to direct action in the streets, eroded the vital center so essential for the politics of compromise and accommodation. Indeed, historians have wondered whether if external war had not come in 1914 England might not have become caught up in civil strife, with fatal damage to her time-honored parliamentary system.

In France, meanwhile, the struggle between the right and the left raged with unabated intensity around the twin issues of the three-year draft and the progressive income tax. As in England, the center of the political spectrum, which in France was multiparty in nature, was being eroded in favor of the two opposing extremes. In particular, the left's strident antimilitarism, which the right construed as a pressing social threat, frightened not only moderate republicans but also radicals into a common political front with the right. In turn, the *enragés* of the left made it increasingly difficult for the socialists to cooperate with the center-left, which stood accused of truckling to antirepublicanism. And, indeed, the right and center joined forces in support of the three-year draft, capitalizing on the appeals of nationalism to impugn the patriotism of the socialists, who advocated a two-year draft. This reordering of political partnerships was reflected in acute cabinet instability and in the antirepublican and protofascist right becoming the backstop for a conservative-leaning regime putting order and defense ahead of reform.

In Italy prewar political and labor disturbances culminated in the explosive Red Week of early June 1914. Especially once this strike wave subsided, and as usually happens in the wake of misfired rebellions, the Italian middle-class nationalists assumed a position of intransigent hostility to the left — including the moderate left — which in 1915 took the form of taking Italy into the war against the will of the vast majority of the Italian nation.

As for Germany's semi-parliamentary system, which was the privileged preserve of conservative nationalists, it was heavily besieged by those parties — the Social Democrats, the *Zentrum*, the Progressives, and the moderate wing of the National Liberals — that denounced Prussia's three-class franchise and clamored for the cabinet's subordination to the Reichstag. Paradoxically, the mounting militancy in certain key trade unions scared off potential converts to political reform. In any case, according to Arthur Rosenberg, the political and social tensions in prewar Germany were "typical of a pre-revolutionary period," and if Germany had not gone to war in 1914 "the conflict between the Imperial Government and the majority of the German nation would have continued to intensify to a point at which a revolutionary situation would have been created."

The power élites in both halves of the Dual Monarchy faced increasingly explosive nationalistic unrest which, in itself, was an expression of spiraling political, economic, and social dysfunctions. Both Otto Bauer and Victor Bibl have argued convincingly that fear of southern Slav insurgency and of intensifying Austro-Czech tensions drove Vienna's political class into trying to overcome its permanent internal crisis by recourse to external war.

Simultaneously the Russian government, firmly controlled by unbending conservatives, confronted rising labor unrest in the major industrial centers alongside heightened restlessness among the peripheral national minorities. It was a sign of the times that during the first seven months of 1914 industrial unrest reached unparalleled scope and intensity, much of it politically and socially rather than economically motivated.

Great care must be taken to distinguish between, on the one hand, the actual scope and intensity of these internal tensions and disturbances, and, on the other hand, their perception, evaluation, and exploitation by the political contestants of the time. It is characteristic of prerevolutionary situations that hardened conservatives and counterrevolutionaries deliberately exaggerate all disorders, including the imminence of their transmutation into full-scale insurrection, in order to press and justify energetic precautionary measures. In turn, advanced reformers and revolutionaries similarly distort and distrust the intentions and actions of their domestic antagonists, charging them with pre-emptive counterrevolutionary designs. But this mutual misrepresentation itself contributed to the polarization between the intransigent forces of order and the revolutionary forces of change, at the expense of the moderate, compromise-seeking center.

In Britain, France, and Italy parliamentary liberalism — the locus of this vital center — was heavily besieged, if not on the verge of collapse. The moderately reformist administrations of all three countries found it increasingly difficult to secure governing majorities. They were buffeted constantly by the parliamentary as well as extraparliamentary pressures of the militant counterrevolutionary right and the militant revolutionary left. In Germany, Austria-Hungary, and Russia, where the ruling power élite considered even the advocates of integral parliamentarism dangerous revolutionaries, the vital center was almost completely emasculated.

It would seem that in these as in other prerevolutionary eras, the specter of revolution precipitated an active counterrevolutionary response among vulnerable status groups — the landed aristocracy, the petty nobility, the petite-bourgeoisie, the artisans, and the bypassed entrepreneurs. In fact, there may well be a certain parallelism between the attitudes and actions of such crisis strata in domestic politics and the attitudes and actions of foreign-policy actors who consider their nation's international power and prestige to be declining. In both instances the threatened parties are particularly prone to force a pre-emptive showdown — armed repression or insurrection at home or preventive war abroad — with the resolve of thereby arresting or reversing the course of history, which they claim to be turning against them.

Admittedly, much has been written about the antiwar agitation that was such a prominent aspect of the prewar thunder on the left. Considerably less is known about the superpatriotic agitation that was so central to the corresponding thunder on the right. To be sure, conventional diplomatic historians have noted the upsurge of nationalism before the war, and its further inflammation during and immediately following the July crisis. Few, however, have bothered to examine systematically the social, economic, and political background of the political organizers and social carriers of this nationalist revival. Surely it is not without significance that nearly all the superpatriots who clamored for preparedness and foreign-policy pugnacity held reactionary, ultraconservative, or protofascist views on domestic affairs. Before the war there were few if any liberal conservatives or reformers in the Navy League, the Tariff Reform League, and the pro-Entente wing of the Unionist and Liberal parties in England; in the *Action française*, the *Ligue des patriotes*, and the *Fédération des gauches* in France; in the Nationalist Party and the *fasci* in Italy; in the Pan-German League and the Conservative Party in Germany; in the war party centering around the Archduke in Austria-Hungary; and in the Assembly of the Russian People and the Black Hundreds in Russia.

Evidently foreign-policy issues became highly politicized, since notwithstanding governmental appeals, the primacy of foreign policy is inoperative under prerevolutionary conditions. Whereas the campaign against the arms race was an integral part of the struggle against the forces of order, the campaign for preparedness was a central feature of the struggle against the forces of change. All along the superpatriots of the two opposing camps did each other's bidding in that they exploited and fomented the mutual suspicion, fear, hostility and insecurity that quickened the European arms race. The Pan-German League and the *Action française* unwittingly helped each other at the expense of heightening international tensions. Domestically, meanwhile, they were instrumental in frightening liberal conservatives and reformists into supporting national preparedness, thereby eroding the vital center. In the parliamentary nations of Western Europe as well as in the autocratic empires of Central and Eastern Europe the prewar governments were particularly responsive to superpatriotic blandishments whenever moderate and advanced reformists threatened a united front, as was the case when Caillaux and Jaurès explored the basis for cooperation. In brief, the center increasingly relied on the right as a backstop, with the powerful encouragement of the upper echelons of the army, the foreign offices, the diplomatic corps, the ministry of the interior, and — in most cases — the church. Almost without exception these time-honored institutions were strongholds of the threatened and intransigent crisis strata rather than of the self-confident and supple business and banking grande-bourgeoisie.

To a not inconsiderable degree, then, throughout Europe the rising international tensions were accompanied by rising internal tensions — by mounting social, political, and economic struggles that radicalized the extremes, eroded the center, and inclined the governments to push preparedness and diplomatic obduracy as part of their efforts to maintain a precarious domestic status quo.

3

THE
BOLSHEVIK
REVOLUTION

The overthrow of the tsarist government in March 1917 came as no surprise. For months the regime had hovered on the point of collapse. Corruption and incompetence at home, defeat and demoralization at the front, had caused widespread discontent. "Revolution was in the air," wrote Buchanan, the British ambassador in Petrograd, "and the only moot point was whether it would come from above or below." The revolution was popular and spontaneous, issuing from food riots and street demonstrations, and it was triumphant, in view of the soldiers' refusal to fire on the crowd. Under the aegis of a provisional government, all political forces were free to compete for power. What came as a surprise, a scant eight months later, was the victory of the Bolshevik wing of the Russian Social Democratic Workers party, the smallest and least impressive of the contenders, whose leaders returned to Russia from abroad or from internal exile after the collapse of the empire. The unexpected victory, which brought the Bolsheviks (or, after they changed their name, the Communists) to the power which they were able to maintain for the next three quarters of a century has been the subject of countless inquiries and serves as the focus of the three readings that follow.

Less closely examined (perhaps because losers in history do not receive quite the same attention as winners) is the question of why revolutionary socialism, with a short-lived exception or two, failed elsewhere in Europe. In Germany, with the prolongation of war misery, Social Democrats and Independent Social Democrats were demanding liberal constitutional reforms and peace without annexations, while a small group on the far left known as the Spartacists openly agitated for revolution. When German sailors refused to set out against the British fleet on a mission they regarded as suicidal and intended only to save the honor of a vanquished navy, and when an independent socialist republic was proclaimed in Bavaria, successful revolution seemed imminent. While events did not go so far in France, Britain, or Italy, it was nevertheless true that formidable labor unrest would soon lead to general strikes in France, have the red flag flying over such industrial centers as Glasgow, and bring about the seizure of factories by workers in northern Italy. Yet revolution, certainly from the left, failed outside of Russia. In his analysis of Bolshevik success, Theodore Von Laue compares conditions in Russia with those in Western and Central Europe and explains why it was only in the former that revolution succeeded.

In the debate over the issue of "inevitability," Von Laue believes that liberal democracy could not have survived in Russia, regardless of whether the provisional government remained faithful to her wartime allies. Other historians have emphasized that government's insistence on continuing to fight a losing war that lacked popular support. George Kennan asks why the Allies, who had hailed the overthrow of the tsar and at once recognized the provisional government, convinced that a popular regime could muster support for a flagging war effort, insisted that the government continue to fight. He concludes that the reasons were not only military ones. In any event, the decision by the government — and its chief minister, Alexander Kerensky — to remain in a wholly unpopular war accounts for the popularity of the Bolsheviks, who could point to the army as already having voted for peace "with its feet" through wholesale desertions. Jerry Hough, in a revision of a well-established book by Merle Fainsod, downplays the belief that superior party organization and German financial support allowed Lenin and the Bolsheviks to prevail.

One might have expected considerable scholarly attention to be given to Lenin and the part he played in the November uprising. Was he the "hero" in this history who by dint of forceful character and strategic brilliance transformed the uncertainties of a chaotic situation into Bolshevik success?[1] Was this success a consequence of his party's superior organization, for which, admittedly, he was responsible? Or was Bolshevik victory the result of his masterful ability to exploit popular unrest by siding with a public opinion he had no intention of following in the future? Given the imperatives of the day, would the results have been the same without Lenin?

The historians cited are providing answers to somewhat different aspects of the larger question of why the Bolsheviks were victorious. Kennan examines the failure of the Western allies to respond to the dilemma faced by the provisional government; Von Laue considers why democracy could not have survived in Russia regardless of what the government did; and Hough asks why the Bolsheviks, though never able to secure a majority, enjoyed substantial popular support.

While reading their analyses, particularly before rushing to judgment on Kerensky and the provisional government, it may be useful to keep the following question in mind. Could this government, under its first chief Prince Lvov, a kindly Tolstoyan type who believed in "non-resistance to evil" and in "bloodless revolution," and then under Kerensky, formerly a bourgeois lawyer who had joined the Socialist Revolutionary party after the tsar's downfall, have undertaken significant reform? It tended in the best liberal tradition to defer decisions to a future constituent assembly, and the reforms agreed to—political amnesty, removal of religious and racial distinctions, and assorted civil liberties—were relatively harmless and readily supported. More controversial issues, especially those of land reform and unilateral withdrawal from the war, were neglected. Under the socialist and former pacifist Kerensky, attempts at sweeping political change were too few and too late; the Achilles' heel of his moderate socialist regime was his stubborn dedication

---

[1]Sidney B. Hook, *The Hero in History* (New York, 1955), pp. 184–228. By "hero," Hook is not making a value judgment; he is referring to "the individual to whom we can justifiably attribute preponderant influence in determining an issue or event . . ." and he devotes a chapter to Lenin to refute the deterministic view of history in orthodox Marxism.

to the war effort, a policy already rejected by the vast majority of the Russian people.

Can we simply conclude that at the heart of the matter is the fact that Lenin was the ultimate revolutionary, that is, prepared to behave as the ultimate opportunist: to take popular stands, to make promises he had no intention of keeping and to enter into alliances he had no intention of maintaining, regardless of how illegal or immoral his actions? This would explain his willingness to violate the promises made to the Allies by previous governments (no matter how irrelevant the promises), to take land from its lawful owners for popular redistribution before lengthy discussions about compensation could be held, and to acquiesce in what amounted to the disintegration of the country by supporting demands for independence by the various ethnic minorities (no matter how legitimate the demands). Lenin defined morality as "that which serves the destruction of the old exploiting society. . . ."[2] Law-abiding liberal that he was, Kerensky could not do these things. He was not a revolutionary.

---

[2] V. I. Lenin, "The Tasks of the Youth Leagues," *Collected Works*, vol. 31 (April–December 1920), (Moscow, 1966), p. 293.

Why Lenin? Why Stalin?

THEODORE VON LAUE

Theodore Von Laue was born in Germany, and received graduate
degrees from Princeton University. He taught at the University of
California at Riverside and at Clark University. A recipient of Guggenheim and Fulbright fellowships, he has published a number of
books including studies on the German historian Von Ranke and
the Russian statesman Sergei Witte. In the book from which this
excerpt is taken, Von Laue contends that the Russian Revolution is
made intelligible only by understanding the internal and external
pressures under which the Russian state and society operate. Why
does Von Laue believe that the failure of democracy in Russia was
"inevitable"? How does he account for the success of radical revolution in Russia and its failure — or absence — in Western Europe?

Liberal democracy in Russia — using the term broadly — had proved
unequal to the task. Since March it had given the country every opportunity to speak its will, and the result had been division, violence, and
a breakdown of government. Spontaneity, leaving the population to its
own devices, had produced anarchy. The invisible resources of unity and
social discipline, which in the western democracies restrained liberty

Excerpts from *Why Lenin? Why Stalin?* by Theodore H. Von Laue. Copyright © 1964,
1971 by Theodore H. Von Laue. Reprinted by permission of Harper & Row, Publishers, Inc.

from degenerating into license and made possible not only effective government in peace but also unprecedented voluntary sacrifices in war, were found wanting in Russia. A few years later they were equally found wanting in Italy, Spain, Poland, or Germany (to mention but a few parallel cases). None of these countries had had a chance in the past of knitting the tight habit of subconscious unity before they copied western democracy. Russia was merely the first case in a long series of similar breakdowns, the one that occurred under the most exceptional circumstances.

Viewing the events of the summer of 1917 in this perspective, we must conclude that the failure of democracy in Russia was inevitable, if not in 1917 then surely in the years following (assuming that a Russian state still survived). Only decades, if not centuries, of relative immunity to the pressures of power politics and an active internal melting pot might have helped the discordant elements to grow together. Now there was no time. In the extreme moments of the twentieth century, a country either possessed that cohesion or had to create it artificially, if it did not want to fall apart.

After the July days, the sole question of Russian domestic politics was whether the heir to autocracy would be a dictator of the right or of the left. The wave of reaction favored the former. It brought to the fore General Kornilov, a distinguished officer whom merit had raised from the peasantry to his high rank and who was by no means a reactionary. He was convinced that only a military dictatorship could save Russia from Germany and from disintegration, an opinion which by now many members of "privilege Russia" (including some socialists) shared. With such backing he began, toward the end of August, to move supposedly reliable army units toward Petrograd, ostensibly in order to strengthen Kerensky but secretly prepared to go further if opportunity opened. Yet as his men approached the capital, they were met by agitators sent by the Soviet, under whose persuasion even the most loyal soldiers lost heart. Against the Petrograd Soviet, Kornilov's troops melted away as had the armies at the front, and his *coup* collapsed. No dictatorship of the right could stem the tide of revolutionary spontaneity as embodied in the soviets. On the contrary, Kornilov revived its impetus, somewhat checked after July, and prepared the way for the dictatorship of the left.

The dictatorship of the proletariat had, of course, been the goal of the Bolsheviks ever since Lenin returned to Russia. At every opportunity, he pressed home the argument that the war was an imperialist war and that it could be stopped, with all its savage hardships, only if the "capitalist" governments in Russia and elsewhere were overthrown. In his eyes, all those Russians who sought to continue the war — and this included Kerensky, the Mensheviks, and most Social Revolutionaries — were "capitalist" warmongers. He gambled on the inability of the Provisional Government to carry out its staggering tasks and on the growing revulsion against the war.

Of all political parties, thus only the Bolsheviks cast their lot with the revolutionary torrent. Their slogan was "All power to the Soviets" until July, when the Soviet leadership turned against the masses. Then they allied themselves with the more radical elements represented in the Petrograd district soviets and the factory committees. In the fall, when they gained control of the city soviets in many parts of Russia, they proclaimed as their goal the dictatorship of the proletariat. They alone dared to profess what the unruly masses wanted and were already trying to achieve by themselves: immediate peace for the soldiers, land to the peasants by Black Partition, self-determination for the minority groups, bread for the hungry, and social justice on their own terms for all those who felt oppressed and exploited. They alone were willing to descend to the language of the *Lumpenproletariat* and, when necessary, to incite its passions to fever pitch. "The Bolsheviks," Trotsky wrote in retrospect, "not afraid of those backward strata now for the first time lifting themselves from the dregs, took people as history had created them." Mercilessly they exploited the ignorance of the masses.

Yet while they placed themselves midstream in the revolutionary tide, they would not be carried away by it. As a revolutionary elite, they had a will of their own. They thought of themselves as the engineers of revolution, harnessing the revolutionary steam power created by the historic conditions of the moment to its true purpose which only revolutionary Marxists could perceive. Whatever the Bolsheviks would do, for their own benefit and that of Russia, they would do through the masses, never against them. But they would also remain inwardly apart, as manipulators, not agents, of the popular will. In this manner, they solved the first of the underlying necessities of modern Russian development, identifying the people with their government and in turn identifying themselves with the people.

Let us ignore at this point the fact that the Bolsheviks were not firmly established for several years, but rather draw a few conclusions about their ascent to power. In the first place one can hardly deny that theirs was a democratic revolution. It established a government that could hope to speak — at least at this fleeting moment — for a majority of Russians. It was a government of "Soviet Russia," as this term has been used here, close to the political instincts of the bulk of the people.

Secondly, the overthrow of the Provisional Government — and of "privilege Russia" in general — was not entirely of the Bolsheviks' own making. It was the result of the elemental torrent of liberation that had broken loose after March. The existing bonds of government and society were all snapping by themselves, in the countryside, the army, the factories, the national minorities, everywhere. No authority was strong enough to stem that tide. All that could possibly be attempted — and that with great difficulty — was to direct it from within until it had run its course.

Thirdly, the elemental revolt aiming at the smashing of the old state machinery was a phenomenon possible only in Russia (or underdeveloped countries like China). Only there did the run of the population still live in relative self-sufficiency, with hardly a stake in the government. "Soviet Russia" had little to lose from the overthrow of the government, neither protection of property or status, nor social security, nor extensive public education, nor any other boon of government. In urban-industrial Europe, on the other hand, the majority of the population had long since acquired such a stake. State, society, and the economy were interwoven a thousandfold; all citizens were patently interdependent for their very livelihood. Thus nearly everyone had a vested interest in order and security, regardless of his political views. Threaten him, in time of crisis and internal disunity, with the overthrow of the government and he would rush headlong into the arms of a Mussolini or Hitler. And if he longed for a change of regime, he would still insist that the transition be accomplished "legally," without disturbing the continuity of the public services. There would never be a chance, in other words, of a Bolshevik revolution in the West.

The Bolshevik seizure of power — to take at this point a long look both backward and forward — marked for Russia the end of an era of revolution from below. The tide of liberation, which assumed hurricane proportions in the fall of 1917 and continued to rage for several years more, had been rising since the start of the century. Autocracy had sacrificed the "Witte system" to it but had itself been forced to give ground in 1905. While seemingly recovering most of its losses, it never succeeded in reestablishing its authority. The trend continued to run against it, even under the pressure of the war. The defeats deepened and strengthened the upsurge until it finally broke all bounds after the sudden fall of the monarchy.

The new freedom liberated the long-suppressed spontaneity of the peoples of Russia. It did not lead, unfortunately, to the self-discipline needed for an effective democratic policy or an industrial economy. Liberation meant throwing off the hated restraints of the old order and being able, for once, to act according to one's deepest feelings.

The war, on which the Bolshevik victory is so often blamed, had rather little to do with that extremist turn of events. It may have contributed to the savagery of the revolt, but it destroyed neither liberal democracy nor Russian "capitalism." Freedom, the heady freedom of the new regime, did that. Given its own ideals, liberal democracy in Russia could never have been more than a brief transition phase. It would always have led to "Soviet democracy," the freedom of the "black people," which signified, under existing conditions, spontaneity carried to the point of anarchy.

By the same logic, however, freedom was bound to destroy itself. If Russia was to survive as a Great Power, with the same universal appeal as the others — these were the harsh terms of the competition — it needed the discipline of cooperation under both government and an industrial economy.

Here lay the central quandary of modern Russia. It was a backward country at the mercy of powerful neighbors. The essence of its backwardness rested in the fact that its people, left to their own devices, could manage neither effective government nor a productive modern economy. Was the Russian Empire then to be dissolved? For the Bolsheviks, at any rate, and many non-Bolsheviks as well, the answer was a passionate No! They craved power for their own survival, for the future of world socialism, and for the integrity of their territorial base in Imperial Russia which they dearly loved. Thus from November, 1917, onward the suppression of spontaneity began anew, slowly at first under Lenin, furiously at last under Stalin. The new harness of Communist rule proved to be far tighter than the tsarist one. The dangers to the country were greater, the ambitions of its rulers bolder, and the progress of the "advanced" countries undiminished; they would not mark time while Soviet Russia tried to catch up.

The essence of industrialism, which stands at the base of modern power, is interdependence and voluntary cooperation throughout the length and breadth of society. Lenin's sociology, although clumsy and extreme, took its cue from the "capitalist" order. Every advanced industrialized society constitutes a vast workshop. Its members voluntarily coordinate their activities under a common law and government — never perfectly, to be sure, yet sufficiently so as to produce a remarkable flow of goods and services. They do this with no more drastic compulsions than submitting to majority rule and earning a living, and sometimes with much nonpecuniary zeal. Submitting to the discipline of their jobs and their political order, they ordinarily do not even feel constricted in their freedom; they are spurred on by the opportunities (the current talk of alienation notwithstanding).

Woe now to a country that requires the results of modern industrialism without possessing among its inhabitants the necessary motivation and self-discipline. It has no choice but to replace the spontaneous self-discipline of the West by a process of deliberate substitution replacing lacking motivation by compulsion. The scope of Communist totalitarianism, as it developed over the years, indicates to what extent, in the judgment of its leaders, the Soviet population still lacks the spontaneous motivation needed for competitive power in world affairs. What it lacks has to be replaced by an artificial, external discipline.

The Bolsheviks would never admit, of course, that they were sacrificing freedom for the sake of power. Their determination to become a superior universal model required that they make an additional effort to represent their Russia as the embodiment of a freedom greater than that found in the "capitalist" West. They had to overtake their model in *all* attributes of superiority, even at the price of stretching the vocabulary of freedom and spontaneity beyond all recognition.

Russia and the West
under Lenin and Stalin

∿⁄∿

GEORGE KENNAN

George F. Kennan accompanied Ambassador Bullitt to Moscow to reopen the American Embassy in 1933, was second secretary, minister-counselor, and from 1952 to 1953 ambassador to the Soviet Union. After twenty-five years in the foreign service, he turned to the writing of diplomatic history. His books have won Pulitzer and Bancroft Prizes for history as well as a National Book Award. Contrast Kennan with Von Laue on the importance of World War I in explaining the Bolsheviks' success.

But Russia was the first great country to crack under the strain of the World War. This meant social and political instability. And the Bolsheviki, being a Russian party, starved for power and success, could not resist the temptation to take advantage of this instability and to make the bid for power. They knew that Russia was scarcely ripe for socialism, in Marxist terms; but they rationalized their action by persuading themselves that a successful seizure of power by Communists in Russia would ignite the smoldering tinder of social revolution in Germany as well.

The Bolsheviki were, of course, by no means the only faction struggling for exclusive power in Russia in 1917. The sudden disintegration of the Tsarist regime had roused to frantic and desperate activity every other political faction active on the Russian scene. In view of the narrow intolerance which has always characterized Russian political thought and activity, the penalty for failure in Russian political life, at crucial moments, can very well be destruction at the hands of others. Once the disintegration of Tsarist power set in, conditions of self-preservation alone would thus have forced every one of these Russian factions to exert its utmost effort, even had ambition for predominance not had this same effect. The result was that Russia was plunged, from the beginning of 1917, into a tremendous domestic-political crisis: probably the greatest that country had ever experienced — certainly the greatest since the so-called "time of trouble" at the end of the sixteenth century. The struggle of the tiny, fanatical Bolshevik faction against all the others was at first only one portion of this huge upheaval.

The things involved in this crisis were of greatest conceivable importance to every individual Russian. The social structure, the system of land ownership, the privileges and property interests of entire classes, were now at stake. There was not a single Russian for whose fate the outcome of this crisis would not have momentous, intimate personal significance.

This being so, it was, of course, the internal crisis which preoccupied the individual Russian from the beginning of 1917 on. The World War had nowhere near the same significance in his eyes. It is difficult, in fact, to see what stake the common people of Russia ever did have in the outcome of the war. A Russian victory would presumably have meant the establishment of Russia on the Dardanelles. For this, the Russian peasant could not have cared less. A German victory would obviously have affected the prestige of the Tsar's government. It might have led to limited territorial changes, and to some German commercial penetration. That any of this would have affected adversely the situation of the Russian peasant is not at all clear; in any case, he was not convinced that it would. Not only this, but he was by now, as a rule, heartily tired of the struggle: of the losses, the hardships, the deprivation. And if this detachment from the issues of the war was true of the ordinary people, how much more true it was of the Bolsheviki, for whom this was the great moment of political existence. They had never had anything but contempt, anyway, for the issues over which people claimed to be fighting in this imperialist war in the West.

How different all this was in the Western countries! Here, war fervor had by 1917 attained a terrific intensity. The Western democracies had by this time convinced themselves, as embattled democracies have a tendency to do, that the entire future of civilization depended on the outcome of the military struggle.

There is, let me assure you, nothing in nature more egocentric than the embattled democracy. It soon becomes the victim of its own war propaganda. It then tends to attach to its own cause an absolute value which distorts its own vision on everything else. *Its* enemy becomes the embodiment of all evil. *Its* own side, on the other hand, is the center of all virtue. The contest comes to be viewed as having a final, apocalyptic quality. If *we* lose, all is lost; life will no longer be worth living; there will be nothing to be salvaged. If we win, then everything will be possible; all problems will become soluble; the one great source of evil — *our* enemy — will have been crushed; the forces of good will then sweep forward unimpeded; all worthy aspirations will be satisfied.

It will readily be seen that people who have got themselves into this frame of mind have little understanding for the issues of any contest other than the one in which they are involved. The idea of people wasting time and substance on any *other* issue seems to them preposterous. This explains why Allied statesmen were simply unable to comprehend how people in Russia could be interested in an internal Russian political crisis when there was a war on in the West. Did the Russians not realize, it was asked in Paris and London, that everything depended on the defeat of the Germans, that if Germany was successful, no one could ever conceivably be happy again, whereas if Germany lost, everyone would somehow or other receive what he wanted?

You saw this well illustrated in the first reaction of President Woodrow Wilson to the news of the seizure of power in Russia by the Communists, in November 1917. "It is amazing to me" — he said —

> that any group of persons should be so ill-informed as to suppose, as some groups in Russia apparently suppose, that any reforms planned in the interests of the people can live in the presence of a Germany powerful enough to undermine or overthrow them by intrigue or force.

There was, of course, an important substantive difference between the issue that interested the early Bolsheviki and that which interested the warring powers in the West. The first was ideological, with universal social and political implications. The Bolsheviki believed that questions of social organization — in particular the question of ownership of the means of production — had an importance transcending all international rivalries. Such rivalries were, in their eyes, simply the product of social relationships. This is why they attached so little importance to the military outcome of the struggle in the West.

.   .   .

The myopia of the Western capitals in the face of Russia's growing agony was well illustrated by the Allied diplomatic conference which took place in Petrograd in January 1917, just one month before the first Revolution. The purpose of this gathering was to stimulate the Russians to new efforts on the eastern front and to co-ordinate these efforts with Western war strategy. Lord Milner and Sir Henry Wilson attended for Great Britain. The French Minister of Colonies, Gaston Doumergue, was there for the French. The Americans were of course not represented, being not yet in the war.

The conference afforded an excellent opportunity for the Allied statesmen to acquaint themselves with the seriousness of the situation in Russia and to take measures betimes to mitigate its effects. Had they looked carefully at the Russian scene at that moment, they could have discerned in it the dilemma that was to be basic to their problem of policy toward Russia throughout the following two years. This dilemma consisted in the fact that not only had Russia become involved in a great internal political crisis, but she had lost in the process her real ability to make war. The internal crisis was of such gravity that there was no chance for a healthy and constructive solution to it unless the war effort could be terminated at once and the attention and resources of the country concentrated on domestic issues. The army was tired. The country was tired. People had no further stomach for war. To try to drive them to it was to provide grist to the mill of the agitator and the fanatic: the last people one would have wished to encourage at such a dangerous moment. The sad fact is that from 1916 on, the demands of the political situation in Russia were in conflict with the demands of the Allied war effort.

At the time of the inter-Allied conference in January 1917, the Russian bureaucracy, themselves partially blind to these realities, had no desire that the Allied governments should pry too deeply into Russia's weaknesses and embarrassments. They were reluctant, in particular, to admit to the real exhaustion of their war effort, being fearful of losing Allied military aid and future support at the peace conference. Instead, therefore, of confessing their real plight, they made efforts to conceal it. They defended themselves against Allied curiosity and Allied demands in the traditional manner: by a combination of extravagant promises of military performance, on the one hand, and a formidable barrage of banquets and other social ordeals on the other. This was a combination guaranteed, by the experience of centuries, to get even the most sanguine Western visitor out of town — exhausted, bilious, empty-handed, but grateful for his escape — within a matter of weeks, if not days. It is a technique, incidentally, which the Soviet government has not hesitated to borrow from its predecessors.

.   .   .

I shall not attempt to describe to you the dramatic circumstances of the February Revolution. I should like only to tell you of two incidents which to my mind reveal the deficiencies of the Allied reaction to what was going on and illustrate the extent to which, as I said earlier, the Russians and the Westerners were preoccupied with different things. Both concern the French ambassador, Paléologue. While he was, as I say, an intelligent man, with much understanding for what was happening, he was first and foremost the representative of his government; he had to follow in his utterances the line his government had laid down for him; and like all Frenchmen he felt very strongly about the war in Europe.

At one point, walking through the streets amid the kaleidoscopic events of the February Revolution, Paléologue found himself surrounded by a group of celebrating students, half-curious, half-suspicious. They evidently first thought him to be some distinguished member of the old regime, and took a hostile attitude. On learning that he was the French ambassador, they called upon him to accompany them to the Tauride Palace, the home both of the Duma and of the Petrograd Soviet, and to do homage there to the red flag of the Revolution which now waved over the building. His answer was eloquently revealing: "I can render no better homage to Russian liberty," he said, "than by asking you to join me in shouting 'Vive la Guerre.'" In other words, "Forget about your Revolution; think of the war."

The second incident took place a few days later. The head of the Russian Duma, Mikhail Rodzyanko, appealed to Paléologue for advice as to the course the Russian moderates should now adopt. Rodzyanko and his friends were men deeply attached to the Allied cause. They really needed advice and help. But Paléologue had to evade the issue. No one in Paris, he realized, would have much understanding for the problems of these men. The words with which he put them off were again revealing. "As ambassador of France," he said, "the war is my principal preoccupation."

In these simple words the principal reason for the bankruptcy of Allied policy in the face of the Russian Revolution — namely, the inability to believe that anything other than the war in Europe could be of real importance — became visible at the start.

.   .   .

Aside from its ideological implications, the Bolshevik seizure of power was, of course, a complete disaster from the standpoint of the Allied war effort. The Bolsheviki were committed to taking Russia out of the war — committed to this not just by their own promises but by the very methods they had used to come into power. They had worked hard and successfully at the demoralization of the armed forces. They had done this in order that the Provisional Government should not have under its control at the crucial moment any sizable body of armed men which could be used as a defense against the violent usurpation of power by the Communists. To this end the Bolsheviki had played for all it was worth the purely demagogic card of land reform, promising the peasant soldier the division of the larger farms and estates and encouraging him to leave the trenches and go back to the village to get his share. This agitation had begun to take effect well before the Bolshevik seizure of power. For days and weeks, the army had been streaming away from the trenches and making its way home as best it could. It was this that caused Lenin to say triumphantly that the army had voted against the war with its feet. By mid-November, when the Communist seizure of power in the main centers was complete, it would have been physically impossible and politically suicidal for the Bolshevik leaders to do anything else but sue for peace. It was therefore natural that the first act of foreign policy of the new regime, taken on the very day of the Revolution, should have been the issuance of the Decree on Peace, calling on all the belligerent peoples and their governments to open negotiations for an immediate cessation of hostilities on the basis of no annexations and no indemnities. With this act, the departure of Russia from the war was really sealed.

Please note how intimately the causes of Kerensky's failure were connected with his effort to continue Russia's participation in World War I. Had he been able to demobilize the Petrograd garrison, and to get its members out of town, he presumably would never have been faced with the July insurrection; nor would the Bolsheviki have been able to organize the final seizure of power in November. But the fact that there was a war on prevented this. Had he not undertaken the summer offensive, he might have permitted the army to demobilize peacefully without raising the fateful problems of military discipline and authority by which he and his regime were bound to be crushed. Had he not endeavored to hold the armed forces together for a military purpose, he might have been able to compete with the Bolsheviki in encouraging the soldiers to return to their villages and in carrying out a prompt and politically effective land reform. The Bolsheviki had, after all, largely stolen the agrarian program of the Socialist-Revolutionary Party, to which Kerensky himself nominally belonged. The only reason they were able to exploit this issue successfully was that they, uninhibited by any loyalty to the war effort, were willing to put this agrarian program into effect at once, whereas Kerensky and his associates felt obliged to ask for delay in deference to the needs of the war effort. In every respect Kerensky's political position would have been eased, and his prospects for resistance to Bolshevik pressure would have been improved, had he been able to take the country out of the war at once.

The question may legitimately be asked: If all this was so, why did Kerensky attempt to continue the war at all? Why did he not flout the wishes of the Allies and address himself exclusively to his internal political problem? I am not sure that I can answer this question. Trotsky alleges that the Provisional Government clung to the tie with the Allies as a means of protecting themselves against the full sweep of the Revolution. This sounds to me forced and unconvincing. Kerensky and other members of the Provisional Government felt themselves bound to the Allies by many bonds. They had no sympathy for the Germans. Feelings of national pride made them reluctant to abandon outright the coalition with which they had been associated. They were urged to continue the war not just by conservative circles in the West but also by the Western Socialists and the representatives of Western labor. Finally, they were well aware that the country over which they presided was at the end of its economic and financial rope; and I am sure that they hesitated to face the future without the assurance that they would have some claim on Western economic assistance after the war.

Like everything else that had to do with the Russian Revolution and Soviet power, Kerensky's final defeat exercised a highly divisive effect on Western opinion. The French and British governments, still swayed predominantly by their interest in the war, tended to sympathize with Kornilov and to blame Kerensky for frustrating what they felt to be the only serious attempt to restore the discipline and fighting capacity of

Russia's armed forces. American circles in Russia, on the other hand, had less natural sympathy for the upper classes, and appreciated dimly the fact that the old Humpty Dumpty of Tsarist Russia could never be put together again. They thought Kornilov's venture doomed to failure in any case. They considered it the height of folly for the Allies to support it: this, they considered, only estranged the workers and peasants without whose support a war effort was unthinkable.

If history has any comment to make on these arguments, from the perspective of forty years, it is that all the parties to these disputes were wrong. The premise from which they all departed — namely, that Russia could and should be kept in the war — was an impossible premise. The sad fact is that by the spring of 1917 nothing the Allies might have done could have made Russia once more a serious factor in the war. The entire Russian economic and political system had by this time been overstrained by the military effort. The prerequisites for a continuation of this effort — spiritual, psychological, and political as well as economic — were simply no longer there. From this standpoint the policies of Paléologue, of Milyukov, and of Kerensky were as futile as those of Buchanan, President Wilson, or Elihu Root. Whichever had been adopted, the results would have been substantially the same, so far as the Russian war effort was concerned. The only point at which Allied statesmanship might, with different policies, have produced a different result was in the political field. It was inevitable that Russia should leave the war in 1917. It was not inevitable that this should have occurred under the chairmanship of the Bolsheviki. This, surely, was at least in part the effect of the blunders of Western statesmanship.

When we inquire, then, into the causality of the Russian Revolution — when we ask ourselves why it was that the Russian political structure broke down in 1917 and why the ensuing situation degenerated within a few months into the rigidities and extremisms of Bolshevism — we see that in each case it was the World War, and specifically the Allied cause in the World War, which was the determining factor. Whatever it may be said to have been that the Western Allies were fighting for, it was this to which the real needs of Russia in these crucial years were sacrificed. The Russian Revolution and the alienation of the Russian people from the Western community for decades to come were only a part of the staggering price paid by the Western people for their insistence on completing a military victory over Germany in 1917 and 1918.

Can it conceivably have been that the end in view was worth this price? I should like to let the discussion of Allied policies toward the Provisional Government rest with this question. The impression I gain after three or four years of immersion in these problems is that in attaching such enormous value to total military victory in 1917 and 1918, the Western peoples were the victims of a great misunderstanding—a misunderstanding about the uses and effects of the war itself. And I suspect that this misunderstanding also lies at the heart of those subsequent developments which have carried the Western community in the space of forty years from a seemingly secure place at the center of world happenings to the precarious and isolated position it occupies today, facing a world environment so largely beyond its moral and political influence.

How the Soviet Union
Is Governed

◈

JERRY F. HOUGH AND MERLE FAINSOD

Merle Fainsod was a Harvard professor of political science whose ground-breaking analysis of the organization of power in Russia, *How Russia Is Ruled*, was published in 1953. In order to take into account recent events and statistics, and to make use of the great amount of scholarly work published since the 1960s, the book was extensively revised and enlarged by Jerry F. Hough, who is a professor of political and policy sciences at Duke University and a senior fellow at the Brookings Institution. It is from this revision that the following excerpt comes. Why, in the opinion of the authors, did the Bolsheviks succeed in winning power in, and after, November 1917?

On no other major event in recent Russian history is there so much general agreement among leading western specialists as there is on the Revolution of 1917. Although there are some differences in emphasis and some variation in interpretation on narrower points, the same general picture emerges from the magnificent and long-standard *The Russian Revolution* written by William Henry Chamberlin in the 1930s, from *How Russia Is Ruled* in the early 1950s, and from the more recent work of such

scholars as Robert Daniels, John Keep, and Alex Rabinowitch. The educated population in the United States also holds a common view of the
Bolshevik revolution, one that is shared by many scholars (including
a number in Russian and Soviet studies). Such unexpected consensus
would be the source of great rejoicing were it not for one unfortunate
fact — namely, that in almost all important respects the consensus of the
educated public is radically different from that of those who study the
revolution.

In the image of the educated public and many scholars, two revolutions occurred in Russia in 1917 — a democratic revolution in March
(or February, according to the Russian calendar of the time) and a Communist coup d'état that overthrew the democratic regime in November
(or October, by the old calendar). The Bolsheviks succeeded, it is believed, not because of popular support (their 25 percent vote in the
Constituent Assembly election of November 1917 is often cited), but
because of their "organizational weapon." The Bolshevik success is attributed to the "fact" that the party of *What Is To Be Done?* had the unity of
views, the military discipline, the narrow elite membership, and the great
conspiratorial leader needed for seizing the levers of power in a time of
chaos and indecisive governmental leadership.

Scholars studying the revolution more seriously, however, have
tended to see only one revolution in Russia in 1917 — a continuing surge
of unrest that overthrew the tsar in March and that, with short periods of
abatement, grew in intensity as the year wore on. It was a time of conflict,
breakdown of authority, polarization of opinion of a type observed more
recently in Chile. These scholars would say that the party was, indeed,
fairly well organized in comparative terms, but they find the Bolsheviks
of 1917 to be a much-divided mass party quite unlike that depicte[1] in
What Is To Be Done? In their explanations of the Bolshevik success, they
emphasize much more the nature of the Bolshevik program. While ac-
knowledging the failure of the party to win majority support, these scholars would argue that the Bolsheviks did have a program that won the
support of half of the inhabitants of Russian cities and the soldiers sta-
tioned near the major urban centers and that satisfied the basic desires of
the peasantry. In this view, the Bolsheviks won because they were the
only party whose radicalism really matched the spirit of the urban majority and the army. Indeed, if the Bolshevik victory is dated by the successful completion of the Civil War in 1921 rather than by the seizure of
power in November 1917 (in many ways, the most reasonable viewpoint),

then one should no doubt give more attention to the millions of peasants who joined the Red army of the Communists instead of their opponents, the Whites.

The contrast between the specialists' view of the revolution and that of the nonspecialist has created a serious problem for western understanding of the Soviet experience. If the social forces that produced the Bolshevik revolution are neglected, as they often are in generalizations about the Soviet system, the new regime inevitably assumes the appearance of a totally alien agent that has grafted itself, like a tumor, onto a helpless organism. The ability of the regime to survive such shocks as collectivization, the Great Purge, and World War II becomes quite incomprehensible, except perhaps in terms of some almost mystical and superhuman totalitarian control. Moreover, of course, if Communist movements in general are seen in light of the nonspecialist's image of the Bolshevik revolution, we may be led into a fundamental misunderstanding of the dynamics of Communist movements in the Third World, sometimes with unfortunate consequences in the foreign policy realm.

.   .   .

Reasons for the Bolshevik Success in 1917

In the brief period of eight months, a tiny band of underground revolutionaries, numbering fewer than 25,000 men on the eve of the March revolution, had gained sufficient support to catapult themselves into a governing authority over nearly 150,000,000 people. The success of the Bolsheviks can be explained on many levels. In one sense, of course, the crucial factor was the revolutionary mood of the time and the way in which the Bolsheviks' opponents responded — or failed to respond — to it. If the Provisional Government had been able to withdraw from the war and carry through a land settlement satisfactory to the peasantry, it is highly doubtful that the Bolsheviks could have been so successful.

Yet, to state this alternative, so plausibly reinforced by hindsight, is to miss the tragic imperatives of 1917. Each of the parties which maneuvered for ascendancy in the months between March and November was the prisoner of its own illusions, its own interests, and its own visions of the future. To a Kadet leader like Miliukov it was inconceivable that Russia could betray her allies and her own national interests by suing for a separate peace; consequently, it was all too easy to believe that his own sense of patriotic exaltation and dedication were shared by soldiers, work-ers, and peasants who had lost their taste for war. To SRs of the right like Kerensky, who in a measure shared Miliukov's illusions, the successful prosecution of the war was paramount, with the agenda of economic reforms to be postponed until properly constituted legal bodies could be assembled to deal with them. To SRs of the center and left, who were much closer to the aspirations and expectations of the villages, land reform brooked no delay. Frustrated by the procrastinations of the Pro-visional Government, the Left SRs were thrown into the arms of the Bolsheviks. For Mensheviks of all shades, still loyal to the orthodox Marxist two-stage panorama of capitalist development, the socialist rev-olution had to be postponed until the bourgeois-democratic revolution was completed. They were left with a program of the establishment of a bourgeois order they described in the harshest of terms and a policy of conducting legal opposition to it—hardly a program for which the wretched and disinherited could develop more than qualified enthusiasm.

Until the arrival of Lenin from exile, the Bolsheviks too were prisoners of ancient formulas. They oriented their policies on a perspec-tive not very different from that of Menshevism. Lenin reversed this course and set the party on the road to the conquest of power. With an unswerving faith in his goal and a readiness to take any measures what-ever to realize it, Lenin, frequently over bitter opposition, managed to transform the party into an instrument that carried out his will.

Despite all its divisions and disorganization, despite all the lack of real direction given to the organization of the revolution in the provinces, despite the fact that "there was little systematic about Bolshevik Party organization during this period," the party still had a sense of discipline that was relatively greater than that of its rivals. On October 30, when a debate on the insurrection broke out at a meeting of Petrograd borough leaders, Sverdlov could say, "The decision of the Central Committee on the uprisings has been made . . . We have not gathered to set aside a decision of the Central Committee, but to consider how we ought to carry it out." It was an appeal that was peculiarly effective to men who had accepted the principle of "democratic centralism" in joining the party. The Central Committee certainly felt that it had the right to debate Lenin's proposals and to disagree with them (as it clearly did, according to the principles of democratic centralism), and the continued presence of a man like Kamenev in the Central Committee despite his opposition to Lenin since April indicates a willingness to maintain a diversity of views within that body. Even the two "strike-breakers" returned to party discipline with the "compromise" of November 2 and Kamenev at least was present at the planning sessions through the night of November 6–7.

Nevertheless, as Fainsod emphasized, the success of the Bolsheviks is to be explained not nearly so much by their discipline as by Lenin's "remarkable talent as a revolutionary strategist . . . [his] unerring sense for the deeply felt dissatisfactions of the masses and a genius for finding the slogans to catalyze grievances into revolutionary energy."

> Except for his insistence on striking at the right moment, Lenin had relatively little to do with the actual mechanics of the insurrection. His great contribution was to set the stage for insurrection by identifying Bolshevism with the major forces of mass discontent in Russian society. Lenin did not create the war-weariness which permeated the army and the nation: the material was at hand; his task was to exploit it. With one word — peace — Lenin and the Bolsheviks fused it into a revolutionary amalgam. The land-hunger of the peasants was an ancient grievance of which all parties were aware. The SRs built their ascendancy in the villages on the promise to satisfy it, but, while they temporized, Lenin stole their program from under their noses . . . With one word — land — Lenin insured the neutrality of the villages . . . With two slogans — bread and workers' control — Lenin captured the allegiance of substantial sections of the industrial workers from the Mensheviks.

The nature of the Bolshevik support — and the limitations on it — were clearly revealed in the elections to the Constituent Assembly, which were held (on the whole) on November 25 to 27 — three weeks after the uprising in Petrograd. All parties participated in the election, and the vote was generally free — a fact attested to by the 25 percent vote that the Bolsheviks received.

While the Bolsheviks were not a majoritarian movement, they did have important pockets of strength. They claimed that they were the party of the proletariat, and it was a claim that they could generally substantiate. The Mensheviks received only 3 percent of the vote in Moscow and Petrograd, and only 1.5 percent of the total vote outside of the Transcaucasus (where they were strong) and a district in which voters were compelled to vote for the Menshevik candidate. In Petrograd and Moscow, the Bolsheviks received 45 percent and 48 percent of the vote respectively, but the Kadets — the party of the middle class and the bourgeoisie — were their major competition here, receiving 26 percent and 35 percent of the vote respectively in the two metropolises.

The Bolsheviks also had strong support among a number of the army units. The Baltic fleet remained a Bolshevik center (63 percent of the vote), as did the army units at the western front (67 percent of the vote) and at the northern front (56 percent of it). In a pattern that was repeated in the peasant vote, the Bolshevik vote declined sharply in units more distant from the metropolitan centers where they had had much less opportunity to present their case. The Bolsheviks received only 30 percent of the vote at the southwest front and only 15 percent of the vote at the Rumanian front, which was the most remote of all. Similarly, the sailors of the Black Sea fleet presented only 20 percent of their votes to Lenin's party.

The picture in the countryside is more mixed. The SRs "won" the election in that they received 38 percent of the total vote, and the bulk of this support came from the peasants. In remote rural areas such as Siberia and the Central Black-Earth region (for example, Kursk and Voronezh), their vote exceeded 75 percent of the total, but in the central and western provinces, where peasant families had more contact with the cities and the army units, the Bolsheviks garnered a substantial number of peasant votes. The latter won 43 percent of the vote in the eleven central and northwest Russian guberniias, and actually carried the rural guberniia of Smolensk with 55 percent of the vote and rural Belorussia with 59 percent. It is hard to avoid the conclusion that the Bolshevik program had strong support among the Russian peasantry whenever the latter were exposed to it in a substantial way.

Social revolution is seldom a matter of winning majority support. In all revolutions there are large numbers who are uninterested, and in the Russian provinces in particular "what emerges," to quote Fainsod, "is a picture of utmost confusion in which passivity and apathy played a much larger role than is commonly assumed." Revolutions are made by active minorities who tap groundswells of discontent, and this the Bolsheviks were able to do; they are successful when the military force supporting the old regime melts away or defects, and this too the Bolsheviks were able to achieve. Russia of 1917 had much in common with the disorder and polarization of the last months of the Allende regime in Chile, but in Chile the soldiers carried out the orders of the "Chilean Kornilov." In Russia they did not, and the war and the war-weariness were surely crucial in this respect.

As William Chamberlin emphasized many years ago, the essence of Lenin's great insight in September and October was an understanding of the meaning of the failure of the Kornilov affair:

> There is no period in Lenin's life when his stature as a leader and his capacity to grasp accurately the basic facts of a new and changing political situation appear so vividly as in the few weeks which elapsed between the Kornilov affair and the Bolshevik stroke for power. He recognized immediately that Kornilov's defeat was Bolshevism's opportunity . . . Living in hiding . . . it was only natural that his judgment should be faulty in connection with some of the details of the projected uprising . . . He seems to have been precipitate with his suggestion that the uprising should have begun at the time of the Democratic Conference, and in his single-track insistence on the organization of insurrection at the earliest possible moment he was somewhat too contemptuous of the expediency of linking up the uprising with the meeting of the Second Congress of Soviets, with its assured Bolshevik majority. But these were minor miscalculations of detail, which could be and were corrected in the development of the action. Lenin's indisputable claim to greatness as a revolutionary leader lies in the fact that he realized immediately after the collapse of Kornilov that the time for action had come, that he drove home this view . . . and that he never relaxed his pressure on the Party Central Committee . . . until the opposition was crushed and the Party organization had swung into line behind his proposals.

To repeat a crucial point, however, the real test of the Bolsheviks came not in November, but in the coming three years. They had to demonstrate an ability to rule that no one expected this group of fractious extremists to have; they had to build an army from a war-weary population after having promised peace; they had to win a Civil War while extracting grain by force from peasants in the countryside, while attempting to reinstitute authority relations in the army and the factory, and while ending the wildly free politics of 1917 and emasculating the soviets in whose name they came to power. It was in 1917–1921 that the Bolshevik revolution was really won.

4

STALIN
AND
STALINISM

One of the most intriguing aspects of President Mikhail Gorbachev's *perestroika*, or restructuring program, is his call for a large-scale return to private farming. Though he has stopped short of rejecting the Soviet experience of agricultural collectivization as a total failure, Gorbachev has boldly detailed the human horror and economic folly of Stalin's rapid collectivization strategy after 1928.

The collectivization of farms was first attempted during the war communism that followed the Bolsheviks' seizure of power. Together with the five-year plans it marked an essential component of Stalin's "Socialism in One Country." State involvement in the economy, however, antedates the Russian Revolution. Peter the Great proposed a five-year plan, and state initiative under the last tsars instigated the industrialization for which the Communists later took credit.

Certainly in the 1920s there was need for drastic economic modernization after years of foreign and civil war. Losses were horrendous: population, which had been 171 million in 1914, was 132 million in 1921, and the loss of Finland, Poland, and the Baltic states also meant a loss of industrial plants, railroads, and farms. Manufacturing in 1920 was thirteen percent of what it had been in 1913. The middle classes had been decimated, and seventy-eight percent of the population worked in (private) agriculture.[1] In the absence of any foreign investment, Stalin believed collectivization was the only way to raise funds for industrial development and to create the substantial military establishment he regarded as vital to confront an anticipated capitalist onslaught.

It also seemed to Stalin the only way to increase the productive capacity of the land. Because primitive methods — plowing with wooden plows, sowing by hand, reaping with sickles, threshing with flails — were still used and the output per acre was among the lowest in Europe, the gathering of scattered holdings into large collective farms (kolkhozy), well-managed and provided with access to government-owned, up-to-date tractors and other machinery seemed an attractive alternative.

Equally desirable among Stalin's far-reaching aims was the great transformation of the petty-bourgeois peasant, a change that would bring the very individualistic, stubborn, and intractable peasant into conformity with the Party's image of the new Soviet man.

What dismayed observers was the frantic haste, the vast increase in state power, the mass terror waged against the *kulaks* (the allegedly well-to-do farmers), the prohibition of all opposition in or out of the Party, and the colossal human costs stemming from forced collectivization and industrialization. The consumers' share of the gross national product was driven down to levels unmatched in modern history, resulting in deprivation of the basic necessities of life. If productivity goals were not achieved, the Party blamed "saboteurs" or "imperialist agents" (including many "Old Bolsheviks"), who were framed-up, hauled into Soviet courts, and later "liquidated" or consigned to the forced labor camps of the "gulag." The widespread destruction of life (Stalin himself estimated that ten million peasants had died in the famine of 1932–33 alone, which came in the wake of refusals to turn land or draft animals

---

[1]Figures cited in Paul Kennedy, *The Rise and Fall of the Great Powers* (New York, 1987), pp. 321–22.

over to the state); agriculture's failure to feed the population adequately; and the loss of individual freedoms for at least the next two generations were not too high a price to pay for Stalin, who, in spite of inflated production figures, could point to many real gains. By the late 1930s, the Soviets' industrial output exceeded that of such nations as France, Japan, Italy, and probably Great Britain, and their military force enabled the USSR to face World War II as a great industrial and military power.

Assessments, appreciations, and criticisms of this so-called "Second Revolution," Stalin's revolution, are found in the readings that follow. In exile Trotsky published a scathing condemnation of Stalin for having betrayed the ideals of Bolshevism. Isaac Deutscher is much less harsh, and while deploring such excesses as the persecution of the old "intelligentsia," finds much to admire in Stalin's achievements. Roy Medvedev contrasts Stalin unfavorably with Lenin, and Bernice Rosenthal traces the changing fortunes of women during the period of Stalinist rule. While reading these interpretations, it is well to bear in mind the great historical question of whether Stalin's revolutionary changes marked a continuation or a perversion of the work begun by Lenin and whether, in view of the human costs incurred, these changes can, as Deutscher argues, be justified.

The Revolution Betrayed

✤

LEON TROTSKY

Leon Trotsky, once Lenin's second-in-command and heir apparent,
the military genius of the Revolution, a significant contributor to
Communist theory, defeated by Stalin in the ideological struggles
of the 1920s, villified and hounded into exile, and ultimately murdered by Stalin's agent, was indeed a titanic but tragic figure in
Russian and twentieth-century history. What is the basis of Trotsky's
condemnation of Stalin? How does he distinguish between Stalin
and Lenin? On what does he blame the degeneration of the Bolshevik Party? Inasmuch as Trotsky had initially called for collectivization himself, how, specifically, does he criticize Stalinist collectivization?

The Degeneration of the Bolshevik Party

The Bolshevik party prepared and insured the October victory. It
also created the Soviet state, supplying it with a sturdy skeleton. The
degeneration of the party became both cause and consequence of the
bureaucratization of the state. It is necessary to show at least briefly how
this happened.

The inner regime of the Bolshevik party was characterized by the
method of *democratic centralism*. The combination of these two concepts,

From *The Revolution Betrayed* by Leon Trotsky, New York, 1945, pp. 94–97, 99–100,
273–279. Reprinted by permission of Pathfinder Press. Copyright © 1972 Pathfinder Press.

democracy and centralism, is not in the least contradictory. The party took watchful care not only that its boundaries should always be strictly defined, but also that all those who entered these boundaries should enjoy the actual right to define the direction of the party policy. Freedom of criticism and intellectual struggle was an irrevocable content of the party democracy. The present doctrine that Bolshevism does not tolerate factions is a myth of the epoch of decline. In reality the history of Bolshevism is a history of the struggle of factions. And, indeed, how could a genuinely revolutionary organization, setting itself the task of overthrowing the world and uniting under its banner the most audacious iconoclasts, fighters and insurgents, live and develop without intellectual conflicts, without groupings and temporary factional formations? The farsightedness of the Bolshevik leadership often made it possible to soften conflicts and shorten the duration of factional struggle, but no more than that. The Central Committee relied upon this seething democratic support. From this it derived the audacity to make decisions and give orders. The obvious correctness of the leadership at all critical stages gave it that high authority which is the priceless moral capital of centralism.

The regime of the Bolshevik party, especially before it came to power, stood thus in complete contradiction to the regime of the present sections of the Communist International, with their "leaders" appointed from above, making complete changes of policy at a word of command, with their uncontrolled apparatus, haughty in its attitude to the rank and file, servile in its attitude to the Kremlin. But in the first years after the conquest of power also, even when the administrative rust was already visible on the party, every Bolshevik, not excluding Stalin, would have denounced as a malicious slanderer anyone who should have shown him on a screen the image of the party ten or fifteen years later.

The very center of Lenin's attention and that of his colleagues was occupied by a continual concern to protect the Bolshevik ranks from the vices of those in power. However, the extraordinary closeness and at times actual merging of the party with the state apparatus had already in those first years done indubitable harm to the freedom and elasticity of the party regime. Democracy had been narrowed in proportion as difficulties increased. In the beginning, the party had wished and hoped to preserve freedom of political struggle within the framework of the Soviets. The civil war introduced stern amendments into this calculation. The opposition parties were forbidden one after the other. This measure, obviously in conflict with the spirit of Soviet democracy, the leaders of Bolshevism regarded not as a principle, but as an episodic act of self-defense.

The swift growth of the ruling party, with the novelty and immensity of its tasks, inevitably gave rise to inner disagreements. The underground oppositional currents in the country exerted a pressure through various channels upon the sole legal political organization, increasing the acuteness of the factional struggle. At the moment of completion of the civil war, this struggle took such sharp forms as to threaten to unsettle the state power. In March 1921, in the days of the Kronstadt revolt, which attracted into its ranks no small number of Bolsheviks, the tenth congress of the party thought it necessary to resort to a prohibition of factions — that is, to transfer the political regime prevailing in the state to the inner life of the ruling party. This forbidding of factions was again regarded as an exceptional measure to be abandoned at the first serious improvement in the situation. At the same time, the Central Committee was extremely cautious in applying the new law, concerning itself most of all lest it lead to a strangling of the inner life of the party.

However, what was in its original design merely a necessary concession to a difficult situation, proved perfectly suited to the taste of the bureaucracy, which had then begun to approach the inner life of the party exclusively from the viewpoint of convenience in administration. Already in 1922, during a brief improvement in his health, Lenin, horrified at the threatening growth of bureaucratism, was preparing a struggle against the faction of Stalin, which had made itself the axis of the party machine as a first step toward capturing the machinery of state. A second stroke and then death prevented him from measuring forces with this internal reaction.

The entire effort of Stalin, with whom at that time Zinoviev and Kamenev were working hand in hand, was thenceforth directed to freeing the party machine from the control of the rank-and-file members of the party. In this struggle for "stability" of the Central Committee, Stalin proved the most consistent and reliable among his colleagues. He had no need to tear himself away from international problems; he had never been concerned with them. The petty bourgeois outlook of the new ruling stratum was his own outlook. He profoundly believed that the task of creating socialism was national and administrative in its nature. He looked upon the Communist International as a necessary evil which should be used so far as possible for the purposes of foreign policy. His own party kept a value in his eyes merely as a submissive support for the machine.

. . .

Of party democracy there remained only recollections in the memory of the older generation. And together with it had disappeared the democracy of the soviets, the trade unions, the co-operatives, the cultural and athletic organizations. Above each and every one of them there reigns an unlimited hierarchy of party secretaries. The regime had become "totalitarian" in character several years before this word arrived from Germany. "By means of demoralizing methods, which convert thinking communists into machines, destroying will, character and human dignity," wrote Rakovsky in 1928, "the ruling circles have succeeded in converting themselves into an unremovable and inviolate oligarchy, which replaces the class and the party." Since those indignant lines were written, the degeneration of the regime has gone immeasurably farther. The G.P.U. has become the decisive factor in the inner life of the party. If Molotov in March 1936 was able to boast to a French journalist that the ruling party no longer contains any factional struggle, it is only because disagreements are now settled by the automatic intervention of the political police. The old Bolshevik party is dead, and no force will resurrect it.

. . .

Bonapartism as a Regime of Crisis

The question we previously raised in the name of the reader: "How could the ruling clique, with its innumerable mistakes, concentrate unlimited power in its hands?"—or, in other words: "How explain the contradiction between the intellectual poverty of the Thermidorians and their material might?"—now permits a more concrete and categorical answer. The Soviet society is not harmonious. What is a sin for one class or stratum is a virtue for another. From the point of view of socialist forms of society, the policy of the bureaucracy is striking in its contradictions and inconsistencies. But the same policy appears very consistent from the standpoint of strengthening the power of the new commanding stratum.

The state support of the kulak (1923–28) contained a mortal danger for the socialist future. But then, with the help of the petty bourgeoisie the bureaucracy succeeded in binding the proletarian vanguard hand and foot, and suppressing the Bolshevik Opposition. This "mistake" from the point of view of socialism was a pure gain from the point of view of the bureaucracy. When the kulak began directly to threaten the bureaucracy itself, it turned its weapons against the kulak. The panic of aggression against the kulak, spreading also to the middle peasant, was no less costly to the economy than a foreign invasion. But the bureaucracy had defended its positions. Having barely succeeded in exterminating its former ally, it began with all its power to develop a new aristocracy. Thus undermining socialism? Of course — but at the same time strengthening the commanding caste. The Soviet bureaucracy is like all ruling classes in that it is ready to shut its eyes to the crudest mistakes of its leaders in the sphere of general politics, provided in return they show an unconditional fidelity in the defense of its privileges. The more alarmed becomes the mood of the new lords of the situation, the higher the value they set upon ruthlessness against the least threat to their so justly earned rights. It is from this point of view that the caste of parvenus selects its leaders. Therein lies the secret of Stalin's success.

.   .   .

The progressive role of the Soviet bureaucracy coincides with the period devoted to introducing into the Soviet Union the most important elements of capitalist technique. The rough work of borrowing, imitating, transplanting and grafting, was accomplished on the bases laid down by the revolution. There was, thus far, no question of any new word in the sphere of technique, science or art. It is possible to build gigantic factories according to a ready-made Western pattern by bureaucratic command — although, to be sure, at triple the normal cost. But the farther you go, the more the economy runs into the problem of quality, which slips out of the hands of a bureaucracy like a shadow. The Soviet products are as though branded with the gray label of indifference. Under a nationalized economy, *quality* demands a democracy of producers and consumers, freedom of criticism and initiative — conditions incompatible with a totalitarian regime of fear, lies and flattery.

Behind the question of quality stands a more complicated and grandiose problem which may be comprised in the concept of *independent, technical* and *cultural creation*. The ancient philosopher said that strife is the father of all things. No new values can be created where a free conflict of ideas is impossible. To be sure, a revolutionary dictatorship means by its very essence strict limitations of freedom. But for that very reason epochs of revolution have never been directly favorable to cultural creation: they have only cleared the arena for it. The dictatorship of the proletariat opens a wider scope to human genius the more it ceases to be a dictatorship. The socialist culture will flourish only in proportion to the dying away of the state. In that simple and unshakable historic law is contained the death sentence of the present political regime in the Soviet Union. Soviet democracy is not the demand of an abstract policy, still less an abstract moral. It has become a life-and-death need of the country.

If the new state had no other interests than the interests of society, the dying away of the function of compulsion would gradually acquire a painless character. But the state is not pure spirit. Specific functions have created specific organs. The bureaucracy taken as a whole is concerned not so much with its function as with the tribute which this function brings in. The commanding caste tries to strengthen and perpetuate the organs of compulsion. To make sure of its power and income, it spares nothing and nobody. The more the course of development goes against it, the more ruthless it becomes toward the advanced elements of the population. Like the Catholic Church it has put forward the dogma of infallibility in the period of its decline, but it has raised it to a height of which the Roman pope never dreamed.

The increasingly insistent deification of Stalin is, with all its elements of caricature, a necessary element of the regime. The bureaucracy has need of an inviolable superarbiter, a first consul if not an emperor, and it raises upon its shoulders him who best responds to its claim for lordship. That "strength of character" of the leader which so enraptures the literary dilettantes of the West, is in reality the sum total of the collective pressure of a caste which will stop at nothing in defense of its position. Each one of them at his post is thinking: *l'état — c'est moi.* In Stalin each one easily finds himself. But Stalin also finds in each one a small part of his own spirit. Stalin is the personification of the bureaucracy. That is the substance of his political personality.

Caesarism, or its bourgeois form, Bonapartism, enters the scene in those moments of history when the sharp struggle of two camps raises the state power, so to speak, above the nation, and guarantees it, in appearance, a complete independence of classes — in reality, only the freedom necessary for a defense of the privileged. The Stalin regime, rising above a politically atomized society, resting upon a police and officers' corps, and allowing of no control whatever, is obviously a variation of Bonapartism — a Bonapartism of a new type not before seen in history.

Caesarism arose upon the basis of a slave society shaken by inward strife. Bonapartism is one of the political weapons of the capitalist regime in its critical period. Stalinism is a variety of the same system, but upon the basis of a workers' state torn by the antagonism between an organized and armed soviet aristocracy and the unarmed toiling masses.

As history testifies, Bonapartism gets along admirably with a universal, and even a secret, ballot. The democratic ritual of Bonapartism is the *plebiscite*. From time to time, the question is presented to the citizens: *for* or *against* the leader? And the voter feels the barrel of a revolver between his shoulders. Since the time of Napoleon III, who now seems a provincial dilettante, this technique has received an extraordinary development. The new Soviet constitution which establishes *Bonapartism on a plebiscite basis* is the veritable crown of the system.

In the last analysis, Soviet Bonapartism owes its birth to the belatedness of the world revolution. But in the capitalist countries the same cause gave rise to fascism. We thus arrive at the conclusion, unexpected at first glance, but in reality inevitable, that the crushing of Soviet democracy by an all-powerful bureaucracy and the extermination of bourgeois democracy by fascism were produced by one and the same cause: the dilatoriness of the world proletariat in solving the problems set for it by history. Stalinism and fascism, in spite of a deep difference in social foundations, are symmetrical phenomena. In many of their features they show a deadly similarity. A victorious revolutionary movement in Europe would immediately shake not only fascism, but Soviet Bonapartism. In turning its back to the international revolution, the Stalinist bureaucracy was, from its own point of view, right. It was merely obeying the voice of self-preservation.

Stalin and
the Second Revolution

ᔥᕊ

ISAAC DEUTSCHER

Isaac Deutscher's biography of Stalin, first published in 1949, remains one of the most important accounts of the leader's rise to
power and of his various accomplishments. Although the author of
an essential three-volume biography of Trotsky and a one-time Trot-
skyist himself, Deutscher attempts to provide a balanced view of
Stalin. He acknowledges the abuses practiced, but argues that the
dictator's policies were no different from those of earlier rulers and
that the steps taken to bring Russia into the twentieth century —
steps which constituted a "second Russian revolution" — were comparable to policies earlier taken in English history. Do you agree
with this analogy and with the conclusions drawn from it? How does
Deutscher evaluate Stalin's policy of forced labor?

Perhaps the most important aspect of his social policy was his fight
against the equalitarian trends. He insisted on the need for a highly
differentiated scale of material rewards for labour, designed to encourage
skill and efficiency. He claimed that Marxists were no levellers in the
popular sense; and he found support for his thesis in Marx's well-known
saying that even in a classless society workers would at first be paid

according to their labour and not to their needs. Nevertheless, a strong strand of equalitarianism had run through Bolshevism. Under Lenin, for instance, the maximum income which members of the ruling party, even those of the highest rank, were allowed to earn equalled the wages of a skilled labourer. That the needs of industrialization clashed with 'ascetic' standards of living and that the acquisition of industrial skill was impeded by the lack of material incentives to technicians, administrators, and workers can hardly be disputed. But it is equally true that, throughout the thirties, the differentiation of wages and salaries was pushed to extremes, incompatible with the spirit, if not the letter, of Marxism. A wide gulf came to separate the vast mass of unskilled and underpaid workmen from the privileged 'labour aristocracy' and bureaucracy, a gulf which may be said to have impeded the cultural and industrial progress of the nation as a whole, as much as the earlier rigidly equalitarian outlook had done.

It was mainly in connexion with Stalin's social policy that his opponents, especially the exiled Trotsky, denounced him as the leader of a new privileged caste. He indeed fostered the inequality of incomes with great determination. On this point his mind had been set long before the 'great change.' As early as 1925 he enigmatically warned the fourteenth congress: 'We must not play with the phrase about equality. This is playing with fire.' In later years he spoke against the 'levellers' with a rancour and venom which suggested that in doing so he defended the most sensitive and vulnerable facet of his policy. It was so sensitive because the highly paid and privileged managerial groups came to be the props of Stalin's régime. They had a vested interest in it. Stalin himself felt that his personal rule was the more secure the more solidly it rested on a rigid hierarchy of interest and influence. The point was also so vulnerable because no undertaking is as difficult and risky as the setting up of a new hierarchy on ground that has just been broken up by the mighty ploughs of social revolution. The revolution stirs the people's dormant longings for equality. The most critical moment in its development is that at which the leaders feel that they cannot satisfy that longing and proceed to quell it. They get on with the job which some of their opponents call the betrayal of the revolution. But their conscience is so uneasy and their nerves are so strained by the ambiguity of their role that the worst outbursts of their temper are directed against the victims of that 'betrayal.' Hence the extraordinary vehemence with which a

Cromwell, a Robespierre, or a Stalin, each hit out against the levellers of his time.

It was only in the late thirties that the fruits of the second revolution began to mature. Towards the end of the decade, Russia's industrial power was catching up with Germany's. Her efficiency and capacity for organization were still incomparably lower. So was the standard of living of her people. But the aggregate output of her mines, basic plants, and factories approached the level which the most efficient and disciplined of all continental nations, assisted by foreign capital, had reached only after three-quarters of a century of intensive industrialization. The other continental nations, to whom only a few years before Russians still looked up, were now left far behind. The industrial revolution spread from central and western Russia to the remote wilderness of Soviet Asia. The collectivization of farming, too, began to yield positive results. Towards the end of the decade the grain crops were thirty or forty million tons higher than those that had been obtained under individual farming. Industry was at last able to supply tractors, harvester combines, and other implements in such numbers that Soviet farming achieved the highest degree of mechanization. The outside world was more or less unaware of the great change and the shift in the international balance of power which it implied. Spectacular failures of the first five-year plan induced foreign observers to take a highly sceptical view of the results of the second and the third. The macabre series of 'purge' trials suggested economic and political weakness. The elements of weakness were undoubtedly there; and they were even greater than may appear when the scene is viewed in retrospect from the vantage point of the late forties. But the elements of strength were also incomparably greater than they were thought to be in the late thirties.

The achievement was remarkable, even if measured only by the yard-stick of Russian national aspirations. On a different scale, it laid the foundations for Russia's new power just as Cromwell's Navigation Act had once laid the foundation for British naval supremacy. Those who still view the political fortunes of countries in terms of national ambitions and prestige cannot but accord to Stalin the foremost place among all those rulers who, through the ages, were engaged in building up Russia's power. Actuated by such motives even many of the Russian White émigrés began to hail Stalin as a national hero. But the significance of the second revolution lay not only and not even mainly in what it meant to Russia. To the world it was important as the first truly gigantic experiment in planned economy, the first instance in which a government undertook to plan and regulate the whole economic life of its country and to direct its nationalized industrial resources towards a uniquely rapid multiplication of the nation's wealth. True enough Stalin was not the originator of the idea. He borrowed so much from Marxist thinkers and economists, including his rivals, that often he might well be charged with outright plagiarism. He was, nevertheless, the first to make of the abstract idea the practical business of government. It is also true that an important beginning in practical planning had been made by the German Government and General Staff in the First World War; and that Lenin had often referred to that precedent as to a pointer to future experiments. What was new in Stalin's planning was the fact that it was initiated not merely as a wartime expedient, but as the normal pattern of economic life in peace. Hitherto governments had engaged in planning as long as they had needed implements of war. Under Stalin's five-year plans, too, guns, tanks, and planes were produced in great profusion; but the chief merit of these plans was not that they enabled Russia to arm herself, but that they enabled her to modernize and transform society.

We have seen the follies and the cruelties that attended Stalin's 'great change.' They inevitably recall those of England's industrial revolution, as Karl Marx has described them in Das Kapital. The analogies are as numerous as they are striking. In the closing chapter of the first volume of his work, Marx depicts the 'primitive accumulation' of capital (or the 'previous accumulation,' as Adam Smith called it), the first violent processes by which one social class accumulated in its hands the means of production, while other classes were being deprived of their land and means of livelihood and reduced to the status of wage-earners. The process which, in the thirties, took place in Russia might be called the 'primitive accumulation' of socialism in one country. Marx described the 'enclosures' and 'clearings' by which the landlords and manufacturers of England expropriated the yeomanry, the 'class of independent peasants.' A parallel to those enclosures is found in a Soviet law, on which Stalin reported to the sixteenth congress, a law which allowed the collective farms to 'enclose' or 'round off' their land so that it should comprise a continuous area. In this way the individual farmers were either compelled to join the collective farms or were virtually expropriated. Marx recalls 'the bloody discipline' by which the free peasants of England were made into wage-labourers, 'the disgraceful action of the state which employed the police to accelerate the accumulation of capital by increasing the degree of exploitation of labour.' His words might apply to many of the practices introduced by Stalin. Marx sums up his picture of the English industrial revolution by saying that 'capital comes [into the world] dripping from head to foot, from every pore, with blood and dirt.' Thus also comes into the world — socialism in one country.

In spite of its 'blood and dirt,' the English industrial revolution — Marx did not dispute this — marked a tremendous progress in the history of mankind. It opened a new and not unhopeful epoch of civilization. Stalin's industrial revolution can claim the same merit. It is argued against it that it has perpetrated cruelties excusable in earlier centuries but unforgivable in this. This is a valid argument, but only within limits. Russia had been belated in her historical development. In England serfdom had disappeared by the end of the fourteenth century. Stalin's parents were still serfs. By the standards of British history, the fourteenth and the twentieth centuries have, in a sense, met in contemporary Russia. They have met in Stalin. The historian cannot be seriously surprised if he finds in him some traits usually associated with tyrants of earlier centuries. Even in the most irrational and convulsive phase of his industrial revolution, however, Stalin could make the claim that his system was free from at least one major and cruel folly which afflicted the advanced nations of the west: 'The capitalists [these were his words spoken during the Great Depression] consider it quite normal in a time of slump to destroy the "surplus" of commodities and burn "excess" agricultural produce in order to keep up high prices and ensure high profits, while here, in the U.S.S.R., those guilty of such crimes would be sent to a lunatic asylum.'

On Stalin and Stalinism

ROY MEDVEDEV

Roy Medvedev's exposé of Stalin's dictatorship, *Let History Judge*, was the first major study of the Stalin era from within the Soviet Union, and was first published in 1969. Medvedev was thereupon expelled from the Communist party. Twenty years later the Party's Control Commission determined that the action was "unfounded," restored his membership, and allowed publication of abbreviated versions of an even more critical revision of the study. In 1989, in the first free election held in the Soviet Union since 1918, Medvedev was sent to both the new Congress of Peoples' Deputies and the Supreme Soviet, the nation's parliament. *On Stalin and Stalinism*, excerpted below, is an assessment of Stalin's character and actions based on sources available only to a Soviet author. Medvedev contends that Stalinism marked a departure from the more benevolent communism envisaged by Lenin, and hence makes a sharp distinction between the two. How does he contrast Lenin and Stalin? Both Medvedev and Deutscher take note of the "second revolution" as taking place in peacetime. How, nevertheless, do their interpretations of it differ? To what extent is Medvedev in agreement with Trotsky?

Stalin himself constantly maintained that he was first and foremost a loyal disciple of Lenin, merely continuing the work of his teacher, and that his activities in every respect represented the implementation of Leninist designs. The same was repeated by people in Stalin's immediate entourage, who additionally made the point that Stalin was the *best* disciple, the one *most steadfast* in his continuation of Lenin's work. However, many none too objective Sovietologists also find it quite tempting to identify Stalinism with Marxism and Leninism and to portray socialism only in its perverted Stalinist form. This is very much the view proclaimed far and wide by Solzhenitsyn, according to whom there never was any such thing as 'Stalinism,' since Stalin always followed in Lenin's footsteps and was only a 'blind, mechanical executor' of Lenin's will. An approach of this kind is convenient not only for those who would like to discredit every variety of socialism as a matter of principle, but also for those who favour the rehabilitation of Stalin and Stalinism. Nevertheless, it is wrong.

Sometimes the urge to identify Stalinism and socialism, Stalinism and communism, can take on truly perverted forms. Certain writers have expressed what amounts to satisfaction that Stalin existed and thereby helped to discredit Marxism and communism.

.   .   .

It should be stated at the outset that the infamous Stalinist system was not the creation of one man alone. Its development was affected by many circumstances and preconditions that were part of Russian life even before the Revolution and also by the experiences of the October Revolution, civil war, and the first six years of Soviet rule. Therefore without making any sweeping generalizations, clearly one cannot avoid identifying some elements of continuity in specific aspects of Leninism and Stalinism, continuity that requires sober, scholarly investigation rather than demagogic assertion. On the whole, Leninism and Bolshevism, both in theory and practice, represented a fundamental departure from the 'classical' social-democratic movements of the nineteenth century, and this allowed Lenin to speak of the creation of a 'party of a new type.' Many of the distinctive characteristics of Leninism resulted from the peculiarities of the Russian environment in which the socialist movement began and developed. Leninism was also influenced by the general international situation: the transition of capitalism to the imperialist stage, the development of monopoly capitalism, the First World War, etc. Quite a number of Lenin's statements and actions were wrong, or appropriate only for specific situations within limited periods of time. Subsequently Lenin admitted some of these errors; others were simply forgotten. But there were certain mistaken notions that he maintained until the end of his life. For example, what Lenin said about communist morality at the Third *Komsomol* Congress can hardly be accepted as a basis for socialist morality: '. . . morality is that which serves the destruction of the old exploiting society. . . . Communist morality is that which serves the struggle [of the proletariat], which unites the workers . . . against every kind of petty ownership . . .'

Furthermore, even in September 1917 Lenin assumed that mass terror and civil war could be averted in the event of a Soviet government coming to power, led by the Bolsheviks. This hope proved to be illusory. Yet the Red terror and the civil war that began in the summer of 1918 were only in part natural measures of self-defence against counter-revolutionary violence and the Intervention; the terror was also intimately connected with serious errors on the part of the first Soviet government in the implementation of important economic and political measures. Government actions provoked opposition and resistance among an overwhelming majority of the petty bourgeois masses of Russia, bringing Soviet power to the brink of catastrophe and compelling those in charge to resort to mass terror.

It is clear that the excesses of this terror were without any justification. Yet we must bear in mind that it is inevitably misleading to judge a revolutionary epoch or wartime situation by the laws and customs normally applicable to peacetime.

If soldiers panic and abandon the trenches under the impact of an enemy onslaught, their commanding officer, brandishing his pistol and shouting 'Go back!,' may shoot three or four soldiers as an example to the others. No one would regard this as a crime if it served to restrain the regiment and make it return to its former position or secure a new line of defence, since otherwise the entire regiment could be killed with nearby regiments and divisions affected as well. In fact, a military tribunal would have the right to try and put before a firing squad a regimental commander who lacked the necessary resolution at the critical moment. However, what was the crime of the unfortunate soldiers who were shot? Were they really more guilty than the others, or did they just happen to be closer to the commander than the real culprits who had been the first to panic? It is perfectly possible that those who were the first to leave the trenches might display exceptional courage in some counterattack only hours later; on the following day they would receive a decoration from the divisional commander or from the same commander of the regiment who had so recently shot down their fleeing comrades. But if the commander of a regiment were to open fire at three or four soldiers in peacetime or on manoeuvres, he would find himself up before a military tribunal.

Considerations of this kind are in many respects applicable to the harrowing years of civil war (1918–20) and to the actions of the Cheka, headed by Dzerzhinsky, and the Council of People's Commissars and the Central Executive Committee, headed by Lenin and Sverdlov. Unfortunately there were a number of situations where Red terror was the only way of avoiding the total destruction of the Soviet state and the triumph of the White terror that would certainly follow. Solzhenitsyn, Shafarevich, and Naum Korzhavin (from his current perspective) understand this well enough — it is simply that they find Kornilov or Denikin preferable to Lenin and Sverdlov, White terror preferable to Red.

But can there really be any comparison between decisions taken at the height of civil war and decisions arrived at in peacetime? Can the Red terror of 1918–20 really be equated with the terror inflicted on the country by Stalin in 1929–32 or in 1936–8? In the first case it was a question of saving the Soviet state from certain downfall; later it was the consolidation of Stalin's one-man dictatorship.

The one-party system was not established without the participation of Lenin, and the same may be said of limitations on freedom of speech and of the press which were introduced immediately after the Revolution and extended during the years of 'war communism.'

One could extend the list of Stalinist measures that in some sense were a continuation of anti-democratic trends in Lenin's time, although there is still the question of different historical circumstances and the fact that we have reason to suppose that Lenin would never have gone as far as Stalin in this direction.

It can easily be shown, for example, how skilfully Stalin managed to manipulate for his own purposes two distinctive characteristics of the Bolshevik Party: centralism and discipline. And yet centralism (which was by no means always 'democratic'), strict discipline, and effective organization were essential aspects of the Leninist party before the Revolution and in the period of Revolution and civil war. Centralism and Party discipline were the crucial weapons that provided victory not only in October but also in the extremely precarious conditions of 1918–19 and during the economic and political crisis of 1920–1. Although the harmful consequences of excessive centralism are quite apparent today, this does not mean that it would have been preferable to have avoided centralism from the very beginning. Lenin believed that centralism was indispensable for the success of the socialist revolution, but he never maintained that the organizational principles of the Party were appropriate for a socialist society. Forms of organization change according to circumstances, and no one understood this better than Lenin. In wartime, ordinary citizens are called up for military service and placed under military discipline. But the war comes to an end, and people returning to normal civil existence are once again subject to other laws and regulations. Stalin not only never modified the centralized system of Party organization, but he extended it to the highest degree of absolutism. This may have suited his personal ambitions and the interests of the apparatus, but it certainly did not correspond to the needs of socialist construction or encourage the creation of a truly just society. Stalin behaved like a Roman general who, instead of disbanding his legions when the war was over, as Roman custom demanded, returned to Italy, took his legions to Rome, and seized power in the Republic.

In most respects, however, there is no continuity between Leninism and Stalinism; they are essentially different political phenomena sharing a common 'Marxist' terminology. Stalin's policies were in no way a reflection of Leninist objectives: the abolition of NEP, the hasty implementation of forced collectivization, mass terror against well-to-do peasants in the countryside and 'bourgeois specialists' in the cities, industrialization largely by harsh administrative rather than economic measures, the prohibition of all opposition both within the Party and outside, the revival of the tactics of 'war communism' in utterly different circumstances — in all this Stalin acted in defiance of clear Leninist directives, particularly those that appeared in his last writings of 1921–2.

I hardly need mention in this context the mass terror against the basic cadres of Party and state in the second half of the thirties. Starting with the annihilation of the leaders and members of all opposition groupings, this terror caused the deaths of more than one million Party members who had borne the brunt of civil war, the transitional period, and the first Five-Year Plan. I hardly need mention Stalin's policy of subordinating the entire Party to the control of the secret police, its power and authority extended beyond measure. Nor is there any need to mention Stalin's revival of Great Russian chauvinism, the deportation of many peoples of the USSR from their native lands, or his anti-Semitic policies which led to the physical destruction of the most brilliant representatives of Jewish culture and his plans for the deportation of all Jews to remote regions of the USSR. It goes without saying that all these and many other criminal political actions have nothing in common either with Marxism or Leninism.

It is certainly not my intention here to portray Lenin as some kind of saint who never committed political mistakes, who never resorted to cruel expedients in the course of political struggle. Many letters and instructions from the civil war period show that Lenin sanctioned the use of terror on a scale that was entirely unjustified. In one of his telegrams of 1918 he ordered the authorities of Nizhny Novgorod to 'evacuate and shoot the hundreds of prostitutes who are getting the soldiers and commanders drunk.' Even when the civil war had come to an end, Lenin proposed that terror be made legitimate in the Criminal Code of the RSFSR; he also advocated a much broader definition of political crime and counter-revolution.

In the spring of 1918 Lenin wrote: 'So long as revolution in Germany is delayed, our task is to learn from German state capitalism to do everything in our power to imitate it without shying away from dictatorial methods in order to accelerate this process. We must even surpass Peter, who hastened the adoption of Westernism by barbaric Rus without stopping at barbarous means in the struggle against barbarism.' It is doubtful whether anyone in the communist movement today would accept the formula that barbarous means are permissible in the struggle against barbarism. And one can hardly imagine that this approach was suitable for the conditions of 1918. It is difficult to accept Lenin's statements on the relativity of all moral concepts.

.   .   .

Undoubtedly Lenin was a man fanatically dedicated to the idea of power, but it was the power of the proletariat, the power of the Communist Party, the power of the workers, and it was never a question of personal power. Lenin was always ready to subordinate his personal interests and ambitions to the interests of the Party, to the interests of the workers, to the interests of the Revolution.

Stalin, on the other hand, was fanatically dedicated to the quest for personal power and was quite prepared to sacrifice any other interests in the process, including the interests of the Party, the proletariat, and the peasantry. Therefore the abuse of power under Stalin was not only on a different scale but was also fundamentally different in character from the abuse of power in Lenin's time. Here, too, there is no continuity.

In essence, Lenin and Stalin have almost nothing in common as human beings or as political personalities. Stalin was brutal, unscrupulous, a boundless cynic and contemptuous of others, no matter whether they were political opponents or members of the Party; consumed by the lust for power, he was a man of morbid vanity with an inferiority complex and a taste for spiteful vengeance. Stalin was not just a political criminal but also a criminal in the ordinary sense of the word; he recognized no rules in political struggle and, above all, in the struggle for personal power. Unfortunately it was just this lack of scruple that gave him an enormous advantage over his opponents and helped him to emerge victorious.

But Lenin was an entirely different person. It would be easy to quote from numerous testimonials by Lenin's comrades, friends, and all those who by right consider themselves to be Marxists and communists.

.   .   .

Leninism was not merely the application of Marxism to Russian conditions. Many aspects of Marxism were enriched and developed by Lenin, in accordance with prevailing conditions in the first quarter of the twentieth century. At the same time, however, Lenin's conception of Marxism was in certain respects a more narrow, one-sided doctrine than that of its founders. In addition, one must keep in mind the fact that classical Marxism was certainly not free of error. But all this bears little relation to Stalinism. I have received a letter from an Old Bolshevik containing the following passage:

> Conservative tendencies and forces have appeared in the socialist movement of the twentieth century that have acted as a brake on the further development of the socialist revolutionary process, in many cases exerting an anti-revolutionary influence. The most striking manifestation of these forces is Stalinism. Stalinism is not just a bureaucratic perversion of Marxism-Leninism in general or the theory and practice of socialist construction in particular. It is a total system of social, political, and economic organization. It is pseudo-socialism.

And this is entirely my own view.

.   .   .

Of course many features of authoritarian rule developed by Stalin first appeared under Lenin and in some cases he played a direct role in introducing them. The one-party system, restrictions on democracy at large and, later, the restrictions on democratic practices and discussion within the Party are all obvious examples. But these are by no means inherent features of Leninism. At first Lenin visualized Soviet power as a pluralist system, allowing all parties with links to the workers (including Right and Left SRs, Mensheviks, Trudoviki, and Anarchists) to compete freely within the Soviets. Even the ban on parties which stood outside the Soviet system was considered to be temporary. Lenin was convinced that the Bolsheviks would prevail over all other parties in an open competition and that this would certainly be the case after the main popular demands had been realized. Before and immediately after October he believed that the Bolsheviks would be able to govern with minimal use of force even in the first phase of the transitional period.

This is not the place to examine the reasons for the civil war or the Bolshevik mistakes that preceded it. Suffice it to say that, as can be seen from his last works, Lenin regarded as *temporary* phenomena much of what became part of our political life as a result of the civil war. For example, he never expected the ban on Party factions or freedom of speech to last. It was Stalin who extended and transformed what Lenin considered to be special measures into permanent and characteristic elements of the system. Stalin was responsible for the barbarous mass terror, the idolization of the 'leader,' the creation of an absolute personal dictatorship, the omnipotent police apparatus controlling even the Party — all those typical features of the regime that today are associated with the concept 'Stalinism.' To be sure, many achievements of the October Revolution were not totally destroyed by Stalinism; pseudosocialism has not managed to root out all elements of socialism from our social, economic, and political life.

Love on the Tractor:
Women in the Stalin Period

ᴠⱽⱽⱱ

BERNICE ROSENTHAL

After the Russian Revolutions of 1917, feminists aspired to a wholly restructured society that would see the liberation of women. In her essay, "Women in the Russian Revolution and After," a young American historian, Bernice Rosenthal, writes that despite greater representation of women in the professions these hopes never really materialized. How does she explain the gradual return to traditional roles for women during the collectivization and industrialization of the 1930s, a period when Stalin, embarking on a course of Russian nationalism and chauvinism, made divorce more difficult and abortion (save for medical reasons) a crime. In the mid-1930s women were officially guaranteed equality within the new system. How did reality differ?

Stalin's accession to power brought the institution of a totally planned economy. Bolsheviks had long viewed massive industrialization as the means to equality. The first Five-Year Plan (1929–1934) aimed to build the infrastructure of a modern Communist society. Featuring heavy industry and collectivization of agriculture, it skimped on consumer goods. Subsequent plans followed the same pattern of deliberately holding down consumption in order to maximize resources for investment.

Until mechanization could occur, hands still had to be used, thus creating a demand for labor. In order to enlist women, the party drew up lists of occupations deemed especially suitable for them (assembly-line work in factories) and strengthened protective legislation. Each year the percentage of women in the labor force increased: from 24 percent in 1928 to 26.7 percent in 1930, 31.7 percent in 1934, 35.4 percent in 1937. Though many women were peasants displaced by collectivization, they made good workers, registering fewer absences, latenesses, and industrial accidents than men did and showing more amenability to factory discipline.

Stalin's first Five-Year Plan had the aura of a military campaign. The slogan "Catch up to and surpass America!" implied that through struggle and sacrifice, Russians could realize their dream of universal prosperity. Despite a sharp drop in the standard of living, they were enthusiastic and believed the privation to be only temporary. In this atmosphere protective legislation was often ignored. Women filled the most arduous jobs: pulling, hauling, digging ditches, maintaining roads. Illiterate and unskilled, they did not qualify for the most attractive positions. Many were simply drafted and sent to work in the wilderness without proper tools, shelters, and food. In four years, young workers, most of them girls, built over 1,500 industrial plants. Popular literature glorified muscular heroines who could do anything a man could do: the idea of "woman's work" became obsolete.

In 1931 efforts were made to upgrade the skills of the entire labor force, including women. Wage differentials for skilled workers replaced identical wages for all workers. The factory training schools established female quotas; by 1934 women comprised 50 percent of their students. In 1935, on a technical proficiency test compulsory for all workers, women outperformed men in the younger age groups. Women were promoted to supervisory positions and, after 1934, became Stakhanovites (workers who markedly exceed their production norms and are held up as models). On the new collective farms, where model statutes decreed that women be paid in their own name, women became tractor drivers, section managers, brigade leaders, and even chairpersons.

An intensified drive to eradicate illiteracy increased opportunities for both sexes. By 1934 a network of primary schools covered the countryside, and the number of secondary schools increased rapidly. Female quotas in technical training institutes and universities made higher education more accessible to women. Each university department reserved

25 percent of its places for women, particularly benefiting women appli-cants in science, mathematics, engineering, and agricultural technology. Though accurate statistics on the number of women before the quotas are unavailable, it is clear that previously few women applied for these fields and even fewer had been admitted.

The party itself made sustained efforts to recruit women and to place them in prominent positions on local soviets, people's courts, and factory committees. Though exact figures are unavailable, women did begin to work their way up. We know that the percentage of women in the party rose from 8.2 percent in 1925 to 15.9 percent in 1932 and that by 1933 girls comprised half the members of the *Komsomol* (Young Com-munist League).

The impact of all these changes varied. For younger women, work provided the means to independence, and increased opportunities for training created the possibility of upward mobility. Many chose not to marry. Jobs and child-care centers in which unmarried women had prior-ity permitted any woman to have children. As a result, some men accused women of flaunting their independence. Older women, on the other hand, expressed bitterness and confusion. They disliked assembly-line work, but for them it was too late to learn new skills. Child-care facilities were included in the first Five-Year Plan, but did not expand rapidly enough to keep pace with demand. Even by 1936 only a small percentage of preschool children could be accommodated, and most married women still did not work. Moreover, the original plan to have twenty-four-hour child-care facilities could not be implemented, so working women could not attend night school or take correspondence courses. As shortages developed, plant managers tended to shift funds from child-care facilities to direct investment in production. By 1935 the hours had been reduced to cover the mother's working time only. Combining work and mother-hood became increasingly difficult, and the birthrate plummeted.

Primitive housing conditions may also account for women's increas-ing reluctance to bear children. The plan did not provide sufficient new housing for the millions of workers flooding into the cities. Often entire families crowded into one room. Few houses had running water or elec-tricity. Hot water and central heating were almost unknown. Carrying water in buckets, chopping wood, hauling fuel for the stove, consumed the woman's time and energy. Factory cafeterias served lunch only. As late as 1935 only 180 laundries existed in all of Russia. Doing the weekly washing involved a full day's work, so working women did it on their day off or at night. Laborsaving devices, like most consumer goods, were not manufactured, and most men refused to help at home with "woman's work." In the newer industrial areas, worse conditions prevailed. At Magnitogorsk, a steel city in the Ural Mountains, tents and dugouts provided the only shelter against the bitter winter winds. Visitors reported waitresses at the workers' cafeteria picking lice out of each other's hair, an example of the abysmal sanitary conditions. At the Dnepestroi Dam site, single women slept on plank beds, in crowded barracks, surrounded by wailing infants.

The family continued to disintegrate. No correspondence existed between formally registering a marriage and its stability, and marriage entailed little status or material advantage for either sex. Being a housewife was condemned, and inflationary pressures created a need for the wife's salary. The economic advantages of shared living expenses, plus sex, were attainable without formal marriage. And marriage did not necessarily denote companionship; industrial plants operated around the clock with no common day off, so a couple working different shifts rarely saw each other. At home, overcrowding frayed the nerves. By 1934, unsupervised children constituted a serious juvenile delinquency problem.

The sexual counterrevolution of the mid-1930s promoted a return to a conventional family structure, a pronatalist policy, and the promotion of a puritanical sexual morality. It resulted from several factors: the hardship suffered by abandoned wives and their children, official dismay at sexual permissiveness, and the precipitous decline in the birthrate after 1934. Sexual individualism and personal hedonism conflicted with the collectivist attitudes desired by the regime.

The 1930 official rehabilitation of the family as a socialist institution turned out to be a harbinger of the new policy. Party theoreticians now emphasized the necessity of a stable family structure but continued to oppose bourgeois patriarchal authority based on women's economic dependence. In 1934, Stalin with great publicity visited his aged mother in the Caucasus and that same year a new law held parents legally liable for the vandalism of their children and gave the entire family collective responsibility for the treason, defection, or state crime of any of its members. Homosexuality became a criminal offense punishable by hard labor. Circular letters had restricted abortion since 1931. At the clinic in Kuznetsk, in eastern Siberia, abortion could be performed only to save the mother's life. The 1936 decrees restricting divorce and abolishing legal abortion culminated the return to traditional morality. "The foul and poisonous idea of the liquidation of the family," Stalin announced in 1936, "is a false rumor . . . spread by enemies of the people." High fees introduced for divorce rose steeply for a second and third instance, and records of divorce were included in the labor books of both parties. The decree abolishing legal abortion stated that since the conditions necessitating the original decree of 1920 had been overcome, "mass abortions for egoistic reasons cannot be tolerated." *Izvestia* and *Pravda* editors scolded women who wrote letters of protest. They denied that childbirth was a personal matter and implied that women who failed to bear many children lacked faith in the socialist future. In a sense, this policy was a logical conclusion of earlier attitudes. Even Kollontai regarded childbearing as a social duty. She believed that a pregnant woman "does not belong to herself . . . she is working for the collective . . . from her own flesh and blood she is producing a new unit of labor." To meet some of the specific protests, Stalin promised increased maternity leave, more and better child-care centers, and improved housing, but not contraceptives. Since Russian women had been using abortion *instead* of birth control, the new law resulted in a steep rise in the birthrate: 18 percent for Russia as a whole, 100 percent in Moscow. However, in 1938, military preparedness led to the reduction of maternity leave to the pre-1936 level.

Women still worked but the new emphasis on motherhood hampered their upward mobility. Anticipating women to be frequently pregnant, managers hesitated to train them. Unallayed domestic responsibilities deflected women's time and energy away from activities leading to promotion. Also, in 1936, Stalin terminated the 50 percent female quotas in the factory training schools and technical institutes. Since women were now equal, he said, special measures were no longer necessary. By 1938 the number of women in technical institutes had dropped to a startling 27 percent; after 1938 these figures ceased to be published. The doors opened to women during the first Five-Year Plan were shut, except to a minority. Only universities made no serious attempt to limit women and their number continued to rise. In 1941 women composed 57 percent of the student body (already reflecting mobilization for the war); they studied teaching, medicine, law, mathematics, agronomy, economics, engineering, and all the sciences. But the majority of women still worked in the lowest-skilled, most easily replaceable job categories, including arduous physical labor.

Literature reflected the new emphasis. Earlier heroines had been almost sexless, the plot being girl meets tractor. Married couples when depicted in bed discussed the Five-Year Plan, their children, if any existed, nowhere in evidence. But the post-1936 female, a kind of superwoman, not only made a "serene home" for her husband but had many children and still equaled her husband's performance on the job. Novels and speeches lauded the joys of motherhood and pitied the childless, while posters of happy, large families appeared all over the Soviet Union. The popular child-care manual, Anton Makarenko's *A Book for Parents*, lauded the large family as the place where collective attitudes are first learned and castigated men who abandoned their wives and children. His pedagogy, stressing discipline and subordination to the group, replaced the more individualistic pedagogy of Lunacharsky, who had been dismissed as commissar of enlightenment in 1931. Makarenko's philosophy emphasized the responsibility of all age groups to society.

Article 122 of the Soviet Constitution of 1936 reads:

> Women in the USSR have equal rights with men in all branches of economic, cultural, social, and political life.
>
> The implementation of these rights of women is assured by granting women the same rights as men to work, to pay, to social insurance and education and by government protection of mothers and children, by paid maternity leave, and by a wide network of maternity homes, children's *crèches*, nursery schools and kindergartens.

Like the entire constitution, this article bore little relation to Soviet reality; at best it can be considered a statement of a still remote ideal. In 1936 the "great terror" began. Women, too unimportant to be purged, numbered only 10 percent of the victims. But this 10 percent included women working their way up the hierarchy and almost all the older generation of women activists, thus removing all but a few women from the higher levels of Soviet society. Moreover, women whose husbands were arrested suffered heavy secondary pressures, such as being fired from their jobs or evicted from their lodgings unless they got divorced.

Mobilization, with its new demands for workers, brought about a renewed effort to recruit women into the work force. Once again they were urged to improve their skills, and after 1941 figures on the number of women in key segments of the economy again became available. For example, in one year, 1941–1942, the percentage of women steam engine operators rose from 6 percent to 33 percent and similar dramatic increases occurred among tractor drivers, locomotive engineers, steam compressor operators, electricians, and welders — all highly paid occupations. By 1945 women composed 56 percent of the labor force, a majority of the miners and a third of the workers in the Baku oil fields. Crucial to the home front, women worked fourteen to eighteen hours a day, often under severe conditions, as in factories hastily evacuated to Siberia with roofs but no walls. Asked if she were tired, a young girl replied: "Tired? Our men are giving their lives for us. How dare I be tired?" Meanwhile, Grandma kept house and minded the children. Women also engaged in actual combat for the Red Army, most often in guerrilla units but also as machine gunners and snipers; no unit lacked women altogether. Women joined the medical and signal corps and several air regiments consisted entirely of women. The unit that captured Hitler's chancellery had a woman major.

After the war, the loss of 20,000,000 men, out of a total population of 170,000,000, severely disrupted the Soviet demographic balance. A woman recalls, "I know of no one — no one — who did not lose a husband, a son, or a lover." Desire to replenish population added to the party's fear of a postwar relaxation of morality and discipline caused a revision of the Family Code in 1944 along still more conservative and pronatalist lines. To prevent wholesale abandonment by returning soldiers in search of younger women, divorce became extremely difficult. As an incentive for the man to stay in the family, other changes made him de facto head of household and favored him in inheritance, which had been gradually reintroduced since the twenties. A reversal of previous policy deprived illegitimate children of inheritance rights and stigmatized them by a line drawn through the space for "father's name" on their identity cards. Women lost their right to file paternity suits. All this was aimed at creating the stable social climate deemed conducive to large families. For women who did not have husbands, however, to stimulate them to bear children and to prevent recourse to illegal abortion, the state assumed direct responsibility for illegitimate children's support at a fixed rate. Two years later, however, the rate was halved, thus shifting the major burden to the mothers. Special honors were provided, including cash subsidies, for large families. Ten children made a woman a Mother Heroine and seven entitled her to an Order of Maternal Glory. The same law introduced family allowances for three or more children and halved their fees for crèches (for children under three), nursery schools, and kindergartens, all financed by a new tax levied on single persons and couples with fewer than three children.

After the war, reconstruction absorbed all resources. The industrial heartland of European Russia lay in ruins and huge tracts of formerly fertile farmland had become scorched earth. Much of the existing housing had been destroyed by the war, and both communal facilities and consumer goods remained unavailable. A significant number of women became doctors, engineers, and scientists; indeed, the shortage of men worked to their advantage professionally. Others continued to be skilled workers; the labor shortage prevented their wholesale displacement by returning war veterans. But these women constituted a small proportion of the total female labor force; the overwhelming majority of women remained concentrated in the lower echelons of the economic ladder. They built the roads, dug the ditches, shoveled the snow, labored on the construction sites, and worked in the fields. As late as the 1950s, women made up four-fifths of the unskilled laborers. And the male deficit militated against equality in personal life as women catered to men.

The experience of Soviet women during the Stalin era brings the question of priorities into sharp focus. True, the planners could not create the material conditions for equality overnight. But they had a choice — between forced-draft industrialization (including collectivization) and a slower but more balanced scheme of economic development that included consumer goods. Despite the fact that stinting on consumer goods and communal amenities weighed particularly heavily on women, they chose forced-draft industrialization for military, ideological, and political reasons. Well before the success of Hitler, Stalin aimed to increase the military might of the Soviet Union. Ideologically, gradual economic development (Bukharin's plan) meant continuing the mixed economy that benefited peasants far more than workers. And the political factor, the tremendous power accruing to those who control the economy, must not be discounted as a reason for Stalin's choice. Not only did women's well-being have low priority in the original plan, but as necessity dictated cuts in the budget, women's needs (length of maternity leave, hours of child-care-center operation) were cut first. And there is no evidence that the sexual counterrevolution, which negated so many of the women's gains, was unpopular in the higher echelons of the party; the planners themselves, apparently, were ambivalent about the equality they preached.

5

THE
NAZIS

When on 30 January 1933 President Hindenburg named Adolf Hitler head of the German government, the Nazi rank and file rejoiced in their triumph and launched an orgy of celebration. Göring proclaimed the rebirth of the Reich, the obliteration of fourteen years of shame, and the founding of a new German state in freedom and honor. That night in Berlin a gigantic torchlight parade of a quarter of a million marched past the führer, while Hindenburg, woodenly expressionless in another window of the chancellery, stood watching the phenomenon to which he had now given his official consecration. The people of Germany watched too, some in fear, some in hope, and all in amazement. Given the horror of the bloodbath into which the regime plunged Europe and the world during its twelve-year existence, historians, political scientists, political sociologists, and others have searched for answers to such questions as how the Nazis came to power, who supported them, and why the German people tolerated their tactics.

What were the reasons for the triumph of Nazism in particular and of fascism in general? Was it the consequence of economic dislocations arising from the depression? If so, why was it not successful in Western Europe as well? Was it rather part of a larger totalitarian movement, an age of dictatorship, which seemed to promise answers to the crises of post-World War I Europe and the depression-ridden "thirties"? Can it best be explained in terms of the German historical past? How did Nazi rule affect the lives of women in comparison to those of men? Whatever the reasons for the Nazi triumph in Germany and its consequences in that country, it had ominous implications for the rest of Europe. The selections that follow not only present different views of the Nazis but may also offer insights into the relationship between the writers and their frameworks of reference.

Women voters by and large continued to support the conservative and religious parties, although many of Hitler's most fanatical followers were women (paradoxically enough in view of what Claudia Koonz was to call the party's "overt misogyny" — its preference for limiting women to traditional roles with *Kinder*, "children," and in *Küche*, "kitchen," if not *Kirche*, "church").[1] In her more general study of women under Nazi rule, Jill Stephenson points out that the call for childbearing nevertheless weakened the stigma attached to unwed motherhood, and insists that the retreat from Weimar's commitment to gender equality began before the Nazi accession to power. Indeed, she argues that the attitude toward women in Germany in the 1930s was influenced more by traditional and economic factors than by Nazi ideology, though this might well have been reversed had the Third Reich endured.

Perhaps the chief question raised by any consideration of the Nazi past is whether its acceptance represented a moral surrender of the German people to authoritarianism or whether it reflected the inability of German democracy to meet the economic and political crises that beset the nation in the early 1930s. Purely historical evidence can neither support nor reject the first answer to this question; the excerpts that follow will prove useful in explicating the second.

---

[1]Claudia Koonz, *Mothers in the Fatherland: Women, the Family, and Nazi Politics* (New York, 1987).

Behometh: The Structure and Practice of National Socialism

∿

FRANZ NEUMANN

Franz Neumann emigrated from Germany to the United States in 1936. He worked for the Office of Strategic Services during World War II and afterwards headed the State Department's German Research Section before becoming a professor of government at Columbia University. His book *Behometh* provides an early analysis of the Nazi phenomenon. What kind of interpretation does Neumann seem to be providing? How does he explain the failure of those who most arduously supported Weimar democracy — the Social Democrats and the trade unions — to organize labor and even the middle classes in defense of the besieged republic?

The main pillars of the pluralistic system were the Social Democratic party and the trade unions. They alone in post-war Germany could have swung the great masses of the people over to democracy; not only the workers but also the middle classes, the section of the population that suffered most from the process of monopolization.

Other strata reacted to the complex post-war and post-revolution situation exactly as one would have expected. The big estate owners pursued a reactionary policy in every field. Monopolistic industry hated and fought the trade unions and the political system that gave the unions

From *Behometh: The Structure and Practice of National Socialism* by Franz Neumann, New York, 1963, pp. 13–17, 33–34. Reprinted by permission of Hippocrene Books, Inc.

their status. The army used every available means to strengthen chauvinistic nationalism in order to restore itself to its former greatness. The judiciary invariably sided with the right and the civil services supported counter-revolutionary movements. Yet the Social Democracy was unable to organize either the whole of the working class or the middle classes. It lost sections of the former and never won a real foothold with the latter. The Social Democrats lacked a consistent theory, competent leadership, and freedom of action. Unwittingly, they strengthened the monopolistic trends in German industry, and, placing complete reliance on formalistic legality, they were unable to root out the reactionary elements in the judiciary and civil service or limit the army to its proper constitutional role.

The strong man of the Social Democratic party, Otto Braun, Prussian prime minister until 20 June 1932 when he was deposed by the Hindenburg-Papen *coup d'état*, attributes the failure of the party and Hitler's successful seizure of power to a combination of Versailles and Moscow. This defense is neither accurate nor particularly skilful. The Versailles Treaty naturally furnished excellent propaganda material against democracy in general and against the Social Democratic party in particular, and the Communist party unquestionably made inroads among Social Democrats. Neither was primarily responsible for the fall of the Republic, however. Besides, what if Versailles and Moscow had been the two major factors in the making of National Socialism? Would it not have been the task of a great democratic leadership to make the democracy work in spite of and against Moscow and Versailles? That the Social Democratic party failed remains the crucial fact, regardless of any official explanation. It failed because it did not see that the central problem was the imperialism of German monopoly capital, becoming ever more urgent with the continued growth of the process of monopolization. The more monopoly grew, the more incompatible it became with the political democracy.

.   .   .

The efficient and powerfully organized German system of our time was born under the stimulus of a series of factors brought into the forefront by the First World War. The inflation of the early '20s permitted unscrupulous entrepreneurs to build up giant economic empires at the expense of the middle and working classes. The prototype was the Stinnes empire and it is at least symbolic that Hugo Stinnes was the most inveterate enemy of democracy and of Rathenau's foreign policy. Foreign loans that flowed into Germany after 1924 gave German industry the liquid capital needed to rationalize and enlarge their plants. Even the huge social-welfare program promoted by the Social Democracy indirectly strengthened the centralization and concentration of industry, since big business could far more easily assume the burden than the small or middle entrepreneur. Trusts, combines, and cartels covered the whole economy with a network of authoritarian organizations. Employers' organizations controlled the labor market, and big business lobbies aimed at placing the legislative, administrative, and judicial machinery at the service of monopoly capital.

In Germany there was never anything like the popular anti-monopoly movement of the United States under Theodore Roosevelt and Woodrow Wilson. Industry and finance were of course firmly convinced that the cartel and trust represented the highest forms of economic organization. The independent middle class was not articulate in its opposition, except against department stores and chains. Though the middle class belonged to powerful pressure groups, like the Federal Union of German Industries, big business leaders were invariably their spokesmen.

Labor was not at all hostile to the process of trustification. The Communists regarded monopoly as an inevitable stage in the development of capitalism and hence considered it futile to fight capital concentration rather than the system itself. Ironically enough, the policy of the reformist wing of the labor movement was not significantly different in effect. The Social Democrats and the trade unions also regarded concentration as inevitable, and, they added, as a higher form of capitalist organization. Their leading theorist, Rudolf Hilferding, summarized the position at the party's 1927 convention: 'Organized capitalism means replacing free competition by the social principle of planned production. The task of the present Social Democratic generation is to invoke state aid in translating this economy, organized and directed by the capitalists, into an economy directed by the democratic state.' By economic democracy, the Social Democratic party meant a larger share in controlling the monopolist organizations and better protection for the workers against the ill effects of concentration.

The largest trusts in German history were formed during the Weimar Republic. The merger in 1926 of four large steel companies in western Germany resulted in the formation of the *Vereinigte Stahlwerke* (the United Steel Works). The *Vereinigte Oberschlesische Hüttenwerke* (the

United Upper Silesian Mills) was a similar combination among the steel industries of Upper Silesia. The *I. G. Farbenindustrie* (the German Dye Trust) arose in 1925 through the merger of the six largest corporations in this field, all of which had previously been combined in a pool. In 1930 the capital stock of the Dye Trust totaled 1,100,000,000 marks and the number of workers it employed reached 100,000.

At no time in the Republic (not even in the boom year of 1929) were the productive capacities of German industry fully, or even adequately, utilized. The situation was worst in heavy industry, especially in coal and steel, the very fields that had furnished the industrial leadership during the empire and that still dominated the essential business organizations. With the great depression, the gap between actual production and capacity took on such dangerous proportions that governmental assistance became imperative. Cartels and tariffs were resorted to along with subsidies in the form of direct grants, loans, and low interest rates. These measures helped but at the same time they intensified another threat. The framework of the German government was still a parliamentary democracy after all, and what if movements threatening the established monopolistic structure should arise within the mass organizations? As far back as November 1923, public pressure had forced the Stresemann cabinet to enact a cartel decree authorizing the government to dissolve cartels and to attack monopolistic positions generally. Not once were these powers utilized, but the danger to privileges inherent in political democracy remained and obviously became more acute in times of great crisis.

The whole process of rationalization, concentration, and bureaucratization had serious repercussions on the social structure. Certainly one of the most significant was the serious weakening of the power of the trade unions, best illustrated by the decline of the strike. The strike weapon has its greatest effectiveness in a period of comparatively free competition, for the individual employer's power of resistance is relatively low. It becomes more difficult to strike successfully as monopolies develop and the strength of employers' organizations grows, and still more so when monopolies reach the scale of international cartels, as in steel. Even stoppage of production on a nation-wide scale can be compensated by the cartel. These are rules of general application.

The pluralism of Weimar led to additional factors in Germany. Growing state intervention in business enterprises gave labor disputes the taint of strikes against the state, while governmental regulation led many workers to consider it unnecessary to join unions. The unions for their part were not eager to fight a state in which they had so much at stake. Above all, monopoly was making major — and for the unions deleterious — changes in the social stratification. The increasing percentage of unskilled and semi-skilled workers (and particularly of women workers); the steady increase in foremen and supervisory personnel; the rise in the number of salaried employees in office positions and in the growing distribution apparatus, many organized in non-socialist unions with a middle-class ideology — all these factors weakened the trade-union movement. The great crisis made matters worse, first because of the tremendous decline in production and the creation of large masses of unemployed, and secondly because the accompanying political tension tended to make every strike a political strike, which the trade unions flatly opposed because of their theories of revisionism and 'economic democracy.'

.   .   .

Every social system must somehow satisfy the primary needs of the people. The imperial system succeeded to the extent and so long as it was able to expand. A successful policy of war and imperialist expansion had reconciled large sections of the population to the semi-absolutism. In the face of the material advantages gained, the anomalous character of the political structure was not decisive. The army, the bureaucracy, industry, and the big agrarians ruled. The divine-right theory — the official political doctrine — merely veiled their rule and it was not taken seriously. The imperial rule was in fact not absolutistic, for it was bound by law, proud of its *Rechtsstaat* theory. It lost out and abdicated when its expansionist policy was checked.

The Weimar democracy proceeded in a different direction. It had to rebuild an impoverished and exhausted country in which class antagonisms had become polarized. It attempted to merge three elements: the heritage of the past (especially the civil service), parliamentary democracy modeled after Western European and American patterns, and a pluralistic collectivism, the incorporation of the powerful social and economic organizations directly into the political system. What it actually produced, however, were sharpened social antagonisms, the breakdown of voluntary collaboration, the destruction of parliamentary institutions, the suspension of political liberties, the growth of a ruling bureaucracy, and the renaissance of the army as a decisive political factor.

Why?

In an impoverished, yet highly industrialized, country, pluralism could work only under the following different conditions. In the first place, it could rebuild Germany with foreign assistance, expanding its markets by peaceful means to the level of its high industrial capacity. The Weimar Republic's foreign policy tended in this direction. By joining the concert of the Western European powers the Weimar government hoped to obtain concessions. The attempt failed. It was supported neither by German industry and large landowners nor by the Western powers. The year 1932 found Germany in a catastrophic political, economic, and social crisis.

The system could also operate if the ruling groups made concessions voluntarily or under compulsion by the state. That would have led to a better life for the mass of the German workers and security for the middle classes at the expense of the profits and power of big business. German industry was decidedly not amenable, however, and the state sided with it more and more.

The third possibility was the transformation into a socialist state, and that had become completely unrealistic in 1932 since the Social Democratic party was socialist only in name.

The crisis of 1932 demonstrated that political democracy alone without a fuller utilization of the potentialities inherent in Germany's industrial system, that is, without the abolition of unemployment and an improvement in living standards, remained a hollow shell.

The fourth choice was the return to imperialist expansion. Imperialist ventures could not be organized within the traditional democratic form, however, for there would have been too serious an opposition. Nor could it take the form of restoration of the monarchy. An industrial society that has passed through a democratic phase cannot exclude the masses from consideration. Expansionism therefore took the form of National Socialism, a totalitarian dictatorship that has been able to transform some of its victims into supporters and to organize the entire country into an armed camp under iron discipline.

The Course of German History

◈

A. J. P. TAYLOR

Alan John Percivale Taylor taught for many years at Manchester and Oxford Universities and published extensively in the areas of European diplomatic, German, and Hapsburg history. He also achieved notoriety as a lecturer for the British Broadcasting Company. The following excerpt, from *The Course of German History*, provides a different perspective from that of Neumann. To what extent is Taylor's approach shaped by the period (World War II) in which he wrote? Do you agree that the Nazis were the product of German historical development?

Certain permanent factors have, indeed, influenced German history, since the time when Charlemagne, by establishing the Holy Roman Empire, advanced German history from the stage of tribal legends. First was their geographic position. The Germans are the peoples of the north European plain, the people without a defined natural frontier. Without the sharp limit of mountain ranges, except at the Alps and the Bohemian mountains, the great plain is intersected by four great rivers (Rhine, Elbe, Oder, Vistula) dividing lines sharp enough to split the German people up among themselves, not rigid enough to confine them within settled frontiers. There is no determined geographic point for German expansion, equally none for German contraction; and, in the course of a thousand years, geographic Germany has gone out and in like a concertina. At times Germany has been confined within the Rhine and the Elbe; at others it has blown itself out to the Pyrenees and to the Caucasus. Every German frontier is artificial, therefore impermanent; that is the permanence of German geography.

Enduring too for a thousand years has been their ethnographical position. Here too the Germans have been the people of the middle; always they have had two neighbours and have shown two faces. To their west was the Roman Empire and its heir, French civilization; to their east, the Slavs, new barbarians pressing on the Germans as the Germans pressed on Rome. To the west therefore the Germans have always appeared as barbarians, but the most civilized of barbarians, eager to learn, anxious to imitate; and the record of German civilization is a story of sedulous and exaggerated imitation of the established order in the west — an imitation which began with Charlemagne's aping of Caesar and has ended in Hitler's aping of Napoleon. To the Slavs of the east, however, the Germans have made a very different appearance: ostensibly the defenders of civilization, they have defended it as barbarians, employing the technical means of civilization, but not its spirit. For a thousand years, again from Charlemagne to Hitler, the Germans have been "converting" the Slavs from paganism, from Orthodox Christianity, from Bolshevism, or merely from being Slavs; their weapons have varied, their method has always been the same — extermination. Most of the peoples of Europe have, at one time or another, been exterminators. The French exterminated the Albigensians in the thirteenth century and the Huguenots in the seventeenth; the Spaniards exterminated the Moors; the English exterminated the North-American Indians and attempted in the seventeenth century to exterminate the Irish. But no other people has pursued extermination as a permanent policy from generation to generation for a thousand years; and it is foolish to suppose that they have done so without adding something permanent to their national tradition. No one can can understand the Germans who does not appreciate their anxiety to learn from, and to imitate, the West; but equally no one can understand Germans who does not appreciate their determination to exterminate the East.

.   .   .

The Empire which Charlemagne founded set the tone for German history from the beginning. It was not intended as a German national state; it claimed to be a universal Empire, a revival of the Empire of the Caesars. The revival did not come from the inhabitants of Rome, of Paris, or of Naples; it came from barbarians, whose only connection with the real empire was that their ancestors had helped to destroy it. The history of the Germans as a civilized people thus began with the deliberate, planned imitation of an institution which had never been theirs. The Empire claimed to be universal. Here too the Germans struck the same note from the beginning. Unlike other peoples, they did not start from their own national state and gradually advance claims to domination: they demanded everything from the beginning. Most typical of all, this Empire — ostensibly the bulwark of Christian civilization and often accepted as such by the peoples of the West both then and since — inaugurated at once the policy of exterminating the Slav peoples of the East. Universalism, aping of foreign traditions, ruthlessness towards the Slav peoples, these three things were to form the pattern of the Reich for more than a thousand years, and to compose the "national character" of the German people. There was nothing innate or mysterious in this. The German character was determined by their geographical position: they were the barbarians on the edge of a great civilization. Hence their anxiety both to master this civilization and to imitate it; hence their barbaric ruthlessness towards the peoples who were pressing on them from behind. They were the people of the middle: dualism was dictated to them.

.   .   .

In nothing was Luther more typical than in his attitude to the princes. Here, more than in any other aspect, did he represent the despair in themselves which had overcome the German middle classes. When, in 1521, Luther went to the Diet at Worms to defend his doctrines, he went under the protection of and as the spokesman of a united and enthusiastic people; never has there been a more tumultuous journey through Germany. The enthusiasm vanished overnight, and Luther crept under the wing of the princes of northern Germany, who became Protestant not as the most advanced, but as the most backward, section of German society — for them Lutheranism was merely a weapon against the political interference either of the Emperor or of the trading classes. Lutheranism, at first a movement of Reform, became, and remained, the most conservative of religions; though it preached the absolute supremacy of the individual conscience within, it preached an equally absolute supremacy for the territorial power without. Luther gave to Germany a consciousness of national existence and, through his translation of the Bible, a national tongue; but he also gave to Germany the Divine Right of Kings, or rather the Divine Right of any established authority. Obedience was the first, and last, duty of the Christian man. The State can do no wrong; therefore, whatever the State orders, that the Christian man can do without danger to his conscience, and, indeed, the more devout the individual, the more eager he will be to carry out the most violent and unscrupulous orders of the prince, God's mouthpiece. In the general decline which was overcoming Germany, the princes represented the one point of stability and order, and the German middle classes, speaking through Luther, surrendered to the princes without reserve. The movement against Rome which Luther personified had sprung from a national resentment against the Papacy, which, by its co-operation with the great feudatories against the Emperor, had prevented national unity. Lutheranism certainly destroyed Papal influence in north Germany, but, lacking confidence in itself, fell into the arms of the princes and thus actually strengthened, indeed made triumphant, the particularism which it had begun by attacking. So the first great expression of the German national spirit repudiated the universalism of the middle ages, only to fall into a particularism which made German unification impossible for centuries.

. . .

Such was the strange work of Luther. He made Germany a nation, but a nation divided against itself. He gave the Germans a spiritual individualism and destroyed for centuries their political independence. He broke with the mediaeval dream of universalism, only to lead Germany into the nightmare of particularism. He taught the Germans to believe in liberty, but he taught them also that liberty is to be found only in the service of the prince. He created the German language, and he used his creation for attacking reason, for expressing hysteria. Like the Germans of a thousand years before and of four hundred years later, Luther was the barbarian who looks over the Rhine, at once the most profound expression and the most decisive creator of German dualism.

. . .

The making of Prussia was the work of the Hohenzollern rulers, almost of one Hohenzollern ruler. Still it could not have been accomplished without the existence of a unique landed class, the Junkers of eastern Germany. No factor is more important in the history of modern

Germany, and no factor is less understood. The Junkers were landowners, lords of great estates. But they had nothing else in common with the French nobles or the Whig aristocrats, the landowners of western Europe. The French and English nobles were a leisured class, the French depending on feudal dues, the English on rents from their tenants. Both spent most of their time away from their estates, the French at court, the English in London. The one produced the French civilization of the eighteenth century, the other the British constitution, the greatest political work of man. The Junkers, however, were not a leisured class, drawing tribute from others. They were, for the most part, without tenants and worked their estates themselves, for they were the owners of colonial lands. The landowners of western Europe were part of a settled community, in which even serfs and copy-holders had some legal existence, but the Junkers had no obligations to the conquered Slav peoples whose land they owned; these peoples had been utterly expropriated and had been degraded not even into tied serfs, but into landless labourers. The Junker estates were never feudal; they were capitalist undertakings, which closely resembled the great capitalist farms of the American prairie — also the result of a colonial expropriation of the American Indians. The Junkers were hardworking estate managers, thinking of their estates solely in terms of profits and efficiency, neither more nor less than agrarian capitalists.

This economic characteristic had a unique political result. Everywhere in Europe the Crown was striving to make the organization of the State more efficient; therefore, despite the king's personal preference for the manners and culture of the nobility, he had to turn for political backing to the capitalist middle classes, who alone possessed the virtues of efficiency and hard work. But these were the very virtues possessed by the Junkers and not possessed to the same degree by the German burghers of the eighteenth century. The German trading classes had abandoned all attempt to keep up with the capitalist triumphs of England, Holland, or even France. Instead they prided themselves on their civic liberties and on the high level of their culture as citizens of the world. These were not assets likely to appeal to Frederick II. But the Hohenzollerns had long ago stamped out the last flickers of aristocratic liberties; and the Junkers had neither the leisure nor the ability to develop a taste for culture — to go to Berlin was merely to leave the threshing floor for the barrack-room. Thus in Prussia alone in Europe, a reforming Crown could carry out its reforms through the agency of great landowners; and the greater the efficiency of the Prussian State, the more it needed the services of the Prussian Junkers. It was no paradox, but an inevitable development, that Frederick, the most efficient of the Hohenzollerns, first made absolute the Junker monopoly of civilian and military office. The State created by Frederick II combined two qualities which were elsewhere opposites. It had, on the one hand, the unscrupulous authoritarianism, the disregard both of humanity and of principle, everywhere characteristic of rule by a privileged upper class; on the other hand, a striving after efficiency and improvement, a rigid devotion to the balancing of accounts, elsewhere associated with the rule of a reforming middle class. The Prussian Junkers, one might say, were politically in the Stone Age; economically and administratively they looked forward to the age of steel and electricity. They were barbarians who had learnt to handle a rifle and, still more, bookkeeping by double entry. Ruthless exploiters of conquered land, they were untouched by European civilization and yet could master every technical improvement which Europe produced. Of course their achievement was not perfect or unbroken. Just as an individual Junker might neglect his estate for culture, or from laziness, and so paid the penalty in bankruptcy, so the Junker governing class sometimes failed to keep up with the times in organization, in military equipment, or even in political pretence. The great disasters of 1807, of 1848, and of 1918, warned them that the anachronism of their survival could be preserved only by ceaseless efficiency; and in each case the lesson was learnt. If the Junkers had owned fat acres instead of sand, if Prussia had ever enjoyed a long period of secure repose in Europe, the habits of leisure and inefficiency would have been too strong to overcome, and eventually at some crisis both Prussian Junkers and Prussian state would have collapsed. But both lived always on the edge of danger and bankruptcy; this bound them together and preserved them.

.   .   .

Eighteen forty-eight was the decisive year of German, and so of European, history: it recapitulated Germany's past and anticipated Germany's future. Echoes of the Holy Roman Empire merged into a prelude of the Nazi "New Order"; the doctrines of Rousseau and the doctrines of Marx, the shade of Luther and the shadow of Hitler, jostled each other in bewildering succession. Never has there been a revolution so inspired by a limitless faith in the power of ideas; never has a revolution so discredited the power of ideas in its result. The success of the revolution discredited conservative ideas; the failure of the revolution discredited liberal ideas.

After it, nothing remained but the idea of Force, and this idea stood at the helm of German history from then on. For the first time since 1521, the German people stepped on to the centre of the German stage only to miss their cues once more. German history reached its turning-point and failed to turn. This was the fateful essence of 1848.

. . .

The refusal of Frankfort to go with the masses, the failure to offer a social programme, was a decisive element in the failure of the German liberals. This refusal and this failure are the theme of *Germany: Revolution and Counter-Revolution*, the pamphlet which Engels wrote for Marx and which is still the best analysis of the events of 1848. But there was another, and even more important cause of failure, a disastrous mistake which Marx, Engels, and most German radicals shared. The National Assembly had come into being when the armed power of Austria and Prussia collapsed; and its prestige waned as Austrian and Prussian armed power revived. These armies won new confidence, no doubt, in the repression of internal disorder. But the prime purpose of armies is foreign war, and it was in foreign war of a sort that Austrian and Prussian absolutism were reborn. Not the social conflict, but the conflict on the national frontiers — in Bohemia, in Poland, and in Slesvig and Holstein — determined the fate of German liberalism. In the struggle against the Czechs, against the Poles, against the Danes, the German liberals unhesitatingly supported the cause of the Prussian and Austrian armies and were then surprised when these weapons were turned against themselves. Liberalism was sacrificed to the national cause.

. . .

The radicals who did not despair of Germany were few. Far more accomplished their own revolution by emigrating to the freedom of the United States. German emigration had already begun on a big scale, more than a hundred thousand a year, in the early 'forties. It dwindled to fifty thousand in 1848, when it seemed that Germany might be at last a place worth living in. After 1848 it soared once more, running at a steady average of more than a quarter of a million a year throughout the eighteen-fifties. These emigrants were the best of their race — the adventurous, the independent, the men who might have made Germany a free and civilized country. They brought to the United States a contribution of inestimable value, but they were lost to Germany. They, the best Germans, showed their opinion of Germany by leaving it for ever.

Like the radical emigrants, most liberals too were disillusioned by their experience of practical politics. Many withdrew to academic studies or served Germany by applying science to practical needs. Some turned from politics to industry and finance. So Hansemann, most liberal of the Prussian ministers of 1848, founded the Discontogesellschaft, one of the greatest of German banks. The liberal politicians who remained politicians resolved to be more moderate and practical than ever. Their faith in the strength of their idea was destroyed; therefore they believed that liberal Germany must be achieved by subtlety and guile. But it would be wrong to suppose that the liberals of Germany vanished or that liberal convictions counted for nothing in Germany after 1848. The professors, the lawyers, the civil servants of the lesser states, remained predominantly liberal: they were still liberal in 1890 and even, for the most part, in 1930. But in 1848 they were a serious and respected political force. After 1848 they counted for less and less and, at last, for nothing at all.

The real significance of the revolution of 1848 was not so much its failure at the time, but the effect of its failure in the future. After 1850 there began in Germany a period of industrial development, after 1871 an industrial revolution. Economic power passed within a generation into the hands of industrial capitalists. Industrial capitalists, it is commonly held, are in politics liberal; but this view is an abbreviation of the real course of events. Industrial capitalists, like all businessmen, judge everything by the standard of success. A good businessman is one who succeeds; a bad businessman is one who "fails." When industrial capitalists enter politics they apply the same standard and adopt as their own the party and outlook which prevails. In England and the United States the struggle between liberalism and arbitrary power had long been fought out. The execution of Charles I, the overthrow of the army, and the Glorious Revolution in England, the defeat of the redcoats and royal government in America, established the great principles of constitutional freedom and the rule of law. The English and American capitalists found the civilian politicians and lawyers in control. Therefore they too became liberals, advocates of individual freedom and upholders of constitutional government. In France, despite the great revolution, the verdict of success was less clear: therefore the industrial capitalists were confused — some became republicans, some Bonapartists, some corrupt and unprincipled. But in Germany there could be no doubt where success lay. The German capitalists became dependants of Prussian militarism and advocates of arbitrary power as naturally and as inevitably as English or American capitalists became liberals and advocates of constitutional authority. Where Anglo-Saxon capitalists demanded *laissez-faire*, German capitalists sought for state leadership; where Anglo-Saxon capitalists accepted democracy, however grudgingly, German capitalists grudgingly accepted dictatorship. This was the fateful legacy of 1848.

.   .   .

There was nothing mysterious in Hitler's victory; the mystery is rather that it had been so long delayed. The delay was caused by the tragic incompatibility of German wishes. The rootless and irresponsible, the young and the violent embraced the opportunity of licensed gangsterdom on a heroic scale; but most Germans wanted the recovery of German power, yet disliked the brutality and lawlessness of the National Socialists, by which alone they could attain their wish. Thus Brüning was the nominee of the Reichswehr and the enemy of the republic, the harbinger both of dictatorship and of German rearmament. Yet he hated the paganism and barbarity of the National Socialists and would have done anything against them — except breaking with the generals. Schleicher, in control of the Reichswehr, was obsessed with German military recovery; yet he contemplated an alliance with the trade unions against the National Socialists and, subsequently, paid for his opposition with his life. The generals, the judges, the civil servants, the professional classes, wanted what only Hitler could offer — German mastery of Europe. But they did not want to pay the price. Hence the delay in the National Socialist rise to power; hence their failure to win a clear majority of votes even at the general election in March 1933. The great majority of German people wanted German domination abroad and the rule of law at home, irreconcilables which they had sought to reconcile ever since 1871, or rather ever since the struggles against Poles, Czechs, and Danes in 1848.

.   .   .

This is the explanation of the paradox of the "Third Reich." It was a system founded on terror, unworkable without the secret police and the concentration camp; but it was also a system which represented the deepest wishes of the German people. In fact it was the only system of German government ever created by German initiative. The old empire had been imposed by the arms of Austria and France; the German Confederation by the armies of Austria and Prussia. The Hohenzollern empire was made by the victories of Prussia, the Weimar republic by the victories of the Allies. But the "Third Reich" rested solely on German force and German impulse; it owed nothing to alien forces. It was a tyranny imposed upon the German people by themselves. Every class disliked the barbarism or the tension of National Socialism; yet it was essential to the attainment of their ends. This is most obvious in the case of the old "governing classes." The Junker landowners wished to prevent the expropriation of the great estates and the exposure of the scandals of the *Osthilfe*; the army officers wanted a mass army, heavily equipped; the industrialists needed an economic monopoly of all Europe if their great concerns were to survive. Yet many Junkers had an old-fashioned Lutheran respectability; many army officers knew that world conquest was beyond Germany's strength; many industrialists, such as Thyssen, who had financed the National Socialists, were pious and simple in their private lives. But all were prisoners of the inescapable fact that if the expansion of German power were for a moment arrested, their position would be destroyed.

But the National Socialist dictatorship had a deeper foundation. Many, perhaps most, Germans were reluctant to make the sacrifices demanded by rearmament and total war; but they desired the prize which only total war would give. They desired to undo the verdict of 1918; not merely to end reparations or to cancel the "war guilt" clause, but to repudiate the equality with the peoples of eastern Europe which had then been forced upon them. During the preceding eighty years the Germans had sacrificed to the Reich all their liberties; they demanded as reward the enslavement of others. No German recognized the Czechs or Poles as equals. Therefore every German desired the achievement which only total war could give. By no other means could the Reich be held together. It had been made by conquest and for conquest; if it ever gave up its career of conquest, it would dissolve. Patriotic duty compelled even the best of Germans to support a policy which was leading Germany to disaster.

Totalitarian Dictatorship
and Autocracy

✧

CARL J. FRIEDRICH AND ZBIGNIEW BRZEZINSKI

Carl J. Friedrich taught at Harvard University for fifty years, and his publications range from a study of the Bronze Age to the philosophy of law to Kant. He was an adviser to General Clay in Germany after World War II and to the European Constituent Assembly in the early 1950s. Zbigniew Brzezinski came to the U.S. from Poland in 1938, and for many years taught government at Harvard University. He was assistant to the president for National Security Affairs from 1977 to 1981, and is now Herbert Lehman Professor of Government at Columbia University. He has written on the Soviet government and on U.S. foreign policy. Brzezinski and Friedrich collaborated on the study from which this excerpt is taken. What is the larger context into which the authors place the Nazi phenomenon? Do you find any relationship between their approach and the Cold War period in which they wrote? How is our understanding of the Nazi phenomenon furthered by focusing on the similarities between Hitler's Germany and Stalin's Russia?

Totalitarian regimes are autocracies. When they are said to be tyrannies, despotisms, or absolutisms, the basic general nature of such

Reprinted by permission of the publishers from *Totalitarian Dictatorship and Autocracy* by C. J. Friedrich and Zbigniew K. Brzezinski, Cambridge, Mass.: Harvard University Press, Copyright © 1956, 1965 by the President and Fellows of Harvard College.

regimes is being denounced, for all these words have a strongly pejora-tive flavor. When they call themselves "democracies," qualifying it by the adjective "popular," they are not contradicting these indictments, except in trying to suggest that they are good or at least praiseworthy. An inspec-tion of the meaning the totalitarians attach to the term "popular democ-racy" reveals that they mean by it a species of autocracy. The leaders of the people, identified with the leaders of the ruling party, have the last word. Once they have decided and been acclaimed by a party gathering, their decision is final. Whether it be a rule, a judgment, or a measure or any other act of government, they are the *autokrator*, the ruler account-able only to himself. Totalitarian dictatorship, in a sense, is the adapta-tion of autocracy to twentieth-century industrial society.

Thus, as far as this characteristic absence of accountability is con-cerned, totalitarian dictatorship resembles earlier forms of autocracy. But it is our contention in this volume that totalitarian dictatorship is histor-ically an innovation and *sui generis*. It is also our conclusion from all the facts available to us that fascist and communist totalitarian dictatorships are basically alike, or at any rate more nearly like each other than like any other system of government, including earlier forms of autocracy. These two theses are closely linked and must be examined together. They are also linked to a third, that totalitarian dictatorship as it actually devel-oped was not intended by those who created it — Mussolini talked of it, though he meant something different — but resulted from the political situations in which the anticonstitutionalist and antidemocratic revolu-tionary movements and their leaders found themselves.

. . .

Totalitarian dictatorship then emerges as a system of rule for real-izing totalist intentions under modern political and technical conditions, as a novel type of autocracy. The declared intention of creating a "new man," according to numerous reports, has had significant results where the regime has lasted long enough, as in Russia. In the view of one lead-ing authority, "the most appealing traits of the Russians — their natural-ness and candor — have suffered most." He considers this a "profound and apparently permanent transformation," and an "astonishing" one. In short, the effort at total control, while not achieving such control, has highly significant human effects.

The fascist and communist systems evolved in response to a series of grave crises — they are forms of crisis government. Even so, there is no reason to conclude that the existing totalitarian systems will disappear as a result of internal evolution, though there can be no doubt that they are undergoing continuous changes. The two totalitarian governments that have perished thus far have done so as the result of wars with outside powers, but this does not mean that the Soviet Union, Communist China, or any of the others necessarily will become involved in war. We do not presuppose that totalitarian societies are fixed and static entities but, on the contrary, that they have undergone and continue to undergo a steady evolution, presumably involving both growth and deterioration.

But what about the origins? If it is evident that the regimes came into being because a totalitarian movement achieved dominance over a society and its government, where did the movement come from? The answer to this question remains highly controversial. A great many explanations have been attempted in terms of the various ingredients of these ideologies. Not only Marx and Engels, where the case seems obvious, but Hegel, Luther, and a great many others have come in for their share of blame. Yet none of these thinkers was, of course, a totalitarian at all, and each would have rejected these regimes, if any presumption like that were to be tested in terms of his thought. They were humanists and religious men of intense spirituality of the kind the totalitarians explicitly reject. In short, all such "explanations," while interesting in illuminating particular elements of the totalitarian ideologies, are based on serious invalidating distortions of historical facts. If we leave aside such ideological explanations (and they are linked of course to the "ideological" theory of totalitarian dictatorship as criticized above), we find several other unsatisfactory genetic theories.

The debate about the causes or origins of totalitarianism has run all the way from a primitive bad-man theory to the "moral crisis of our time" kind of argument. A detailed inspection of the available evidence suggests that virtually every one of the factors which has been offered by itself as an explanation of the origin of totalitarian dictatorship has played its role. For example, in the case of Germany, Hitler's moral and personal defects, weaknesses in the German constitutional tradition, certain traits involved in the German "national character," the Versailles Treaty and its aftermath, the economic crisis and the "contradictions" of an aging capitalism, the "threat" of communism, the decline of Christianity and of such other spiritual moorings as the belief in the reason and the reasonableness of man — all have played a role in the total configuration of factors contributing to the over-all result. As in the case of other broad developments in history, only a multiple-factor analysis will yield an adequate account. But at the present time, we cannot fully explain the rise of totalitarian dictatorship. All we can do is to explain it partially by identifying some of the antecedent and concomitant conditions. To repeat: totalitarian dictatorship is a new phenomenon; there has never been anything quite like it before.

The discarding of ideological explanations — highly objectionable to all totalitarians, to be sure — opens up an understanding of and insight into the basic similarity of totalitarian regimes, whether communist or fascist. They are, in terms of organization and procedures — that is to say, in terms of structure, institutions, and processes of rule — *basically alike.* What does this mean? In the first place, it means that they are *not wholly alike.* Popular and journalistic interpretation has oscillated between two extremes; some have said that the communist and fascist dictatorships are wholly alike, others that they are not at all alike. The latter view was the prevailing one during the popular-front days in Europe as well as in liberal circles in the United States. It was even more popular during the Second World War, especially among Allied propagandists. Besides, it was and is the official communist and fascist party line. It is only natural that these regimes, conceiving of themselves as bitter enemies, dedicated to the task of liquidating each other, should take the view that they have nothing in common. This has happened before in history. When the Protestants and Catholics were fighting during the religious wars of the sixteenth and seventeenth centuries, they very commonly denied to one another the name of "Christians," and each argued about the other that it was not a "true church." Actually, and in the perspective of time, both were indeed Christian churches.

The other view, that communist and fascist dictatorships are wholly alike, was during the cold war demonstrably favored in the United States and in Western Europe to an increasing extent. Yet they are demonstrably not wholly alike. For example, they differ in their acknowledged purposes and intentions. Everyone knows that the communists say they seek the world revolution of the proletariat, while the fascists proclaimed their determination to establish the imperial predominance of a particular nation or race, either over the world or over a region. The communist and fascist dictatorships differ also in their historical antecedents: the fascist movements arose in reaction to the communist challenge and offered themselves to a frightened middle class as saviors from the communist danger. The communist movements, on the other hand, presented themselves as the liberators of an oppressed people from an existing autocratic regime, at least in Russia and China. Both claims are not without foundation, and one could perhaps coordinate them by treating the totalitarian movements as consequences of the First World War. "The rise [of totalitarianism] has occurred in the sequel to the first world war and those catastrophies, political and economic, which accompanied it and the feeling of crisis linked thereto." As we shall have occasion to show in the chapters to follow, there are many other differences which do not allow us to speak of the communist and fascist totalitarian dictatorships as wholly alike, but which suggest that they are sufficiently alike to class them together and to contrast them not only with constitutional systems, but also with former types of autocracy.

Before we turn to these common features, however, there is another difference that used to be emphasized by many who wanted "to do business with Hitler" or who admired Mussolini and therefore argued that, far from being wholly like the communist dictatorship, the fascist regimes really had to be seen as merely authoritarian forms of constitutional systems. It is indeed true that more of the institutions of the antecedent liberal and constitutional society survived in the Italian Fascist than in the Russian or Chinese Communist society. But this is due in part to the fact that no liberal constitutional society preceded Soviet or Chinese Communism. The promising period of the Duma came to naught as a result of the war and the disintegration of tsarism, while the Kerensky interlude was far too brief and too superficial to become meaningful for the future. Similarly in China, the Kuomingtang failed to develop a working constitutional order, though various councils were set up; they merely provided a facade for a military dictatorship disrupted by a great deal of anarchical localism, epitomized in the rule of associated warlords. In the Soviet satellites, on the other hand, numerous survivals of a non-totalitarian past continue to function. In Poland, Czechoslovakia, Hungary, and Yugoslavia we find such institutions as universities, churches, and schools. It is likely that, were a communist dictatorship to be established in Great Britain or France, the situation would be similar, and here even more such institutions of the liberal era would continue to operate, for a considerable initial period at least. Precisely this argument has been advanced by such British radicals as Sidney and Beatrice Webb. The tendency of isolated fragments of the preceding state of society to survive has been a significant source of misinterpretation of the fascist totalitarian society, especially in the case of Italy. In the twenties, Italian totalitarianism was very commonly misinterpreted as being "merely" an authoritarian form of middle-class rule, with the trains running on time and the beggars off the streets. In the case of Germany, this sort of misinterpretation took a slightly different form. In the thirties, various writers tried to interpret German totalitarianism either as "the end phase of capitalism" or as "militarist imperialism." These interpretations stress the continuance of a "capitalist" economy whose leaders are represented as dominating the regime. The facts as we know them do not correspond to this view. For one who sympathized with socialism or communism, it was very tempting to depict the totalitarian dictatorship of Hitler as nothing but a capitalist society and therefore totally at variance with the "new civilization" that was arising in the Soviet Union. These few remarks have suggested, it is hoped, why it may be wrong to consider the totalitarian dictatorships under discussion as either wholly alike or basically different. Why they are basically alike remains to be shown, and to this key argument we now turn.

The basic features or traits that we suggest as generally recognized to be common to totalitarian dictatorships are six in number. The "syndrome," or pattern of interrelated traits, of the totalitarian dictatorship consists of an ideology, a single party typically led by one man, a terroristic police, a communications monopoly, a weapons monopoly, and a centrally directed economy. Of these, the last two are also found in constitutional systems: Socialist Britain had a centrally directed economy, and all modern states possess a weapons monopoly. Whether these latter suggest a "trend" toward totalitarianism is a question that will be discussed in our last chapter. These six basic features, which we think constitute the distinctive pattern or model of totalitarian dictatorship, form a cluster of traits, intertwined and mutually supporting each other, as is usual in "organic" systems. They should therefore not be considered in isolation or be made the focal point of comparisons, such as "Caesar developed a terroristic secret police, therefore he was the first totalitarian dictator," or "the Catholic Church has practiced ideological thought control, therefore . . ."

The totalitarian dictatorships all possess the following:

- An elaborate ideology, consisting of an official body of doctrine covering all vital aspects of man's existence to which everyone living in that society is supposed to adhere, at least passively; this ideology is characteristically focused and projected toward a perfect final state of mankind — that is to say, it contains a chiliastic claim, based upon a radical rejection of the existing society with conquest of the world for the new one.

- A single mass party typically led by one man, the "dictator," and consisting of a relatively small percentage of the total population (up to 10 percent) of men and women, a hard core of them passionately and unquestioningly dedicated to the ideology and prepared to assist in every way in promoting its general acceptance, such a party being hierarchically, oligarchically organized and typically either superior to, or completely intertwined with, the governmental bureaucracy.

- A system of terror, whether physical or psychic, effected through party and secret-police control, supporting but also supervising the party for its leaders, and characteristically directed not only against demonstrable "enemies" of the regime, but against more or less arbitrarily selected classes of the population; the terror whether of the secret police or of party-directed social pressure systematically exploits modern science, and more especially scientific psychology.

- A technologically conditioned, near-complete monopoly of control, in the hands of the party and of the government, of all means of effective mass communication, such as the press, radio, and motion pictures.

- A similarly technologically conditioned, near-complete monopoly of the effective use of all weapons of armed combat.

- A central control and direction of the entire economy through the bureaucratic coordination of formerly independent corporate entities, typically including most other associations and group activities.

The enumeration of these six traits or trait clusters is not meant to suggest that there might not be others, now insufficiently recognized. It has more particularly been suggested that the administrative control of justice and the courts is a distinctive trait; but actually the evolution of totalitarianism in recent years suggests that such administrative direction of judicial work may be greatly limited. We shall also discuss the problem of expansionism, which has been urged as a characteristic trait of totalitarianism. The traits here outlined have been generally acknowledged as the features of totalitarian dictatorship, to which the writings of students of the most varied backgrounds, including totalitarian writers, bear witness.

Political Man:
The Social Bases of Politics

∾⫯⫰

SEYMOUR MARTIN LIPSET

Seymour Martin Lipset, a professor of political science and sociology, has taught in numerous American universities, most recently at Stanford. He has published extensively on the social origins of political behavior, on the American Revolution, the student rebellions in the 1960s, and on other subjects. In compiling this account, he consulted the findings of writers who relied on German voting records to provide a social and political analysis of Nazi party supporters in the last elections held in the Weimar Republic. Who did vote for the Nazis? Why? How do Lipset's conclusions differ from Neumann's?

The classic example of a revolutionary fascist party is, of course, the National Socialist Workers' party led by Adolf Hitler. For Marxian analysts, this party represented the last stage of capitalism, winning power in order to maintain capitalism's tottering institutions. Since the Nazis came to power before the days of public opinion polls, we have to rely on records of the total votes to locate their social base. If classic fascism appeals largely to the same elements as those which back liberalism, then the previous supporters of liberalism should have provided the backing for the Nazis. A look at the gross election statistics for the

From Seymour Martin Lipset, *Political Man: The Social Bases of Politics*, The Johns Hopkins University Press, Baltimore/London, 1981, pp. 138–147.

German Reich between 1928 and 1933 would seem to verify this. (See table.)

Although a table like this conceals changes by individuals which go against the general statistical trend, some reasonable inferences may be made. As the Nazis grew, the liberal bourgeois center parties, based on the less traditionalist elements of German society — primarily small

PERCENTAGES OF TOTAL VOTE RECEIVED BY VARIOUS GERMAN PARTIES, 1928–1933, AND THE PERCENTAGE OF THE 1928 VOTE RETAINED IN THE LAST FREE ELECTION 1932*

Party	Percentage of Total Vote					Ratio of 1928 to Second 1932 Election Expressed as Percentage
Conservative Party	1928	1930	1932	1932	1933	
DNVP	14.2	7.0	5.9	8.5	8.0	60
Middle-class Parties						
DVP (right liberals)	8.7	4.85	1.2	1.8	1.1	21
DDP (left liberals)	4.8	3.45	1.0	.95	.8	20
Wirtschaftspartei (small business)	4.5	3.9	0.4	0.3	†	7
Others	9.5	10.1	2.6	2.8	.6	29
Total proportion of middle-class vote maintained:						21
Center (Catholic)	15.4	17.6	16.7	16.2	15.0	105
Workers' Parties						
SPD (Socialist)	29.8	24.5	21.6	20.4	18.3	69
KPD (Communist)	10.6	13.1	14.3	16.85	12.3	159
Total proportion of working-class vote maintained:						92
Fascist Party						
NSDAP	2.6	18.3	37.3	33.1	43.9	1277
Total proportion of increase in Fascist party vote:						1277

*The basic data are presented in Samuel Pratt, *The Social Basis of Nazism and Communism in Urban Germany* (M.A. thesis, Dept. of Sociology, Michigan State University, 1948), pp. 29, 30. The same data are presented and analyzed in Karl D. Bracher, *Die Auflösung der Weimarer Republik* (Stuttgart und Düsseldorf: Ring Verlag, 1954), pp. 86–106. The 1933 election was held after Hitler had been chancellor for more than a month.
†The *Wirtschaftspartei* did not run any candidates in the 1933 elections.

business and white-collar workers — completely collapsed. Between 1928 and 1932 these parties lost almost 80 per cent of their vote, and their proportion of the total vote dropped from a quarter to less than 3 per cent. The only center party which maintained its proportionate support was the Catholic Center party whose support was reinforced by religious allegiance. The Marxist parties, the socialists and the Communists, lost about a tenth of their percentage support, although their total vote dropped only slightly. The proportionate support of the conservatives dropped about 40 per cent, much less than that of the more liberal middle-class parties.

An inspection of the shifts among the non-Marxist and non-Catholic parties suggests that the Nazis gained most heavily among the liberal middle-class parties, the former bulwarks of the Weimar Republic. Among these parties, the one which lost most heavily was the *Wirtschaftspartei*, which represented primarily small businessmen and artisans. The right-wing nationalist opponent of Weimar, the German National People's party (DNVP), was the only one of the non-Marxist and non-Catholic parties to retain over half of its 1928 proportion of the total vote.

The largest drop-off in the conservative vote lay mainly in the election districts on the eastern border of Germany. The proportion of the vote obtained by the German National People's party declined by 50 per cent or more between 1928 and 1932 in ten of the thirty-five election districts in Germany. Seven of these ten were border areas, including every region which fronted on the Polish corridor, and Schleswig-Holstein, fronting on the northern border. Since the party was both the most conservative and the most nationalist pre-Nazi opponent of the Versailles Treaty, these data suggest that the Nazis most severely weakened the conservatives in those areas where nationalism was their greatest source of strength, while the conservatives retained most of their voters in regions which had not suffered as directly from the annexations imposed by Versailles and in which, it may be argued, the party's basic appeal was more conservative than nationalist. The German-American sociologist Rudolf Heberle has demonstrated in a detailed study of voting patterns in Schleswig-Holstein that the conservatives lost the backing of the small property owners, both urban and rural, whose counterparts in nonborder areas were most commonly liberals, while they retained the backing of the upper-strata conservatives.

Some further indirect evidence that the Nazis did not appeal to the same sources as the traditional German right may be found in the data on the voting of men and women. In the 1920s and 1930s the more conservative or religious a party, the higher, in general, its feminine support. The German National People's party had more female backing than any party except the Catholic Center party. The Nazis, together with the more liberal middle-class parties and Marxist parties, received disproportionate support from men.

More direct evidence for the thesis is given in Heberle's study of Schleswig-Holstein, the state in which the Nazis were strongest. In 1932 *"the Conservatives were weakest where the Nazis were strongest and the Nazis were relatively weak where the Conservatives were strong.* The correlation in 18 predominantly rural election districts between percentages of votes obtained by the NSDAP [Nazis] and by the DNVP [Conservatives] is negative (minus .89). . . . It appears that the Nazis had in 1932 really succeeded the former liberal parties, like the *Landespartei* and Democratic party, as the preferred party among the small farmers . . . while the landlords and big farmers were more reluctant to cast their vote for Hitler."

A more recent analysis by a German political scientist, Günther Franz, identifying voting trends in another state in which the Nazis were very strong — Lower Saxony — reported similar patterns. Franz concluded:

> The majority of the National Socialist voters came from the bourgeois center parties. The DNVP [conservatives] had also lost votes, but in 1932, they held the votes which they received in 1930, and increased their total vote in the next two elections. They were (except for the Catholic Center) the only bourgeois party, which had not simply collapsed before the NSDAP. . . .

This situation in Schleswig-Holstein and Lower Saxony also existed in Germany as a whole. Among the thirty-five electoral districts, the rank-order correlation of the proportionate Nazi gain with the liberal parties' loss was greater (.48) than with the conservatives' loss (.25).

Besides the liberal parties, there was one other group of German parties, based on the *Mittel-stand*, whose supporters seem to have gone over almost en masse to the Nazis — the so-called "federalist" or regional autonomy parties. These parties objected either to the unification of Germany or to the specific annexation of various provinces like Hesse, Lower Saxony, and Schleswig-Holstein to Prussia. In large measure they gave voice to the objections felt by the rural and urban middle classes of provincial areas to the increasing bureaucratization of modern industrial society and sought to turn the clock back by decentralizing government authority. At first glance, the decentralist aspirations of the regional autonomy parties and the glorification of the state inherent in fascism or Nazism seem to reflect totally dissimilar needs and sentiments. But in fact both the "state's rights" ideology of the regionalists and the Nazis' ideological antagonism to the "big" forces of industrial society appealed to those who felt uprooted or challenged. In their economic ideology, the regional parties expressed sentiments similar to those voiced by the Nazis before the latter were strong. Thus the *Schleswig-Holsteinische Landespartei*, which demanded "regional and cultural autonomy for Schleswig-Holstein within Germany," wrote in an early program:

> The craftsman [artisan] has to be protected on the one hand against capitalism, which crushes him by means of its factories, and on the other hand against socialism, which aims at making him a proletarian wage-laborer. At the same time the merchant has to be protected against capitalism in the form of the great department stores, and the whole retail trade against the danger of socialism.

The link between regionalism as an ideology protesting bigness and centralization, and the direct expression of the economic self-interest of the small businessmen may be seen in the joining of the two largest of the regional parties, the Lower Saxon *Deutsch-Hanoverischen Partei* and the Bavarian *Bauern und Mittelstandsbund*, into one parliamentary faction with the *Wirtschaftspartei*, the party which explicitly defined itself as representing the small entrepreneurs. In the 1924 elections the Bavarian regionalists and the small businessmen's party actually presented a joint electoral ticket. As Heberle points out about these parties: "The criticism of Prussian policy . . . the demand for native civil servants, the refusal to accept Berlin as the general center of culture, were all outlets for a disposition which had been formed a long time before the war. . . . At bottom the criticism against Prussia was merely an expression of a general antipathy against the social system of industrial capitalism. . . ."

The appeal of the Nazis to those elements in German society which resented the power and culture of the large cities is also reflected in the Nazis' success in small communities. A detailed ecological analysis of voting in German cities with 25,000 or more population, in 1932, indicates that *the larger the city, the smaller the Nazi vote*. The Nazis secured less of their total vote in cities over 25,000 in size than did any of the other five major parties, including the Catholic Center and the conservative DNVP. And Berlin, the great metropolis, was the only predominantly Protestant election district in which the Nazis received under

25 per cent of the vote in July 1932. These facts sharply challenge the various interpretations of Nazism as the product of the growth of anomie and the general rootlessness of modern urban industrial society.

Examination of the shifts in patterns of German voting between 1928 and 1932 among the non-Marxist and non-Catholic parties indicates, as we have seen, that the Nazis gained disproportionately from the ranks of the center and liberal parties rather than from the conservatives, thus validating one aspect of the thesis that classic fascism appeals to the same strata as liberalism. The second part of the argument, that fascism appeals predominantly to the self-employed among the middle strata, has been supported by three separate ecological studies of German voting between 1928 and 1932. Two American sociologists, Charles Loomis and J. Allen Beegle, correlated the percentage of the Nazi vote in 1932 in communities under 10,000 in population in three states with the percentage of the labor force in specific socioeconomic classes and found that "areas in which the middle classes prevailed [as indicated by the proportion of proprietors in the population and the ratio of proprietors to laborers and salaried employees] gave increasingly larger votes to the Nazis as the economic and social crises settled on Germany."

This high correlation between Nazi vote and proprietorship holds for farm owners as well as owners of small business and industry in Schleswig-Holstein and Hanover, but not in Bavaria, a strongly Catholic area where the Nazis were relatively weak. Heberle's study of Schleswig-Holstein, which analyzed all of the elections under Weimar, concluded that "the classes particularly susceptible to Nazism were neither the rural nobility and the big farmers nor the rural proletariat, but rather the small farm proprietors, very much the rural equivalent of the lower middle class or petty bourgeoisie (*Kleinbuergertum*) which formed the backbone of the NSDAP in the cities."

The sociologist Samuel Pratt's excellent study of urban voting prior to the Nazi victory related the Nazi vote in July 1932 to the proportion of the population in the "upper middle class," defined as "proprietors of small and large establishments and executives," and to the proportion in the "lower middle class," composed of "civil servants and white-collar employees." The Nazi vote correlated highly with the proportion in both middle-class groups in different-size cities and in different areas of the country, but the correlations with the "lower middle class" were not as consistently high and positive as those with the "upper middle." As Pratt put it: "Of the two elements of the middle class, the upper seemed to be the more thoroughly pro-Nazi." The so-called upper class, however, was predominantly composed of small businessmen, so that the correlation reported is largely that of self-employed economic status with Nazi voting. This interpretation is enhanced by Pratt's finding that the Nazi vote also correlated (+ .6) with the proportion of business establishments with only one employee — in other words, self-employment. "This would be expected, for plants of one employee are another measure of the proprietorship class which was used in measuring the upper middle class."

The occupational distribution of the membership of the Nazi party in 1933 indicates that it was largely drawn from the various urban middle-class strata, with the self-employed again being the most overrepresented. (See table.) The second most overrepresented category — domestic servants and nonagricultural family helpers — also bears witness to the party's appeal to small business, since this category is primarily composed of helpers in family-owned small businesses.

The relation of German big business to the Nazis has been a matter of considerable controversy, particularly since various Marxists have attempted to demonstrate that the movement was from the outset "fostered, nourished, maintained and subsidized by the big *bourgeoisie*, by the big landlords, financiers, and industrialists." The most recent studies suggest that the opposite is true. With the exception of a few isolated individuals, German big business gave Nazism little financial support or other

THE RATIO OF THE PERCENTAGE OF MEN IN THE NAZI PARTY TO THE PERCENTAGE IN THE GENERAL POPULATION FROM VARIOUS OCCUPATIONS, 1933*

Occupational Category	1933
Manual Workers	68%
White-collar Workers	169
Independents[†]	187
Officials (civil servants)	146
Peasants	60
Domestic servants, and nonagricultural family helpers	178

*Computed from a table in Hans Gerth, "The Nazi Party: Its Leadership and Composition," in Robert K. Merton, *et al.*, eds., *Reader in Bureaucracy* (Glencoe: The Free Press, 1952), p. 106.
[†]Includes self-employed businessmen, artisans, and free professionals.

encouragement *until* it had risen to the status of a major party. The Nazis did begin to pick up financial backing in 1932, but in large part this backing was a result of many businesses' policy of giving money to all major parties except the Communists in order to be in their good graces. Some German industrialists probably hoped to tame the Nazis by giving them funds. On the whole, however, this group remained loyal to the conservative parties, and many gave no money to the Nazis until after the party won power.

Women in Nazi Society

∿

JILL STEPHENSON

Jill Stephenson's thoroughly researched study of women in Nazi society was first presented as a thesis to the University of Edinburgh. She has also written a book on women's organizations associated with the Nazi party. The excerpt below reveals the Nazi emphasis on domestic roles for women, but also some less well known aspects of Nazi policy in this area. What accounts for the inconsistencies in Nazi attitudes toward the roles assigned to German women in the "thousand-year Reich"?

It can only be surmised what the position of women in a 'thousand-year Reich' would have been. Clearly, the Nazis' chief concern with women was for their capacity as childbearers. Women with a full-time job might be reluctant to start or add to a family, and so women were to be encouraged to give up work to spend their time in the home, and to have many children in order to fill this time. Girls with an academic education might be reluctant to forego the opportunity of an interesting, responsible, and possibly well-paid career, even if they were married; accordingly, the emphasis was to be shifted away from the study of academic subjects, and where a preponderance of these remained in a curriculum, girls were

From Jill Stephenson, *Women in Nazi Society*, London, 1975, pp. 189–193, 195–197. Reprinted by permission of Croom Helm Ltd.

also to be reminded of their maternal role at every opportunity, by taking compulsory courses in domestic science and by mixing socially in the organisations and usefully in the Labour Service with girls and women from different backgrounds, who would be more interested in human relationships than in physics or foreign languages. Above all, women were to be kept physically healthy for childbearing, and had therefore to be removed from work that was actually or potentially damaging to their reproductive capacity.

The motive was world domination; one of the means to this was to be a dramatic increase in the population, by means of creating an atmosphere in which procreation was considered natural and was rewarded in both material and psychological terms, and by attempting to make any means of conception control beyond total abstinence from sexual intercourse unavailable. But some of the side effects were desirable. For example, the Nazis were considered puritanical in their condemnation of tobacco and alcohol — no doubt partly influenced by Hitler's abstinence from and aversion to them — but they were medically correct in urging pregnant women not to smoke or to drink alcohol. While the Nazis claimed to advocate temperance rather than abstinence with regard to alcohol, they were uncompromising in their opposition to cigarette smoking, at a time when it was accepted as fashionable among women as well as men, and before the health hazards directly connected with it were widely accepted. Foreigners were mildly amused by the zeal of some of the Party faithful in encouraging cafes to hang notices prominently on their premises bearing the legend 'The German woman does not smoke,' but it was the Rector of Erlangen University, whose own field was medicine, who stated unequivocally that 'For a woman, smoking is without doubt a vice.'

Another aspect of social mores which seemed to the Nazis to have implications for the birth rate was women's clothing. They condemned the foreign influences — of Paris and the United States — which, they claimed, had encouraged German women to adopt a style of dressing that was either frivolous or else an imitation of men's clothes, and was in any case decadent and not conducive to a healthy rate of population growth (*fortpflanzungsfeindlich*); the reasoning behind this assertion was not explained. To give guidance about the kind of clothing that was considered desirable in the Nazi State, the German Fashion Bureau was opened in Berlin in the spring of 1933, under the honorary presidency of Magda Goebbels, who claimed that she was 'trying to make the German woman more beautiful.' At first, there was emphasis on the creation of a 'German style' for German women, but the women's magazines continued to carry fashion articles featuring clothes which were considered fashionable in Paris and London, and eventually in 1937 the DFW denied that there had been, or should be, attempts to devise a 'German style.' These ideas, however, were not new in the 1930s; during the Great War there had been criticism of the 'improper' clothes that some women and girls were wearing, and the call went out for the creation of a 'German style.' The objections were against something which was clearly too terrible to be described explicitly, but the implication was that new styles were being adopted which were at once unpatriotic — presumably imported from enemy countries — and morally risky.

The ideal type of woman in Nazi theory was the peasant wife, whose peaceful, wholesome life was devoted to her work on the land and, above all, her family. The picture of this woman at her spinning wheel was offered as the alternative to the city bred chic sophisticates of the decadent 1920s. To encourage the simple perfection embodied — it was quite unrealistically believed — in this rural figure, edicts were issued castigating and ridiculing women who 'shave their eyebrows, use rouge, dye their hair' in an altogether foreign manner. The Party's puritans conducted a vigorous campaign against cosmetics, although Hitler was apparently not averse to women's using them. Himmler, however, maintained a strict attitude, giving instructions that the mothers in the SS's *Lebensborn* homes should not be permitted to use lipstick, to paint their nails, or to shave their eyebrows. It was further made clear that the SS expected the future wives of its members to demonstrate their wholesomeness by achieving the Reich Sport Medal, since the kind of woman who was suitable for the nation's elite to marry was not the one 'who can dance nicely through five-o'clock teas, but who has proved her fitness by sports activity. For good health, the javelin or the pole-vault are of more value than the lipstick.' This motif ran throughout Nazi speeches about women — naturally enough, since it was directly relevant to the function regarded as most important, childbearing, the function to which all Nazi thought about women was ultimately related.

It is this consistent obsession that renders comprehensible some of the apparent inconsistencies in Nazi thought and practice; for example, while some Nazis undoubtedly took a more puritanical view of social and sexual life than others, there was general acceptance that the family was the essential basic unit of society, to be maintained and protected by every possible means. But the very existence of the family was an obstacle to the Nazis' attempt at totalitarian control, and so the Nazi organisations had to try to exert some influence over individual members of the family in the hope that the family unit as a whole would be permeated by National Socialist ideas and would grow in corporate loyalty to the Nazi regime. A strict line of demarcation was, however, to be drawn between business and pleasure: Hess repeatedly reminded Party members that they were not allowed to wear Party uniform when out on social occasions with women, unless the function was an official one to which wives were invited. Hess particularly condemned those who wore Party uniform when taking their wives for a ride in a car, and ordered that on no account was a woman to be driven in an open car with her husband when he was in uniform. This potential source of petty family friction was, however, trivial compared with the apparent threat to the family unit by some Nazi social policies.

The more tolerant attitude towards unmarried motherhood and the introduction of 'irretrievable breakdown' as a ground for divorce in the Third Reich alarmed some of those who had believed Nazi promises of restoring respectability to German life after the permissiveness of the Weimar Republic. They were, in fact, policies which were more similar to those of liberals and even Communists than to the standard Christian morality of conservatives who had supported Hitler in preference to socialists of any colour. No doubt Himmler and the SS and Hess were in a small minority in the NSDAP in positively encouraging unmarried motherhood, but the Party clearly, after some initial hesitation, moved to a position where it accepted that motherhood was desirable, therefore those women who became mothers out of wedlock should not be discriminated against, even if they should equally not be acclaimed as examples worthy of imitation. The result was more humane treatment of unmarried mothers, of the kind advocated particularly by radical feminists both before and after the Great War and by Communists, in imitation of the Soviet Russian example. On the whole, the Nazis recognised that there was an implicit contradiction in their claim to be upholding the family unit and their attempt to diminish prejudice against the unmarried mother; but their overriding desire for children led them to welcome any 'racially valuable' child, regardless of the marital status of its parents, and therefore to value the parents themselves.

Population policy, again, underlay the peculiar situation which arose from the Nazis' being more concerned with the health and welfare of women workers than some of the avowed champions of women's rights. While the Communists and the Socialists were, like the Nazis, anxious to develop schemes of labour protection for women, particularly for pregnant women and nursing mothers, the radical feminists of the Open Door International, who were the first to claim that the Nazis had no regard for women and aimed to subject them fully to male domination, denied that special provision for women's welfare was anything other than a device for discriminating against women. Thus, the most militant feminists were prepared to countenance a situation where women and girls were free to work during the day or at night for as many hours as they chose, regardless of the damage they might do to their health. Indeed, they, along with the Communists, demanded equal pay for equal work, which might have discouraged employers from using women for heavy work since men were more obviously fitted for it; but it was the Nazis who actually introduced equal pay in some cases for this very purpose. And the radical feminists never suggested that their aim in agitating for equal pay was to discourage employers from using female labour on the same terms as male. In the end — always for the natalist motive — the Nazis showed more concern for the physical well-being of women.

Perhaps this helps to account for the acceptance of the Nazis by women generally, and even by some of those who had been opposed to the Nazis in the pre-1933 period.

. . .

It is one of the many ironies of National Socialism that its policies and its defeat created a situation in which discrimination against women in many areas, particularly in employment, was not a practical proposition. The need for many women to assume the role of breadwinner after the Second World War, in the absence of men who were dead, incapacitated, or in prison, led to the opening up of new opportunities for women in the Federal Republic. In the Democratic Republic, that which so many of the Nazis' supporters had feared above all, and which the Nazis had been pledged to prevent, the victory of Communism, has meant that there has been a much more decisive change of policy, so that women have — within the limits of a new dictatorship — equal rights and equality of opportunity. The Nazis, then, unwittingly acted as the agents of the kind of changes they had aimed to prevent or reverse, and women became more self-reliant and were accorded a greater degree of legal and social equality. But the Nazis had certainly given the impression of arresting developments in the direction of greater equality for women; it remains to decide how far this was true.

In the first place, progress was made in improving opportunities for women even before 1914, notably in education; 'emancipation' did not suddenly begin in 1918. After the Great War far less progress was made than feminists had hoped for and conservatives had feared. Indeed, certain areas of activity were opened to women for the first time, including full participation in politics and entry to the legal profession. But the progress made in winning real influence for women in politics and significant representation for them in professions other than teaching, where they were already well-established, was slow and gradual, as it was bound to be, while the provisions of the Imperial Civil Code continued to affirm the superiority of the male sex in society, and especially in marriage. In addition, no sooner were modest reforms introduced after the Great War than the forces of reaction asserted themselves, so that German women — insofar as they were interested — were, like the nation as a whole, bitterly divided between those who resented even cautious change, associating it with 'Bolshevism,' and those who poured contempt on the small improvements that were effected. Even moderate feminists, who accepted that evolution was the best course, but a slow one, began to be disillusioned by the later 1920s, and to be alarmed in the early 1930s when the effects of the depression seemed to many justification — or excuse — for a retreat from the Weimar Constitution's commitment to equal rights for members of both sexes. The conservatives, the Churches, and even some trade unionists were very ready to see in, for example, the deliberate discrimination against the employed married woman the solution to Germany's problems which were, in the view of the Churches and the conservatives, at least, not merely of an economic nature but political and moral as well.

Thus, the clock was stopped not in 1933 but in 1930. The Nazis, with their weird, backward looking philosophy, benefited from attitudes which had already developed and hardened, and found at least tacit — and often open — support for their promised policy of restoring women to a position of security, decency and domesticity. But it was not their intention, they repeatedly asserted, to restrict women to the traditional 'three K's' — *Kinder, Küche, Kirche* (nursery, kitchen, church) — as conservatives hoped. Once again, German conservatives had mistaken the Nazis for old style, nationalist reactionaries like themselves, failing to comprehend the essentially revolutionary nature of Nazism. Certainly, in the Nazi State women were to concern themselves to a considerable degree with children and with household matters; but a regime which aspired to totalitarian control had to urge all its citizens to look outward from their private lives, to surrender their privacy and allow themselves to be imbued with the Nazi *Weltanschauung*, and to accept the primacy of the needs of the State as interpreted by the Nazi leadership. Thus, German women were to be less 'requisites of German men' than — like German men — agents at the disposal of the Nazi regime. It was crucial to women's position that the needs of the regime became such that women could be discriminated against to only a very limited extent.

In the Third Reich, men were, after all, controlled and confined to the same extent as women, and often, given the relative immunity of the housewife from official surveillance, even more. If men monopolised positions of power in the Nazi State, only a minority of men exercised power, and the great mass of men were excluded in the same way as women. Male and female opponents and victims of Nazi racist policies were discriminated against and persecuted on an equal basis. Certainly the Nazis were determined to persuade as many women as possible, in the early years, at least, that their natural sphere of activity was the home and family; but it is often overlooked that the majority of women choose to marry and have children in the absence of official pressure to do so. The Nazis were starting their campaign with the advantage of women's biological character and natural disposition on their side. Their aim was to reverse the evident trend towards contempt for the *nur-Hausfrau* (the woman who is 'only a housewife'), which was a side effect of the provision of more opportunities for women outside the home. In this, they to some extent succeeded; where they were wrong was in trying to coerce women into complying with their policy, by limiting opportunities outside the home and by trying to remove all means of birth control.

Attempts to limit opportunities for women outside the home were made, at a time when the massive unemployment problem made them doubly attractive. But the change which came in the economic situation in the mid-1930s made even the campaign against employed married women first redundant and then positively harmful. Similarly, the steps taken to reduce the academic content of girls' school curricula — a reaction against the strong emphasis there had been on academic ability after the Great War — proved to be damaging even before the Second World War gave rise to an urgent demand for girl students in all disciplines. In the later 1930s, women were not only to be given the opportunity to work and to study, whether they were married or single, but were to be positively encouraged to do these things. The motive was, as ever, the serving of the needs of the Nazi State at the time, not the improvement of opportunities for women; but such an improvement was in fact a result.

The unrealistic and ideologically motivated barriers raised against women's advancement in the highest echelons of the civil service and to the practice of law by women were indeed indicative of what was, in the Nazi view, ideal, and of what would no doubt have been their aim in the 'thousand-year Reich,' if other policies had permitted it. But these instances were exceptions, and the result of the abnormal 1930s — abnormal in political and economic terms and culminating in war — was that women's position in employment outside the home, including the professions as a whole, was consolidated, not eroded, while, in addition, the status of the housewife and mother was raised.

6

APPEASEMENT:
The Munich Pact

The Munich Conference of 29–30 September 1938 included Germany, Italy, France, and Great Britain, represented respectively by Hitler, Mussolini, Daladier and Chamberlain. It called for the annexation by Germany of the Sudetenland, the western end of Czechoslovakia, whose population contained a majority of German-speaking people. After signing the agreement, Daladier and Chamberlain told the Czech representatives, who had been left waiting in an anteroom, that their country had been partitioned. Signed by Chamberlain and Hitler the next day, the official statement, which saw the agreement "as symbolic of the desire of our two peoples never to go to war with one another again," marked the touchstone of the appeasement policy pursued by Britain and France during much of the decade. On their return to London and Paris, Chamberlain and Daladier were cheered by huge crowds for having prevented war. "No conqueror returning from a victory on the battle-field," said the London *Times* on 1 October, "has come home adorned with nobler laurels than Mr. Chamberlain from Munich yesterday" and most newspapers published that day on both sides of the English Channel shared the sentiment. Only a few agreed with Winston Churchill when he told the House of Commons that "we have suffered a total and unmitigated defeat. All is over. Silent, mournful, abandoned, broken Czechoslovakia recedes into the darkness. . . ." Indeed, for that country which had remained faithful to her democratic belief and had relied on her friends in the West, the betrayal was a cruel one. Unconsulted, ignored, she lost her fortifications, three-quarters of her heavy industry, her vital transportation, and, of course, what remained of the morale of her people. The German press exulted in the gains made: a dangerous enemy neutralized, the Versailles monstrosity removed, the Reich's power revealed, quantities of men and material added to her military, and all accomplished without bloodshed. In the future, the word "appeasement," once a wholly honorable diplomatic alternative designed to minimize the outbreak of armed conflict, became a term of oppobrium and conjured up a hateful and despicable policy. The "Munich analogy" would be made countless times in the years to come to show the consequences of yielding to a dictator.

Should the British and the French have realized that Hitler's demands on Czechoslovakia presaged his ultimate goal of European conquest? Or did the two democracies act in the most appropriate manner given existing circumstances? The four excerpts which follow provide four different views. While not defending appeasement in theory, two support the Munich Accord, although for different reasons. The other two see the policy as wrong from beginning to end but do not question the appeasers' sincerity or honesty, only their policy and their wisdom.

What, then, are the "lessons" of Munich? That nations must behave honorably and fulfill commitments (Churchill)? That to be effective, statesmen must have an understanding of history (Rowse)? That to have freedom of action a great power must support a sufficient defense establishment (Butler)? That democracies cannot enter wars without full public support (Weinberg)? Politicians and the public at large have concluded that Munich teaches us that dictators cannot be appeased. But the most important lesson may well be that historical lessons themselves, rather than historical realities, influence events — and that their consequences can be more unpleasant historical lessons.

The Gathering Storm

⍉

WINSTON CHURCHILL

Sir Winston Churchill, active for many years in British politics, led his country in war from 1940 to 1945. A noted historian, he published extensively, and his multi-volume memoirs of World Wars I and II constitute invaluable sources. The following is drawn from the first volume of the latter. On what grounds does Churchill condemn Chamberlain? What are his arguments for calling a halt to appeasement in 1938?

Chamberlain returned to England. At Heston where he landed, he waved the joint declaration which he had got Hitler to sign, and read it to the crowd of notables and others who welcomed him. As his car drove through cheering crowds from the airport, he said to Halifax, sitting beside him, "All this will be over in three months"; but from the windows of Downing Street he waved his piece of paper again and used these words, "This is the second time there has come back from Germany to Downing Street peace with honour. I believe it is peace in our time."

.   .   .

We have now also Marshal Keitel's answer to the specific question put to him by the Czech representative at the Nuremberg Trials:

> Colonel Eger, representing Czechoslovakia, asked Marshal Keitel: "Would the Reich have attacked Czechoslovakia in 1938 if the Western Powers had stood by Prague?"
>
> Marshal Keitel answered: "Certainly not. We were not strong enough militarily. The object of Munich [i.e., reaching an agreement at Munich] was to get Russia out of Europe, to gain time, and to complete the German armaments."

.   .   .

Hitler's judgment had been once more decisively vindicated. The German General Staff was utterly abashed. Once again the Fuehrer had been right, after all. He with his genius and intuition alone had truly measured all the circumstances, military and political. Once again, as in the Rhineland, the Fuehrer's leadership had triumphed over the obstruction of the German military chiefs. All these generals were patriotic men. They longed to see the Fatherland regain its position in the world. They were devoting themselves night and day to every process that could strengthen the German forces. They, therefore, felt smitten in their hearts at having been found so much below the level of the event, and in many cases their dislike and their distrust of Hitler were overpowered by admiration for his commanding gifts and miraculous luck. Surely here was a star to follow, surely here was a guide to obey. Thus did Hitler finally become the undisputed master of Germany, and the path was clear for the great design. The conspirators lay low, and were not betrayed by their military comrades.

.   .   .

It may be well here to set down some principles of morals and action which may be a guide in the future. No case of this kind can be judged apart from its circumstances. The facts may be unknown at the time, and estimates of them must be largely guesswork, coloured by the general feelings and aims of whoever is trying to pronounce. Those who are prone by temperament and character to seek sharp and clear-cut solutions of difficult and obscure problems, who are ready to fight whenever some challenge comes from a foreign Power, have not always been right. On the other hand, those whose inclination is to bow their heads, to seek patiently and faithfully for peaceful compromise, are not always wrong. On the contrary, in the majority of instances they may be right, not only morally but from a practical standpoint. How many wars have been averted by patience and persisting good will! Religion and virtue alike lend their sanctions to meekness and humility, not only between men but between nations. How many wars have been precipitated by firebrands! How many misunderstandings which led to wars could have been removed by temporising! How often have countries fought cruel wars and then after a few years of peace found themselves not only friends but allies!

The Sermon on the Mount is the last word in Christian ethics. Everyone respects the Quakers. Still, it is not on these terms that Ministers assume their responsibilities of guiding states. Their duty is first so to deal with other nations as to avoid strife and war and to eschew aggression in all its forms, whether for nationalistic or ideological objects. But the safety of the State, the lives and freedom of their own fellow countrymen, to whom they owe their position, make it right and imperative in the last resort, or when a final and definite conviction has been reached, that the use of force should not be excluded. If the circumstances are such as to warrant it, force may be used. And if this be so, it should be used under the conditions which are most favourable. There is no merit in putting off a war for a year if, when it comes, it is a far worse war or one much harder to win. These are the tormenting dilemmas upon which mankind has throughout its history been so frequently impaled. Final judgment upon them can only be recorded by history in relation to the facts of the case as known to the parties at the time, and also as subsequently proved.

There is, however, one helpful guide, namely, for a nation to keep its word and to act in accordance with its treaty obligations to allies. This guide is called *honour*. It is baffling to reflect that what men call honour does not correspond always to Christian ethics. Honour is often influenced by that element of pride which plays so large a part in its inspiration. An exaggerated code of honour leading to the performance of utterly vain and unreasonable deeds could not be defended, however fine it might look. Here, however, the moment came when Honour pointed the path of Duty, and when also the right judgment of the facts at that time would have reinforced its dictates.

For the French Government to leave her faithful ally, Czechoslovakia, to her fate was a melancholy lapse from which flowed terrible consequences. Not only wise and fair policy, but chivalry, honour, and sympathy for a small threatened people made an overwhelming concentration. Great Britain, who would certainly have fought if bound by treaty obligations, was nevertheless now deeply involved, and it must be recorded with regret that the British Government not only acquiesced but encouraged the French Government in a fatal course.

Appeasement:
The Art of the Possible

ᘛ

R. A. BUTLER

Richard Austen Butler was born in India in 1902, and served as
undersecretary for India in the Conservative government of 1932–
1937 and as undersecretary for foreign affairs from 1938 to 1941. He
was accordingly very much involved in the appeasement policy practiced during the pre-World War II period. He was minister of education during the war and afterwards a candidate for, but never
attained, the leadership of the Conservative party. Why does Butler
believe that at the time there was no real alternative to appeasement? What advantages does he say were gained by Britain as a
result of postponing the outbreak of war?

Within a few days of my going to the Foreign Office, Hitler had
given us one more indication of the shape of things to come by his forcible
incorporation of Austria into Germany. The *Anschluss*, I told the assembly at Chatham House, had increased my conviction that 'This country
must be strong, strong of purpose and strong in arms. We are living in
critical times and it is therefore no more than the plain duty of the
government to press ahead with our rearmament programme so that we
may have the strength to back our policy and so that in case of need we
shall be able to defend ourselves.' Churchill had at last been listened to

From R. A. Butler, *The Art of the Possible. The Memoirs of Lord Butler*, Copyright © Lord
Butler 1971. Reprinted by permission of Hamish Hamilton Ltd., publisher.

with rapt attention and respect when he warned the House of Commons that we were confronted with a nicely calculated and carefully timed programme of aggression, unfolding stage by stage. There was general agreement and apprehension that the next stage would involve Czechoslovakia. Accordingly the Prime Minister asked the Chiefs of Staff for a report on the new military situation following the *Anschluss*. They specified that the Czechoslovak frontier of 2,500 miles could not be protected from a German attack, thus confirming Austen Chamberlain's warning in 1936 that 'If Austria goes, Czechoslovakia is indefensible.' They also advised that Britain was not in a position to wage war, particularly in view of our unreadiness in the air. Later in the summer they reported to the Committee of Imperial Defence that it was of vital importance for us to gain time for the completion of the defence programme. The government was therefore faced with a categorical warning that the country was not ready for war, especially if this involved (as was expected or feared) not only a German front, but conflict in the Mediterranean with Italy and trouble in the Far East with Japan.

This was the unpalatable military appreciation which Chamberlain and Halifax gave to the representatives of France — who alone had a direct treaty obligation to the Czechs — when they came to London at the end of April. The main result of these Anglo-French conversations was therefore a decision to make a joint *démarche* in Prague to secure the maximum concessions from President Beneš. It has been wrongly assumed that Chamberlain believed such concessions would inevitably forestall a German military invasion of Czechoslovakia. On the contrary, he was fully aware, as were all the best of our diplomatic advisers, that the Sudeten problem might not be the real issue and that Hitler might have ambitions far beyond the restoration of Sudeten rights. Chamberlain felt that this was a situation which would have to be faced if it came, but that a world war could not be fought to maintain inviolate the ascendancy of seven million Czechs over an almost equal multitude of discontented minorities. The boundaries of Czechoslovakia had been drawn, as Churchill himself testified, in flagrant defiance of the doctrine of self-determination. There is no doubt that the government of the new State kept the three million Germans in a position of political, educational and cultural inferiority, and that bitterness was exacerbated by the economic depression of the 'thirties which hit the German industrialized areas (the Sudentenland) more severely than elsewhere. These grievances were outrageously exploited by the Nazis and their Sudeten puppet,

Henlein; but the grievances were real. In the week of the *Anschluss*, Basil Newton, our Ambassador in Prague, advised us (correctly, as was seen in 1945) that the *status quo* in Czechoslovakia could not be perpetuated even after a victorious war. On 22nd March I wrote to Lord Brabourne in India questioning whether we could defend by force a feature of the Peace Treaties which was in fact indefensible. I indicated that I had tried to get the Cabinet Committee involved to issue a statement saying that we were prepared to seek revision of the Treaties. I also said, 'To summon the League, talk to Litvinov, or act as mediator between Germans and Czechs, is likely to bring down on our heads more trouble than standing aloof.' This letter proved, alas, to be prophetic.

I was not myself a prime mover in the complex and dramatic events of the succeeding months. As a junior Minister I was little consulted about their cause or course. My role was sometimes that of a sceptical spectator, as when I stood in the Foreign Secretary's room in July studying the glass-fronted bookcase and heard Lord Runciman accept his impossible mediating mission to Prague with the words, 'I am being cut off like a small rowing boat from a great liner.' Throughout the fateful weeks of September I was off-stage in Geneva where, however, I conducted two important interviews with the Foreign Ministers of the Soviet Union and of France. The former convinced me that Russia had no intention of coming to the help of the Czechs, even if the Czechs had wanted this, which they didn't; the latter gave me the measure of France's political unreliability. These two factors were interrelated, since a French declaration of war was stipulated by the Russians to be a condition of their own intervention. I am thus convinced that Sir John Wheeler-Bennett's conclusion about the inevitability of the Munich agreement was correct and, in view of his own vehement and sustained reaction to appeasement, all the more creditable to his historical mastery. 'Let us say of the Munich Settlement,' he wrote, 'that it was inescapable; that, faced with the lack of preparedness in Britain's armaments and defences, with the lack of unity at home and in the Commonwealth, with the collapse of French morale, and with the uncertainty of Russia to fight, Mr. Chamberlain had no alternative to do other than he did; let us pay tribute to his persistence in carrying out a policy which he honestly believed to be right. Let us accept and admit all these things, but in so doing let us not omit the shame and humiliation that were ours; let us not forget that, in order to save our own skins — that because we were too weak to protect ourselves — we were forced to sacrifice a small Power to slavery.' In the light of the events of March 1939 the defenders of Munich, of whom I have always been one, cannot be morally blind to the savage impeachment of those concluding words; but in the light of the political and strategic realities of 1938 the critics of Munich, though deserving all respect, persevere in passion by denying its historical inevitability.

.   .   .

I was left in no doubt that the Russians themselves did not mean business. Litvinov had been deliberately evasive and vague, except when he had said that if France acted the Soviet would act too. Since his conversations with his opposite number had been far more numerous and dispiriting than mine, this was tantamount to saying that if Bonnet threw himself off the Eiffel Tower Litvinov would be there to catch him. It seemed to me preposterous for him to pretend ignorance of Soviet military preparations. He was, and gave the clear impression of being, much nearer the centre of power than any other Russian Foreign Minister with whom I have had dealings, and he had been at his desk in the Kremlin in the first week of September. He was perfectly well aware that, in the absence of a common frontier between Russia and Czechoslovakia, the 'barrier' policy of Poland and Roumania would limit Soviet aid to modest air support. Nor is there any evidence that if the railways through the Carpathian Mountains had been available to Russian forces, they would have been capable of rendering effective aid. Appreciations arriving at the Foreign Office from our Embassy in Moscow warned that the great purges of 1937 had had a disastrous effect on the morale and efficiency of the Red Army which, 'though no doubt equal to a defensive war within the frontiers of the Soviet Union, is not capable of carrying the war into the enemy's territory with any hope of ultimate success or without thereby running the risk of endangering the régime.' We now know that precisely similar appreciations were reaching Berlin from the German Ambassador.

Nevertheless, the theory that we deliberately 'excluded Russia from Europe' and that this played a decisive part in the ultimate tragedy was widely held by political opinion at home. It was endorsed after the war by Churchill who, advancing a somewhat medieval interpretation of history, argued that Stalin wanted to help Beneš because in 1936 the latter had revealed a plot against his life. The murders and massacres of his régime hardly reveal Stalin as so warm-hearted a man even in matters concerning his own family. Nor was this hypothetical affection and affinity reciprocal. As Beneš told the French Ambassador in Prague, and as Litvinov admitted more or less explicitly to the League, the Czechs did not wish to accept Soviet intervention unless France acted first. Many Czechs had fought against the Bolsheviks in 1918 and feared Soviet domination. General Jan Syrovy is on record as saying, 'We don't want the Russians in here as we shall never get them out.' Though, in the light of subsequent history, no sentiment compels readier or sadder assent, it was of secondary significance to the British in 1938. For us the criterion was whether Russia intended to oppose the German army, whether indeed she could afford to fight. My interview with Litvinov only confirmed our conclusion that, both on political and military grounds, the U.S.S.R. could not be trusted to wage war in defence of interests that were not bound up with her own security.

It is true that none of the diplomatic negatives I have exhibited were to be any less in evidence in 1939 than they were in 1938. In neither year could any reliance have been placed on the League of Nations to deter aggression. In either year the worm-eaten fabric of French political society and the self-seeking duplicity of the Soviet régime would have combined to leave us alone to face at close quarters the onslaught of the Luftwaffe. But the crucial change that came about as a result of the year's delay was in our preparedness to meet this onslaught. The 'special importance of preparation in the air and of developing the passive resistance of our population,' which had been my theme at Chatham House in April 1938, proved indeed to be the key factors. In September 1938 the R.A.F. had only one operational fighter squadron equipped with Spitfires and five in process of being equipped with Hurricanes; by the summer of 1939, thanks to Lord Swinton's earlier tenure of the Air Ministry, it had twenty-six squadrons of modern eight-gun fighters, and a year later forty-seven. Our ground defences against air attack were also substantially strengthened in this period. The provision of anti-aircraft guns was increased fourfold to 1,653, of which more than half were the newer 3.7- and 4.5-inch guns, and barrage balloon defence was completed in London and extended outside. More important was the fact that, by the time war broke out, the chain of radar stations, which during the Munich crisis had been in operation only in the Thames estuary, guarded the whole of Britain from the Orkneys to the Isle of Wight. Meanwhile, the administrative talents of John Anderson had wrought corresponding transformations in civilian A.R.P., and plans for evacuating schoolchildren and finding emergency hospital beds were completed.

These preparations extended to the pace and scope of British rearmament generally, as Professor Postan has described in his official history of British war production. But I stress them here both because they

undoubtedly constituted the most important defence achievement between Munich and the outbreak of war and because, though we now
know that the figures of German strength quoted by our professional
advisers and our critics alike to have been greatly exaggerated, they did
provide the indispensable means by which we won the Battle of Britain.
On this reckoning Munich was not, in Wheeler-Bennett's phrase, a 'pro-
logue to tragedy,' but the pause, however inglorious, which enabled
Churchill when his time came to lead the nation through the valley of
the shadow to victory. Nor was the military breathing-space the only
gain. There were subtler but equally significant changes of opinion at
home and abroad. During 1938 it had been possible to argue, and I argued
myself, that the principles of self-determination for which the previous
war had ostensibly been fought could not be denied to the Sudetens
simply because they were Germans or even because they were supported
by Nazis. The Treaty of Versailles still weighed heavily. By 1939 the
morality was quite clearly all on one side. There could no longer be any
doubt in any mind that the ambitions of Germany stretched far beyond
its ethnic frontiers and that it had indeed, in Chamberlain's phrase, 'made
up its mind to dominate the world by fear of its force.' These considerations affected not only the will and conscience of our own people but the
attitudes of Commonwealth governments and of enlightened leaders in
foreign countries, most notably in the U.S.A.

Appeasement:
A Study in Political Decline

࢞

A. L. ROWSE

Alfred Leslie Rowse, noted British historian and writer, has published extensively on Elizabethan England, on Shakespeare, and on
other historical and cultural subjects including his Cornish child-
hood. His account of Britain's appeasement policy has been praised
for its intensity and sense of personal commitment. Unlike other
critics, Rowse is especially interested in the appeasers themselves.
Why, in his view, did they behave the way they did?

What was characteristic of this inner group, especially of Chamberlain, Simon and Hoare, but of the egregious Runciman, Kingsley
Wood and Ernest Brown too — the Chamberlainites as such? There were
several things that united them. They were 'men of peace,' *i.e.* no use
for confronting force, or guile, or wickedness. That they did not know
what they were dealing with is the most charitable explanation of their
failure; but they might at least have taken the trouble to inform themselves. There were plenty of people to tell them, but they would not listen. They all shared a Nonconformist origin, and its characteristic self-
righteousness — all the more intolerable in the palpably wrong. These
things are more important than people realise; to the historian they are

Reprinted from *Appeasement, A Study in Political Decline, 1933–1939*, by A. L. Rowse, by
permission of W. W. Norton & Company, Inc. Copyright © 1961 by A. L. Rowse. Copyright renewed 1989 by A. L. Rowse.

significant elements. One way or another they had none of the old 18th-century aristocracy's guts — they were middle-class men with pacifist backgrounds and no knowledge of Europe, its history or its languages, or of diplomacy, let alone of strategy or war. Of the most ennobled of them, also middle-class on his paternal side, Churchill has a verbal comment; 'Grovel, grovel, grovel! First grovel to the Indians, then grovel to the Germans; next grovel to the Americans, then it's grovel to the Russians.' The plain truth is that their deepest instinct was defeatist, their highest wisdom surrender.

·   ·   ·

All the same people were shocked when on 7 September 1938 *The Times* came out with Dawson's notorious leader — Amery describes it as 'mischievous' — advocating the cession of the Sudeten areas: at that juncture a plain invitation to Hitler to take them. John Walter, of the old *Times* tradition, wrote a formal protest to Dawson: 'I felt that our leader on Czechoslovakia yesterday must have come as a shock to many readers of *The Times*, advocating as it did the cause of the Wolf against the Lamb, on the ground of Justice. No wonder there is rejoicing in Berlin.' He received a pretty disingenuous reply — and Dawson could be pretty disingenuous (like Simon) when he tried. After expressing surprise that there was not more criticism of the leader — actually the press rocked with it, 'but personally I think the leader was right. My own impression is that neither Hitler nor Henlein wants a revision of frontiers!' What was the value of Dawson's 'impression' any way? All that we wanted from him was that he should stand for the urgent interests of this country, which were one with the interests of Europe and civilisation. In truth, Hitler wanted not a mere revision of frontiers: he wanted the lot. These people were bent on helping him to it, and nothing could stop them. *The Times History* says that John Walter's 'remonstrance had no effect on their policy'; and anyway they had all the Astors with them all the time.

The Times History admits the sensation the leader caused in Europe — taken everywhere as evidence of retreat beforehand. The Foreign Office had to put out an assurance that no such cession was contemplated; but who would believe its assurance now? Dawson assured B.-W. that Halifax 'does not dissent privately from the suggestion that any solution, even the secession of the German minorities, should be brought into free negotiations at Prague.' More humbug: anyone might know that there could be no free negotiation in these circumstances. The only step that could strengthen our hands in the negotiation would be to call in Russia, and that these people would never do. Dawson's biographer says, 'Geoffrey was certainly influenced too by the thought that Nazi Germany served as a barrier to the spread of Communism in the West.'

This was what was so short-sighted and confused their minds. The immediate and overwhelming danger to Britain was Hitler's Germany. To call Russia into the balance was the only way to contain him, perhaps overthrow him. Amery noted at the time, 'A really definite declaration from the British and French governments any time in the last three weeks might have saved the situation. German generals have actually risked their lives secretly sending word to us that we should make such a declaration in order to stop Hitler in his wild career.' If a break had come inside Germany, as it still could have been forced by resisting Hitler, it is true that the German Army, the generals and conservative forces would have come out on top. Such a Germany, retaining the decencies of civilisation though conservative and resting on the Army, would have been a strong counterpoise to Russia. It was letting Hitler get away with it, until nothing would stop him except war, that let the Russians into the centre of Europe.

These people had no sense of strategy any more than they had of history. Their very pursuit of peace at any price brought the war down on them. Amery noted of Chamberlain's craven speech at the time, harping on the horror of war 'because of a quarrel in a far-away country between people of whom we know nothing': 'Poor Neville. He described himself as a man of peace to the inmost of his being, and that he assuredly is. If ever there was an essential civilian, a citizen accustomed to deal with fellow citizens on City Council or in Cabinet, and a man quite incapable of thinking in terms of force, or strategy or diplomacy, it is Neville. If he survives his efforts as a Foreign Minister I wonder how long he can survive as a war leader.'

.   .   .

Considerations on the other side were totally ignored. Amery tells us that 'the heads of the German Army were convinced that they could not possibly have faced a war at that time. General Beck considered it hopeless, as Marshal von Keitel also declared in his evidence at the Nuremberg trial.' The group of generals at this time planned Hitler's arrest; 'at the same time they sent a succession of envoys, more particularly a German Conservative leader, Herr von Kleist, who came over in

August "with a rope round his neck" and saw Vansittart and Churchill to tell them that the German Army and people were unanimous against war, but could only stop Hitler if we made our attitude quite clear.' So far from attaching any importance to such information, Chamberlain's environment preferred Lindbergh's. 'The only result was to encourage Chamberlain in his determination to see Hitler personally. This entirely disorganised the generals' coup, which had actually been planned for the very day when Chamberlain flew to Berchtesgaden.' The Mayor of Leipzig, Goerdeler, who was to have been Chancellor in Hitler's place could only comment 'by refusing a take a small risk Chamberlain has made war inevitable.'

These were the circumstances in which Chamberlain was fool enough to go to the footstool, with nothing to negotiate with, never even considering the only possible counterpoise to bring into the balance. Nothing could be more condemnatory than his friend Amery's summing up of it all. 'Inflexibly dedicated to his self-imposed mission, he ignored the warnings of the Foreign Office, dominated his colleagues, overrode wavering French Ministers, brushing aside their moral compunctions as lacking realism, and, to the last moment, refused to acknowledge failure. It was only in that fixed determination that he could persuade himself, in spite of all evidence to the contrary, that Hitler's pledges were sincere, or shut his eyes to the dishonourable aspect of his treatment of the Czechs or to the worthlessness of the guarantees which he persuaded himself at the time he had secured for their future independence and which he afterwards cynically repudiated. . . . Russia's attitude throughout the crisis was perfectly clear. Litvinov had consistently backed the conception of collective security — in effect an alliance between Russia and the Western Powers to meet the growing danger from Germany. . . . Only sheer infatuation with appeasement at almost any price can explain the cold shouldering of Russian offers of help when things were already on the eve of war.'

But Chamberlain was bent on going. He wrote to his sister, 'Afterwards I heard from Hitler himself, and it was confirmed by others who were with him, that he was struck all of a heap, and exclaimed, "I can't possibly let a man of his age come all this way; I must go to London." Of course, when he considered it further, he saw that wouldn't do, and indeed it would not have suited me, for it would have deprived my coup of much of its dramatic force. But it shows a side of Hitler that would surprise many people in this country.' No wonder Hitler used to call him, so Adam von Trott told me, *der Arschloch* [the arsehole]. It was this kind of smug vanity that made us hate him, apart from the mortal danger he was to his country. His biographer, Feiling, can do no better for him than to say, 'simple he was, as his letters show, and obstinately sanguine in that he was bent on finding decency even in dictators.' He reported himself of his first meeting with Hitler, 'I had established a certain confidence, which was my aim, and on my side, in spite of the hardness and ruthlessness I thought I saw in his face, I got the impression that here was a man who could be relied upon when he had given his word.' Vain old fool — his *impression* against all the evidence of perjury, torture, murder, thuggery that had accumulated since 1933, and was there before!

Those of us who understood knew that so far from being 'Peace for our time,' Munich made war certain and in the worst possible conditions — minus thirty-five Czech divisions and without an ally, save a France utterly unnerved and divided within. *The Times* thought that Chamberlain had done better than Sir Edward Grey in 1914; even Halifax repeats this piece of Tory meanness about the Liberal government of 1914. Apropos of the guarantee to Poland in 1939 he says, 'There was in that no room for misunderstanding of the British position as there had been in 1914.' All the historian needs to observe is that in 1914, under a Liberal government, this country entered the war with both France and Russia as allies and shortly gained Italy too to our side; after twenty years of Tory domination and virtually unbroken Tory government — smart they were at elections — this country was on the verge of war with both Germany and Italy, alone save for a France that *we* had broken, only half at our side.

.   .   .

How to account for this prolonged aberration of the most eminent?

It is indeed a strange case, and takes some explaining: yet it has its historical significance, and was something of a symptom, a pointer to the future too. These men came at the end of an age; they were late Victorians by birth and upbringing, sharing to the full the standards of that era, with all their limitations, public-spirited and respectable, conventional and unimaginative. Indeed, they distrusted imagination and intellectualism; it was not good form to hammer things out in discussion, perhaps even to think things out. The contrast here with Churchill is very marked. *The Times History* bears this out in Dawson, the most powerful man of them all. 'His remarkable capacity to decide quickly the innumerable questions that present themselves every day was accompanied by a strong reluctance to discuss in detail the serious questions of the time. In conversation it was imperative that such questions be handled lightly. If anyone attempted to entrap him in discussion, or hold forth to him, he was swift in closing the interview. Those in professional contact with him were soon made conscious of particular forms of Dawsonian disapproval. Those lacking a hereditary sense of social tact were briefly dealt with. It was a serious obstacle to a man's progress in the office if he were so unfortunate as to qualify for the description of "Bore."'

That is completely accurate. As I observed Dawson, I regarded him as an empiricist, with no principles, properly speaking, to guide him in a world profoundly changing, where the Victorian landmarks were toppling over, their values inapplicable. What was the point of attaching so much importance to social convention? (He used to observe of one Cabinet, half-humorously, that it had all too few Etonians, and not one 'wet-bob' among them — but it was only *half*-humorously.)

G. M. Trevelyan has several times suggested one line of explanation for them — there is no excuse — and that perhaps the fairest and best. These decent good men did not know what kind of men they were dealing with in Hitler and his kind. I dare say that is true. But they were told often enough: why would they not take telling?

This leads us nearer the heart of the problem.

As I have said, they were ignorant of Europe and European history; they had read Greats at Oxford, then Dawson went to South Africa and Simon to the Bar. All this group knew more about the Empire than they did about Europe, or the world. In addition, some of them were much influenced by Cecil Rhodes's insistent (and ignorant) pro-Germanism.

There is a further consideration of some interest for political thought — or for those who are interested in English processes of political thought. In this story we see the decadence of British empiricism, empiricism carried beyond all rhyme or reason. In general I am in sympathy with empiricism in politics; I much prefer it to doctrinairism. The practical way of looking at things, not looking too far in advance (*pace* Amery), not rocking the boat, and other clichés that do duty for thinking ahead, may serve well enough in ordinary, normal times. But our times are not 'normal' in the good old Victorian sense, and never will be again. And this habit of mind in politics will certainly not serve in times of revolution, perpetual stress and conflict, war, the reshaping of the world. This conventional British way of looking at things was simply not equal to the times, and it caught these men out badly.

Even so, the empirical habit of mind, that considered itself so much more practical — E. H. Carr in his writings at the time thought these people more 'realist' in their estimate of Hitler! — need not have equated itself with ignorance. Not one of these men in high place in those years ever so much as read *Mein Kampf*, or would listen to anybody who had. They really did not know what they were dealing with, or the nature and degree of the evil thing they were up against. To be so uninstructed — a condition that arose in part from a certain superciliousness, a lofty smugness, as well as superficiality of mind — was in itself a kind of dereliction of duty.

They would not listen to warnings, because they did not wish to hear. And they did not think things out, because there was a fatal confusion in their minds between the interests of their social order and the interests of their country. They did not say much about it, since that would have given the game away, and anyway it was a thought they did not wish to be too explicit about even to themselves, but they were anti-Red and that hamstrung them in dealing with the greater immediate danger to their country, Hitler's Germany.

There is a rider to add to this point about class. These men, even Halifax, were essentially middle-class, not aristocrats. They did not have the hereditary sense of the security of the state, unlike Churchill, Eden, the Cecils. Nor did they have the toughness of the 18th-century aristocracy. They came at the end of the ascendancy of the Victorian middle-class, deeply affected as that was by high-mindedness and humbug. They all talked, in one form or another, the language of disingenuousness and cant: it was second nature to them — so different from Churchill. This, and the essential pettiness of the National Government, all flocking together to keep Labour out, was deeply corrupting, both to them and the nation. It meant that they failed to see what was true, until too late, when it was simply a question of survival.

What I had under observation, then, in all those years was a class in decadence. These eminent specimens of it, be-ribboned and be-coroneted — all except Dawson, who, as editor of *The Times*, was above such things — with the best will in the world well-nigh ruined their country and reduced it to a second-rate place in the world.

The total upshot of their efforts was to aid Nazi-Germany to achieve a position of brutal ascendancy, a threat to everybody else's security or even existence, which only a war could end. This had the very result of letting the Russians into the centre of Europe which the appeasers — so far as they had any clear idea of policy — wished to prevent. Of course their responsibility was a secondary one. The primary responsibility was all along that of the Germans: the people in the strongest strategic position in Europe, the keystone of the whole European system, but who never knew how to behave, whether up or down, in the ascendant arrogant and brutal, in defeat base and grovelling.

These men had no real conception of Germany's character or malign record in modern history. Quite simply, we owe the wreck of Europe's position in the world to Germany's total inability to play her proper rôle in it.

That was no reason why these Englishmen should — largely out of ignorance and confusion of mind — have done everything to aid the process; in the event bringing down the British Empire with it too, for which they cared infinitely more than ever they did for Europe or Europe's place in the world.

Munich after 50 Years

～√I_~

GERHARD L. WEINBERG

Gerhard Weinberg was born in Germany and educated in the U.S. He has taught at the Universities of Chicago and Michigan, and is currently on the faculty of the University of North Carolina, where he specializes in modern German and diplomatic history. He is best known for his two-volume study of the foreign policy of Nazi Germany. The article in the respected journal *Foreign Affairs*, from which the following is taken, was written on the fiftieth anniversary of the Munich Accord. How does Weinberg challenge the traditional conception of the pact? Why was Hitler disappointed in the diplomatic settlement reached? Is Weinberg defending the decision taken by Chamberlain and Daladier?

Half a century after the Munich conference, that event lives in the public memory as a series of interrelated myths. For most people, Munich represents the abandonment of a small country, Czechoslovakia, to the unjust demands of a bullying and powerful neighbor by those who would have done better to defend it. It is believed that the Allies, by the sacrifice of one country, only whetted the appetite of the bully whom they had to fight anyway, later and under more difficult circumstances. The "lesson"

Reprinted by permission of *Foreign Affairs*, Fall, 1988. Copyright 1988 by the Council on Foreign Relations, Inc.

derived from this widely held view is that it makes far more sense to take action to stop aggression at the first opportunity.

.   .   .

Three aspects of the Munich conference that developed more fully afterward, or on which we are now better informed, suggest that this traditional interpretation warrants a closer look.

In the first place, it was after all the same two Allied leaders who went to Munich, Chamberlain of Great Britain and Edouard Daladier of France, who one year later led their countries into war against Adolf Hitler's Germany, something no other leader of a major power did before his own country was attacked. The Italians, who under Benito Mussolini thought of themselves as a great power, joined with Hitler in June 1940 in what Mussolini saw as an opportunity to share the spoils of victory. Joseph Stalin was sending the Nazis essential war supplies until a few hours before the German invasion of June 1941 awoke the Kremlin from its confidence in an alignment with Hitler. Franklin D. Roosevelt, who had repeatedly but vainly warned the Soviet leader of the German threat, had worked hard to rouse the American people to the dangers facing them; but until confronted by a Japanese surprise attack and by German and Italian declarations of war, he had hoped that Americans might be spared the ordeal of war.

Only Britain and France went to war with Germany out of calculations of broader national interest instead of waiting to be attacked; and it is perhaps safe to argue that without the lead from London, the French government would have backed off in 1939 and awaited a German invasion of its own territory. It is rather ungracious, especially for Americans whose country would not take action to defend either Czechoslovakia or Poland, and which had provided by law that it would not help anyone who did, to condemn as weaklings the only leaders of major powers who mustered up the courage to confront Hitler on behalf of another country.

A second factor that prompts us to take a new look at the 1938 crisis is the view that Hitler, the man usually thought to have triumphed at Munich, is now known to have held of it. The opening of German archives and the new availability of important private papers provide a picture rather different from the one commonly held.

We now know that Hitler had never been particularly interested in helping the over three million people of German descent living inside Czechoslovakia, but only in the ways they might help him in his project to isolate Czechoslovakia from outside support, create incidents that would provide a pretext for the invasion and destruction of that country, and thereafter provide manpower for additional army divisions. The new divisions, in turn, he considered useful for the great war he planned to wage against the powers of Western Europe as the prerequisite for the quick and far easier seizure of enormous territories in Eastern Europe.

Hitler believed that German rearmament was far enough advanced by late 1937 and early 1938 to make this first little war against Czechoslovakia possible. While spreading propaganda on behalf of the ethnic Germans of Czechoslovakia, Hitler was counting on the threat of Japan's advance in East Asia and Italy's support in Europe, and the reluctance of France and England to fight another great war, to isolate Czechoslovakia from outside support. It is understandable in this context that the successful and peaceful annexation of Austria in March 1938 (which left Czechoslovakia even more vulnerable than before), followed by a dramatic reaffirmation of Germany's alignment with Italy during Hitler's visit to Rome, produced Hitler's decision in the second week of May 1938 to go to war that year. We are not ever likely to know whether his belief that he was suffering from throat cancer contributed to his haste; he was certainly a man with a mission in a hurry who would explain later in 1938 that he preferred to go to war at the age of 49 so that he could see the whole issue through to resolution!

But there proved to be inner flaws in his strategy. The prospective allies he had selected turned out to be reluctant. The Japanese at that time wanted an alliance against the Soviet Union, not against the Western powers. Poland and Hungary both hoped to obtain pieces of Czechoslovakia but wanted them without a general European war. The Italians, furthermore, were not as enthusiastic as Hitler thought. Mussolini had given a hostage to fortune by committing large forces to the support of Francisco Franco in the Spanish Civil War, forces certain to be lost in a general war in which they would be cut off from their homeland.

The basic miscalculation of the German government was, however, of a different type: it was integrally related to the issue that Hitler deliberately placed at the center of public attention, the Sudeten Germans living in Czechoslovakia. The purpose of this focus was obvious. The constant attention in both publicity and diplomacy to the allegedly mistreated millions of Germans living in Czechoslovakia was designed to make it politically difficult, if not impossible, for Britain and France to come to Czechoslovakia's assistance when it was eventually attacked.

How could democracies contest the principle of self-determination that they had themselves proclaimed? Would they act to turn a small war into a huge one on the unproven assumption that a big war inevitably would come anyway?

But there were aspects of this program that might, from Hitler's perspective, cause problems. One was that the continued diplomatic focus on the Sudeten Germans, which was needed to assure the isolation of Czechoslovakia, might eventually make the transition from diplomacy to war more difficult. The other was that, despite the number and significance of the Germans inside the Czechoslovak state, there were obviously far more Czechs and Slovaks. If ever the real as opposed to the pretended aim of German policy became clear, the very same concept of self-determination that worked against support of Czechoslovakia as long as its German-inhabited rim was under discussion would shift in favor of Prague once the undoubtedly non-German core came into question. It was in this regard that the crisis of the end of September 1938 came to be so dramatic and its resolution, in Hitler's eyes, so faulty.

We now know that Hitler had originally planned to stage an incident inside Czechoslovakia to provide Germany with a pretext for invading that country with the objective of destroying it all rather than merely annexing the German-inhabited fringe. He was influenced by the experience of 1914, when Austria-Hungary had taken the assassination of the Archduke Francis Ferdinand as an excuse to attack Serbia.

.   .   .

What, then, went wrong? Why was there no transition from propaganda and diplomacy to war?

The constant emphasis on the Sudeten Germans in Nazi propaganda brought too late a response from the government in Prague, which until August left the initiative to Berlin. And this in spite of a formal and explicit, but confidential, warning to Prague from the French government in July that under practically no circumstances would it come to the defense of its Czechoslovak ally. Keeping this message undisclosed — and it was one of the few secrets that did not leak out in the Paris of the 1930s — was of course essential to the official French pretense that it was the British who were holding them back from full support of Prague, a pretense that turned to panic when the British position hardened and could no longer provide a fig leaf for French unwillingness to act.

The centrality of the nationality issue also created a terrible dilemma for London. Canada, Australia and the Union of South Africa

(as it was then known) all made it absolutely clear to the British government that they would not go to war alongside Britain over the Sudeten
German question. The British chiefs of staff strongly argued against
the risk of military action. If war were to come, it would have to come
under circumstances that made the issues clear to the public in Britain
and the dominions, and, as the British learned in September 1938, to
the French.

It was under these circumstances that on September 13 Neville
Chamberlain decided to fly to Germany, originally planning not even to
tell Berlin that he was coming until after his plane had taken off. The
Germans were startled enough even when notified in advance, and they
were trapped by their own propaganda that there were nationality issues
to discuss. Moreover, those who genuinely believed in the fairy tale of the
"stab in the back" — that Germany had not been beaten at the front in
World War I, but had instead lost the war because of the collapse of the
German home front — could not risk starting a second war unless German
public opinion could be convinced that such a war, with all its costs in
lives and treasure, was everybody else's fault.

So the British prime minister had to be received at Berchtesgaden.
All he could be told, of course, was the official public line that something
had to be done for the poor Sudeten Germans. While Chamberlain set
about getting the agreement of France and Czechoslovakia to having the
German-inhabited portions of Czechoslovakia ceded to Germany, Hitler
began plotting other ways to arrange for war in spite of the meddlesome
Englishman. When at their second meeting, on September 22 at Bad
Godesberg, Chamberlain offered Hitler an Allied capitulation to his
ostensible demands — the French, Czechoslovak and British governments
had all agreed to the transfer of the Sudeten territory — the German
dictator was dumbfounded and raised new and obviously preposterous
conditions for a peaceful settlement.

It was at this point that the issue shifted conspicuously from the
fate of the Sudeten Germans to that of the Czechs and Slovaks. Here
Hitler was indeed trapped by his own strategy. He now had either to risk
a war with Britain and France as well as Czechoslovakia or pull back, call
off the planned invasion, and settle for what Prague, London and Paris
had already agreed to.

It was not only Germany's military and diplomatic leaders who
urged caution on the Nazi dictator. Troubled by the prospect of a general

war when the German people gave every sign of being unenthusiastic about it, Hitler's closest political associates, Hermann Göring and Joseph Goebbels, argued for a peaceful settlement. The prospective allies of Germany in this crisis were hesitant, now that war was a real and not merely a theoretical possibility. The Poles certainly wanted a piece of Czechoslovakia, but not at the risk of breaking completely with their French ally and Great Britain. The Hungarians were watering at the mouth over the possibility of realizing their extensive territorial demands: all of the Slovak and Carpatho-Ukrainian portions of the Czechoslovak state and a few additional pieces if they could get them. The authorities in Budapest, however, were very conscious of having only recently begun their own rearmament; they were also fairly certain that Britain and France would go to war over a German invasion of Czechoslovakia and that such a general war would end in a German defeat.

Hitler never forgave the Hungarians, whose resolution, in his eyes, was not commensurate with their appetite, but he was even more astonished by the defection of his most important ally, Italy. Mussolini's urging him to settle for the German-inhabited fringe of Czechoslovakia instead of attacking that country as a whole — when Hitler had expected encouragement to go forward, along with a full promise of support — appears to have played a major part in his decision to recall the orders for war, already issued, and instead agree to a settlement by conference at Munich.

Precisely because he had not tested the predictions of those who had warned against an attack on Czechoslovakia, Hitler was then and ever after angry over having pulled back. He projected his own reticence onto others, denouncing as cowards those whose advice he had followed instead of testing his own concept in action, and despising the British and French leaders before whose last-minute firmness he had himself backed down.

If the Munich agreement, which others then and since have regarded as a great triumph for Germany, appeared to Hitler then and in retrospect as the greatest setback of his career, it was because he had been unwilling or unable, or both, to make the shift from propaganda and diplomacy to war as he had always intended. He had been trapped in a diplomatic maze of his own construction and could not find the exit to the war that he sought. In the last months of his life, in 1945, as he reviewed what had gone wrong and caused the dramatic descent from Germany's earlier heights of victory, he appears to have asserted that his failure to begin the war in 1938 was his greatest error, contributing to the eventual collapse of all his hopes and prospects.

In the intervening years he was most careful not to repeat what he considered were the great errors of 1938. A massive campaign was begun to rally the German people for war. As Hitler put it on November 10, 1938, meeting with the German press, the peace propaganda designed to fool others had carried in it the risk of misleading his own people into thinking that peace, not war, was intended. Thereafter, Hitler would sometimes postpone but would never again call off an attack on another country once ordered, and he would never again allow himself to be trapped in diplomatic negotiations.

In 1939 German ambassadors were kept away from London and Warsaw; they were in fact forbidden to return to their posts. The incident the Nazis had planned as the pretext for war against Poland — an assault on a radio station inside Germany — would be organized and managed directly from Berlin. Furthermore, as Hitler explained to his military leaders on August 22, 1939, he had things organized so well that his only worry was that at the last minute some *Schweinehund* would come along with a compromise and again cheat him of war. The allusion to Chamberlain and Munich was unmistakable. And it ought to be noted that this "lesson" of Munich remained with him. When the Soviet Union made desperate efforts in 1941 to avert war with Germany, by volunteering the most extensive concessions, by offering to join the Tripartite Pact and by soliciting diplomatic approaches from Berlin, Hitler once again claimed to be worried about only one thing: a last-minute compromise offer that would make it difficult for him to continue on the road to yet another extension of the war.

As for the remainder of Czechoslovakia, he was even more determined that it be destroyed. The German government devoted itself in the months after Munich to accomplishing that objective, never realizing that, in the face of universal relief over the avoidance of war, the violation of the agreement just signed would make any further step by Germany the occasion for war. In 1939 no one listened to Nazi tales of persecuted Germans in Poland; the Germans themselves had demonstrated to everyone that such propaganda was merely a pretext for actions with entirely different objectives. And when soundings were taken in London before the invasion of Poland, the answer was that Czechoslovakia must have its independence back first before any negotiations; similar soundings after the German conquest of Poland were answered with the demand that both Czechoslovakia and Poland be restored to independence. Since Hitler and his associates had not been interested in the fate of those who had been used as propaganda instruments, they never could understand that others had taken the issue seriously — but only once.

A third facet of the Munich agreement as we look back on it from the perspective of fifty years is the light shed on events by the opening of wartime archives and the progress of research. The account of German policy presented here is in large part based on materials that became available after World War II. The British archives have also been opened and show a government hoping against hope for a peaceful settlement, but prepared to go to war if there were an invasion of Czechoslovakia in spite of all efforts at accommodating what were perceived as extreme but not entirely unreasonable demands. We now know that Chamberlain was correctly reported as willing to contemplate the territorial cession of the German-inhabited portions of Czechoslovakia in early May 1938, and that the British knew that there was no serious French military plan to assist Czechoslovakia — the only offensive operation planned by the French if war broke out was into Libya from Tunisia. It is now also known that in June 1938 Winston Churchill explained to a Czechoslovak official that it was essential for Czechoslovakia to work out an agreement with Konrad Henlein, the leader of the Sudeten Germans, and that although he, Churchill, was criticizing Chamberlain, he might well have followed the same policy if he had held the responsibilities of power.

It is also clear that there were serious doubts within the British government — which may or may have not been justified — about the ability of Britain and France to defeat Germany, and a determination that if war came and victory were attained, the German-inhabited portions of Czechoslovakia would *not* be returned to Prague's control.

The question of whether or not Britain and France would have been militarily better off had they gone to war in 1938 will remain a subject for debate for historians. Most would agree that the defenses of Czechoslovakia would have proved more formidable in 1938 than those of Poland in 1939, but then the question remains whether, since there was to be no attack by the French in the west in 1938, a somewhat longer Czechoslovak resistance would have made any significant difference. It can be argued that the Germans used the last year of peace more effectively than the British and the French, but it must also be recalled that new British fighter planes and radar defenses would not in any case have been available to meet a German onslaught in 1939 as they were for the Battle of Britain in 1940. And the excellent Czechoslovak tanks Germany acquired must be weighed against Poland's essential 1939 contribution to breaking the German Enigma-machine code.

RESISTANCE
OR
COLLABORATION?

The Example
of Vichy France

I n one sense Vichy stands as a classic example of collaboration in World
War II; in another it is unique, for no lawfully constituted government
of any other occupied country chose to cooperate with the victorious
enemy. France fell a scant six weeks after the German attack that began
10 May, 1940. Fearful that a continuation in North Africa of what appeared to be a hopeless struggle might provoke civil unrest, Marshal
Philippe Pétain, the hero of the Battle of Verdun in World War I, formed
a government and negotiated an armistice. On 11 July, at the resort town
of Vichy in unoccupied France, a remnant of the French legislature by a
large majority voted Pétain full power to issue a new constitution. The
next day he took the title chief of state, repealed the Constitutional Laws
of 1875, and indefinitely adjourned the Chamber of Deputies and the
Senate. On the initiative of Pierre Laval, who had been appointed vice

premier, Pétain met with Hitler at Montoire on 24 October. The Vichy regime, as it became known, attempted to replace France's Third Republic with a new order, the "National Revolution," and disenchantment with the prewar Popular Front electoral coalition of Socialists, Communists, and Liberals induced many Conservatives to follow Pétain in his quest. The motto "Work, Family, Country" replaced the revolutionary slogan of "Liberty, Equality, Fraternity," and "The French State" (L'Etat français) superseded "The Republic." Anti-Semitic and anti-Communist decrees were passed, as were laws establishing rigid censorship and vast increases in state power.

Pétain's appeal defies simple explanation. His supporters assert that at times he tried to resist the harshest forms of Nazi pressure and intimidation, for example, by dismissing Laval in December 1940 and by writing to Hitler defining the limits of collaboration. (However, under German threats, Laval was replaced by men whose willingness to collaborate was beyond doubt, and Laval himself was subsequently reappointed.) There are still people in France, like the concierge Madame Lucie, who praise Pétain for having saved her sons: "While de Gaulle left us, the Marshal stayed with us, though he was an old man."[1]

Others, however, opposed Pétain and chose to resist, aware that any amount of collaboration, though it might seem a lesser evil than the "Polandization" of France, must lead the French down a slippery moral slope and result in Vichy France becoming Germany's most important supplier of both goods and manpower during the war years.

The story of the Resistance fell subject to mythology in the decades after the war, when apparently nearly everyone had been a resister. Then in the 1970s came demythologizing with a vengeance, as highlighted by such films as Marcel Ophuls' *The Sorrow and the Pity*, and Robert Paxton's history of Vichy, which revealed the extent to which so many of the French collaborated, or supported collaboration. Most recently, some historians have rejected the belief that Vichy enjoyed wide support; they consider misleading both the Gaullist view of France as a nation of resisters and the revisionist view of a nation of collaborators.

What is one to conclude from these samples, drawn over a thirty-five year span, from the histories of the Vichy experience? That much

---

[1]Bonnie Smith, *Confessions of a Concierge. Madame Lucie's History of Twentieth Century France* (New Haven, 1985), p. 64.

depends on how one defines collaboration and resistance? That history may be distorted because it is written by those on the winning side, in this case the Gaullists who created the myth of a nation of resisters? That revisionists may sometimes distort history as well? That if there were minorities committed to Vichy or the Resistance, a majority of the French was motivated by self-interest, which would explain the growth of resistance movements as Allied victory became more probable? Although there were collaborators in all the occupied countries, why was Vichy the only example of official government collaboration? To what extent was Vichy a reflection of an indigenous fascism? Finally, what should be said about the moral dilemma confronted by the French? Does not the dramatic historical situation represented by Vichy reinforce the validity of Sartre's existential interpretation: that every person has the freedom to choose a course of action, but what is not possible is not to choose, for this too is a choice?

The Vichy Regime

∿⟋⟍

ROBERT ARON

Robert Aron participated in both the rival Giraud and de Gaulle movements in Algiers during World War II. He published many works of history including material on Vichy and on the liberation of France. He also wrote studies of Jesus, Waterloo, and French socialism. How legitimate is it to present French collaborationists and particularly Pétain as victims of circumstance doing their best to shield France from Nazi tyranny? How does Aron distinguish between Pétain and Laval, and how does he explain the Marshal's willingness to face his accusers as the war drew to an end?

Very early, on Thursday 24th October (1940), the Head of the State left Vichy. He did not conceal his great satisfaction at meeting the Führer.

.   .   .

The conversation that followed bore little relation to that between Hitler and Laval. A difference which, with an interval of only two days, was due to three causes.

In the first place, Hitler had returned weary and disappointed from his interview with Franco. For nine hours, the two men had discussed the

From Robert Aron, *The Vichy Regime, 1940–1944*, pp. 216, 218–221, 224–225, 310–311, 460–463, 514–515, 517. Permission granted by The Bodley Head, Publishers for Putnam & Co. Ltd.

conditions for Spain's entry into the war. Franco, forewarned by Pétain, and determined not to yield, put forward demands which made agreement impossible. He asked for the whole of French Morocco and part of Algeria. For all their polite words, Franco inflicted a complete defeat on Hitler on the 23rd October. On the 24th, when he met Pétain, the Führer was still suffering from his disappointment: he had none of that dynamism which, two days before, had so impressed Laval.

A second difference between the interview of the 22nd and 24th was that the principal negotiator with the Chancellor had changed. Instead of it being Laval, whose attitude was precise and who was ready to take his stand at the side of Germany, it was now the Marshal who, having decided to refuse military collaboration with the Reich, avoided making any precise promises.

Resolved not to yield on the essential points, Pétain was led to make a concession on a matter which he judged to be of secondary importance, without realising its gravity. It consisted, on Hitler's demand, of making a broadcast extolling collaboration.

Hitler opened the interview with one of his customary monologues.

"I am certain of winning the war, but I must finish it as soon as possible, for nothing is more ruinous than war. England will have to pay the greater part of the cost. But every European country will suffer from its prolongation.

"It is therefore in their interest to form a continental community with the object of shortening the duration of hostilities.

"What position does the French Government propose to adopt?"

Pétain saw in this an excellent opportunity for replying vaguely: certainly, he was prepared to accept collaboration in principle, but he could not immediately specify to what extent France could participate; ways and means must be studied by his Government.

.   .   .

Pétain cleverly took the opportunity of making a diversion: since the Führer had spoken of peace, would he state in what terms he envisaged the final treaty, "in order that France might know her fate and the two million prisoners return as soon as possible to their families?"

As, no doubt, the Marshal expected, Hitler avoided answering: the final treaty could only be considered after the ultimate defeat of England. Pétain then observed that, while waiting upon events, measures must be taken to assure the early return of the prisoners at least, to ameliorate the situation with regard to the demarcation line, which was creating an intolerable situation, and to reduce the indemnity for the occupation.

To these questions, which for Pétain were the real object of the interview, Hitler did not reply with an immediate refusal: he agreed to study them.

The fate of the prisoners was, he knew, one of the means of exerting pressure to which Pétain was most sensitive. Hitler, also, by this shift, re-introduced the problem of collaboration and put the deal squarely before the Marshal: "If France and Germany achieve an agreement on collabo-ration, France may expect concessions on all the points the Marshal has mentioned."

At this point, Laval intervened: "Thanks to the Führer's offer, France is no longer face to face with a blank wall. . . . However, in spite of my own personal desire to do so, I recognise that there are difficulties in declaring war on England. . . . Public opinion must grow accustomed to the idea and then, in accordance with constitutional law, we need the consent of the National Assembly."

There followed a long speech by Laval, who repeated almost word for word his declarations of two days before and reaffirmed his desire to collaborate. Pétain listened without saying a word and only spoke again to demand the return to France of the departments in the north which had been attached to the military government in Belgium; he was less precise over Alsace-Lorraine.

Hitler finally promised to make known in writing his position on the various points raised; the Marshal, for lack of any more concrete promises, would make a radio appeal inviting the French to collaborate with Germany and thus, for lack of the reality, content himself with words. So the interview came to an end. Pétain, throughout, had been extremely reticent. Having obtained from Marshal Keitel the freeing of General Laure and an authorisation to visit a Prisoners' Camp near Amboise, the Marshal left for Vichy, where he arrived on the evening of the 25th and, on the 26th October, informed the Council of Ministers of the results of the interview. The impression he gave them was very differ-ent from that given by Laval in the Council of the 23rd after the first meeting at Montoire.

For Pétain, there was no question of military collaboration with Germany: Montoire had merely been an opportunity to make contact. The Marshal had not gone beyond the limits he had set himself.

.   .   .

Thus, the Montoire interview aggravated and lent precision to the initial disagreements which, since the 25th June, 1940, had separated Pétain and Laval.

For the Marshal, the armistice was not and could not be more than a pause, which allowed France to exist provisionally, while awaiting the outcome of the war between England and the Axis; Montoire, looked at from his point of view, was but an episode and made no change in his policy towards Germany.

For Laval, on the other hand, the armistice permitted of a reversal of alliances, of which Montoire, in the most definite way, was to mark the beginning.

It is clear that Montoire was the origin of a triple misunderstanding whose consequences were to weigh heavily upon the whole Vichy drama.

Misunderstandings between Pétain and Laval, which were soon to come to a head in the clash of the 13th December; misunderstandings between Hitler and the Marshal on the exact meanings of "collaboration" and Franco-German relations, which would bring in their train the occupation of the free zone in November, 1942, the scuttling of the Fleet and, in August, 1944, the removal of Pétain by the Germans.

But there was also another misunderstanding, more grievous and more eventful in its dramatic and long term consequences for France, more complex and profound, though perhaps involuntary, between Pétain and public opinion. The majority of Frenchmen did not and could not understand what Pétain's real attitude, after Montoire, was towards the occupying power.

They did not know that by his secret message to Franco, Pétain had tried to torpedo the interview before even going to it.

They did not know that at Montoire he had not agreed to the proposals put forward by Hitler and Laval.

They did not know that, at the same time, he was carrying on negotiations with London.

They only knew of his spectacular statements on the French radio in which he extolled in words the collaboration he had been constrained to accept, but which he had decided never to allow to become military engagements.

Certain words have a terrifying and injurious power, when the head of a vanquished State, after an interview with the conqueror, expresses himself as did Pétain on the 30th October:

"It is in all honour and in order to maintain the unity of France — a unity of ten centuries within the framework of the constructive activity

of the new European Order — that I am today pursuing the path of collaboration. . . . This collaboration must be sincere. It must bring with it
patient and confident effort. An armistice, after all, is not peace. France
is constrained by the many engagements she has taken towards the conqueror. At least, she remains sovereign. This sovereignty imposes upon
her the duty of defending her soil, to extinguish divergency of opinion
and to diminish the number of dissidents in her colonies. This policy is
mine. The Ministers are only responsible to me. It is I alone whom history
will judge.

"Until today I have spoken to you the language of a father. Today I
speak to you in the language of a leader. Follow me. Put your faith in
France eternal."

These words, even admitting that they were only words, were fateful in their consequences.

Montoire is perhaps the principal cause of the appalling crises of
conscience that Vichy imposes on public opinion.

It explains why, for instance, certain patriots, who were originally
loyal to Pétain, now tore up their photographs of the Marshal, who had,
during the first months, been the object of their veneration and in whom
they had placed their hopes. At Vichy itself, it brought about the resignation of the Secretary-General of the Ministry of Foreign Affairs,
François Charles-Roux.

Conversely, it justified to some extent the actions of all those who
believed that, by collaborating, they were obeying the Marshal and serving the country. This speech of the 30th October incited many Frenchmen to take a path that was to be fatal to them.

.   .   .

Pétain and Darlan tried to negotiate, each on his own level, as
Pétain and Laval had done after the armistice.

Darlan used Benoist-Méchin as intermediary to establish contact
with Ribbentrop and Keitel. But Keitel said to the French emissary:

"If France does not give Germany the control she demands in North
Africa, she will be treated like Yugoslavia."

And, a fortnight before, between the 6th and 8th April, the Luftwaffe had bombed Belgrade, even though the capital of Yugoslavia had
been declared an open town; it had caused 12,000 casualties.

Pétain had recourse to the good offices of a certain German art
historian, Erckmann, a confidant of Hitler's, in order to get a letter to the

Führer in which he complained in violent terms of the German proceedings in France. This letter remained unanswered.

At the same time, Pétain made a speech over the radio in which he was categorical: "Honour," he said on the 11th April, "demands that we should not undertake anything against our old allies."

Similarly, on the 14th February, he had assured the Caudillo, during the course of an interview at Montpellier, that he would never let the Germans enter North Africa.

．　　．　　．

On the 4th December, Otto Abetz reappeared on the scene, having been recalled from disgrace by Ribbentrop.

．　　．　　．

In an interview which lasted half an hour, the Ambassador gave the Marshal a letter from Ribbentrop dated 29th November. It was a long document, which took the Marshal to task for his permanent resistance to the occupying power.

Ribbentrop began by recapitulating the crisis of the 13th November: it denoted a state of mind "in open contradiction to the policy of collaboration between France and Germany." Then he transmitted, on behalf of the Führer, an ultimatum containing five points:

1. The Chancellor opposed all remitting of power to the National Assembly "which, in September, 1939, had declared war on Germany without any cause whatever, and of which a not negligible proportion of members are again fighting against Germany."

2. Since no election could take place in time of war, there existed, and could exist, "no legal body capable of exercising the functions which the proposed broadcast wished to confer on it, and which, for this purpose, could be recognised by Germany."

3. The Führer took the opportunity of declaring that the Marshal had not remained loyal to the spirit of collaboration envisaged at Montoire, but had on the contrary shown "permanent resistance." "The policy of the supreme controllers of the French State at Vichy has pursued a direction which the Government of the Reich cannot approve and which it will not accept in the future in its capacity as occupying power, in view of the fact that it is responsible for the maintenance of order and public calm in France."

After these threats, here are the terms of the ultimatum:

4. "The Government of the Reich is compelled to demand that the supreme direction of the French State should in future submit all

proposed modifications of laws to the agreement of the Government of the Reich [a statute for a Protectorate]; that, moreover, Monsieur Laval, should be charged with re-organising the French Cabinet without delay in a manner acceptable to the German Government as a guarantee of collaboration. This Cabinet must thereafter enjoy the unreserved support of the supreme directorate of the State.

"Finally, the supreme direction of the French State will be responsible for taking measures to eliminate immediately all elements obstructive to the important work of recovery in the influential posts of the administration and also for appointing persons worthy of confidence to these posts."

After this ultimatum, clause 5 was an insolent piece of blackmail.

"Today, the one and only guarantee for the maintenance of public calm and order in the interior of France and thereby the security of the French people and its regime against revolution and Bolshevik chaos is the German Wehrmacht . . . I pray you to take such action that Germany will be able to safeguard these interests in all circumstances by one means or another."

In conclusion, there was a formal recognition of the "freedom" left to the Marshal: "If however you do not consider that you are in a position to respond favourably to the German demands mentioned above, or if our rejection of your proposed law, directed against German interests, should decide you to consider yourself afterwards as before prevented from exercising your functions, I am to inform you, in the name of the Führer, that he leaves you entirely free to draw what conclusions you please. . . ."

It was an invitation, couched in barely diplomatic terms, to submit or resign.

Pétain's reaction was dignified. With his hands clasped, he replied: "I perfectly understand the meaning of this letter and as a soldier I cannot admit what you say. But it has taken three weeks to give me this answer. It raises extremely delicate questions which I want to consider. I would like to see you again tomorrow morning to give you my reply."

Abetz agreed to the delay, but not without inflicting two somewhat specious arguments on the Marshal. If Pétain refused, he was playing the game of the Communists. While the summoning of the National Assembly in the case of the Marshal's death placed a premium upon it. The "British Intelligence Service" would not fail to make use of it. "Do you think so?" said the Marshal.

"Yes, Monsieur le Maréchal, and we wish to preserve you."

All this did not unduly alarm the Head of the State; hardly had Abetz left when he openly took Romier for a little walk and confided in him as follows:

"Really the Germans are not clever politicians and Monsieur Laval is absurd to hang on to them. If he thinks that Churchill and the Americans will sit down at the same table as himself, he's making a big mistake. He'll prevent my welcoming them, and that's all he'll succeed in doing. If he was really intelligent, he would have taken the opportunity I gave him of flying to the Argentine or elsewhere."

.   .   .

Alone of all the survivors of Vichy, Pétain wished at all costs to return to France. The Marshal, while still at Sigmaringen, had learned on 5th April, by the radio, that his trial would begin in Paris on the 24th April. Far from wishing to avoid appearing, he desired to reply personally to the accusations.

"Monsieur le Chef de l'Etat Grand Allemand," he immediately wrote to Hitler, "I have just learned that the French authorities propose to put me on trial in my absence before the High Court of Justice. The trial will begin on the 24th April. This news imposes an obligation on me which I look on as imperative and I ask your Excellency to facilitate my accomplishing my duty.

"I received on the 10th July, 1940, from the National Assembly, a mandate which I have fulfilled to the best of my ability in the circumstances. As Head of the Government in June, 1940, at Bordeaux, I refused to leave France. As Head of the State, when grave hours once more faced my country, I decided to remain at my post in Vichy. The Government of the Reich compelled me to leave on the 20th August, 1944.

"I cannot, without forfeiting my honour, allow it to be believed, as some tendentious propaganda is insinuating, that I sought refuge in a foreign country in order to evade my responsibilities. It is only in France that I can answer for my actions and I am the only judge of the risks that this attitude may entail.

"I therefore have the honour of earnestly asking your Excellency to give me this opportunity. You will naturally understand the decision I have reached of defending my honour as Head of the State and of protecting by my presence all those who have followed me. It is my only object. No argument can make me abandon this decision.

"At my age, there is only one thing one still fears: it is not to have done all one's duty, and I wish to do mine."

.   .   .

At the agreed hour, a leading French official, the Commissaire de la République of Dijon, entered Swiss territory to meet Pétain and inform him that a warrant had been issued against him: the Marshal was to be placed under surveillance.

At the Frontier, the barrier rose; the cars entered France and stopped.

A few soldiers and policemen hesitated, uncertain whether they should present arms or not. A General came forward and asked the Marshal to get out of his car: it was General Koenig, whom Pétain did not know.

Having placed his foot to earth, the Marshal extended his hand. Koenig refused to take it.

Vichy France;
Old Guard and New Order

∿ℓ∾

ROBERT PAXTON

Robert Paxton, a professor at Columbia University, has published three books on Vichy France. The one from which the following excerpts are drawn has had considerable impact both in the English original and in the French translation, and, unlike earlier works on the Vichy government, has made extensive use of German archival material. How does Paxton attempt to debunk the myth that France was a nation of resisters? In what way does his view of Pétain differ from Aron's? How, specifically, does he treat the rationales for collaboration made by Vichyites? In his opinion, what was the real explanation for their decision to collaborate?

The prospect of liberation by the sword, under the auspices of "brigands," was anything but alluring to many Frenchmen. Some 45,000 volunteered for the infamous Milice in 1944, partly, perhaps, to escape from labor service, partly for fanaticism, but at least in part to help defend "law and order." Counting police and military guard units as well, it is likely that as many Frenchmen participated in 1943–44 in putting down "disorder" as participated in active Resistance. Almost every Frenchman wanted to be out from under Germany, but not at the price of revolution.

Under these conditions, the number of active Résistants was never very great, even at the climactic moment of the Liberation. After the war, some 300,000 Frenchmen received official veterans' status for active Resistance service: 130,000 as deportees and another 170,000 as "Resistance volunteers." Another 100,000 had lost their lives in Resistance activity. This brings the total of active Resistance participation at its peak, at least as officially recognized after the war, to about 2 percent of the adult French population. There were no doubt wider complicities. But even if one adds those willing to read underground newspapers, some two million persons, or around ten percent of the adult population, seem to have been willing to take even that lesser risk. Let nothing said here detract from the moral significance of those who knew what they had to do. But the overwhelming majority of Frenchmen, however they longed to lift the German yoke, did not want to lift it by fire and sword.

.   .   .

In the end, one must make some overall judgment of the immediate results of collaboration for Frenchmen. With all its one-sided social favors and with all its complicity in the brutal last stages of nazism's paroxysm, did it not save many Frenchmen from still worse direct German administration? Was it not better to have Frenchmen administering Frenchmen than the tender ministrations of a gauleiter? Did not the Vichy regime save France from "Polandization"? Did it not "éviter le pire"?

.   .   .

Pierre Laval, in his turn before the High Court, claimed that his government had managed to "éviter le pire," to act as a "screen" between the conqueror and the French population. The refrain was taken up by succeeding defendants before the High Court and by a stream of self-exculpating memoirs.

Despite these partisan origins, the material advantage theory has been quite widely accepted. Robert Aron, trying to strike a reasonable balance on the basis of the trial records, the only sources available in 1954, argued that life was easier, statistically speaking, for Frenchmen than for others in occupied Europe. The reproaches against Vichy, he said, are moral rather than material.

In its most widespread form, the material advantage thesis argues that Vichy kept France from "Polandization," and everyone knows that the Poles suffered more in World War II than the French. Nazi contempt for Slavic Untermenschen makes Poland an invalid comparison with

France, however. Nazi purists might well cast aspersions upon French "mongrelization" and lack of racial self-consciousness, but they did not contemplate French extinction. The shield theory must be understood in terms of actual German demands, rather than in terms of vaguely infinite possibilities of evil. It can be validly tested only in comparison with fully occupied Western countries like Belgium, Holland, or Denmark, or other collaborating regimes like Quisling's Norway. If incomplete occupation or the existence of a quasiautonomous indigenous administration spared France any of the rigors of direct German rule, those favors should show up in comparison with fully occupied Western countries without an indigenous collaborationist regime.

One can suppose two ways in which Vichy France could have suffered less than France under a gauleiter. The German occupation authorities might have asked for less in order to reward and solidify a useful collaborationist regime. Of if the German occupation authorities asked no less of France than of fully occupied Western nations, the Vichy regime might have been better able or more willing to refuse excessive demands than would a gauleiter. A hard comparative look at the material conditions of life in Western occupied countries fail to show any important advantage for France, either granted by or extorted from Berlin.

Frenchmen were no better nourished than other Western occupied countries. Comparison of caloric intakes in France and fully occupied Western nations is, of course, treacherous ground, for access to food depended greatly on one's location, ready cash for the black market, or connections — and a cousin on the farm might be more useful in that respect than a cabinet minister. Average figures mean even less in this case than in most, and agricultural statistics are certainly less reliable for French *paysans* than for Danish dairy farmers. Nevertheless, it appears that French caloric intake was the lowest in Western Europe, with the exception of Italy, which is astonishing for so rich an agricultural country. Furthermore, in Eastern Europe, Rumania, Bulgaria, Hungary, and the Protectorate of Bohemia-Moravia seem to have eaten better than France. French caloric intake is estimated to have descended under the occupation as low as 1,500 calories a day where there was access to black market supplies and even lower for city populations where there was not.

Not all the French hunger can be attributed directly to German occupation policy, of course. With much food production in the hands of a notoriously small, independent, and secretive peasantry, France suffered as much from maldistribution as from genuine shortages. Moreover,

France had depended before the war upon imports of some staples, such as vegetable oils, so that Allied blockade and shipping shortages made matters worse.

There is no sign, however, that Vichy managed to win significant concessions in those areas where German policy added to French hunger. The armistice provision (copied from that of 1918) that French prisoners of war should not be repatriated until the peace produced a serious labor shortage in agriculture, keeping French agricultural production from ever returning to prewar figures. The petroleum shortage prevented the replacement of farm laborers with machines. Moreover, the gigantic German requisitions of French foodstuffs, for the occupying army and for export to the Reich, were among Germany's most important single sources of nourishment. France supplied more foodstuffs to Germany, both absolutely and relatively, than did even Poland.

It was indeed explicit German policy that the French should have a lower standard of living than the Germans. Both Goering and Abetz, as we have seen, thought that Frenchmen should have less to eat than Germans. Abetz stated early in July 1942 that French wages must remain lower than those in Germany (which had been the lowest in industrial Europe in the 1930s) so that French workmen would go to work in Germany.

It begins to look as if material conditions of life in occupied Europe depended less upon avoiding total occupation and having an indigenous regime than upon Germany's ethnic feelings about the occupied power and upon simple opportunity. Bargaining by Vichy was quite incapable of preventing increases in Germany's food delivery quotas in France in the summer of 1942 and in early 1943 or of preventing France, the richest agricultural producer of the occupied nations, from experiencing localized malnutrition.

·   ·   ·

There remains the somber business of the Jewish Final Solution. It is true, as Xavier Vallat claimed, that a larger proportion of the Jewish populations of totally occupied Holland, Belgium, Norway, and Italy (totally occupied after 1943) perished than that of France, even taking refugees and citizens together. The real question, however, is not whether fewer Jews were deported from France than from the totally occupied countries, but whether more Jews were deported from France because of Vichy preparations and assistance than would have been the case if the Germans had had to do it all alone. Vichy bears a heavy burden of responsibility, seen in these terms.

It is true that the unoccupied zone of France provided a refuge of sorts for tens of thousands of Jewish refugees from Germany and Eastern Europe for the first two years. Republican France having taken over from England the role of Europe's refugee haven in the late nineteenth century, German Jews and then, after September 1939, Polish Jews, followed a well-worn path to the west. The fact that the armistice and the division of France into two zones kept many of these refugees one jump ahead of the German armies was not the result of any Vichy sentimentality about the refugees. In fact, Vichy objected vigorously when the Germans delivered more expatriate Jews into the unoccupied zone in the fall of 1940. After protest, Vichy acquiesced in Article 19 of the armistice, which empowered Germany to demand the extradition of German citizens who had sought refuge in France. Under this provision, such prominent figures as Herschel Grynspan (who had assassinated a German diplomat in Paris in 1938) and the socialist economist and Weimar minister Rudolf Hilferding were delivered back into German hands — an ominous first warning about the precariousness of asylum in Vichy France. Moreover, Vichy did everything possible to encourage the further emigration of Jewish refugees. At a time when French Jews were being uprooted from the economy, there was no possibility of foreigners settling. Vichy also revoked some recent citizenships, enlarging the number of Jews in France without the protection of citizenship. Finally, Vichy gathered destitute Jewish refugees into work camps. Although Pétain spared them the yellow star, thousands were waiting behind barbed wire when the Germans came into the unoccupied zone in November 1942. Only those with money had managed to use southern France as a springboard for safer havens. For the rest, the French tradition of refuge made the unoccupied zone a trap.

The possibilities of sheltering Jews in southern France were far greater, say, than in the ghetto of Amsterdam. Furthermore, by the time the Germans actually arrived in southern France, in November 1942, there had been ample time for emergency arrangements. The final irony is that Italian-occupied Alpine France provided the cover in 1943 that Vichy refused. Many French citizens did the same, but the Vichy authorities deserve none of their credit. Vichy bears the guilt for not having used its opportunity for the kind of escape operation that the totally occupied Danes managed to carry out by moving almost the entire Jewish population by small boat to Sweden in September 1943.

This survey suggests that the shield theory hardly bears close examination. The armistice and the unoccupied zone seemed at first a cheap way out, but they could have bought some material ease for the French population only if the war had soon ended. As the war dragged on, German authorities asked no less of France than of the totally occupied countries. In the long run, Hitler's victims suffered in proportion to his need for their goods or his ethnic feelings about them, not in proportion to their eagerness to please. Vichy managed to win only paltry concessions: a few months of the *relève* instead of a labor draft, exemption from the yellow star for Jews in the unoccupied zone, slightly lower occupation costs between May 1941 and November 1942, more weapons in exchange for keeping the Allies out of the empire. Judged by its fruits, Vichy negotiation was barren.

In the last analysis, fruitful negotiation depends upon some comparable capacity of each party to threaten the other with damage if acceptable compromises are not made and to withhold that damage if acceptable compromises are made. Vichy's one serious threat — to take fleet and empire over to the Allied side — lacked credibility. Vichy leaders could not exercise it without suffering more than the Germans. To be sure, the Germans did not want the effort and expense of a total occupation of France. Vichy leaders could delude themselves for the first months that France had found a cheap way out of the war. Even after the sufferings increased, however, they could not flee abroad without sacrificing the National Revolution, their commitment to internal order, and, after the Gaullists took over the empire from the Giraudists, their personal liberty and even life.

.   .   .

There is, finally, a grave moral case to be made against the Vichy elite. There is, first of all, the charge of using the defeat of 1940 for narrowly sectarian purposes, to seek revenge upon the Popular Front and to remake France along new lines, no less partisan than the old and in the service of narrower interests. This does not mean that they had plotted the defeat of France in advance. But their domestic enmities were so all-consuming, after four years of the Popular Front and its successors, that they committed the most elementary of political errors. They wrote new laws under an armed foreign occupation.

There is also the charge of abetting the further internal division of France. No other major occupied country entered the war so torn; no other major occupied country used the occupation as the occasion for such a substantial restructuring of domestic institutions. When biographies of Marshal Pétain began to appear in 1966, it became regular practice to blame the poisons of division attending the Liberation upon de Gaulle's rigorous sectarianism and the upwelling of revenge encouraged by Resistance lawlessness. A will to healing reconciliation coexisted within the Liberation forces alongside a well-justified determination to purge and punish the collaborators, however. It was most visible in the Liberation army, a successful amalgam of Armistice Army, Free French, and Forces Françaises Libres under two ex-Pétiniste officers (Marshals de Lattre de Tassigny and Juin) and one Gaullist officer (Marshal Leclerc de Hauteclocque). If that will to reconciliation did not prevail over the will to revenge in 1944, it was very largely because the Vichy regime had not been the mere caretaker regime in 1940–44 that its defenders claim. Vichy waged another round in the virtual French civil war of the 1930s. Then, its geopolitical gamble having failed and war having ended neither in German victory nor in a French-mediated compromise but in total Allied victory, Vichy reaped the winds of sectarian passion that it had sown.

There is, finally, the issue of complicity. Continually repurchasing its shadow sovereignty at a higher and higher price, the Vichy regime made many Frenchmen accomplices in acts and policies that they would not normally have condoned. Marshal Pétain, in particular, was a figure to whom millions of Frenchmen looked with more than usual confidence. After the total occupation of France in November 1942, or at least after the constitutional crisis of November–December 1943, it was time to cease lending the stamp of one's approval to an enterprise that no longer worked. "Old age is a shipwreck," as de Gaulle observed, but Germans who met Pétain in 1943 still found him fresh and alert. Moreover, he was surrounded by men whose brilliance of preparation and of administrative career made them superior to the Third Republic leadership of the late 1930s. These able and intelligent men led other Frenchmen deeper into complicity with the besieged Third Reich's last desperate paroxysms: the Final Solution, forced labor, reprisals against a growing resistance. What can explain such egregious choices?

Tactical motives, the hope of saving France from worse, can not explain that complicity after November 1942. Of the four elements composing the Vichy bargaining position — military defeat, continuation of others in the war, the stranglehold of German occupation upon the richest two-thirds of France, and the exclusion from German grasp of the French fleet and empire — only the last one was ever within Vichy's control. After the total occupation of France, the scuttling of the French fleet, and the return of French North Africa to war in November 1942, Vichy no longer had even that leverage. Life was clearly no easier for Frenchmen by then than for the totally occupied Western European countries.

Clearly other motives led Frenchmen deeper into that final complicity. Bureaucratic inertia and blindness to considerations beyond the efficiency of the state were among them. Beyond that was the attraction of the National Revolution for its partisans.

At bottom, however, lay a more subtle intellectual culprit: fear of social disorder as the highest evil. Some of France's best skill and talent went into a formidable effort to keep the French state afloat under increasingly questionable circumstances. Who would keep order, they asked, if the state lost authority? By saving the state, however, they were losing the nation. Those who cling to the social order above all may do so by self-interest or merely by inertia. In either case, they know more clearly what they are against than what they are for. So blinded, they perform jobs that may be admirable in themselves but are tinctured with evil by the overall effects of the system. Even Frenchmen of the best intentions, faced with the harsh alternative of doing one's job, whose risks were moral and abstract, or practicing civil disobedience, whose risks were material and immediate, went on doing the job. The same may be said of the German occupiers. Many of them were "good Germans," men of cultivation, confident that their country's success outweighed a few moral blemishes, dutifully fulfilling some minor blameless function in a regime whose cumulative effect was brutish.

Readers will prefer, like the writer, to recognize themselves in neither of these types. It is tempting to identify with Resistance and to say, "That is what I would have done." Alas, we are far more likely to act, in parallel situations, like the Vichy majority. Indeed, it may be the German occupiers rather than the Vichy majority whom Americans, as residents of the most powerful state on earth, should scrutinize most unblinkingly. The deeds of occupier and occupied alike suggest that there come cruel times when to save a nation's deepest values one must disobey the state. France after 1940 was one of those times.

Choices in Vichy France

✳

JOHN SWEETS

John Sweets received his two graduate degrees from Duke University, and since 1977 has been teaching at the University of Kansas. How may his view of the Vichy regime be compared with that of Aron? What is the nature of his disagreement with Paxton and how does the question of defining a resister help explain this disagreement?

In describing their eventual fate and by treating them apart from the earlier discussion of the National Revolution, I do not wish to imply that the SOL [Service d'Ordre Légionnaire, which became the Milice Française, collaborationist groups] or the Milice — nor, for that matter, the Parisian collaborationists — were somehow foreign to the true French experience, or mere creatures of the occupation, unrelated to the French past. The best of recent scholarship has demonstrated conclusively that the history of Vichy is best understood as a whole. There was not a "Vichy of Pétain" in contrast to a "Vichy of Laval," but a regime that evolved over time in an increasingly authoritarian direction within a framework of changing conditions. The growing literature on the phenomenon of collaboration has established beyond question that these movements, representing to varying degrees a French form of fascism, although drawing special advantages from the occupation era, were firmly rooted in the French past. On the other hand, I do hope readers will see that these collaborationist organizations represented a very small minority of the French population. Most French people were unwilling to accept the ideology and programs associated with Vichy's National Revolution. A still greater number, indeed an overwhelming majority, rejected the more aggressive and violent designs of the collaborationist parties and the Milice, who, for themselves, rarely had any illusions about their unpopularity and isolation within the national community.

As often occurs with problems of historical interpretation, in recent years there has been a shift away from an earlier, particularly Gaullist perspective, which had portrayed France during the occupation as a nation of resisters with only a handful of rascally collaborators to mar the nation's behavior during this tragic era. A wave of films in the 1960s and 1970s — notably *The Sorrow and the Pity*, which purported to re-create the experience of Clermont-Ferrand during the war and occupation — and several important studies of collaborationist movements and individual collaborationist leaders have focused much more attention on those aspects of the era that were considered less pleasant, perhaps even better forgotten. We should not ignore the fascism, anti-Semitism, and other disreputable phenomena that rose to the surface in occupied France with generic French origins; but these should be placed in proper perspective. In otherwise excellent accounts, some of the authors of this recent literature on the collaborationists have exaggerated the strength of collaborationism, sometimes subtly by implication, or more directly by a questionable interpretation of statistics concerning membership in collaborationist groups. Although no serious study of which I am aware argues that collaborationists were more than a tiny minority of the population, we are led to believe that there were roughly as many collaborationists as resisters in France. As the liberation approached, the feud between these two extremist minorities erupted in a bloody civil war. Reaching this point, the pendulum of historical interpretation has swung far beyond a version that can be supported by a careful scrutiny of the evidence. If one were forced to choose a myth, the Gaullist version of a "nation of resisters" would be far more accurate than the new myth of a "nation of collaborators." Although there was a great deal of excitement and some violence, there was no "Franco-French civil war" at the liberation for the very good reason that there was virtually no one around anxious to fight for Vichy's New Order, much less for the more extreme visions of the ultracollaborationists. The tremendous surge of enthusiasm for the resistance was almost universal and represented a genuine following out of all proportion to the small comfort the population had afforded the collaborationist groups in their prime.

The status of the extreme right in France, at least as measured by the size of its constituency, *fell* during the German occupation, even though some of their ideas were incorporated into governmental policy, public activity on the part of their prewar rivals to the left was dissolved and prohibited, and they received some support from the Germans. In the 1930s Doriot's PPF [Parti Populaire Français] and Colonel de la Rocque's Parti Social Français (PSF) each attracted far more adherents than all of the wartime collaborationist groups combined. The PPF and the other collaborationist organizations were much less popular under the occupation, no doubt because they were linked so closely to the German conquerors in the popular mind. That so many people considered the collaborationists creatures of the Germans during the occupation helps to explain how they were so easily dismissed as "un-French" after the liberation. A brief discussion of the membership, motivations, and activities of the collaborationist groups at Clermont-Ferrand will suggest a theme of some continuity of leadership with past extremist organizations and demonstrate the futility of efforts by these groups to obtain popular support. Although the relative strength of these movements was undoubtedly greater in other parts of the country, local studies of collaborationist groups elsewhere indicate that the feeble response to collaborationist organizations at Clermont-Ferrand was not inconsistent with the general pattern for France.

.   .   .

In order to successfully convey the atmosphere or reconstitute the history of France under the German occupation, a reformulation of the definition of resistance is required. The notion of a small band of activist conspirators must be made to square with, or be incorporated into, a broader perspective that will account for the existence of an atmosphere in 1943–1944 in which resistance was nurtured by massive and widespread popular complicity, while collaboration, its polar opposite, was discouraged, and collaborators were made to feel like outcasts in their own land. The existence of an extensive network of sympathizers and accomplices beyond the framework of the organized resistance has sometimes been overlooked or underestimated in scholarly accounts of the Vichy period. The problem at one level is simply one of counting, where documentation is incomplete and often unreliable. Beyond that basic consideration are problems of definition and interpretation. We know that many individuals who were not members of resistance movements committed acts of opposition to the Vichy regime or to the Germans. How many such actions were necessary for one to be considered a resister? Or was membership in an organized group required before acts of opposition could be described as resistance? A definition that is limited to active members of organized groups has the advantage of greater precision, but such a limitation may prohibit an adequate appreciation of the *phenomenon of resistance*. A broader construction of the term *resistance*, involving a concept of *active opposition* to the Vichy regime and the Germans, is admittedly unwieldy. But it is also truer to the complex reality of the resistance in France.

To illustrate the methodological and interpretative issues involved, let us consider the conclusions of one of the most objective and fair-minded general histories of the Vichy period. Starting with what seems to be an unchallengeable proposition that most people in France were neither active resisters nor active collaborators, and repeating an earlier scholarly estimate that perhaps 400,000 persons, or 2 percent, of the adult population of France belonged to the resistance, Robert Paxton has written that if one lumps together volunteers for the Milice, regular police, and French guard units, "it is likely that *as many Frenchmen participated in 1943–44 in putting down 'disorder' as participated in active Resistance*," adding that "the overwhelming majority of Frenchmen, however they longed to lift the German yoke, did not want to lift it by fire and sword." Other authors, taking their cue from Paxton, or following a similar logic, have posited the concept of a "Franco-French" civil war at the liberation. According to this scenario, extremists on either side fought it out, while the vast majority of the population stood aside, uncommitted and uninvolved. Insofar as these perspectives have served to revise an earlier viewpoint — the myth that all the French were resisters during the Nazi occupation of France — they have served a useful purpose. Our study of Clermont-Ferrand and the Auvergne suggests that the revision has been overdrawn, that the idea of a "nation of resisters," while unquestionably an exaggeration, cannot be dismissed out of hand.

.   .   .

Consider, for example, that at least 543 persons, not included in the preceding figures [for members of resistance organizations], were executed (*fusillés*) "for acts of resistance" in the Auvergne (238 in the Puy-de-Dôme, 120 in the Cantal, 27 in the Haute-Loire, and 158 in the Allier); more than 1000 persons were arrested by the Germans in the Puy-de-Dôme in 1943 and 1944; and at least 1171 were deported from the Puy-de-Dôme to concentration camps in Germany or central Europe for political motives or resistance, as were hundreds of other suspected resisters in the other three departments of the region. If one adds several hundred persons the French police arrested on suspicion of Communist propaganda or "antinational" activity, many of whom were sent to internment camps, and recalls the massive opposition to the forced labor draft from which several thousand Auvergnats escaped by direct acts of disobedience, the total numbers of individuals *actively involved* in opposition to Vichy and the German occupation, although still a minority, becomes a substantial minority. Moreover, to this point we have dealt only with individuals who, after a great deal of painstaking research, could be identified and counted individually. What of those men and women who, while not found on the membership lists of a resistance formation, nor on the lists of deported, executed, or outlawed, contributed in a meaningful way to the resistance? Can one omit the doctors in the Puy-de-Dôme, who although not usually members of resistance movements, sabotaged the operation of the STO [Service du Travail Obligatoire] and the attempted requisition of men for railroad guard duty by signing hundreds of certificates of physical incapacity for individuals who the police complained continued "to pursue as usual their occupations"? What of the village priests who were credited by the resisters with numerous acts of bravery in sheltering those sought by French and German authorities, or those men and women who gave work, food, and shelter to maquis groups or individuals forced to live off of the land?

On Armistice Day 1943, in response to tracts signed by the CGT [Confédération Général du Travail, the largest trade union federation], MUR [Mouvements Unis de la Résistance, a major national resistance group], the Front National, and the Socialist Party, hundreds of workers at Ollier, Bergougnan, Michelin, and the other major factories at Clermont-Ferrand stopped working for ten or fifteen minutes at 11:00 A.M. in a symbolic protest, and even the thirty saleswomen at Prisunic joined them by crossing their arms in silence. Several months before that, when Marcel Michelin had been arrested by the Germans, all 7000 employees of the Michelin firm were preparing to go out on strike until the management convinced them that such an action might bring further harm to

Monsieur Michelin. Beyond such specific incidents, of which there are other examples, how can one quantify the amount of passive resistance involved in high worker absence from the workplace? Especially during the last months of the occupation, absence rates were 20 percent or more above normal in the mines and factories of the Puy-de-Dôme. Although loud explosions were more likely to draw attention to resistance sabotage, some resisters believed that much had been accomplished by workers in silent, but more subtle actions, such as faulty wiring of precision parts for airplane motors that were machined ever so slightly under specifications. Interestingly, at Clermont-Ferrand's most important industrial center, the Michelin works, management insisted that there be no sabotage in terms of inferior workmanship. The company was very concerned that Michelin uphold its reputation for making only "the best tires." On the other hand, the company produced far fewer tires than it was capable of manufacturing and was able to hide fairly significant quantities of material from German overseers. And, of course, the resistance movements had contacts in the factory who informed them when shipments of tires were scheduled for delivery, so that large quantities of "the best tires" would not arrive in Germany.

One could continue to enumerate an impressive array of individuals responsible for actions not attributable to the organized resistance — the fifteen-year-old girl who on her own initiative burned the records of hundreds of young men scheduled to be drafted for the STO, public employees charged with collecting and melting down metal statues who saved them from destruction by delays and falsification of records, directors and staff at Clermont-Ferrand's central hospital who were suspected by police of "a tacit connivance" with the resisters and political prisoners who seemed to escape with a remarkable frequency when in treatment there, or numerous PTT [Postes Télégraphes et Téléphones] agents singled out for particular praise by resistance leaders because of their courageous and timely warnings concerning military or police movements by German or French forces. A comprehensive listing would be at least as impressive as those more spectacular sabotage or guerilla actions of the organized resistance formations.

What was the cumulative impact of all of these isolated acts of opposition to the Vichy regime and the German occupation? In terms of "effectiveness" in hindering the German war machine, the value of such actions is impossible to calculate. Who knows how many, if any, airplane motors failed in flight or tanks broke down on the eastern front as a result of the sabotage of workers in factories at Clermont-Ferrand? We do know that factories in the city producing goods for Germany were constantly behind schedule in filling orders, despite the careful supervision of German officials. No one would claim that the hundreds of thousands of French men and women who listened to the BBC or read and passed on to friends copies of underground newspapers were great heroes, no more than were those who participated in symbolic strikes of short duration or mingled anonymously among crowds that gathered in city squares for fleeting demonstrations on May Day or Bastille Day. Yet these actions were illegal under Vichy France, and they signified a choice consciously made, and never entirely without risk.

Eugène Martres has concluded that one in six persons in the Cantal was associated with the resistance in one way or another as a sympathizer or active participant, suggesting that there were perhaps ten sympathizers for every resister. I have been unable to arrive at a satisfactory estimate of that kind for the Puy-de-Dôme, although resistance membership and the range of its activity was certainly higher there than in the Cantal. After more than fifteen years of research into the matter, I have become convinced that (short of a roll call in the hereafter) we will never have an entirely satisfactory statistical description of the French resistance. Even the rosters of FFI [Forces Françaises de l'Intérieur, resistance movement] and lists of the various resistance medals awarded after the liberation are highly untrustworthy gauges for minimum calculations. For example, at Clermont-Ferrand when Alphonse Rozier was asked by the prefect of the Puy-de-Dôme to suggest members of the Front National who had been particularly distinguished in their service to the resistance, Rozier suggested the name of a young woman, killed by the Germans, who had been an intelligence informant for his organization, and was a prostitute. The prefect apparently felt that there was something undignified or improper about awarding a resistance medal to a prostitute, and consequently Rozier refused to submit other names or accept a commendation himself. Therefore, the numbers of people active in the Front National are understated in "official" records of resistance membership. The problem, really, is not to add some names to one roster or subtract others where claims of resistance derring-do have been exaggerated. One must go beyond the ultimately insoluble issue of precise head counts to an appreciation of the general atmosphere, the climate in which resistance operated in the last two years of the German occupation.

Earlier chapters of this study have demonstrated the relatively rapid disenchantment of the Auvergnat population with Vichy's New Order and the patent failure of most of the regime's policies, the increasingly hostile reaction to German troops and occupation policies, the overwhelmingly negative response to genuine collaborationist groups, and the evolution of public opinion toward enthusiasm for a Gaullist political alternative. Therefore, it was not surprising that disgruntled police officers reported time after time that they were unable to obtain help from the local population in their efforts to fight resistance in the Auvergne. Gendarmes in the countryside cited "enormous difficulty in the search for information about the terrorists," and referred to "a veritable conspiracy of silence and a pretense of ignorance." Their colleagues in the cities remarked that witnesses to robberies or sabotage never seemed to remember license numbers and were never able to describe vehicles used by resisters, and they noted "a tacit complicity on the part of the population." Numerous documents originating from central police headquarters at Vichy indicated that this situation was not peculiar to the Auvergne — that "the individuals being sought often benefit from the sympathy of the population and start off with numerous accomplices."

If one is looking for heroes, a choice to remain silent was certainly not comparable to full-time commitment to resistance activism. Still, in the conditions of occupied France, the cumulative weight of such decisions was significant. Moreover, when one considers the other side of the coin, the climate in which the "forces of order" were operating, the difference was striking. As surely as a simple enumeration of membership in the FFI understates the size of the resistance in France, calculations of the total number of Milice, GMR [Gardes Mobiles de Réserve, an anti-resistance organization], and French police overstate the number of those *actively opposing* the resistance. First, effective Milice membership has often been greatly exaggerated. Instead of the more than 1000 adherents suggested by some accounts, no more than 250 men actually fought resisters in Milice formations drawn from the Puy-de-Dôme. According to the careful records of the officer in charge of all uniformed security forces for the Puy-de-Dôme, with headquarters at Clermont-Ferrand, 2237 men and officers were available for duty in the summer of 1944. Not only was this number well below the number of armed resisters in the department, but, for reasons that were discussed earlier in this chapter, these men were by no means reliable upholders of public order.

Not without reason had the Vichy regime begun to threaten its own servants with harsher and harsher penalties for failure to carry out the government's orders. In addition to the desertions on D-Day of large numbers of police and gendarmerie units surrendering their arms to maquis units, the verdicts of postliberation purge committees for the police and gendarmerie offer another indication of how little substantial support the Vichy regime enjoyed in its last months. Since the commission included a significant number of resisters, lenient treatment of officers who had actively fought the resistance was unlikely. Individual notations concerning those police examined by the purge commission suggest that it was almost impossible to be maintained on the police force if one had fired a weapon in operations against the maquis. Officers who had participated in such operations, but had shown no zeal in action versus the resistance, were not usually penalized. Under that sort of careful scrutiny, only 244 policemen in the Auvergne were sanctioned by loss of their job, transfer to another region, or some other form of punishment. In other words, aside from the Milice and a few GMR units, in the last months of the occupation resisters in the Auvergne did not find Vichy's "forces of order" to be serious threats, except, of course, when they operated in conjunction with German troops or the Gestapo.

No "Franco-French" civil war took place at the liberation in the Auvergne (nor for that matter elsewhere in France) because no one was left to fight for Vichy once the German troops had departed, taking with them the last diehard supporters of a French and European New Order. The liberation of France brought the establishment of the government of Charles de Gaulle without the widespread disorder and even chaos that some had predicted. No one should have been surprised. What a minority of French men and women had fought for during four long years was what almost everyone wanted — the Germans driven out of their country and freedom to choose their own way in the future. They had given scant aid and comfort to the enemy and little more to the government of Pétain and Laval. And when a skeptic asked, "What did you do when the Germans were there?" and thought that many seemed to embrace too eagerly the myth of a nation of resisters, most French people could answer honestly: "Our hearts were in the right place."

8

THE
HOLOCAUST

One would think that unlike other topics in this anthology the Holocaust does not lend itself to varying and conflicting interpretations. Except to a handful of perverse or anti-Semitic writers who deny it occurred, the facts seem clear. Nazi racial policy was described by Hitler in *Mein Kampf*, in which he stated his belief in Aryan racial supremacy and his contempt for "lesser" peoples. At the bottom rank, below that occupied by Slavs, were Jews and gypsies, as well as homosexuals from all racial and religious groups. In the 1930s, legislation was enacted to exclude German Jews from public life and to try to force them to emigrate. There is evidence that in conversations, in a speech, and in a memorandum dated 25 January, 1939, Hitler spoke of his intention to destroy the Jews. After World War II began and millions of Jews were brought under German control, thousands were murdered by SS troops.

A "final solution," that is, the annihilation of the Jews, was ordered in the summer of 1941. However, it soon became clear that such methods as machine-gun fire presented technical obstacles to genocide because of the large numbers of victims involved. In early 1942, at a conference in Wannsee, a Berlin suburb, plans were formulated by high-ranking Nazis for assembly-line destruction of the Jews by gassing. Six centers were established, the largest at a Polish rail center near the village of Auschwitz where an average of twelve to fifteen thousand deaths per day could be managed. From roundup points, Jews from everywhere in conquered Europe were dispatched by trains, and with horrible efficiency about six million were killed, approximately two thirds of the previous Jewish population of Europe and about two fifths of all the Jews in the world. Most came from Poland (three million) and the Soviet Union (one-and-a-half million), but with some exceptions, such as Denmark, Jews in other countries died in proportionate numbers. How mass extermination was carried out with ruthless efficiency is the subject of Raul Hilberg's meticulous and authoritative investigation.

Questions can nevertheless be raised. How did Nazi anti-Semitism evolve into mass murder? Hitler's racial ideology notwithstanding, was the Nazi leadership influenced by the additional millions of Jews in the newly conquered lands and by the imperatives of an inefficient bureaucracy? Exactly how important was Hitler's own role? Persecution could not have been effective without the participation — or acquiescence — of ordinary German men and women. How do we explain this? The debate between "intentionalists," convinced that mass destruction was decided on from the outset, and "functionalists," who see it as the end of an evolutionary process, is discussed by Michael Marrus. Of equal concern is the reaction, or lack of it, by the Allies, even when confronted with evidence that mass murder was taking place. Why did the Allies not aggressively try to save Jews before the war's end? Why did they refuse, for example, to bomb the rail facilities at Auschwitz? These issues are explored by Walter Lacqueur in the final reading.

The Destruction
of the European Jews

ᴗᴸᴢ

RAUL HILBERG

Raul Hilberg is a professor of political science at the University of Vermont. He came to the United States from Vienna, served in the U.S. Army, and, as a member of the War Documentation Project, examined masses of German records. He began work on *The Destruction of the European Jews* in 1948, and has published several studies concerning the fate of European Jews. He served as a member of the U.S. Holocaust Memorial Council, and testified for the Department of Justice in cases against individuals implicated in the killings. The following excerpt comes from the revised edition of *The Destruction of the European Jews*, a book concerned with the *process* by which the Holocaust took place. The "machinery" of destruction is recounted in sequential steps: the definition of who were Jews, their expropriation, their deportation, and, finally, their annihilation. The excerpt which follows describes the clearing of the ghettos Jews were forced to inhabit and the subsequent transportation to the extermination centers.

In the Reich-Protektorat area [most of Czechoslovakia], considerable difficulties were caused by privileged or semiprivileged categories of Jews. No such encumbrances hindered the deportations in Poland.

From Raul Hilberg, *The Destruction of the European Jews* (New York: Holmes and Meier, 1985) pp. 489–91, 492, 493–4, 497. Reprinted by permission of Holmes and Meier, Publishers, Inc.

There was no Mischling problem [half-Jew, of which there were different categories], no mixed-marriage problem, no old-Jews problem, no war-veterans problem. There were only a handful of foreign Jews in Poland, some of whom were pulled out of the ghettos at the very last minute and some of whom were shipped to killing centers by mistake. Only one major difficulty arose in connection with any particular group of Jews, and that problem did not become acute until the end of 1942: the labor shortage. Arrangements had to be made to keep a few skilled laborers alive a little longer. These arrangements, which were concluded at the close rather than at the beginning of the deportations, will be discussed later.

As the ghetto-clearing operations began, notice of roundups would sometimes be given to the Polish population in announcements posted a day or so in advance. The Poles were told that any ghetto passes in their possession were canceled, and they were warned against lingering in the streets or opening windows while the evacuation was in progress. Anyone interfering with the operation or giving shelter to Jews was going to be punished by death, and any unauthorized presence in a Jewish apartment was going to be construed as pillage.

Inside the ghettos, the policemen and their helpers had to cope with another problem: filth, sewage, and vermin. In the words of the Gettoverwaltung, the work was "nauseous in the extreme [*im äussersten Grade ekeleregend*]." In the Galician ghettos the police were confronted by vast epidemics. In the ghetto of Rawa Ruska, the Jewish population had concealed its sick in holes in the hope of saving them from deporta-tion. Before the Rawa Ruska Aktion was over, the SS and Police had dragged 3,000 sick and dying Jews out of their hiding places. We have no overall figures for German losses incurred by reason of the epidemics, but in Galicia alone SS and Police Leader Katzmann reported that one of his men had died of spotted fever and that another 120 had fallen ill with the disease.

After a ghetto was cleared of Jews, the police and municipal officials had to reenter the Jewish quarter and clean it up. Although Poles and Jews could be used for some of the dirtiest labor, the job was still far from pleasant. A large ghetto could be emptied in two or three days, but the cleanup operation required weeks or even months. Thus the Lublin ghetto was disbanded and its inhabitants deported April 17–20, 1942, but the cleanup action (*Säuberungsaktion*) was still in progress two months later.

The operation was carried out in stages. First, a demolition Kom-mando entered the ghetto and blew up all uninhabitable buildings. Next came the salvage crew (*die Lumpensammelkolonne*), which collected all sorts of junk left behind by the deportees. This detachment was followed by a clearing Kommando (*die Aufräumungskolonne*), which had to do the hardest work: the cleaning of the latrines. In some latrines the feces were piled up to a height of three feet. The Aufräumungskolonne had to use hoses to clean up the mess. The fourth crew consisted of carpenters and glass workers who sealed hermetically all doors and windows in order to enable the gas column (*Vergasungskolonne*) to kill all vermin in the apartments. Finally, the cleanup column (*Reinmachungskolonne*) was called up to remove the dead rats, mice, flies, and bugs, and to tidy up the place.

Still, the dilapidation in the ghettos was a comparatively minor annoyance in the total picture, and the bureaucrats were not much concerned with it. Their primary worry was the progress of the deportations, the rate at which Jewry was disappearing. The top men were interested only in speed. As early as June 18, 1942, Staatssekretär Dr. Bühler asked Higher SS and Police Leader Krüger when he would finish. Krüger replied that in August he would be able to "survey" the situation.

Krüger was a bit cautious because just then he was experiencing his first *Transportsperre*, a complete shutdown of traffic in deportation trains. The *Transportsperre* was instituted for only two weeks, and Krüger managed even then to wangle a few trains from Präsident Gerteis of the Ostbahn. Moreover, after the lifting of the restrictions, Krüger expected to resume the deportations with redoubled effort. Then, in July, another hitch occurred when the railway line to the killing center of Sobibór, on the Bug, broke down and had to be repaired. The SS and Police had hoped to deport several hundred thousand Jews to Sobibór.

On July 16, 1942, Obergruppenführer Wolff, chief of Himmler's Personal Staff, telephoned Staatssekretär Dr. Ganzenmüller of the Transport Ministry for help. Ganzenmüller looked into the situation and found that the matter had already been settled locally. Three hundred thousand Warsaw ghetto Jews had been diverted from Sobibór to Treblinka. Beginning on July 22, 1942, a daily train crammed with not fewer than 5,000 Jews per run was to leave Warsaw for Treblinka, while twice weekly another train carrying 5,000 Jews was to run from Przemyśl to Belzec. When Wolff received this news, he wrote the following letter of thanks:

> Dear Party Member Ganzenmüller:
>   For your letter of July 28, 1942, I thank you — also in the name of the Reichsführer-SS — sincerely [*herzlich*]. With particular joy [*mit besonderer Freude*] I noted your assurance that for two weeks now a train has been carrying, every day, 5,000 members of the chosen people to Treblinka, so

that we are now in a position to carry through this population movement [*Bevölkerungsbewegung*] at an accelerated tempo. I, for my part, have contacted the participating agencies to assure the implementation of the process without friction. I thank you again for your efforts in this matter and, at the same time, I would be grateful if you would give to these things your continued personal attention.

With best regards and

Heil Hitler!
Your devoted
W.

At the end of 1942, when the deportations were already two-thirds over, the SS and Police offices were confronted by another breakdown. Urgently, Krüger wrote to Himmler:

> SS and Police Leaders today report unanimously that by reason of Transportsperre every possibility of transport for Jewish resettlement is cut off from December 15, 1942, to January 15, 1943. Because of this measure, our master plan for Jewish resettlement is severely jeopardized.
>
> Obediently request that you negotiate with central offices of Armed Forces High Command and Transport Ministry for allocation of at least three pairs of trains for this urgent task [*dass mindestens 3 Zugpaare für die vordringliche Aufgabe zur Verfügung stehen*].

Apparently the negotiations were not very successful this time, for on January 20, 1943, Himmler wrote to Ganzenmüller for more trains. The Reichsführer pointed out that he knew under what strain the railway network was operating but that the allocation of the trains was, in the last analysis, in Ganzenmüller's own interest. The Jews, said Himmler, were responsible for all the railway sabotage in the Generalgouvernement, the Białystok district, and the occupied eastern territories. Hence the sooner the Jews were "cleared out," the better for the railways. While writing about the eastern Jews, Himmler also took occasion to remind Ganzenmüller that unless trains were made available for the Jews of the western occupied areas, sabotage would break out there too.

While the shortage of transport was a particularly pressing problem in the planning of the whole operation, a host of complications was to arise after the organizational problems were solved. These ramifications developed like shock waves from a single point of impact: the discovery by outsiders of the true nature of the "resettlements."

If concealment was difficult within the German-Czech area, it was doubly difficult in Poland. The Reich-Protektorat area had no death camps and most Reich transports were moving out to the east. Poland, on the other hand, was the home of all six killing centers and Polish transports were moving in short hauls of not more than 200 miles in all directions. Many eyes were fixed on those transports and followed them to their destinations. The deputy chief of the Polish Home Army (London-directed underground force), General Tadeusz Bor-Komorowski, reports that in the spring of 1942 he had complete information about the Kulmhof (Chełmno) killing center in the Warthegau. When the Germans cleared the Lublin ghetto, the Polish underground traced the transports to Bełżec. The underground command could not find out what was going on inside Bełżec, but, estimating that 130,000 Jews had been shoved into the camp, the Poles concluded that it "was not big enough to accommodate such a large number of people." In July 1942 the Home Army collected reports from railroad workers that several hundred thousand Jews had disappeared in Treblinka without a trace.

Sometimes the information spilling out of the camps was quite specific. In the Lublin district the council chairman of the Zamość ghetto, Mieczysław Garfinkiel, was a recipient of such news. During the early spring of 1942 he heard that the Jews of Lublin were being transported in crowded trains to Bełżec and that the empty cars were being returned after each trip for more victims. He was asked to obtain some additional facts and, after contacting the nearby Jewish communities of Tomaszów and Bełżec, was given to understand that 10,000 to 12,000 Jews were arriving daily in a strongly guarded compound located on a special railroad spur and surrounded by barbed wire. The Jews were being killed there in a "puzzling manner." Garfinkiel, an attorney, did not give credence to these reports. After a few more days, two or three Jewish strangers who had escaped from Bełżec told him about gassings in barracks. Still he did not believe what he heard. On April 11, 1942, however, there was a major roundup in Zamość itself. Counting the remaining population of his ghetto, Garfinkiel calculated a deficit of 3,150 persons. The next day, the thirteen-year-old son of one of the council functionaries (Wolsztayn) came back from the camp. The boy had seen the naked people and had heard an SS man make a speech to them. Hiding, still clothed, in a ditch, the young Wolsztayn had crawled out under the barbed wire with the secret of Bełżec.

What the Home Army had found out through its investigations, and what Garfinkiel had discovered almost unwittingly, ordinary people were suspecting without much proof. The population drew its conclusions quickly and spread them as rumors throughout the occupied Polish territory. By late summer of 1942 almost every inhabitant of Poland, whether outside or inside a ghetto, had some inkling of what was going on. In the end even children knew the purpose of the deportations. When, during the summer of 1944 in the Łódź ghetto, the children of an orphanage were piled on trucks, they cried, "*Mir viln nisht shtarbn!* [We don't want to die!]"

·   ·   ·

The Jewish leadership in the Polish ghettos stood at the helm of the compliance movement, and ghetto chiefs were the implementors of the surrender. Always they delivered up some Jews to save the other Jews. Having "stabilized" the situation, the ghetto administration would bisect the remaining community. And so on. Moses Merin, president of the Central Council of Elders for Eastern Upper Silesia, presided over such a shrinking process. On the eve of the first deportations, Merin made his first decision. "I will not be afraid," he said, to "sacrifice 50,000 of our community in order to save the other 50,000." During the summer of 1942 the other 50,000 Jews were lined up in a mass review, from which half were sent to Auschwitz. Merin commented after that deportation: "I feel like a captain whose ship was about to sink and who succeeded in bringing it safe to port by casting overboard a great part of his precious cargo." By 1943 there were only a few survivors. Merin addressed them in the following words: "I stand in a cage before a hungry and angry tiger. I stuff his mouth with meat, the flesh of my brothers and sisters, to keep him in his cage lest he break loose and tear us all to bits."

Throughout Poland the great bulk of the Jews presented themselves voluntarily at the collecting points and boarded the trains for transport to killing centers. Like blood gushing out of an open wound, the exodus from the ghettos quickly drained the Polish Jewish community of its centuries-old life.

However, in an operation of such dimensions not everybody could be deported so smoothly. As the circle of Jewish survivors shrank, the awareness of death increased, and the psychological burden of complying with German "evacuation" orders became heavier and heavier. Toward the end of the operations increasing numbers of Jews hesitated to move out, while others fled from the ghettos or jumped from trains to find refuge in the woods. In the Warsaw ghetto a few of the surviving Jews rallied in a last-minute stand against the Germans.

The Germans reacted to the recalcitrant Jews with utmost brutality. Howling raiders descended upon the ghettos with hatchets and bayonets. In the Warthegau the police were sent into such actions in a half-drunken stupor. Every Gestapo man assigned to ghetto-clearing duty received daily an extra ration of a little over half a pint of brandy. The Gettoverwaltung in Łódź demanded a brandy allocation for its employees, too, on the ground that employment without such brandy was "irresponsible." In Galicia the Jews were particularly aware of their fate because they had already witnessed the mobile killing operations in 1941. In the words of the SS and Police report, they "tried every means in order to dodge evacuation." They concealed themselves "in every imaginable corner, in pipes, chimneys, even in sewers." They "built barricades in passages of catacombs, in cellars enlarged to dugouts, in underground holes, in cunningly contrived hiding places in attics and sheds, within furniture, etc."

In the Galician operations massacres were interspersed with deportations, particularly during the *Transportsperren* in the early summer of 1942 and in December–January 1942–43. Often, the old and infirm Jews were not transported at all, but shot in the course of the roundup. The general mode of procedure in Galicia may be illustrated by events in three towns.

In Stanisławow, about 10,000 Jews had been gathered at a cemetery and shot on October 12, 1941. Another shooting took place in March 1942, followed by a ghetto fire lasting for three weeks. A transport was sent to Bełżec in April, and more shooting operations were launched in the summer, in the course of which Jewish council members and Order Service men were hanged from lampposts. Large transports moved out to Bełżec in September and October, an occasion marked by the bloody clearing of a hospital and (according to reports heard by a German agricultural official) a procession of Jews moving to the train station on their knees.

The Galician town of Rawa Ruska, only about twenty miles from Bełżec, was a railway junction through which deportation trains passed frequently. A survivor, Wolf Sambol, recalling scenes of shootings in the town, quotes a drunken Gendarmerie man shouting at the victims: "You are not Jews anymore, you are the chosen. I am your Moses and I will lead you through the Red Sea." He then opened fire at the victims with an automatic weapon. The same survivor remembers a little girl under the corpses, pushing herself out covered with blood, and looking carefully to the right and left, running away. Transports moved out of Rawa Ruska as soon as the *Sperre* [blockade] was lifted in July 1942. Although the nature of Bełżec was no longer a secret that summer, the Rawa Ruska Jewish Council pursued a cooperative course, and large numbers of Jews gathered at the collecting point for transport. Their wish, said Sambol, was to live half an hour longer (*Ihr Wunsch ist es, eine halbe Stunde älter zu sein*). Several thousand others, however, sought to hide, and many jumped from trains.

One transport pulled out from the southern Galician town of Kołomyja on September 10, 1942. In its fifty cars it carried 8,205 deportees. Some of the victims had been driven to the train on foot from villages in the area, while others had been waiting in the town itself. Neither group had had much to eat for days before departure. The slowness of the train, pulled by an underpowered locomotive that periodically had to stop, contributed to the agony of the Jews inside. They stripped off their clothes in the heat, ripped off the barbed wire at the aperture near the ceiling of the car, and tried to squeeze through and jump out. The Order Police Kommando, consisting of one officer and fifteen men, shot all of its ammunition, obtained more rounds from army personnel along the way, and finally hurled stones at escapees. When the train arrived in Bełżec, 200 of those aboard were dead.

Such scenes aroused people in the entire district. Once a Polish policeman related his experiences freely to an ethnic German woman who then wrote anonymously to Berlin. Her letter reached the *Reichskanzlei*. The Polish policeman, she wrote, had asked her whether she was not finally ashamed of being an ethnic German. He had now become acquainted with German culture. During the dissolution of the ghettos, children had been thrown on the floor and their heads trampled with boots. Many Jews whose bones had been broken by rifle butts were thrown into graves and covered with calcium flour. When the calcium began to boil in the blood, one could still hear the crying of the wounded.

The Holocaust in History

∿∕∕∾

MICHAEL MARRUS

Michael Marrus teaches at the University of Toronto. He has published a book on the assimilation of the French Jews at the time of
the Dreyfus Affair, and has co-authored an acclaimed study of the
Jews and Vichy France. The work from which the following is taken,
The Holocaust in History, received widespread applause for its assessment of scholarly knowledge on the Holocaust. Do the arguments
of the "intentionalists" or those of the "functionalists" seem the
more persuasive? Why? What appears to be Marrus' view?

For an important body of historical opinion, the questions asked
about the emergence of the Final Solution can be answered easily with
reference to Hitler's anti-Jewish rhetoric, drawn from various points in
his career but seen to reflect a consistent murderous objective. In this
view, Hitler is seen as the driving force of Nazi anti-semitic policy, whose
views indicate a coherent line of thought from a very early point. Hitler
is also seen as the sole strategist with the authority and the determination
to begin the implementation of the Final Solution. In what is probably
the most widely read work on this subject, Lucy Dawidowicz argues that
the Führer set the stage for mass murder in September 1939, with the

From Michael Marrus, *The Holocaust in History*, pp. 34–38, 40–46. First published by
University Press of New England, 1987. Copyright © 1987 Michael Marrus. Reprinted by
permission of the author.

attack on Poland. "War and the annihilation of the Jews were interdependent," she writes. "The disorder of war would provide Hitler with the cover for the unchecked commission of murder. He needed an arena for his operations where the restraints of common codes of morality and accepted rules of warfare would not extend." September 1939, therefore, saw the beginning of "a twofold war": on the one hand there was the war of conquest for traditional goals such as raw materials and empire; on the other there was the "war against the Jews," the decisive confrontation with the greatest enemy of the Third Reich. Orders to begin Europe-wide mass murder, issued in the late spring or summer of 1941, are seen as flowing directly from Hitler's idea on Jews, expressed as early as 1919. On various occasions his "program of annihilation" may have been camouflaged or downplayed. But Dawidowicz insists that it was always his intention: "Once Hitler adopted an ideological position, even a strategic one, he adhered to it with limpetlike fixity, fearful lest he be accused, if he changed his mind, of incertitude, of capriciousness on 'essential questions.' He had long-range plans to realize his ideological goals, and the destruction of the Jews was at their center."

Borrowing from the British historian Tim Mason, Christopher Browning was the first to dub this interpretation "intentionalist," linking it to other historiographical themes in the history of the Third Reich. This line of thought accents the role of Hitler in initiating the murder of European Jewry, seeing a high degree of persistence, consistency, and orderly sequence in Nazi anti-Jewish policy, directed from a very early point to the goal of mass murder. Like much of the interpretative literature on Nazism, this explanation of the Final Solution rests on quotations and depends, in the final analysis, on the notion of a Hitlerian "blueprint" for future policies, set forth in *Mein Kampf* and other writings and speeches. Critics of this approach, referred to as "functionalists," are rather impressed with the evolution of Nazi goals, with the sometimes haphazard course of German policies, and with the way that these are related to the internal mechanisms of the Third Reich.

Intentionalism, it may be supposed, was born at Nuremberg in 1945, when American prosecutors first presented Nazi crimes as a carefully orchestrated conspiracy, launched together with the war itself. At that time American legal experts hoped to prove that there had been a deliberate plan to commit horrendous atrocities as well as other breaches of international law; in this way they expected to designate certain German organizations and institutions as part of a criminal conspiracy, vastly

simplifying the work of future prosecutions. Years later, after much historical analysis, many historians still accept the notion of an unfolding
Hitlerian plan. In his detailed critique of David Irving, for example,
Gerald Fleming sees an "unbroken continuity of specific utterances"
leading from Hitler's first manifestations of anti-semitism "to the liquidation orders that Hitler personally issued during the war." A major
task of Fleming's work is the collection of such utterances, which the
author hopes will tear away the camouflage covering Hitler's primary
responsibility.

One can sympathize with an effort to remind a sometimes negligent
audience of Hitler's incessant, raving hatred of Jews. And it is similarly
valuable to expose the Nazis' linguistic perversions — distortions intended
to conceal the killing process from the victims, from the Allies, and from
the German public as well. Nevertheless, the problem of interpreting
Hitlerian rhetoric still remains. For the fact is that Hitler was forever
calling for the most ruthless action; for sudden, crushing blows; for the
complete annihilation of his foes; or evoking his irrevocable, ironlike
determination to do this or that. We cannot ignore Hitler's amply demonstrated blood lust, and there is no doubt that the contemplation of
mass killing inspired him on more than one occasion. In retrospect,
historians have little difficulty in tracing "direct lines," but it is much
more problematic to ascertain what Hitler actually intended and how he
acted on such expressions at specific moments. In May 1938, for example,
Hitler told his generals of his "unalterable decision to destroy Czechoslovakia by military action in the foreseeable future." According to Gerhard
Weinberg, the Nazi leader indeed wanted military action, but believed he
could avoid a general war. When he learned in September, on the eve of
his attack, that a general war threatened, that neither Mussolini nor the
German public were likely to follow him, and that he could achieve a
stunning success peacefully, he changed his mind. So "unalterable decisions" could be altered. The implication is that Hitler's words should
indeed be taken seriously, but that they must also be seen in the context
of his actions and the concrete situations he faced.

This is a reasonable reply to the use made of Hitler's famous speech
of 30 January 1939 by intentionalist historians such as Dawidowicz and
Fleming. Adopting a characteristically "prophetic" tone in his address to
the Reichstag, Hitler issued a terrible warning: "One thing I should like
to say on this day which may be memorable for others as well as for us
Germans: In the course of my life I have very often been a prophet, and I

have usually been ridiculed for it. During the time of my struggle for power it was in the first instance the Jewish race which only received my prophecies with laughter when I said that I would one day take over the leadership of the State, and with it that of the whole nation, and that I would then among many other things settle the Jewish problem. Their laughter was uproarious, but I think that for some time now they have been laughing on the other side of their face. Today I will once more be a prophet. If the international Jewish financiers outside Europe should succeed in plunging the nations once more into a world war, then the result will not be the bolshevization of the earth, and thus the victory of Jewry, but the annihilation of the Jewish race in Europe."

Fleming is certainly right to stress the importance of Hitler's self-portrayal as a "fighting prophet," and Hitler's subsequent references to this speech in the middle of the war indicate a conscious desire, once the Final Solution was under way, to assert a continuity of actions against the Jews. This is but one of many pieces of evidence that suggest Hitler insisted on a definitive solution to the Jewish question, and in this sense the speech is an important measure of his priorities. Less clear, however, is what the January speech tells us about Hitler's objectives at the time. A look at his words in context shows that Hitler spoke for several hours, but devoted only a few minutes to the Jews. Speaking in the wake of the Munich conference, Hitler focused mainly on economic matters, in an address judged by the British ambassador to be relatively conciliatory. One of the purposes of Hitler's address was likely to sow confusion and division among the Western powers. He probably did envisage war in Europe as his "prophecy" suggested; but this was likely not a world war, but rather a fight over Poland, which would be over quickly. As Uwe Dietrich Adam points out, Hitler and other Nazi leaders looked to an even more ruthless crackdown on Jews in the event of war. We shall never know for certain precisely what plans lurked in Hitler's consciousness and whether his reference to "annihilation" at that particular time should be taken literally. But it is not at all plain that he had fixed upon mass murder, which presumably would have to begin once the short Polish campaign was over. And it is even less likely that Hitler thought concretely about Europe-wide killings, which he was not in a position to undertake until his stunning military successes in 1940–41.

.   .   .

Against this interpretation, so-called functionalist historians present a picture of the Third Reich as a maze of competing power groups, rival bureaucracies, forceful personalities, and diametrically opposed interests engaged in ceaseless clashes with each other. They see Hitler as a brooding and sometimes distant leader, who intervened only spasmodically, sending orders crashing through the system like bolts of lightning. While in theory the power of the Führer was without limit, in practice he preferred the role of arbiter, according legitimacy to one or another favorite or line of conduct. Add to this Hitler's curious leadership style — his inability to mount a sustained effort, his procrastination, his frequent hesitation — and one can understand the reluctance of many to accept the idea of a far-reaching scheme or ideological imperative necessitating the Final Solution. Few historians of this school doubt that Hitler was murderously obsessed with Jews; they question, however, whether he was capable of long-term planning on this or any other matter, and they tend to look within the chaotic system itself for at least some of the explanation for the killing of European Jews.

Reflecting this perspective, Martin Broszat's 1977 critique of David Irving's *Hitler's War* presented to a wide public a serious interpretation of the origins of the Final Solution in which Hitler did not have full operational responsibility. Broszat's approach was hardly an exculpation of the Nazi leader. On the contrary, he took Irving to task for his "normalization" of Hitler and pointed to dangerous forces within the German Federal Republic that utilized the apologetic drift in the British historian's work. Broszat reasserted Hitler's "fanatical, destructive will to annihilate" that traditional historiography has always seen at the core of the Führer's personality. He stressed Hitler's "totally irresponsible, self-deceiving, destructive and evilly misanthropic egocentricity and his lunatic fanaticism." As the author of a 1969 work, *Der Staat Hitlers*, Broszat had no doubt about who was in charge and what kind of a person he was.

Nevertheless, the heart of Broszat's argument was that the Final Solution was not begun after a single Hitlerian decision, but arose "bit by bit." He suggested that deportations and systematic killings outside the sphere of the Einsatzgruppen in Russia started through local Nazi initiatives, rather than a directive from the Führer. According to this view, Hitler set the objective of Nazism: "to get rid of the Jews, and above all to make the territory of the Reich *judenfrei*, i.e., clear of Jews" — but without specifying how this was to be achieved. In a vague way, the top Nazi leadership hoped to see the Jews pushed off to the east, and uprooted large masses of people with this in mind. Top Nazi officials had "no clear aims . . . with respect to the subsequent fate of the deportees," however. Their policy was "governed by the concept that the enormous spaces to be occupied in the Soviet Union would . . . offer a possibility for getting rid of the Jews of Germany and of the allied and occupied countries," but they also toyed with other schemes, such as the Madagascar Plan, to achieve their objectives. Expectations of an early resolution heightened during the Russian campaign, which was supposed to finish in a matter of weeks. Deportation trains carrying Jews from the Reich began to roll eastward. Yet by the autumn these plans were upset. Military operations slowed, and then came to a standstill. Transportation facilities were over-loaded. Nazi officers in the occupied east, receiving shipments of Jews from the Reich, now complained that they had no more room in the teeming, disease-ridden ghettos. It was then, in Broszat's view, that Nazi officials on the spot started sporadically to murder the Jews who arrived from the west. Killing, therefore, "began not solely as the result of an ostensible will for extermination but also as a 'way out' of a blind alley into which the Nazis had manoeuvered themselves." In its early stages, annihilation was improvised, and its execution was marked by confusion and misunderstanding. Only gradually, in early 1942, did Himmler and the SS establish the coherent structures of the Final Solution, coordinated on a Europe-wide basis.

Among functionalists, Hans Mommsen has presented the most forceful case for a Führer uninvolved in and perhaps incapable of administration, concerned rather with his personal standing and striking propaganda postures. Mommsen goes even further than Broszat in suggesting that Hitler had little directly to do with anti-Jewish policy. While not denying the Führer's intense hatred of Jews, Mommsen sees the Nazi leader as thinking about the Jews mainly in propagandistic terms, without bothering to chart a course of action. The Final Solution, he observes, resulted from the interaction of this fanatical but distant leader with the chaotic structure of the Nazi regime. In the Third Reich, office was piled upon office, and underlings were left to find their way in a bureaucratic and administrative jungle. The only guide to success, and a compelling one, was fidelity to the Hitlerian vision. Underlings competed for the favor of this ideologically obsessed, but essentially lazy leader. Given the Führer's mad compulsions, this competition programmed the regime for "cumulative radicalization," a process that ended ultimately, of course, in its self-destruction. Hitler's heightened rhetoric prompted others to realize his "utopian" ravings about Jews and undoubtedly stimulated murderous excesses. But he issued no order for the Final Solution and had nothing to do with its implementation.

.   .   .

The crisis came with Barbarossa, not only because of the apocalyptic character of the campaign, but also because it promised to bring hundreds of thousands more Jews within the hegemony of the Reich. What were the Germans to do with them? During the early course of the campaign Hitler tipped the scales for mass murder. The decision to massacre the Soviet Jews was probably taken in March, as part of the Barbarossa planning process. Before the end of July, Hitler, buoyed up by the spectacular successes of the Wehrmacht in the early part of the Russian campaign, probably issued his order for Europe-wide mass murder. At that point, the Führer likely felt, everything was possible. On 31 July, Göring authorized Heydrich to prepare a "total solution" (*Gesamtlösung*) of the Jewish question in the territories under the Nazis' control. Before long, work began on the first two death camps — at Belzec and Chelmno, where construction started in the autumn. On 23 October, Himmler issued a fateful order that passed along the Nazi chain of command: henceforth there would be no Jewish emigration permitted anywhere from German-held territory. On 29 November, invitations went out to the Wannsee Conference, intended to coordinate deportations from across Europe. The Final Solution was about to begin.

Browning and others have criticized the work of various functionalists on three grounds. First, they challenge Adam's notion that pushing great masses of Jews off "to the east" was still an option for the Nazis in the summer of 1941. No concrete preparations for such a massive deportation have ever been discovered, and it is unlikely that serious planning for it could have been under way without leaving a trace in the historical record. Göring's authorization to Heydrich on 31 July to prepare a "total solution" could hardly have referred to such expulsions, they say, since Heydrich already had such authority and had been expelling Jews on a smaller scale since the beginning of 1939. Seen in the context of the furious killings then under way by the Einsatzgruppen, Göring's communication appears rather like a warrant for genocide. Like many, Klaus Hildebrand finds it difficult to distinguish between the gigantic operations of the killing teams in Russia and the other aspects of the Final Solution. "In qualitative terms the executions by shooting were no different from the technically more efficient accomplishment of the 'physical final solution' by gassing, of which they were a prelude." Second, historians have challenged Broszat's idea of locally initiated mass murders. Not only does it seem unlikely that the systematic killing of Jews from the Reich, for example, could have been undertaken without the Führer's agreement, there is also too little evidence of local initiatives with which to sustain this theory. As Eberhard Jäckel noted recently, there is rather "a great deal of evidence that some [local officials] were shocked or even appalled when the final solution came into effect. To be sure, they did not disagree with it. But they agreed only reluctantly, referring again to an order given by Hitler. This is a strong indication that the idea did not originate with them."

Third, Browning contends that the decision for Europe-wide mass murder was taken in the summer of 1941, in the euphoria of the first victories in the Barbarossa campaign, and not a few months later. He draws upon postwar evidence from Rudolf Höss, the commandant of Auschwitz, and Adolf Eichmann, from the start a key official in the bureaucracy of the Final Solution, to the effect that the Führer's mind was made up during the summer. This sense of timing differs notably from functionalists who conclude that the Final Solution arose from disappointment with the outcome of the fighting in Russia. Adam, for example, sees the Nazis depressed by the prospect of having to spend another winter with the Jews; the journalist Sebastian Haffner imagines, much less plausibly, that Hitler saw as early as the end of 1941 that the European war could not be won and that the other contest, "the war against the Jews," could at least be pursued to its final conclusion.

Outsiders to these disputes may well suspect that some of the sharp edges of the controversy are wearing off and that there is more agreement among these historians than meets the eye. Opinion is widespread that there was some Hitlerian decision to initiate Europe-wide killing. The range of difference over timing extends across only a few months, with intentionalists positing a Führer order sometime in March 1941, with Browning and others opting for the summer, and with a few, such as Adam, looking toward the early autumn. What finally precipitated this decision, however, is likely to remain a mystery. Military historians tell us that, despite the extraordinary successes of the Wehrmacht in the first weeks of the Barbarossa campaign, the Germans found the going difficult as early as mid-July 1941. Although their forces advanced great distances and destroyed much of their opposition, they were surprised at the extent and efficacy of Soviet resistance and were greatly slowed by faulty intelligence, poor roads and bridges, and marshes. Chief of the army general staff Franz Halder portrayed an exasperated Führer after only six weeks of fighting, and it seems likely that by late August Hitler already knew that the war would continue well into 1942. This was a major setback, even though the Germans did not taste real defeat until December. Whether euphoria or disappointment prompted the decision is therefore difficult to say. On the other hand, the idea of Hitler breaking the logjam caused by an ill-defined policy rings true, given what we know of his leadership style. Students of Hitler's behavior in other areas have been struck by his preference for sudden, unexpected, spectacular coups. His was the method of the supreme gambler, "forever looking for short cuts." For someone as ruthless and fanatical as Hitler, a decision for the Final Solution can well be imagined in the apocalyptic atmosphere of Barbarossa, the war to settle once and for all the fate of the thousand-year Reich.

"La guerre révolutionna la Révolution," French historian Marcel Reinhard once wrote about the revolutionary impact of the war of 1792 on the revolutionaries in Paris. So it has been observed that the war against the Soviet Union revolutionized the Third Reich, and it is not surprising that this campaign transformed Nazi Jewish policy as well. It is difficult to follow the process of political and ideological radicalization in detail, for this was a period of extensive fluidity — even for a regime that, as Karl Dietrich Bracher has said, "remained in a state of permanent improvisation." Ian Kershaw observes that "the summer and autumn of 1941 were characterized by a high degree of confusion and contradictory interpretations of the aims of anti-Jewish policy by the Nazi authorities." It seems useful, however, to understand Jewish policy in this period as evolving within a genocidal framework — extending beyond Jews to include the incurably ill, Soviet intelligentsia, prisoners of war, and others as well. In this fevered atmosphere, incredible as it may seem, an "order" to send millions of people to their deaths may have been no more than a "nod" from Hitler to one of his lieutenants.

The Terrible Secret

⬥

WALTER LAQUEUR

Walter Laqueur was born in Germany but left in 1938. A distinguished professor of history, he is an eminent commentator and an expert in international affairs. He chairs the International Research Council of the Center for Strategic and International Studies at Georgetown University and edits the *Washington Quarterly*, a review of strategic and international issues. He also directs the Institute of Contemporary History and the Wiener Library in London, co-edits the *Journal of Contemporary History*, and teaches contemporary history at Tel Aviv University. His books include studies on European history, the Middle East, guerrilla movements, Zionism, terrorism, fascism, nationalism, and human rights. Do all of Laqueur's answers appear equally valid, or are some more credible than others?

The evidence gathered so far shows that news of the 'final solution' had been received in 1942 all over Europe, even though all the details were not known. If so, why were the signals so frequently misunderstood and the message rejected?

The fact that Hitler had given an explicit order to kill all Jews was not known for a long time. His decision was taken soon after he had made up his mind to invade Russia. Victor Brack, who worked at the time in Hitler's Chancellery, said in evidence at Nuremberg that it was no secret in higher party circles by March 1941 that the Jews were to be exterminated. But 'higher party circles' may have meant at the time no more than a dozen people. In March 1941, even Eichmann did not know, for the preparations for the deportations and the camps had not yet been made. First instructions to this effect were given in Goering's letter to Heydrich of 31 July 1941. The fact that an order had been given by Hitler became known outside Germany only in July 1942 and even then in a distorted form: Hitler (it was then claimed) had ordered that no Jew should be left in Germany by the end of 1942. But there is no evidence that such a time limit had ever been set. It would not have been difficult, for instance, to deport all Jews from Berlin in 1942, but in fact the city was declared empty of Jews by Goebbels only in August 1943. Witnesses claimed to have seen the order, but it is doubtful whether there ever was a written order. This has given rise to endless speculation and inspired a whole 'revisionist' literature — quite needlessly, because Hitler, whatever his other vices, was not a bureaucrat. He was not in the habit of giving written orders on all occasions: there were no written orders for the murderous 'purge' of June 1934, for the killing of gypsies, the so-called euthanasia action (T4) and on other such occasions. The more abominable the crime, the less likely that there would be a written 'Führer order.' If Himmler, Heydrich or even Eichmann said that there was such an order, no one would question or insist on seeing it.

The order had practical consequences, it affected the lives or, to be precise, the deaths of millions of people. For this reason details about the 'final solution' seeped out virtually as soon as the mass slaughter started.

The systematic massacres of the *Einsatzgruppen* [mobile killing units] in Eastern Galicia, White Russia, the Ukraine and the Baltic countries became known in Germany almost immediately. True, the scene of the slaughter was distant and it took place in territories in which at the time civilians and foreigners were not freely permitted to travel. But many thousands of German officers and soldiers witnessed these scenes and later reported them and the same is true of Italian, Hungarian and Romanian military personnel. The German Foreign Ministry was officially informed about the details of the massacres; there was much less secrecy about the *Einsatzgruppen* than later on about the extermination camps. The Soviet Government must have learned about the massacres within a few days; after several weeks the news became known in Western capitals too, well before the Wannsee Conference. The slaughter at Kiev (Babi Yar) took place on 29–30 September 1941. Foreign journalists knew about it within a few days; within less than two months it had been reported in the Western press. The massacres in Transniestria became known almost immediately. Chelmno, the first extermination camp, was opened on 8 December 1941; the news was received in Warsaw within less than four weeks and published soon afterwards in the underground press. The existence and the function of Belzec and Treblinka were known in Warsaw among Jews and non-Jews within two weeks after the gas chambers had started operating. The news about the suicide of Czerniakow, the head of the Warsaw *Judenrat*, reached the Jewish press abroad within a short time. The deportations from Warsaw were known in London after four days. There were some exceptions: the true character of Auschwitz did not become known among Jews and Poles alike for several months after the camp had been turned into an extermination centre. At the time in Poland it was believed that there were only two types of camps, labour camps and extermination camps, and the fact that Auschwitz was a 'mixed camp' seems to have baffled many.

If so much was known so quickly among the Jews of Eastern Europe and if the information was circulated through illegal newspapers and by other means — there were wireless sets in all major ghettos — why was it not believed? In the beginning Russian and Polish Jewry were genuinely unprepared, and the reasons have been stated: Soviet Jews had been kept uninformed about Nazi intentions and practices, Polish Jews believed that the massacres would be limited to the former Soviet territories. At first there was the tendency to interpret these events in the light of the past: persecution and pogroms. The Jewish leaders in Warsaw who learned about events in Lithuania and Latvia in early 1942 should have realized that these were not 'pogroms' in the traditional sense, spontaneous mob actions, nor excesses committed by local commanders. There are few arbitrary actions in a totalitarian regime. The *Einsatzgruppen* acted methodically and in cold blood. The majority of Jewish leaders in Eastern Europe did not yet realize that this was the beginning of a systematic campaign of destruction. The whole scheme was beyond human imagination; they thought the Nazis incapable of the murder of millions. Communication between some of the ghettos was irregular; Lodz ghetto, the second largest, was more or less isolated. But rumours, on the other hand, still travelled fast. If the information about the 'final solution' had been believed it would have reached every corner of Poland within a few days. But it was not believed and when the 'deportations' from Polish ghettos began in March 1942 it was still generally thought that the Jews would be transported to places further East.

.   .   .

Jewish leaders and the public abroad (Britain, America and Palestine) found it exceedingly difficult in their great majority to accept the ample evidence about the 'final solution' and did so only with considerable delay. They too thought in categories of persecution and pogroms at a time when a clear pattern had already emerged which pointed in a different direction. It was a failure of intelligence and imagination caused on one hand by a misjudgment of the murderous nature of Nazism, and on the other hand by a false optimism. Other factors may have played a certain role: the feeling of impotence ('we can do very little, so let us hope for the best'), the military dangers facing the Jewish community in Palestine in 1942. If the evidence was played down by many Jewish leaders and the Jewish press, it was not out of the desire to keep the community in a state of ignorance, but because there were genuine doubts. As the worst fears were confirmed, there was confusion among the leaders as to what course of action to choose. This was true especially in the US and caused further delay in making the news public. In Jerusalem the turning point came with the arrival of a group of Palestinian citizens who had been repatriated from Europe in November 1942. The leaders of the Jewish Agency, who had been unwilling to accept the written evidence gathered by experienced observers, were ready to believe the accounts delivered by chance arrivals in face-to-face meetings.

.   .   .

Millions of Germans knew by late 1942 that the Jews had disappeared. Rumours about their fate reached Germany mainly through officers and soldiers returning from the eastern front but also through other channels. There were clear indications in the wartime speeches of the Nazi leaders that something more drastic than resettlement had happened. Knowledge about the exact manner in which they had been killed was restricted to a very few. It is, in fact, quite likely that while many Germans thought that the Jews were no longer alive, they did not necessarily believe that they were dead. Such belief, needless to say, is logically inconsistent, but a great many logical inconsistencies are accepted in wartime. Very few people had an interest in the fate of the Jews. Most individuals faced a great many more important problems. It was an unpleasant topic, speculations were unprofitable, discussions of the fate of the Jews were discouraged. Consideration of this question was pushed aside, blotted out for the duration.

Neutrals and international organizations such as the Vatican and the Red Cross knew the truth at an early stage. Not perhaps the whole truth, but enough to understand that few, if any, Jews would survive the war. The Vatican had an unrivalled net of informants all over Europe. It tried to intervene on some occasions on behalf of the Jews but had no wish to give publicity to the issue. For this would have exposed it to German attacks on one hand and pressure to do more from the Jews and the Allies. Jews, after all, were not Catholics. In normal times their persecution would have evoked expressions of genuine regret. But these were not normal times and since the Holy See could do little — or thought it could do little — even for the faithful Poles, it thought it could do even less for the Jews. This fear of the consequences of helping the Jews influenced its whole policy.

.   .   .

Neither the United States Government, nor Britain, nor Stalin showed any pronounced interest in the fate of the Jews. They were kept informed through Jewish organizations and through their own channels. From an early date the Soviet press published much general information about Nazi atrocities in the occupied areas but only rarely revealed that Jews were singled out for extermination. To this day the Soviet Communist party line has not changed in this respect: it has not admitted that any mistakes were made, that the Jewish population was quite unprepared for the *Einsatzgruppen*. It is not conceded even now that if specific warnings had been given by the Soviet media in 1941 (which were informed about events behind the German lines) lives might have been saved. As far as the Soviet publications are concerned the Government and the Communist Party acted correctly — Soviet citizens of Jewish origin did not fare differently from the rest under Nazi rule, and if they did, it is thought inadvisable to mention this. The only mildly critical voices that have been heard can be found in a few literary works describing the events of 1941–42. Some Western observers have argued that the (infrequent) early Soviet news about anti-Jewish massacres committed were sometimes dismissed as 'Communist propaganda' in the West and that for this reason the Soviet leaders decided no longer to emphasize the specific anti-Jewish character of the extermination campaign. This explanation is not at all convincing because Soviet policy at home was hardly influenced by the *Catholic Times*, and it should be stressed that domestically even less publicity than abroad was given to the Jewish victims from the very beginning.

In London and Washington the facts about the 'final solution' were known from an early date and reached the chiefs of intelligence, the secretaries of foreign affairs and defence. But the facts were not considered to be of great interest or importance and at least some of the officials either did not believe them, or at least thought them exaggerated. There was no deliberate attempt to stop the flow of information on the mass killings (except for a while on the part of officials in the State Department), but mainly lack of interest and disbelief. This disbelief can be explained against the background of Anglo-American lack of knowledge of European affairs in general and Nazism in particular. Although it was generally accepted that the Nazis behaved in a less gentlemanly way than the German armies in 1914–18, the idea of genocide nevertheless seemed far fetched. Neither the *Luftwaffe* nor the German navy nor the Afrika Korps had committed such acts of atrocities, and these were the only sections of the German armed forces which Allied soldiers encountered prior to 1944. The Gestapo was known from not very credible B-grade movies. Barbaric fanaticism was unacceptable to people thinking on pragmatic lines, who believed that slave labour rather than annihilation was the fate of the Jews in Europe. The evil nature of Nazism was beyond their comprehension.

But even if the realities of the 'final solution' had been accepted in London and Washington the issue would still have figured very low on the scale of Allied priorities. Nineteen forty-two was a critical year in the course of the war, strategists and bureaucrats were not to be deflected in the pursuit of victory by considerations not directly connected with the war effort. Thus too much publicity about the mass murder seemed undesirable, for it was bound to generate demands to help the Jews and this was thought to be detrimental to the war effort. Even in later years when victory was already assured there was little willingness to help. Churchill showed more interest in the Jewish tragedy than Roosevelt and also more compassion but even he was not willing to devote much thought to the subject. Public opinion in Britain, the United States and elsewhere was kept informed through the press from an early date about the progress of the 'final solution.' But the impact of the news was small or at most shortlived. The fact that millions were killed was more or less meaning-less. People could identify perhaps with the fate of a single individual or a family but not with the fate of millions. The statistics of murder were either disbelieved or dismissed from consciousness. Hence the surprise and shock at the end of the war when the reports about a 'transit camp' such as Bergen-Belsen came in: 'No one had known, no one had been prepared for this.'

.   .   .

One of the questions initially asked was whether it would have made any difference if the information about the mass murder had been believed right from the beginning. It seems quite likely that relatively few people might have been saved as a result and even this is not absolutely certain. But this is hardly the right way of posing the question, for the misjudgment of Hitler and Nazism did not begin in June 1941 nor did it end in December 1942. The ideal time to stop Hitler was not when he was at the height of his strength. If the democracies had shown greater foresight, solidarity and resolution, Nazism could have been stopped at the beginning of its campaign of aggression. No power could have saved the majority of the Jews of the Reich and of Eastern Europe in the summer of 1942. Some more would have tried to escape their fate if the informa-tion had been made widely known. Some could have been saved if Hitler's satellites had been threatened and if the peoples of Europe had been called to extend help to the Jews. After the winter of 1942 the situation rapidly changed: the satellite leaders and even some of the German offi-cials were no longer eager to be accessories to mass murder. Some, at least, would have responded to Allied pressure, but such pressure was never exerted. Many Jews could certainly have been saved in 1944 by bombing the railway lines leading to the extermination centres, and of course, the centres themselves. This could have been done without de-flecting any major resources from the general war effort. It has been argued that the Jews could not have escaped in any case but this is not correct: the Russians were no longer far away, the German forces in Poland were concentrated in some of the bigger towns, and even there their sway ran only in daytime — they no longer had the manpower to round up escaped Jews. In short, hundreds of thousands could have been saved. But this discussion belongs to a later period. The failure to read correctly the signs in 1941–42 was only one link in a chain of failures. There was not one reason for this overall failure but many different ones: paralyzing fear on one hand and, on the contrary, reckless optimism on the other; disbelief stemming from a lack of experience or imagination or genuine ignorance or a mixture of some or all of these things. In some cases the motives were creditable, in others damnable. In some instances moral categories are simply not applicable, and there were also cases which defy understanding to this day.

9

THE
OUTBREAK
OF THE
COLD WAR

I f the controversies of the Cold War show signs of receding into the "historical" past, historians remain divided with regard to its origins and—as time will doubtless reveal—its impact. Even its chronological outbreak remains a subject of contention, although most will agree that the seeds of confrontation were sown in the years following the Bolshevik Revolution. Certainly Stalin's Russia had less in common with the Western capitalist democracies than with Hitler's Germany, and it may well be that what requires explanation is not how the wartime Allies fell apart but how such an uneasy alliance could have been maintained. With the disappearance of the wartime necessity to maintain the alliance, and with the West and the Soviet Union for all practical purposes sharing a common border soon after the German surrender, was it understandable, if not inevitable, that old tensions and antagonisms would resurface?

From Stalin's point of view and based on his experiences with the West, he had little reason to trust their intentions vis-à-vis the Soviet Union, and hence his determination to secure his borders with friendly buffer states. The "atomic diplomacy" practiced by the United States beginning in the summer of 1945 and President Truman's staunch anti-communism reinforced these suspicions. From the standpoint of the Western Allies, the absorption of the Eastern European states into the Russian empire and their transformation into Soviet satellites attested to Stalin's imperialist ambitions and his drive for European, if not world, hegemony. Given this mutual distrust and the personalities involved with decision making on both sides, conflict becomes more comprehensible, and this should be kept in mind when approaching the historical interpretations that follow.

Regardless of whether one believes that a U.S.–USSR confrontation was inevitable, historians stress that the last year of World War II and the two or three years immediately afterwards were crucial in determining subsequent relations between the two superpowers. Prior to at least the Yalta Conference in February 1945, the Western Allies emphasized military considerations in their relations with the Soviet Union. By July of that year, however, at the time of the Potsdam Conference, the situation had changed and "immediate decisions on the future of Europe could no longer be set aside in favor of more congenial discussions of military progress."[1] It was these decisions that began to make the Cold War a visible reality.

If the atmosphere had changed, historians disagree as to whether American policy had. More or less reflecting the views of the American government, Herbert Feis maintains that while the successful testing of an atomic bomb strengthened Truman's resolve at Potsdam, American policy was defined by officials who, having given little consideration to the bomb until it was exploded on Hiroshima, remained consistent. Gar Alperovitz, on the other hand, states unequivocally that the bomb changed American foreign policy and even suggests that it was dropped on Japan not so much for the military purpose of ending the Pacific war as quickly as possible but to bring political pressure on Russia. The elaboration and defense of both positions are found in the first two readings.

---

[1]Robert O. Paxton, *Europe in the 20th Century*, 2nd ed. (San Diego, 1985), p. 502.

A larger perspective is taken in the two that follow, in which the writers attempt to assess responsibility for the Cold War. Reflecting the views of such revisionist historians as William Appleman Williams and Gabriel Kolko, Ronald Steel points to U.S. policy (especially as formulated by Dean Acheson) as seeing the world in ideological terms, and specifically the Truman Doctrine and the decision to create a new state in West Germany as hardening existing mistrust and hastening the division of Europe. In contrast, Vojtech Mastny blames Stalin and the Soviet system (of which Stalin was a product) for the wish to build an empire, which understandably provoked a Western response.

Rather than encourage the student to take sides in regard to the outbreak of the Cold War, these readings should raise larger questions about the subject and also about the process of writing history. For example, how inevitable was the Cold War? Were there identifiable turning points which transformed suspicions into confrontations? What motivated each side to take the stand it did and were these motives ideological biases or more traditional power politics? Or were miscalculations to blame? Should the purpose of sorting through piles of evidence be simply to prove a historical point, as Alperovitz was one of the first to try to do for the atomic bomb, or to seek understanding of the larger process at work, that is, of why things happen? It may well be that the major question here is why a decision was never taken to prevent use of the bomb; diplomatic considerations alone are too limiting to provide an answer.[2] Perhaps we must investigate not only the political but the personal context (for example, Stalin's paranoia and the differences between Roosevelt and Truman), not only the scientific but also the institutional forces at work, and in so doing change the nature of diplomatic history itself.

---

[2]Martin J. Sherwin, "Old Issues in New Editions," *Bulletin of the Atomic Scientist* 41 (December, 1985), p. 44.

Between War and Peace

ᴺᴵᴶ

HERBERT FEIS

Herbert Feis is an economist, influential government adviser, and Pulitzer Prize-winning historian. From 1931–43 he advised the State Department on international economic affairs, was chief technical adviser to the American delegation at the World Economic and Monetary Conference in London, special consultant to the Secretary of War from 1944–47 and a member of the State Department's policy planning staff during 1950–51. He has written extensively on U.S. diplomatic history. In *From Trust to Terror* he tries to summarize and analyze the factors that contributed to the breakdown in relations among the victorious Allies after 1945. Because he was allowed to use unpublished State Department papers and papers of U.S. policymakers not then available to other scholars, this and his other works show the government's point of view and possess something of a quasi-official character. How does Feis reject the charge that the atomic bomb was used against Japan not for military but for political purposes?

While the Conference at Potsdam was assembling, the American Government, after five years of gigantic effort, had successfully tested an atomic bomb, of destructive power, explosive and radiating, far greater than any weapon hitherto known.

Reprinted from *From Trust to Terror, The Onset of the Cold War, 1945–1950*, by Herbert Feis, by permission of W. W. Norton & Company, Inc. Copyright © 1970 by Herbert Feis.

. . .

Roosevelt had briefly seemed all but persuaded to inform the Russians what we had accomplished before the bomb was demonstrated and used; to get started on direct discussions with them of what should be done, as a matter of common concern, before the Communists could suspect that the bomb was going to be used in the service of national diplomacy, and therefore conclude that they must make a breakneck effort to emulate us. But Churchill had rejected this course as naïve; naïve because it would nullify this great weapon which power-bent Communists would respect, and certainly seek to secure. In September 1944 Roosevelt had abruptly changed his mind and agreed with Churchill that no knowledge about the atomic bomb project should be disclosed before a permanent policy was determined.

Truman, who had known nothing about the bomb project, had been compelled to reckon with the coming event in a great hurry. The first informing memo which Secretary of War Stimson, who had been the supervising mentor of the whole effort, gave him (Apr. 25th) should have been startling. "Within four months we shall in all probability have completed the most terrible weapon ever known in human history, one bomb of which could destroy a whole City." The new President had been impressed but not astounded. Unlike Stimson, he was not flung into sleepless nights of anxiety about problems of policy.

The wish to know whether we actually possessed this awesome weapon may have been, and probably was, one of the reasons why Truman deferred his meeting with Churchill and Stalin to discuss postwar settlements. The question of whether, when, and how much to tell the Russians had been left in abeyance. There lurked in everyone's mind the thought that when Truman met Stalin at Potsdam, he might open up on the subject.

The impressions formed at Potsdam by Truman, Byrnes, Stimson, and Marshall of the harsh ways of a Communist police regime and of the sprawl of Russian aims, caused them to decide that the Russians should be told only enough to avert future accusations of malevolent deception, until they had a clearer idea of what the Russian policy would be.

Truman had waited a week after learning of the successful test in New Mexico to tell Stalin about the bomb, and then casually and laconically. To Truman's surprise, Stalin's response was equally off-hand; he had not shown any curiosity about the nature of the weapon, or given any hint that he perceived it might affect the contest for national advantage and position. The President inferred that Stalin did not grasp the significance of what he had been told. But later revelations make it seem far more probable that Stalin was dissimulating; that he did not wish by quiver or inquiry to allow Truman and Churchill to conclude that Soviet diplomacy would be affected by the fact that the West now had a supreme weapon. We know now that by the time of Potsdam Soviet scientists and engineers with capable knowledge of the theory of atomic structure and fission were hard at work designing laboratory apparatus to produce a chain reaction.

In short, the evasions at Potsdam now seem clearly to forecast the devious direction that subsequent discussions about the control of atomic energy would take. The nations were to be frightened tenants in a house that at any time might be blown to pieces by a monstrous force rather than trust each other as caretaker.

Here the narrative may be briefly interrupted to take note of accusations that our primary purpose in using the bomb against Japan was not to shock the Japanese leaders into acceptance of our demand for unconditional surrender, but to end the war before the Soviet Union entered. And conjunctively to impress and frighten the Soviet Government so that it would be more yielding to American and British diplomatic designs and wishes.

Rather careful study seems to me amply to justify dismissal of these allegations. They are distorted inferences from the acknowledged fact that after American negotiators at Potsdam knew they had the weapon, they no longer thought it necessary to worry over whether the Soviet Government would enter the Pacific War in time to save American lives, or to offer additional inducements to do so. His knowledge that the bomb had been tested did make Truman firmer in his refusal to cede some of the more grasping Soviet claims at Potsdam and after. But the American Government did not change its policies or expand its claims because it had acquired the bomb; it faithfully followed the course defined by officials who had known nothing about the bomb until it was exploded on Hiroshima.

·   ·   ·

The crisis of decision came abruptly.

Ever since 1820, when Greece had fought for and won independence from the Ottoman Empire, Great Britain had been its friend and protector. The enduring admiration for ancient classical Greece in the hearts of English scholars and statesmen had shed a glow upon the moves of British strategists and soldiers. But now — in 1947 — Britain, itself in a sorry plight, felt compelled to relinquish the role.

.   .   .

The American Ambassador in Greece, Lincoln MacVeagh, in well phrased messages, stressed the urgency of the situation. So did Paul Porter, who was head of the American Mission which had been advising the Greek Government about economic affairs, and Mark Ethridge, who had been sent by Truman to investigate the political turmoil in the Balkans. All three discerned signs of an impending move of the Communists to take over the country. Unless the Greek Government received immediate and enough military and financial aid, they foresaw that it would go down under the effects of surging inflation, strikes, riots, and public panic, giving the Communist guerillas their chance to win control of the country. In the same messages they warned that our aid would not save the situation unless used wisely and honestly. Therefore they recommended that the American Government should stipulate that its aid be administered by an American group large and expert enough, and granted sufficient authority to bring about a thorough reorganization of the Greek economy, public administration, and military direction.

While the American civilian leaders who read these messages from their colleagues in Greece were worrying over the political effect of the downfall of the Greek and Turkish Governments, American military authorities were pondering the strategic consequences. They discerned the possibility that if the Communists secured control of Greece, they might in concert with Bulgaria threaten Turkey and cause it to grant the Soviet Union control of the Dardanelles and a base there. Possibly also the Greek Communists might make Salonika available as a Soviet naval and air base.

Turkey was, our Ambassador in Ankara continued to stress, also vulnerable to Communist agitation and pressure. American assistance was urgently needed for the equipment and enlargement of the army; and beyond that, to shore up the spirit of resistance of the people, and to relieve their poverty.

Marshall was convinced by the reports of our missions in Greece and Turkey, and satisfied with the recommendations of the concerned groups in Washington. Truman agreed that it was vital to American security that the Communists be thwarted in Greece and Turkey. Within hours he approved the proposed program of action.

But he thought with trepidation about what the congressional response might be to the costly hazardous ventures which all those about him were advocating. He therefore asked the two ranking members of the Senate Foreign Relations Committee, Arthur Vandenberg and Tom Connally, and other members of the Congress to meet with Marshall, Acheson, and himself. Admiral Leahy was also present.

Marshall, in his cryptic and dry way, described the situation and explained why he thought it imperative that the United States come to the support of the Greek and Turkish Governments. Incisively, he remarked: "The choice is between acting with energy or losing by default." Most of his auditors were impressed. But some remained unconvinced. They thought the proposed action was not essential to protect American security, being activated rather by Britain's design to salvage its imperial interest. The well-worn question "Aren't we just pulling the British chestnuts out of the fire?" was heard once again.

Acheson took over the presentation. He stretched the panorama of the Communist purpose and saturated it with dread. The Communists, he averred, were trying to get control not only of Greece and Turkey, but of Iran and other Arab countries of the Middle East. They might be on the verge of winning in Italy. They held important places in the French Cabinet; they were extending their area of control in China. If they won in Greece and Turkey, he predicted, it would make it more likely they would win elsewhere — and ultimately everywhere. The fall of the dominoes could be heard as he talked along.

Most of the members of Congress present expressed willingness to support the administration's resolve to aid the Greek and Turkish Governments, quickly and in a substantial way. But the Republican Speaker of the House of Representatives, Joseph Martin, remained opposed, and the Republican Chairman of the Foreign Relations Committee, Senator Vandenberg, did not regard himself as committed. Admiral Leahy, who was against acceptance of the risk and responsibility, recounted in his Diary, "The consensus of opinion of the members of Congress present was that such action could obtain the support of the American people only by a frank, open, public announcement that the action was taken for the purpose of preventing an overthrow of the subject governments by the Communists."

.   .   .

The three Foreign Ministers met in Paris at the end of June. Each day the British Foreign Office let the American Government know how their talks were going.

Bidault proposed they be guided by Marshall's statement that the countries of Europe should take the initiative and together reach a joint accord among themselves about the needs and the aims. In this program it would be expected that each would both help itself and the others. Molotov then suggested that the American Government be asked how much it would give. Bevin demurred. He stubbornly maintained that the context of Marshall's statement made it clear that before answering this question the American Government would want to know what constructive joint plan the European governments themselves were able to conceive. By doing their best to help themselves not only individually but as a group, they could, he stressed, limit to a minimum the amount of aid they must ask of the United States.

At the next session (June 28th) Molotov insinuated that the American Government was activated by a wish to enlarge exports in view of the economic crisis he saw approaching in the United States. Then he strongly objected to the procedure whereby the European countries in conference would draw up a general economic program to which American help would be adjunct. Rather he urged that each country should continue as before to decide for itself the best ways to improve its condition. France and Britain, he said, each had its economic plan as did the Soviet Union, whose successive five-year plans were being realized and would assure constant increase in Soviet prosperity. Let each country, therefore, draw up its own statement of what it needed in the way of American aid. In conference thereafter, the European countries could consider the national statements and draw up a list of their total requirements and ascertain the possibility of getting such help from the United States. The Bidault-Bevin proposals would inevitably, he alleged, bring unwarranted outside interference with their national affairs. Moreover, the needs of those countries that had fought Germany and been occupied should have prior considerations and be the first group invited to take part in the prospective program. He was aggrieved because it was contemplated that Germany would be associated with the program, on the basis of information to be provided by the commanders of the four zones.

To this version of the answer to be made to Marshall, the Soviet officials clung. Russia was proudly maintaining the outward semblance of strength, although its people were in sore need of almost everything — food, clothing, housing, which was appallingly short, tools, transport. Food was so scarce because of the drought in the summer of 1946 that the Soviet Government had been compelled to continue bread rationing and to change its plans so as to give agriculture priority over heavy industry. But a good harvest in 1947 was in prospect, and enough reserve remained to carry over under strict control. Russia was defying its own wants, concealing its own deficiencies, rather than allowing itself to appear dependent on the bounty of capitalist United States. The use of men, materials, and machines for armaments was cramping; the Soviet Government was keeping the fear of war alive, so that its people should work hard, though weary and bewildered.

Molotov grew more open in his accusations. On July 2nd — the first day of their talks — he alleged that the British and French Governments were trying to use Marshall's proposal as a pretext to create a new organization which could interfere in the affairs of independent countries and direct their development. The possibility of any country's securing an American credit, he argued, would be dependent on its "docile" conduct toward this organization and its Director. As examples he said the suggested arrangement would enable them to bring pressure on Poland to produce more coal and retard the growth of other industries; on Czechoslovakia to increase its production of food and reduce its production of machines; or on Norway to give up plans to create a steel industry on the grounds that this would better suit certain foreign steel companies. In such ways a combined plan would be an invasion of the sovereignty of all and end their economic independence.

This appraisal ignored the fact that no country would be coerced to agree to features of the combined plan it thought unacceptable, or into joining in it. Each would be free to judge for itself whether the benefits obtained would not outweigh any adaptations required of it.

Behind Molotov's arguments could be detected unwillingness to subject the Russian economic situation and program to discussion. But beyond that the Soviet spokesmen were posing as the defenders — against the American imperialists — of any of Russia's satellites who might be tempted to join in order to get American help (Poland, Czechoslovakia, and Hungary were tempted). He warned Bevin and Bidault that the participants in the combined program being considered would be separated from other European countries. Europe would be divided; one group would be opposed against another. This, he said, might seem advantageous to certain great powers (the United States) who wanted to dominate others.

Milovan Djilas, an emissary of Tito's, was in Paris at the time. In his book *Conversations with Stalin*, he offers an explanation of why Molotov during the previous days had appeared to be considering some kind of compromise procedure. Djilas states that Molotov told him that the Soviet Government was going to refuse to join the conference which was being proposed and that he, Djilas, said Yugoslavia would also do so. But Molotov was turning over another tactic in his mind. He was wondering ". . . whether a conference should not be called in which the Eastern countries would also participate, but only for propaganda reasons, with the aim of exploiting the publicity and then walking out of the conference at a convenient moment. I was not enthusiastic about this variation either, though I would not have opposed it had the Russians insisted. . . . However, Molotov received a message from the Politburo in Moscow that he should not agree even to this." There are corroboratory accounts of the receipt of a message which agitated Molotov and instructed him to cease discussion of Russian participation.

There was in Molotov's demeanor and response, as there had been in so many of the Communist denunciations of the United States, a *jealous* rage. The U.S. could offer what the Soviet Union could not.

Atomic Diplomacy

∿

GAR ALPEROVITZ

Gar Alperovitz presides over the National Center for Economic Alternatives. In his controversial *Atomic Diplomacy*, a scrutiny of a critical four-month period in the closing days of World War II, from spring to September, 1945, he tries to show that the atomic bomb played a major role in the formation of a tougher American policy towards Russia, pointing out Truman's new confidence when he met with Stalin at Potsdam. Alperovitz was criticized for making an unobjective evaluation of the records and for taking remarks out of context. It was to counter these criticisms that, in 1985, he published a revised edition of his book that generally reinforces the author's original account. Does the evidence presented fully support the interpretation offered? Because his book begins with Roosevelt's death, does Alperovitz's omission of the original assumption that the bomb would be used in wartime weaken his argument?

The political developments after August 1945, like the later (mid-1946), ill-fated attempts to control atomic energy, cannot here be analyzed. And, unfortunately, Admiral Leahy's summary judgment that the Cold War began in the Balkans can only be tested with further research.

However, at this point the major conclusions to be drawn from a study of American policy during the first five months of the Truman administration can be briefly summarized. It is also possible to attempt to define certain other problems which, with presently available materials, can be stated but cannot be conclusively resolved.

The most important point is the most general: Contrary to a commonly held view, it is abundantly clear that the atomic bomb profoundly influenced the way American policy makers viewed political problems. Or, as Admiral Leahy has neatly summarized the point, "One factor that was to change a lot of ideas, including my own, was the atom bomb . . ." The change caused by the new weapon was quite specific. It did not produce American opposition to Soviet policies in Eastern Europe and Manchuria. Rather, since a consensus had already been reached on the need to take a firm stand against the Soviet Union in both areas, the atomic bomb *confirmed* American leaders in their judgment that they had sufficient power to affect developments in the border regions of the Soviet Union. There is both truth and precision in Truman's statement to Stimson that the weapon "gave him an entirely new feeling of confidence."

This effect was a profoundly important one. Before the atomic bomb was tested, despite their desire to oppose Soviet policies, Western policy makers harbored very grave doubts that Britain and America could challenge Soviet predominance in Eastern Europe. Neither Roosevelt nor Truman could have confidence that the American public would permit the retention of large numbers of conventional troops in Europe after the war. (And Congressional rejection of Truman's military-training program later confirmed the pessimistic wartime predictions.) Thus, at the time of the Yalta Conference, as Assistant Secretary of State William L. Clayton advised Secretary Stettinius, "a large credit . . . appear[ed] to be the only concrete bargaining lever for use in connection with the many other political and economic problems which will arise between our two countries."

That this lever of diplomacy was not sufficiently powerful to force Soviet acceptance of American proposals was amply demonstrated during the late-April and early-May crisis over Poland. Despite Truman's judgment that "the Russians needed us more than we needed them," Stalin did not yield to the firm approach. Hence, without the atomic bomb it seemed exceedingly doubtful that American policy makers would be able substantially to affect events within the Soviet-occupied zone of Europe.

It may well be that, had there been no atomic bomb, Truman would have been forced to reconsider the basic direction of his policy as Churchill had done some months earlier.

Indeed, Churchill's 1944 estimate of the power realities usefully illuminates the problems faced by Western policy makers as they attempted to judge their relative strength vis-à-vis the Soviet Union. As soon as Roosevelt rejected Churchill's desperate pleas for an invasion through the Balkans, the Prime Minister understood that he would have little power in Southeastern Europe, and that, indeed, the British position in Greece was seriously threatened. As he told Roosevelt, "the only way I can prevent [utter anarchy] is by persuading the Russians to quit boosting [the Communist-oriented] E.A.M." Again, there was overwhelming logic in his parallel 1944 argument: "It seems to me, considering the Russians are about to invade Rumania in great force . . . it would be a good thing to follow the Soviet leadership, considering that neither you nor we have any troops there at all and that they will probably do what they like anyhow." As he later recalled, before the atomic test, "the arrangements made about the Balkans were, I was sure, the best possible."

As I have attempted to show, by the time of the Yalta Conference, somewhat reluctantly, and against the wishes of the State Department, Roosevelt came to the same conclusion. Even the State Department was forced to adopt the official view that "this Government probably would not oppose predominant Soviet influence in [Poland and the Balkans]." And one high-ranking official went beyond this judgment; substituting his concern for Western Europe for the Prime Minister's specific fears about Greece, he stated: "I am willing to sponsor and support the Soviet arguments if it will save . . . the rest of Europe from the diplomacy of the jungle which is almost certain to ensue otherwise." As Truman's Balkan representative recalled the Yalta Conference, it was "fateful that these discussions should have been held at a time when Soviet bargaining power in eastern Europe was so much stronger than that of the western allies." But it remained for Byrnes to summarize the early-1945 relative strengths of the powers: "It was not a question of what we would *let* the Russians do, but what we could *get* them to do."

As I have shown, this appraisal was radically changed by the summer of 1945. Since Byrnes advised Truman on both the atomic bomb and the need for strong opposition to the Russians in Eastern Europe before the President's first confrontation with Molotov, the new weapon's first impact possibly can be seen as early as the April showdown. However, no final judgment can be rendered on this point, using the evidence presently available. But there is no question that by the middle of July leading American policy makers were convinced that the atomic bomb would permit the United States to take a "firm" stand in subsequent negotiations. In fact, American leaders felt able to demand *more* at Potsdam than they had asked at Yalta. Again, Churchill's post-atomic appraisal is in striking contrast to his view of the pre-atomic realities: "We now had something in our hands which would redress the balance with the Russians." And Byrnes's new advice to Truman was quite straightforward: "The bomb might well put us in a position to dictate our own terms. . . ."

.   .   .

To recall the judgments of Stimson and Eisenhower in the autumn of 1945 is to state the ultimate question of to what extent the atomic bomb affected the entire structure of postwar American-Soviet relations. But it is not possible at this juncture to test Secretary Stimson's September view that "the problem of our satisfactory relations with Russia [was] not merely connected with but [was] virtually dominated by the problem of the atomic bomb." Nor can the issue of why the atomic bomb was used be conclusively resolved.

This essay has attempted to describe the influence of the atomic bomb on certain questions of diplomacy. I do not believe that the reverse question — the influence of diplomacy upon the decision to use the atomic bomb — can be answered on the basis of the presently available evidence. However, it is possible to define the nature of the problem which new materials and further research may be able to solve.

A fruitful way to begin is to note General Eisenhower's recollection of the Potsdam discussion at which Stimson told him the weapon would be used against Japan:

> During his recitation of the relevant facts, I had been conscious of a feeling of depression and so I voiced to him my grave misgivings, first on the basis of my belief that Japan was already defeated and that dropping the bomb was completely unnecessary, and secondly because I thought that our country should avoid shocking world opinion by the use of a weapon whose employment was, I thought, no longer mandatory as a measure to save American lives. It was my belief that Japan was, at that very moment, seeking some way to surrender with a minimum loss of "face."

"It wasn't necessary to hit them with that awful thing," Eisenhower concluded.

Perhaps the most remarkable aspect of the decision to use the atomic bomb is that the President and his senior political advisers do not seem ever to have shared Eisenhower's "grave misgivings." As we have seen, they simply assumed that they would use the bomb, never really giving serious consideration to not using it. Hence, to state in a precise way the question "Why was the atomic bomb used?" is to ask why senior political officials did *not* seriously question its use as Eisenhower did.

The first point to note is that the decision to use the weapon did not derive from overriding military considerations. Despite Truman's subsequent statement that the weapon "saved millions of lives," Eisenhower's judgment that it was "completely unnecessary" as a measure to save lives was almost certainly correct. This is not a matter of hindsight; *before the atomic bomb was dropped each of the Joint Chiefs of Staff advised that it was highly likely that Japan could be forced to surrender "unconditionally," without use of the bomb and without an invasion.* Indeed, this characterization of the position taken by the senior military advisers is a conservative one.

General Marshall's June 18 appraisal was the most cautiously phrased advice offered by any of the Joint Chiefs: "The impact of Russian entry on the already hopeless Japanese may well be the decisive action levering them into capitulation . . ." Admiral Leahy was absolutely certain there was no need for the bombing to obviate the necessity of an invasion. His judgment after the fact was the same as his view before the bombing: "It is my opinion that the use of this barbarous weapon at Hiroshima and Nagasaki was of no material assistance in our war against Japan. The Japanese were already defeated and ready to surrender . . ." Similarly, through most of 1945 Admiral King believed the bomb unnecessary, and Generals Arnold and LeMay defined the official Air Force position in this way: Whether or not the atomic bomb should be dropped was not for the Air Force to decide, but explosion of the bomb was not necessary to win the war or make an invasion unnecessary.

Similar views prevailed in Britain long before the bombs were used. General Ismay recalls that by the time of Potsdam, "for some time past it had been firmly fixed in my mind that the Japanese were tottering." Ismay's reaction to the suggestion of the bombing was, like Eisenhower's and Leahy's, one of "revulsion." And Churchill, who as early as September 1944, felt that Russian entry was likely to force capitulation, has written: "It would be a mistake to suppose that the fate of Japan was settled by the atomic bomb. Her defeat was certain before the first bomb fell . . ."

The military appraisals made before the weapons were used have been confirmed by numerous postsurrender studies. The best known is that of the United States Strategic Bombing Survey. The Survey's conclusion is unequivocal: "Japan would have surrendered even if the atomic bombs had not been dropped, even if Russia had not entered the war, and even if no invasion had been planned or contemplated."

That military considerations were not decisive is confirmed — and illuminated — by the fact that the President did not even ask the opinion of the military adviser most directly concerned. General MacArthur, Supreme Commander of Allied Forces in the Pacific, was simply informed of the weapon shortly before it was used at Hiroshima. Before his death he stated on numerous occasions that, like Eisenhower, he believed the atomic bomb was completely unnecessary from a military point of view.

Although military considerations were not primary, as we have seen, unquestionably political considerations related to Russia played a major role in the decision; from at least mid-May American policy makers hoped to end the hostilities before the Red Army entered Manchuria. For this reason they had no wish to test whether Russian entry into the war would force capitulation — as most thought likely — long before the scheduled November invasion. Indeed, they actively attempted to delay Stalin's declaration of war.

Nevertheless, it would be wrong to conclude that the atomic bomb was used simply to keep the Red Army out of Manchuria. Given the desperate efforts of the Japanese to surrender, and Truman's willingness to offer assurances to the Emperor, it is entirely possible that the war could have been ended by negotiation before the Red Army had begun its attack. But, again, as we have seen, after Alamogordo neither the President nor his senior advisers were interested in exploring this possibility.

One reason may have been their fear that if time-consuming negotiations were once initiated, the Red Army might attack in order to seize Manchurian objectives. But, if this explanation is accepted, once more one must conclude that the bomb was used primarily because it was felt to be politically important to prevent Soviet domination of the area.

Such a conclusion is very difficult to accept, for American interests in Manchuria, although historically important to the State Department, were not of great significance. The further question therefore arises: Were there other political reasons for using the atomic bomb? In approaching this question, it is important to note that most of the men involved at the time who since have made their views public always mention *two* considerations which dominated discussions. The first was the desire to end the Japanese war quickly, which, as we have seen, was not primarily a military consideration, but a political one. The second is always referred to indirectly.

In June, for example, a leading member of the Interim Committee's scientific panel, A. H. Compton, advised against the Franck report's suggestion of a technical demonstration of the new weapon: Not only was there a possibility that this might not end the war promptly, but failure to make a combat demonstration would mean the 'loss of the opportunity to impress the world with the national sacrifices that enduring security demanded.' The general phrasing that the bomb was needed 'to impress the world' has been made more specific by J. Robert Oppenheimer. Testifying on this matter some years later he stated that the second of the two "overriding considerations" in discussions regarding the bomb was "the effect of our actions on the stability, on our strength, and the stability of the postwar world." And the problem of postwar stability was inevitably the problem of Russia. Oppenheimer has put it this way: "Much of the discussion revolved around the question raised by Secretary Stimson as to whether there was any hope at all of using this development to get less barbarous relations with the Russians."

Vannevar Bush, Stimson's chief aide for atomic matters, has been quite explicit: "That bomb was developed on time . . ." Not only did it mean a quick end to the Japanese war, but "it was also delivered on time so that there was no necessity for any concessions to Russia at the end of the war."

In essence, the second of the two overriding considerations seems to have been that a combat demonstration was needed to convince the Russians to accept the American plan for a stable peace. And the crucial point of this effort was the need to force agreement on the main questions in dispute: the American proposals for Central and Eastern Europe. President Truman may well have expressed the key consideration in October 1945; publicly urging the necessity of a more conventional form of military power (his proposal for universal military training), in a personal appearance before Congress the President declared: "It is only by strength that we can impress the fact upon possible future aggressors that we will tolerate no threat to peace . . ."

If indeed the "second consideration" involved in the bombing of Hiroshima and Nagasaki was the desire to impress the Russians, it might explain the strangely ambiguous statement by Truman that not only did the bomb end the war, but it gave the world "a chance to face the facts." It would also accord with Stimson's private advice to McCloy: "We have got to regain the lead and perhaps do it in a pretty rough and realistic way. . . . We have coming into action a weapon which will be unique. Now the thing [to do is] . . . let our actions speak for themselves." Again, it would accord with Stimson's statement to Truman that the "greatest complication" would occur if the President negotiated with Stalin before the bomb had been "laid on Japan." It would tie in with the fact that from mid-May strategy toward all major diplomatic problems was based upon the assumption the bomb would be demonstrated. Finally, it might explain why none of the highest civilian officials seriously questioned the use of the bomb as Eisenhower did; for, having reversed the basic direction of diplomatic strategy *because* of the atomic bomb, it would have been very difficult indeed for anyone subsequently to challenge an idea which had come to dominate all calculations of high policy.

At present no final conclusion can be reached on this question. But the problem can be defined with some precision: Why did the American government refuse to attempt to exploit Japanese efforts to surrender? Or, alternatively, why did they refuse to test whether a Russian declaration of war would force capitulation? Were Hiroshima and Nagasaki bombed primarily to impress the world with the need to accept America's plan for a stable and lasting peace — that is, primarily, America's plan for Europe? The evidence strongly suggests that the view which the President's personal representative offered to one of the atomic scientists in May 1945 was an accurate statement of policy: "Mr. Byrnes did not argue that it was necessary to use the bomb against the cities of Japan in order to win the war . . . Mr. Byrnes's . . . view [was] that our possessing and demonstrating the bomb would make Russia more manageable in Europe. . . ."

Russia's Road to the Cold War

❦

VOJTECH MASTNY

Vojtech Mastny was born in Prague and became an American citizen. He did graduate work at Columbia University, and taught at the University of Illinois and the U.S. Naval War College. A Guggenheim and Danforth Fellow, he directs the Institute for East Central Europe. He has published works on the Czechs under Nazi rule and on the Benes-Stalin-Molotov conversations of 1943. In *Russia's Road to the Cold War*, he focuses on Soviet wartime aims and policies in Eastern Europe. To what extent does Mastny see the Cold War as an inevitable result of leadership and policies (especially Soviet leadership and policies) as early as the 1941–45 period? How sensitive is he to the realities of a coalition war when he condemns the U.S. and Great Britain for failing to challenge Soviet territorial demands in the last years of World War II?

The crucial years of the Stalin–Hitler pact left a durable imprint on both the content and the style of Soviet foreign policy. It was in collusion and competition with his congenial Nazi rival that Stalin had formulated the main objectives of that policy in Europe and had developed the means for their attainment as well. Those objectives had not proved very different from the traditional goals of Russian imperialism.

Nor had the principal means — the pursuit of a balance of power, with a special predilection for the time-honored device of spheres of influence — been unknown in the arsenal of the "old diplomacy." Nonetheless, in pursuing his goals Stalin had added and perfected a blend of opportunism and savagery that was peculiarly his own. He did not regard it as his fault that the mixture had failed to protect him from Hitler; therefore neither his aims nor his methods were likely to alter in the future — provided, that is, that he could survive the catastrophe he had been so instrumental in bringing on the heads of his people.

.   .   .

Of the new perspectives that the Red Army's ascendancy had opened to Stalin in 1943, a separate peace leading to a Soviet–German condominium over Europe had been of interest to him only during the brief span of time between Stalingrad and Kursk. The alternative possibility of using that ascendancy to advance the cause of Communism also did not appeal to the cautious dictator. Thus a gradual and "orderly" growth of Soviet strength from an eastern European base — perhaps with the help of his Communist followers in different countries but not at the cost of a confrontation with his powerful Western allies — emerged as the most desirable goal. The ever more accommodating Western attitude toward a possible division of the continent into spheres of influence abetted Stalin's quest for power and influence. Yet what exactly was worth striving for, in the wide range between his minimum aims and the enticing prospect of Russia's possible hegemony over a prostrate Europe, still remained undecided. The many unanswered questions were to be clarified at the great Allied conferences scheduled in Moscow and in Teheran later that year.

.   .   .

The flurry of diplomatic activities at the end of 1943 had shaped Stalin's outlook in a curious way. There was an irony in the relationship between his original expectations and the results of Moscow and Teheran. He had sought, above all, Western military commitments that would shorten the war, and only secondarily looked for political gains to facilitate the growth of Soviet power and influence in postwar Europe. On his first priority he believed he had accomplished less, and on his second priority more, than he had been bargaining for. In reality, his gains were the opposite: the promise of the Second Front was definite whereas the Anglo-American recognition of his freedom of action in eastern Europe was not. Nor could Czechoslovakia's willing subordination, a windfall rather than a viable precedent, provide the desired model for other countries. Nonetheless, Stalin's peculiar illusions and misperceptions continued to shape his view of the relationship between military and political affairs for several more months.

.   .   .

Stalin's grasping for a unilateral solution to the Polish question highlighted the profound change in his outlook that had been brought about by the advent of the Second Front. In shaping his long-term aims, the Normandy landings proved an even greater landmark than Stalingrad. After the elaborate Soviet blandishments to induce the enemy to surrender had come to naught, the compelling Anglo-American commitment to further struggle at last prompted Stalin to order his armies beyond the frontier of June 1941 and conquer the lands that would eventually become components of his new empire. With the Rubicon crossed, any premature end to hostilities now would only serve to reduce the potential rewards of the conquest. For the first time since the war began, concern for those rewards started to outweigh Soviet military considerations. It was at this moment that the uprising in Warsaw posed starkly the dilemma between political and military imperatives, with all its grave implications for Stalin's nascent empire.

.   .   .

The empire that Nazi folly and Western forbearance had prompted Stalin to seek was his triumph and his nemesis. By military action and inaction, he had by the fall of 1944 secured Russia's supremacy in all the countries he regarded as vital for its security, and beyond. However, on the issue of how the West could be persuaded to sanction that supremacy permanently, the Soviet ruler showed a disturbing reluctance to define the extent of his inflated security needs. Nor did the Western powers act with the necessary determination to clarify the extent of their tolerance, Churchill's elusive percentages deal notwithstanding. They would all have a further chance at another summit meeting, on whose success the future of the alliance now hinged.

.   .   .

If we may draw an analogy with Germany's responsibility for World War I, the Soviet Union "willed" the post-Yalta crisis, much though the West helped to "cause" it. The conflict would not have arisen if Stalin had not all along regarded the suppression of majority will in the neighboring countries as indispensable for the pursuit of what he defined as the Russian national interest. Nor would the situation have deteriorated so precipitously if, once the sham of Yalta had been exposed, Stalin had chosen the path of conciliation rather than confrontation. Even so, the process he had set in motion was not yet irreversible; the impending common victory over Nazism had many dangers but also many opportunities for continued, though strictly limited, collaboration. In determining which trend would prevail, the remaining weeks of the war were crucial.

.   .   .

In guiding Russia on its road to the Cold War, Stalin was both a victim and an accomplice. He was a victim in the sense that his 1945 military triumph fell short of his hopes — inflated hopes, to be sure, because of his exaggerated and quixotic notion of security. But he was also an accomplice, for he had provoked the adverse Western reaction which, contrary to his expectations, had frustrated those hopes. He might have acted with more restraint if, as Litvinov noted, the Western powers had taken a firm and unequivocal stand early enough. By not doing so, they too had become both accomplices and victims, for their own pious hopes for a stable relationship with Moscow had likewise been frustrated. There was an element of predestination in all this: Stalin could have taken a more enlightened view of what security means — but only if he had not been Stalin. And the Western statesmen could have acted with fewer scruples — but then *they* would have had to be akin to Stalin. Wielding so much greater control over Russian policies than they did over theirs, the dictator may still seem to have been capable of steering away from confrontations more easily. But in the last analysis, his hands were tied by the Soviet system which had bred him and which he felt compelled to perpetuate by his execrable methods; that system was the true cause of the Cold War.

What are the lessons of the Cold War? For better or for worse, they are lessons of an irrevocable past; it is remarkable how much those events, hardly more than thirty years old, already have the unmistakable air of another era. In pondering the thoughts and actions of the statesmen of the time, one cannot help noticing how small and simple their world was in comparison with ours. How modest were their tools, how rudimentary their perceptions. Certainly the Americans and Russians have since learned a great deal about one another. It is this sense of a distance traveled that makes irresistible a broad appraisal of the perspectives lost and found.

The longer the perspectives, the more does June 1941 appear as one of the great turning points in history. Not only did Hitler's gratuitous aggression open the door through which the Soviet Union eventually stepped out to become the world's mightiest and perhaps last imperial power; it also provided the dubious justification for Stalin's imperialism. The humiliation of his life, the Nazi treachery imbued Stalin with an extraordinary drive to justify in retrospect the wisdom of the expansionistic policies he had initiated during his abortive association with the German dictator. The experience thus perpetuated rather than discredited the mixture of cynical opportunism and ruthless power politics, disregarding the interests of other nations, that had been the hallmark of the association. Neither Stalin nor his successors have ever repudiated this legacy.

The enduring memory of a narrow escape from catastrophic defeat in 1941 nurtured a cult of military strength in the Soviet Union. The cult has since burgeoned into a militarism so pervasive that critics have sometimes wondered whether it may have acquired a momentum beyond the leaders' ability to control. Having created the biggest war machine the world has ever seen, the Russians have far exceeded any reasonable security requirements. Whether their feeling of security has increased proportionately is doubtful; that such a feeling among other nations has diminished as a consequence is certain.

In bringing the war against Nazi Germany to a victorious end, Stalin created the Soviet empire as a by-product. He had not originally sought a military conquest of the whole area he won. He would have preferred to advance his power and influence there, as elsewhere, by less risky and more subtle means, although he never ruled out resorting to force if the conditions were right; in this respect, his approach differed from that of his successors less than it may seem. But Stalin was unable (contrary to his hopes) to satisfactorily project his power abroad except by force of arms and to maintain it except by putting in charge vassal Communist regimes; as a result, he saddled his country with a cluster of sullen dependencies whose possession proved a mixed blessing in the long run.

Far from providing the ultimate protective shield, the empire enlarged the area whose integrity the Russians had to uphold and also diluted its internal cohesion. In coping with the ensuing challenges, the

Soviet leaders since Stalin had greatly refined the art of penetrating other countries without outright conquest and of controlling those previously conquered without excessive resort to force. Despite the refinements, however, the fundamental dilemmas of imperialism they inherited from him are still very much with them, with no resolution in sight. The recurrent Soviet setbacks in uncommitted countries and the smoldering discontent throughout eastern Europe suggest a disconcerting lack of alternatives to force.

In masterminding Russia's ascent during World War II and its aftermath, Stalin proved an accomplished practitioner of the strategy of minimum and maximum aims, a strategy his heirs then continued to pursue with variable success. Apt at both exploiting the existing opportunities and creating new ones, he let his aspirations grow until he realized that he had misjudged the complacency of his Anglo-American partners — as they had misjudged his moderation. So he plunged his country into a confrontation with the West that he had neither desired nor thought inevitable. Not without reason were tributes to his diplomatic proficiency conspicuously missing among the accolades that he afterward stage-managed to impress his subjects by the multiple facets of his presumed genius.

Since Stalin, in pursuing his rising aspirations, took into close account the actual and anticipated Western attitudes, his coalition partners contributed their inseparable share to a development that they soon judged was detrimental to their own vital interests. If the Soviet ruler did not rate nearly so high as a diplomat as his reputation suggested, his American and British opposite numbers surely rated even lower. The great war leaders, Roosevelt and Churchill, failed not so much in their perceptions as in their negligence to prepare themselves and their peoples for the disheartening likelihood of a breakdown of the wartime alliance. The British Prime Minister, whose perceptions were keener, is that much more open to criticism than the American President. In any case, by their reluctance (however understandable) to anticipate worse things to come, the Western statesmen let matters worsen until the hour of reckoning was at hand.

The undistinguished performance of Britain's World War II diplomacy is perhaps the main revelation so far to come out from the recently opened London government archives. Quite apart from the substance of policies, the striking decline of professionalism makes the preceding blunders of appeasement appear less as temporary aberrations than as symptoms of the same unsurmounted crisis of adjustment to the eclipse of power. Nor, to be sure, did the American diplomacy of those days exactly shine. Its shortcomings were largely those of innocence and inexperience, as its subsequent coming of age demonstrated. Since then the United States foreign policy has, for all its persisting deficiencies, drawn on an expertise beyond any comparison with that available thirty years ago — surely one of the most encouraging differences between then and now.

It has been a commonplace to observe that nothing could have prevented the Russians from overrunning the countries they did and installing there regimes of their choice. Indeed, compelling reasons can be cited to explain why the development was inevitable. But this "realistic" argument, which overlooks the difference between Soviet capability and Soviet aims, is a poor guide to both understanding history and inspiring action.

Commissar of the Cold War

RONALD STEEL

Ronald Steel has written extensively on American politics and
foreign policy. His books include *Pax Americana* and the award-
winning biography, *Walter Lippman and the American Century*. Educated at Northwestern and Harvard Universities, he has been a
visiting professor at several U.S. universities. The following is taken
from his lengthy review of Dean Acheson's memoirs, *Present at the
Creation*. Insofar as Steel's account touches on such pivotal episodes
in the Cold War as the Truman Doctrine, the Marshall Plan, and
the Berlin Blockade, it offers a useful and concise summary of how
revisionist historians interpret these events. How do Steel's analyses
of the Truman Doctrine and the Marshall Plan compare with those
of Feis?

The first testing of the new diplomacy came early in 1947 when the
British informed Washington that they could no longer afford the cost of
supporting the Greek royalist government against communist insurgents.
Acheson, substituting for Secretary Marshall, convinced Truman of the
need to preserve the Western sphere of influence in the eastern Mediterranean. Congress was asked to provide $400 million for emergency aid

to Greece, with Turkey thrown in for good measure. During the initial briefing, the Congressmen were skeptical about providing help for Britain's client state. Instead of arguing that the balance of power required US intervention, an argument which he evidently assumed his audience would not understand, Acheson chose to scare them with the specter of communism running rampant. "Like the apples in a barrel infected by one rotten one," he told the skeptical legislators,

> the corruption of Greece would infect Iran and all to the East. It would also carry infection to Africa through Asia Minor and Egypt, and to Europe through Italy and France, already threatened by the strongest domestic communist parties in Western Europe. The Soviet Union was playing one of the greatest gambles in history at minimal cost. It did not need to win all the possibilities. Even one or two offered immense gains. We and we alone were in a position to break up the play. These were the stakes that British withdrawal from the eastern Mediterranean offered to an eager and ruthless opponent.

Of course, as Milovan Djilas later pointed out, not only was Stalin not instigating the communist uprising in Greece, but he was actually trying to discourage it and told the Yugoslavs to stop supporting it. "What do you think," Djilas quotes Stalin as saying in February 1948, "that Great Britain and the United States — the United States, the most powerful state in the world — will permit you to break their line of communication in the Mediterranean? Nonsense. And we have no navy. The uprising in Greece must be stopped, and as quickly as possible."

But Acheson was not interested in such subtleties at the time, nor is he now. His lurid analysis scared the legislators, and the Greek-Turkish aid bill was sent to Congress on March 12, 1947, encapsuled in the message that came to be known as the Truman Doctrine. In his pride over the doctrine, Acheson neglects to mention what one learns from Charles Bohlen's recently published *The Transformation of American Foreign Policy* — that General Marshall, who was at the time en route to Moscow with Bohlen, thought the message unduly severe and asked Truman to change it:

> When we received the text of the President's message, we were somewhat startled to see the extent to which the anti-communist element of this speech was stressed. Marshall sent back a message to President Truman questioning the wisdom of this presentation, saying he thought that Truman was overstating the case a bit. The reply came back that from all his

contacts with the Senate, it was clear that this was the only way in which the measure could be passed.

In assessing the Truman Doctrine it is important to remember that in the spring of 1947 the discord between Russia and the West had not yet hardened into the confrontation of the Cold War. The division of Europe was not yet completed, and at the time many believed that the Truman Doctrine was hastening it. Walter Lippmann asked whether the President had laid down a policy or was launching a crusade, and scored what he called "big hot generalities." What particularly troubled him was the sentence, which later came to be considered the key part of the Doctrine, in which Truman declared:

> I believe that it must be the policy of the United States to support free peoples who are resisting attempted subjugation by armed minorities or by outside pressures.

In this seemingly innocuous sentence Lippmann saw what others later discovered: a formula for the repression of revolutionary movements. Gradually the American people became convinced, above all by the propaganda of their own government, that they were involved in a life-or-death struggle with an ideology. Communism, whatever its form, became equated with a threat to America's survival.

The fault lies with the Cold War liberals such as Acheson. They treated the American people cynically, thinking they could be manipulated, giving them injections of anti-communism in order to get through military appropriations they felt inadequate to explain otherwise. Acheson is not the only offender, but he is among the worst, for he was intelligent enough to know what he was doing. With a distaste for public opinion bordering on contempt, he did not tell the truth to Congress and he did not tell the truth to the people. The wave of anti-communism Acheson helped to unleash proved far too powerful for him to handle, especially after McCarthy appeared on the scene. It paralyzed him as Secretary of State, discredited the office he held, justly drove the Democrats from office, and made it virtually impossible for the nation to follow a rational foreign policy. Treat the people with contempt, and you will be treated contemptuously in return. That is the lesson of Dean Acheson's presence at the creation, and the greater misfortune is that we have all been paying for it ever since.

In selling the Truman Doctrine to a skeptical Congress, Acheson laid down the basic tenets of American post-war foreign policy: the ideological division of the world, the equation of "freedom" with American strategic and political interests, the belief that every outpost of the empire (the "free world"), however unimportant it might be in itself, must be prevented from falling under communist control lest the entire structure be threatened (collective security). These were Acheson's justifications for Korea, as they are for Vietnam.

.   .   .

The Marshall Plan is, of course, considered an unprovocative act of enlightened self-interest that saved Western Europe from falling into the communist orbit. But at the time many Europeans, despite the economic crisis they were facing, feared American assistance presented in a form that might antagonize Moscow. As Louis Halle has observed, "When the offer of rescue came at last, in the form of the Marshall Plan, it undoubtedly did contribute to the final fall of Czechoslovakia and its incorporation in the Russian empire." To Stalin's mind the Marshall Plan, coming hot on the heels of the Truman Doctrine, was a design for an anti-communist Western Europe backed up by American military power. This, one recalls, was at a moment when the United States still had an atomic monopoly, and when certain high officials in the government were calling for a "preventive" nuclear strike against the Soviet Union. We cannot know what effect a different American posture would have had on Stalin's plans. But from the record available to us it seems clear that the hardening American attitude reinforced traditional Russian fears of isolation by hostile forces and led the Kremlin to tighten its grip on the territories already under its control. The Russians rejected Washington's call to cooperate in the European Recovery Program and forbade their satellites from participating—just as Washington expected they would. As Charles Bohlen further notes in *Transformation*:

> Kennan and I . . . said we were convinced that the Soviet Union could not accept the plan if it retained its original form, because the basis of self-help and the fact that the United States was to have a voice with the receiving country as to how the aid was used would make it quite impossible for the Soviet Union to accept . . .

Russia's rejection was greeted with relief in Washington and saved the Marshall Plan from almost certain Congressional dismemberment. The breach was widened.

The division of Europe was sealed in the winter of 1948 by the coup in Czechoslovakia and the blockade of Berlin. Today it is assumed that the blockade was an unprovoked act of Soviet aggression to push the

Western allies out of Berlin. But it was not that clear-cut. In retrospect, the Russian aim was to prevent the United States, together with Britain and France, from establishing an independent, anti-communist West German state. Nothing that happened during this or any other period can excuse the ruthlessness with which Soviet puppet regimes treated the peoples of Eastern Europe and East Germany. For the most part, however, Russia's diplomatic moves were made in response to Western initiatives, as the sequence of events reveals: In May 1947 the US and Britain fused their occupation zones into an economic union. The next month General Marshall proposed the European Recovery Program in his speech at Harvard, and a month later Washington announced that the German economy was to be self-sustaining. In August the Germans were allowed to increase production to the 1936 level, and at this point the French agreed to fuse their zone with the other two. "By November," Acheson reports, "the three allies were able to present a solid front to the Russians."

The inability of the Western allies to work together with Russia in governing Germany led to discussions in London in February and March 1948 toward the creation of an independent German state in the Western zones: the so-called "London Program." That same February the Russians gave the go-ahead for the coup in Czechoslovakia, and, upon the allies' signing the Brussels Defense Pact, walked out of the Allied Control Council in Berlin. The US, Britain, and France proceeded with the integration of their zones, and in June announced they would proceed to form a West German government with "the minimum requirements of occupation and control." As a first step they set up a separate currency for West Germany.

This, in Acheson's words, "triggered the final break with the Soviet Union in Germany." Five days after the announcement of the Western currency reform, the Russians set up their own currency system for East Germany and all Berlin. The Allies responded by extending the West German currency reform to Berlin (still under four-power control). The next day the Russians imposed a full blockade on Berlin.

For Acheson, this sequence of events, culminating in a separate West German state, was a triumph of US diplomacy. But it solidified the division of Europe. Was it entirely the fault of the Russians, or was Moscow reacting defensively? According to George Kennan, chief of the policy planning staff of the State Department at the time,

> There can be no doubt that, coming as it did on top of the European recovery program and the final elaboration and acceptance of the Atlantic

alliance, the move toward establishment of a separate government in Western Germany aroused keen alarm among the Soviet leaders. It was no less than natural that they should do all in their power to frustrate this undertaking and to bring the three Western powers back to the negotiating table in order that Russia might continue to have a voice in all-German affairs.

Kennan feared that the "London Program," providing for a separate West German state, would induce the Russians to set up a rival government in the East, and "the fight would be on for fair; the division of Germany, and with it the division of Europe itself, would tend to congeal." Instead of a separate arrangement for Berlin, he favored a settlement for Germany as a whole involving the withdrawal of Russian troops. In November 1948 the Planning Staff presented a package entitled "Plan A," which provided for a new provisional German government under international supervision, withdrawal of allied forces to garrisons on the periphery of Germany, and complete demilitarization of the country. Kennan says the plan was never seriously considered. "Mr. Acheson, if I read his mind correctly in retrospect, regarded it as no more than a curious . . . aberration," while "the London Program . . . was being rushed frantically to completion with the scarcely concealed intention that it should stand as a *fait accompli* before the Big Four foreign ministers."

Acheson's formula for German reunification, expressed at the foreign ministers' meeting in Paris in May 1949, was "to extend the Bonn constitution to the whole country." This would, of course, not only have eliminated the pro-Soviet regime in the eastern zone, but have brought a unified Germany into the Western camp. As Acheson was no doubt aware, this possibility was anathema not only to the Russians but to the East (and even West) Europeans who had twice been invaded by Germany in this century and were opposed to reunification under any conditions.

Of course Acheson did not seriously expect the Russians to accept. He wanted to anchor West Germany firmly to NATO and feared that unification through neutrality would lead to European neutrality, if not communization. In his eyes there was nothing to negotiate, other than a Russian withdrawal from Eastern Europe — for which he was willing to give up nothing in return. He believed the United States must stand firm everywhere the status quo was tested, such as Berlin, and later in such places as Korea and Vietnam, lest the Soviets be tempted to make even greater incursions elsewhere.

Like his followers Rusk and Rostow, Acheson saw every situation as a global confrontation. There were no local contests, but only localized testing of America's will to resist Soviet (or Chinese, or simply "communist") aggression. As part of his policy of creating situations of strength, Acheson was engaged in a race against time to build up German and European military power before the participants lost interest, "to achieve the European Defense Community and end the occupation in Germany before ebb tide in Europe and America lowered the level of will too far."

A momentary threat to these plans came in March 1952 when Stalin sought four-power talks on a German peace treaty. Stalin's proposal differed from previous ones in calling for a reunified Germany free of foreign troops, neutralized, demilitarized, and with the boundaries agreed upon at Potsdam. Acheson surmised, quite correctly, that this was designed to prevent the further integration of Germany into the West. It was, in his words, "a spoiling operation." Rather than a unified neutral Germany, Acheson, like Adenauer, wanted a divided Germany with the strongest segment linked to the West. If Stalin were really serious, German unification would have meant abandoning NATO. The price was too high.

Although he knew better, Acheson persisted in equating communism with Soviet imperialism even in cases where it obviously did not apply. This helped him to squeeze foreign and military aid out of a recalcitrant Congress and to justify policies which might otherwise have seemed unjustifiable. "Of course we opposed the spread of communism," he writes of US policy in Asia with the marvelous assurance of one whose hypocrisy has moved on to the higher plane of self-congratulation. "It was the subtle, powerful instrument of Russian imperialism, designed and used to defeat the very interests we shared with the Asian peoples, the interest in their own autonomous development uncontrolled from abroad."

To show our concern for the interests of the Asians, Acheson in May 1950 called for American military and economic aid to France to help put down Ho Chi Minh's independence movement. This was justified under the catch-all strategy of blocking Soviet imperialism. "The United States government," the official State Department document declared,

> convinced that neither national independence nor democratic evolution can exist in any area dominated by Soviet imperialism, considers the situation to be such as to warrant its according economic aid and military

equipment to the Associated States of Indochina and to France in order to assist them in restoring stability and permitting these states to pursue their peaceful and democratic development.

Helping French colonialism caused him no moral pain, although he continually griped about the stubbornness of the French in wanting to run their colony themselves rather than turn it over to American "advisers." His sympathies naturally seem to lie with the colonizers rather than with those being colonized. By the time Acheson left office, the United States was paying nearly half of France's military bill in Indochina. "I could not then or later," he explains of this policy, "think of a better course." After all that has happened there since, he still cannot.

10

THE END
OF EUROPEAN
EMPIRE

Decolonization refers to the "process by which the peoples of the Third World gained their independence from their colonial rulers"[1] and in so doing brought an end to almost 500 years of European empire. Nearly all of it took place in the decade or two after the end of World War II, although its origins may be found well before that time. An age of colonization was over, one which despite the brutalities of imperialism had placed its stamp on Western civilization as the first to relate all the peoples of the globe. Whether independence was achieved by the willingness of the European powers to grant it, or whether it was forced upon the powers by national movements (Third World countries prefer the term "national liberation" to decolonization) remains a subject of

---

[1]M. E. Chamberlain, *Decolonization. The Fall of the European Powers* (Oxford, 1985), p. 1.

controversy. In any case, as shown by Rudolf von Albertini, World War II provided the colonies with their opportunity. The devastating setbacks incurred by Britain, France, and Holland in the early years of the war shattered the myth of Western invincibility, and if many colonials once more sided with their "mother countries," after 1945 the latter faced a choice between providing concrete reforms or promising future independence.

Was the age of imperialism in fact over or has the dominance of the Western nations over their former colonies continued under other forms? "Neocolonialism," that is, continued economic domination or control by foreigners, may be more invidious than direct colonization in that a colony at least had an opportunity to seek redress for its grievances. Certainly the colonial power that had exercised direct rule assumed that the newly sovereign state would maintain the strong political and economic ties established during the period of colonial rule. Even when these ties were severed with the former mother country, direct rule by colonial powers, as Wolfgang Mommsen observes, was often replaced by the indirect rule of the post-World War II superpowers. Resentment against any kind of foreign involvement was particularly strong in the cases of former colonial governments taken over by new leaders who had not been associated with the "colonial tradition" and who in many cases rejected Western culture and Western political forms.

Developing countries have claimed that their relationships with the superpowers are at best uneven and that economic control, whether practiced by foreign nations or multinational corporations, is even more damaging than political control because it perpetuates dependency. The former president of Ghana, Kwame Nkrumah, was an articulate and forceful spokesman for an African view of Third World problems.

To what extent does either the colonial legacy or neocolonialism explain the precarious economic position of many Third World countries? Can their economic — and perhaps also political — problems be explained, as sociologist Immanuel Wallerstein has argued, by the impossibility of all states developing simultaneously, a theory that has won favor with some Marxists?[2] Other developmental economists have argued that

---

[2] Immanuel Wallerstein, *The Modern World System: Capitalist Agriculture and the Origins of the European World Economy in the Sixteenth Century* (New York: 1976). Briefly, Wallerstein points to the historical division of the world into core, periphery, and semiperiphery states that possess unequal political and military power and consequently engage in unequal exchange relationships. Two other volumes, published in 1980 and 1989, carry the story through the 1840s.

"periphery countries" have failed to develop because they produce largely for export and have neglected the growth of a home market. Or was it imperialist control that destroyed indigenous industry and brought a halt to domestic agricultural production for home consumption? Could these economies have been sufficiently protected from international competition or exploitation, or both, to develop a sound economic footing? In view of a mounting awareness of global interrelatedness in a rapidly shrinking world, such questions are of primary concern.

The Impact of Two World Wars
on the Decline of Colonialism

∖∪⁄

RUDOLF VON ALBERTINI

In an important book published in German in 1966 and translated
as *The Administration and the Future of the Colonies, 1919–1960* (New
York, 1971), Rudolf von Albertini was one of the first to explore the
decolonization process. In the article from which the following is
taken, he summarizes developments in the thirty years before the
colonies achieved independence, placing particular emphasis on the
importance of the two world wars. To what extent does von Albertini recognize the importance of indigenous national movements in
the colonies as explanations of their independence? To what extent
does he hold responsible such domestic developments in the colonial
powers as the rise of mass democracy and the welfare state? What,
precisely, was the impact of the two world wars?

It did not escape the notice of political observers in the interwar
years that the first world war had brought the 'revolt of the coloured man'
into prominence or at least hastened its coming. So much was clear even
without the speculative gaze of Spengler or the analytical elaborations of
Paul Valéry. Discussions about the European forfeiture of power and
prestige and the 'rising tides of colour' became a commonplace, although

From Rudolf von Albertini, "The Impact of Two World Wars on the Decline of Colonialism," *Journal of Contemporary History* (1969 4(1)), pp. 17, 19–22, 25–30, 32–35. Reprinted
by permission of the publisher.

for preference the responsibility was at first placed on outside influences: President Wilson's 'right of self-determination,' Pan-Islam, the Russian Revolution; whilst German commentators stressed above all the Allies' 'criminal' employment of coloured troops against white ones. Today's preference is for examining individual areas of Asia and Africa and arguing in favour of an indigenous emancipation movement. A few comparative observations would therefore seem of value, for only against the wider horizon of world affairs does the emancipation of the colonies reveal its full relevance.

.   .   .   .

The outbreak of war in Europe — and this should be emphasized — did not however lead to rebellions or unrest, nor did the national élites at once make use of it to advance radical demands. On the contrary, the manifestations of loyalty and readiness to give military and financial aid were many and doubtless in the initial phase genuine, perhaps because an introduction to western culture had forged emotional links with the colonial power despite a simultaneous assertion of national consciousness, perhaps because England and France were successful in presenting a credible picture of the war as one forced upon them in defence of freedom and justice against an autocratic Germany. German attempts to form links with the nationalists, in India and North Africa, met with only scant success. Especially striking was the attitude of Gandhi who, landing in London on 6 August 1914 on the way back from South Africa, took an active part in organizing an Indian ambulance unit and, unlike Mrs. Besant, categorically declined to make use of Indian loyalty to 'extort' reforms: as late as summer 1918 Gandhi supported the British recruitment drive, even at the risk of losing the respect of the more radical nationalists and the masses.

Troops were withdrawn from India, Indochina, North and West Africa, while from Indochina to West Africa a general recruitment drive for native soldiers was opened in these areas. In the course of the war India provided 1.3 million (combatants and labourers); Indochina 150,000; Algeria 300,000; and French West Africa 200,000. This recruitment of volunteers presented at first few difficulties, no doubt because it was possible to appeal to the military tradition of certain tribes (nobody envisaged a long hard war), and because joining seemed at first advantageous. In the ensuing period, however, recruitment met with growing opposition, and open or veiled compulsion was necessary. Attempts to avoid war service, the flight of young men at the sight of recruiting agents, and even open rebellion leading to bloody punitive expeditions, are recorded in the cases of Indochina, Algeria, and Black Africa. In India recruiting had been concentrated on the Punjab, a factor often overlooked in the growing unrest and disaffection which in 1919 provoked the Amritsar massacre. The forced recruitment of camel drivers in Egypt made it easy for the nationalists in 1919 to spread agitation among the fellaheen too. The compulsory draft into the Carrier Corps in Kenya was detested: it drove whole families to seek refuge in the bush and resulted in very heavy loss of life, and at the same time gave the settlers the opportunity to recruit urgently needed African labour.

It seems to me that the significance of this more or less compulsory draft for the emancipation movement in the colonies has often been overrated, quite apart from the fact that the British in India and the French in North and West Africa were astute enough to treat the war veterans as a privileged group, thereby binding them more closely to the colonial power. On the other hand there can be no doubt that hundreds of thousands were uprooted from their traditional and rigidly defined society, confronted by totally new experiences and discoveries, and made socially and psychologically mobile enough to become receptive to the slogans put out by the educated élite.

However, war and the consequences of war changed the composition of the nationalist movements, which managed in a relatively short time to gain a solid footing among the masses. The 'complementary' pattern of trade between colony and mother country was disrupted, industries developed or were expanded, the number of wage-earners increased sharply, the trade union movement took root. Prices rose and additional problems of adaptation at the end of the war sharpened a social ferment which found an outlet in strikes and local disturbances. The radicalization of the Congress Party can be precisely traced in its choice of presidents and their opening addresses. Thus in 1917 at the Calcutta Congress Mrs. Besant pointed emphatically to India's achievements in the war—'the condition of India's usefulness to the Empire is India's freedom'—but also to the 'awakening of Asia' before and during the war; England, she said, had rewarded India's loyalty with nothing but 'distrust,' and the Allied struggle for freedom was apparently meant to benefit only the Dominions, but not India. At the same time she was able to observe a change in the attitude of the business world represented by Tata which, annoyed at the restrictions and shortage of credit, but also at the government's refusal to compensate firms formerly trading with Germany for their losses, had given its support to the nationalist movement. India would be able to meet future Japanese competition only if she enjoyed home rule, that is, had administrative control over taxation and revenue policy. At the 1918 Congress President Malaviya enumerated Wilson's 14 points and referred to the appointment of Sinha as India's representative at the peace conference, but did not fail to mention that Sinha was responsible to the government of India and not to the Indian people.

The British government could not let matters rest at vague promises of reform: after the surprising agreement of Congress Party and Moslem League in the Lucknow Pact of 1916 and the grave Mesopotamia crisis, London found itself forced into the 'Declaration on India' of 20 August 1917, which proclaimed for the first time officially that the aim of British policy in India was 'responsible government' and opened the way for the 1918–19 Montagu-Chelmsford reforms. In this dialectic of challenge and response the accelerating effect of the war is particularly noticeable. Whereas in 1912 'representative government' had been decisively rejected and autocratic rule, relaxed somewhat by the presence of representatives of Indian interests, had been considered natural and necessary for at least decades to come, by the end of the war London was committed to withdrawal from India; and though every concession might be made reluctantly, with reservations and delaying tactics, there could be no going back.

.   .   .

As Great Britain and France found themselves obliged during the war either to introduce concrete reforms at once or to lay down the principles for future decolonization — assimilation and integration in the French sphere; self-government in the British — problems peculiar to the settler colony began to take shape, although they were at first not widely recognized for what they were. In Algeria the *évolués* who favoured assimilation were opposed by the closed ranks of the Franco-Algerians, who in their turn could also point to their sacrifices in the war and who in 1918–19, in collaboration with the conservative colonialist groups in the mother country, were able to water down the reforms which had originally been generous in their intentions, and above all prohibit the grant of citizenship if personal status under Islamic law was retained. In Southern Rhodesia London was willing to concede 'responsible government' rather than bear the cost of reimbursing the South Africa Company and the colonial administration, thus clearing the way for responsible government and the plebiscite of 1923. In Kenya it was felt that the colonists should be compensated for their economic hardships and military aid during the war, and in 1916 they were granted the right to vote in the Legislative Council, which later made it difficult to block the further step of an unofficial majority as a preliminary to responsible government. In other words, in the settler colonies the war propelled events in the opposite direction in the sense that a relaxation of colonial rule benefited the whites.

A further aspect deserves consideration: immediately after the war the colonial élite found that its hopes of liberal reforms had been illusory, or realized that it had overrated the readiness for such reforms. Only then did the social and psychological effects of the war make their full impact, just at the time when conservative governments faced with revolutionary forces in their own countries showed little inclination to yield to nationalist pressure. The Algeria Act of 1919 by no means fulfilled the 1915 proposals of Clemenceau and Leygues and disappointed even the moderate *évolués*; the Montagu-Chelmsford reforms were well received in India, especially by Gandhi, but they were accompanied by the Rawlatt Bills and Amritsar, which indicated the administration's opposition to reform and its belief in repression. Only when this became clear did Gandhi, who had had complete faith in England's liberal intentions, make final the break with the colonial power and give the signal for passive resistance. London's refusal to accept the Milner Report on Egypt shut the door to any remaining possibilities of an understanding with the nationalists. Liberal governors in Indochina and Indonesia gave way to conservative ones. The natural relationship of tension between colonial power and emancipation, between reaction and progress, hardened into a policy of immobility, so typical of the interwar years.

If we take Ludwig Dehio's interpretation of the second world war as a new and final attempt to achieve hegemony in Europe, an attempt which, in a system of states already disintegrating (Holborn), inevitably took particularly destructive forms and hastened the assertion of hegemony by the flanking powers, then the recent acceleration in the process of colonial evolution and devolution can be more easily understood. This war was truly global, a conflict in which the colonial territories of Southeast Asia were the scene of decisive military action; but most important of all, the chief colonial powers suffered disastrous setbacks. France collapsed, although the Vichy government was able to hold on to a number of positions in North Africa and Indochina, and de Gaulle's Free France gained its first territorial foothold in Equatorial Africa. Great Britain suffered a shattering defeat in Singapore. In the perspective of world affairs the fall of this bastion of Southeast Asia can be seen to be of great significance, as it not only cleared the way for Japan to occupy the entire region, but also seemed symbolically to herald the collapse of the colonial system as a whole, and revealed the decline, hitherto to a great extent concealed, of England as a world maritime power.

Despite growing nationalist agitation in the thirties, national leaders once more opted almost unanimously for the Allied cause, and, with a few exceptions, showed no sympathy with the Axis powers. This was true of Gandhi and the avowed anti-fascist Nehru, but also of the moderate Burmese, who enjoyed a share of government and administration, of the moderate Indonesians, of Bourgiba and the Neo-Destour of Tunisia, of Ferat Abbas in Algeria, and the *évolués* in British and French Africa. Recruitment and mobilization of colonial troops again passed off with no great difficulty. The manifestations of loyalty were however clearly linked this time with demands for reform. The war offered a suitable opportunity for demanding autonomy or even independence, and this no longer as a mere promise to follow after the war, but effectively and at once. Refusal by the colonial powers to concede such incisive changes during the war resulted, for example in India, in a gradual sharpening of the tension with Congress and led to the 1942 'Quit India' movement, even though the possibility of a Japanese advance into India remained real. England clamped down hard but at the same time recognized that withdrawal from India was no longer to be avoided; and the question was thus reduced to the 'when' and 'how' of the transfer of power. The Cripps mission to India, which even envisaged that country's withdrawal from the Commonwealth, was dispatched as a move to counter the Japanese advance and in answer to American pressure.

In North Africa the Vichy government allowed little scope for nationalist movements, and de Gaulle too was for a long time reluctant to commit himself to future emancipation. After the Allied landing, however, the nationalists learned how to exploit France's weakness and the tensions within the Allied camp. During the temporary occupation of Tunisia by the Axis powers, the Sultan and Bourgiba 'collaborated' and took action against France, whilst the Sultan of Morocco attempted with American backing to put in his claim for independence before the protectorate could be re-established. Even more symptomatic of this trend was the change in attitude of the Algerians; Ferat Abbas dropped

his plea for integration and assimilation and demanded the establishment
of an Algerian state, announcing in the Algerian Manifesto of 10 February 1943 a programme which, if not tantamount to a complete and
open break with France, was clearly Algerian and nationalist in spirit.
De Gaulle sought to counter it by granting civil rights with retention of
Islamic personal status, which in reality meant implementation of the
1936–37 popular front programme.

President Roosevelt and his colleagues openly favoured anti-
colonialism, supporting the Congress Party in India and the Sultan in
Morocco, and extended expressly to the colonial territories the right of
self-determination embodied in the Atlantic Charter which Churchill
had wished to apply only to the nations of Europe liberated from the
Axis. It was only natural that the nationalists should seize upon this,
and, disappointed by Churchill and by the discrepancy between Allied
declarations and the effective measures taken, should rely upon future
American support. The significance of American anti-colonialism has
however been perhaps exaggerated; the war alone, with all its political
and social implications and repercussions, was enough to break the stagnation of the interwar years and hasten or set in motion the process of
decolonization.

This was especially true in Southeast Asia where the Japanese
occupation created entirely new conditions. Whereas in North and West
Africa, in India and Ceylon, the colonial administration was weakened
but managed to survive, in Southeast Asia it was completely destroyed,
and this alone had epoch-making consequences. The unexpected collapse of the colonial power was seen as the 'failure of a divine mission'; it
awakened millennial expectations which were immediately identified
with the expulsion of foreigners and necessarily made any rule reimposed
by force appear questionable. Ties of loyalty were broken, the passive
endurance of an established system of rule rejected, whilst on the other
hand mass forces were released which lent an undreamed-of impetus to
the emancipation movement. Moreover, as part of their war effort and
their concept of co-prosperity, the Japanese mounted a systematic campaign of anti-western and anti-white propaganda and sought also with
great skill to accommodate nationalist aspirations. Japanese procedure in
fact varied considerably in the different regions but created similar situations. Thus the disappearance of the European ruling cadres — by retreat
in Malaya and Burma, by internment in Java — and the shortage of Japanese personnel, opened the way to advancement for countless minor

native officials and led at least temporarily to a collaboration of expediency with the occupying power. At the same time the 'inferiority complexes' inherent in the 'colonial situation' were cured and the determination to achieve self-government strengthened.

In Indochina the French administration did in fact continue, since the Japanese were content with military occupation and indirect control, but Admiral Decoux found himself obliged to employ Vietnamese in order to woo them away from the anti-French opposition movement. The Japanese replaced the languages of the European rulers with national languages and awakened hopes that independence would soon be granted. A good part of these hopes was in fact not realized, or realized only shortly before the Japanese defeat; forced labour and forced recruitment led the rural population in particular to resent Japan. In Java the nationalists released from Dutch internment took part in government only as 'advisers,' but they gained new opportunities of influencing the masses: anti-imperialist slogans were aimed with characteristic ambivalence both at the Allies and at Japan, and their ultimate effect was to benefit the nationalist movement. Japan set up its own mass organizations, and among other things a radio network which for the first time made the rural population politically accessible. These served to propagate the 'co-prosperity' idea but were taken over by the nationalists just as Japan was preparing to consider independence and the formation of a national government, enabling the group around Sukarno and Hatta to mobilize the villages. As Japan also encouraged military training and created native armed forces in Burma, Malaya, and Indonesia, the nationalists had at their disposal a readymade instrument of power for their encounter with the returning colonial power.

At the same time the leadership of the nationalist movements passed to those radical groups which before the war had either formed an unimportant minority or had been crippled by police action. In Burma this was accompanied by a generational change: the moderate Burmese politicians and the Indian bourgeoisie who had retreated with the British were succeeded by the Thakin group under the young Aung San, a product of the extremist student nationalism of the late thirties. The group had established links with Japan and had marched with a 'national liberation army' into Burma, but had then ceased its collaboration and finally fought on the side of the Allies against Japan. It thus had control of a cadre which was immediately able to take on administrative duties and assured the group of mass peasant support, so that when the Japanese capitulated, Great Britain was confronted with a *fait accompli*. In Indo-china the Communist party of Ho Chi Minh, though small, was able to profit from the 'strange alliance' and, operating from China, to consolidate a maquis position in Upper Tongking which, on the retreat of the Japanese in 1945, but just before the arrival of the French, enabled it together with other nationalist groups to declare an Indochinese Republic which, in the agreement of 6 March 1946, received from France a pledge of extensive autonomy. The attempt to get round this reluctant concession and to neutralize Ho Chi Minh's position by incorporating his republic into a French-controlled federation led in 1946 to war.

.   .   .

Once again the part played by the veterans was considerable if difficult to evaluate. After years of absence they were alienated from traditional society; often dissatisfied with their conditions of discharge and with insufficient opportunities for work in the towns, they formed an important element of social and political unrest in the critical phase immediately after the war, clearly discernible in for example the Accra riots of 1948. The national élite became more broadly based. The old notables and the few educated Africans were now replaced by younger leaders, often students, and by representatives of the African middle class — small businessmen, officials, teachers — who used new methods of organization and propaganda, founded trade unions, and began to build up modern parties. In Africa, too, wartime loyalty and service by African troops were recalled when political demands were presented. Representatives of the important student body in London and of the youth organizations in Africa started to criticize the administration sharply, especially its racial discrimination, and pressed for more rapid africanization and the expansion of the educational system, and in the political field for swift redemption of the pledge of self-government. During a visit to London in 1943 Azikiwe, the spokesman of Nigerian nationalism, handed the colonial secretary a memorandum with the significant title 'The Atlantic Charter and British West Africa,' containing a claim for full independence within fifteen years. Thus challenged, London began gradually to adopt a new line: it helped to establish the trade unions, took in hand the modernization of local government, and prepared new constitutions. The details are of no interest here. What is important is the remarkable acceleration caused by the war. As late as 1938 a colonial secretary could regard centuries (!) of British rule as necessary and — apparently — possible; during the war London actually accepted an African majority in the Legislative Council (the Burns constitution for the

Gold Coast, 1944–46), thus recognizing by implication the transition to responsible government. The analogy with the situation in India in 1914–19 needs no emphasis.

In the French sphere the initiative came much more strongly from the mother country: Free France, impelled by a revolutionary urge for renewal, attempted to break through the stagnation of the Third Republic; at the same time an effective programme of reform had to be found to counter American anti-colonialism. The Brazzaville conference of governors in 1944 laid down the post-war policy for Africa; the traditional concept of decolonization was upheld and the colonies, despite decentralization measures and the formation of local assemblies, were to be integrated into Greater France, with extension of civil rights and the election of African representatives to the Paris parliament. It was then that political life in French West Africa really began, since the elections necessitated parties and the new electorate had to be mobilized. The role of the second world war as an accelerating factor was revealed perhaps even more strikingly in French West Africa than in British Africa.

Only slowly are we beginning to grasp the last 50–60 years as a kind of historical unity. We are easily tempted to isolate particular events, or to devote our attention to one single country or area — Europe, America, or Asia. The complex as a whole, but also the numerous reciprocal effects within it, tend to remain outside our field of vision.

It is historical fact that the first world war saw the collapse of the European system of states. But that was not all. It is equally well known, although detailed research is only just beginning, that the creation of armies numbering millions, the wartime economy necessitating intervention by the state and sweeping changes in production, the movement of prices and incomes, the radicalization in the labour movement and the emancipation of women — all these, among other things, stirred the bourgeois-liberal society of the pre-1914 years into movement. The interwar years appear to us today as a period of crisis and adjustment during which, although it was possible to check the wave of revolution released by the war, the new mass society achieved neither economic nor political stability: the open or latent crisis of west European democracy and the fascist-authoritarian movements in central, east, and southern Europe are clearly to be viewed against the broader horizon. Only in the second world war, and not least as a consequence of that war, did the breakthrough to the welfare state follow after 1945 in the advanced industrialized countries of Europe and America, still based on the individualist-capitalist economic system, but supplemented by planning mechanisms and stabilized with the aid of an extensive machinery of state intervention.

The world wars as factors hastening the decline of colonialism should therefore not be considered in isolation, since the movement towards emancipation in the colonies was accompanied by a parallel change of structure in the colonial powers which, in the changing composition of élites and the mobilization of human masses, can be seen as an analogous phenomenon. This suggests completely new perspectives for a comparative historical approach concerned with sociological and politological issues. There has already been an interesting attempt by Professor Arno Mayer to analyse specific variants of nationalism in the years following the first world war, in which he draws attention to a similarity between the new states of central and eastern Europe and the states which gained independence after 1945; in both instances predominantly agrarian societies ruled by traditional élites were subjected to a rapid process of modernization, resulting in the sudden and unforeseen achievement of independence, which brought into the open national problems of integration (frontiers, minorities) as well as the conflict between old and new élites. In the absence of strongly cohesive internal forces, structural economic and social change led to a personalization of political power and to the subsequent emergence of military dictatorship as a way out of internal difficulties.

The first world war, the interwar years, and the second world war, but also Europe and the world outside Europe, are thus drawn closer together. The emancipation of Asia and Africa should not be understood as a mere by-product of the wars in Europe, but as an integral part of the structural change in the world political constellation which had been developing since the turn of the century, characterized on the one hand by a transfer of power from Europe to the non-European world, on the other hand by a Europeanization or westernization of this latter world.

The Continuity of Imperialism

∿

WOLFGANG MOMMSEN

Wolfgang J. Mommsen is a distinguished German historian who has published among other things an important book on Max Weber and German politics. In association with a colleague, Jürgen Oster-hamel, he edited a collection of essays by historians and political scientists exploring the continuities and discontinuities between the imperialist domination of the Third World in the nineteenth and early twentieth centuries and the external relations of the dependent states that emerged from the decolonization of the post-World War II decade. The excerpt that follows comes from Mommsen's introduction to this collection. Like many of the contributors, he argues that the dominance of the old imperialist powers and the dependence of the newly emerged states on them are no longer based on formal imperialism but on informal means of control. Where does one draw the line between informal means of control and the ordinary exercise of power among unequal actors in the international system, that is, in the theory and practice of international politics as a whole?

Strategies of Imperialist Rule

A recently published study on European imperialism in the nineteenth and twentieth centuries begins with the observation, 'the "age of Imperialism" is over,' only to add that 'on the other hand, "imperialism"

From Wolfgang J. Mommsen and Jürgen Osterhammel, eds., *Imperialism and After. Continuities and Discontinuities*, pp. 333–335, 342–347, 348–350, 353–354. London, 1986. Reprinted by permission of the publisher, Unwin Hyman Ltd.

itself, as a variety of human political and economic behaviour, appears to be quite alive, judging from events in Vietnam and Afghanistan.' Furthermore, it points out that many people hold the view that 'the dissolution of the colonial empires in our own time was simply the end of a phase in the history of imperialism,' not of imperialism itself. Apparently there is no easy answer to these questions. There can be little doubt that the ending of formal colonial rule by the Western powers with but few remnants of their former colonial possessions still intact is a crucial cæsura in the history of mankind. This is true equally of the peoples formerly subjected to imperialist control and of the European peoples.

The break-up of the European colonial empires which had been built up in the course of more than four centuries was associated with Europe's loss of hegemony over the globe which had been so noticeable in the eighteenth and nineteenth centuries. Two new superpowers, the United States and, with some delay, the Soviet Union, had stepped in. Their rise to hegemonial status in world affairs, particularly since the Second World War, can well be described as the emergence of two new varieties of informal and, for the most part, indirect imperialism. While there will be disagreement as to whether the hegemony exercised by the United States over much of the Western world since 1945 should be described as imperialism, formal or informal, few people will object to assessing the Soviet bloc as an empire of a new sort, one which displays striking continuities with its tsarist predecessor. Whatever the case, the process of decolonization was intimately connected to the rise of these two antagonistic powers to the world power status which they enjoy today.

The cæsura marked by decolonization and the end of empire, that is to say, the forfeiting of all direct control by the former colonial powers, appears to be a very marked one. But on closer inspection, it evaporates to some extent. The formal granting of independence did not change social reality at the periphery overnight; instead it was merely a stage, though an important one, in the painful and difficult struggle for emancipation in a world still dominated by the West economically, culturally and, at least to some degree, politically, though perhaps no longer to the same extent as before 1940.

This fact becomes all the more apparent if the end of empire is seen against the backcloth of the reality of imperialist rule during the classical age of imperialism. The classical interpretations of imperialist rule which stressed, above all, formal imperialist domination were far too simplistic. None of the imperialist powers ever established a full system of direct rule in their colonial possessions directly comparable to classic European patterns of government; instead, they all relied upon various combinations of formal and informal, direct and indirect rule which could not do with out the partly enforced, partly voluntary collaboration of indigenous élites.

According to Robinson and Gallagher's famous definition, European imperialism proceeded according to the paradigm 'informal control if possible, formal rule if necessary.' That is to say, the establishment of imperialist control was a gradual process. Initially it was effected by informal techniques with a minimum of governmental interference, if any at all. The establishment of formal and direct rule was only the ultimate stage in this process of extending imperial control, a stage which from the point of view of the metropolitan society did not necessarily turn out to be the most profitable one. For, as Robinson has so aptly put it, 'if empire could not be had on the cheap, it was not worth having at all.' It has by now been established beyond doubt that there was a continuity of expansion, however slow, at the periphery throughout the nineteenth century, irrespective of what metropolitan governments might say about it, and of whether public opinion was in favour of further imperialist expansion, or, as was the case in the early Victorian period in Britain and elsewhere, against it. In many instances, trade paved the way for the eventual establishment of formal colonial rule, in others it was prepared for by missionary activity, or by a combination of both, whilst in only a relatively small number of cases strategic considerations played a decisive role. It was the rivalry between the European powers which eventually made it necessary to formalize imperialist rule and establish proper bureaucratic administrations by which the usually vast and often thinly populated territories in Asia and Africa could be effectively controlled.

In fact most, if not all, of the imperialist powers found that the cooperation of indigenous élites was not only convenient, but indispensable for the administration of the territories in question. Direct rule, that is, administration without the assistance, however limited, of indigenous élites or social groups with an independent standing in the respective polity, was the exception rather than the rule. Britain is commonly held to have invented and practised widely the strategy of 'indirect rule,' whilst France allegedly acted according to the theory of 'assimilation.' In fact, however, all the imperialist powers employed techniques of subsidiary rule in administering their colonial possessions, though in differing ways, which were conditioned by local circumstances and the availability of indigenous governmental systems or collaborative élites suitable for the colonial power's purposes; sometimes these even had to be created artificially. Almost everywhere we find rather colourful and complex combinations of direct or near-direct rule and indirect or subsidiary rule with the assistance of indigenous puppet regimes. The Indian principalities, which were sometimes arranged like a chessboard, provide one example of this. Not surprisingly the European powers often preferred to exercise imperial control in the form of a protectorate, however fictitious this may have been. Often this fiction was maintained right to the very end in the face of actual reality, as was done by Britain in the case of Egypt, and by France in the case of Morocco.

.   .   .

The Transfer of Power

On the whole, the transfer of power to the new nationalist élites which began in 1947, but rapidly took on the proportions of an avalanche, was implemented fairly smoothly. However, nobody (with the possible exception of the Portuguese who took a little longer to realize what was on the cards) wanted to retain full imperial control in their major colonial dependencies any longer than was absolutely necessary. This led to a series of dramatic crises, the most disastrous being the transfer of power in the Belgian Congo in 1960 which led to chaotic conditions in Zaire, as it was henceforth to be called. In the case of Algeria decolonization was achieved only after a bitter struggle, and furthermore it led to a severe crisis of the French political system. In the majority of cases, however, the transfer of power aroused only limited controversy in metropolitan societies, largely because governments acted upon the assumption that the new indigenous regimes would retain existing political and economic ties with the former mother country and that, by and large, business would be carried on as usual.

However, the formal handing over of power to the leaders of the nationalist movements cannot be considered a total watershed as far as imperialist control is concerned. From the African or Asian point of view, it was very often no more than a new 'bargain' struck with those sections of the indigenous élites which had been 'acculturated' to Western values and Western political traditions rather than with the people as a whole. It could be seen as a new sort of 'collaboration' designed to maintain traditional cultural, economic and political ties with the former mother country and, in many cases, it was in fact so.

It was in the interests of the West to have the former colonial peoples take over the political institutions of Western parliamentary government. It was also considered to be in the interests of the new nations to maintain existing economic links with the industrialized world, particularly those with the former mother country; in many cases this may indeed have been the case. But naturally the nature of the relationship with the former imperial power soon became a matter of serious internal dispute, which intensified as the anticipated immediate beneficial effects of independence on the indigenous economy turned out to be a chimera. The heritage of the Western nation-state with its rational bureaucratic administration and the idea of national unity transcending all tribal differences initially benefited the new Westernized intellectual élites, but often at the expense of other indigenous groups less well placed in the post-colonial systems which emerged in the 1960s.

In a variety of cases this final 'bargain,' as it were, between the former imperial power and the new nationalist movements did pay off. The new states accepted membership of the British Commonwealth of Nations, or the Union Française, thereby maintaining, at least symbolically, a formal tie with the former metropolitan country. The latter was, therefore, often able to maintain a limited degree of actual influence, however informal it may have been; in addition, membership of these new federations amounted to a guarantee that existing informal economic and cultural links would be maintained and perhaps even intensified.

These new forms of relations between metropolitan and peripheral countries can surely not be considered straight-forwardly 'imperialist,' but neither did they represent a clearcut break with the past, particularly if continuing informal links, that is, those of an economic nature, are taken into consideration. Often the granting of independence took place on the unspoken assumption that any substantial violation of the rights of nationals of the former mother country who were to stay in the newly independent state would amount to a breach of this 'contract' which, in turn, would establish the right of intervention by whatever means considered suitable by the former colonial power. Furthermore, it was expected that the new country would remain in the West's political camp. Often co-operation in military affairs and the supply of military technology in the future was considered a necessary corollary.

From the point of view of the non-Westernized sections of the indigenous population it could be argued that the final break with the imperialist past came only much later when the groups who had contracted the 'bargain' marking the granting of independence had gradually been replaced by other, more lowly placed sections of society. In the same vein, parliamentary institutions were either relinquished or reduced to a mere façade behind which new authoritarian power structures emerged. This is exactly what happened in the great majority of cases: there was a takeover by new leaders no longer directly associated with the colonial tradition, who had not been brought up under Western political institutions and under the influence of Western culture. All that remained was the use of sophisticated Western military technology, partly as a source of prestige, partly in order to engage in aggressive policies carried out using imperialist tactics on a regional basis. Sometimes these new regimes, often of a massively dictatorial nature, associated themselves with either the Soviet bloc or other major powers. Hence, formal emancipation from imperialist control of the classical kind at times led straight into an acceptance of the informal imperialist paramountcy of one of the superpowers which presently dominate the international arena.

The transfer of power to the new nationalist élites did constitute a cæsura in the development of relations between the West and the Third World. Yet, as we have described, it is far less marked than is usually assumed. It must be conceded that one key element of imperialist rule was formally abdicated, at least in principle, namely the right to use coercion and, if necessary, military force in the event of flagrant violations of the 'bargains' relating to the transfer of power. In a way the classic paradigm of imperialist rule had changed, it was now to be 'informal control wherever possible, while formal control no longer applies.' But even this was a matter of degree, rather than of clearcut principles. It was in fact only the emergence of a new international system dominated by two rival superpowers, both professedly anti-imperialist, that denied the Western powers the possibility of direct imperialist intervention in formally independent countries in order to maintain informal control, economic or otherwise.

Neither the United States nor the Soviet Union was henceforth prepared to permit direct intervention by third powers in Third World countries to any great extent. In this respect, the Suez crisis of 1956 represented a turning point: British intervention had to be abandoned in the face of joint pressure from the United States and the Soviet Union. Since this juncture, open imperialist interventions based upon historical claims acquired during the age of imperialism have become extremely rare, if not impossible. None the less they do occur, as the cases of Vietnam, Afghanistan, the Falkland Islands and recently the revival of

American interventionist policies in Central America demonstrate. But now a legitimation for intervention, perhaps a cry for help by some indigenous group or movement, whether it be engineered or genuine, is usually indispensable. For today, imperialist action is no longer considered morally justified; it cannot be carried out with anything like the self-righteousness which was typical of nineteenth-century imperialism.

Legacies of Empire and Dependency

But can the age of imperialism be considered finally closed (regardless of the fact that some remnants of former colonial rule still linger on) because informal imperialist control, whether it takes economic, cultural, political, or some other form, can no longer be backed up, if necessary by force? This would perhaps be premature. On the economic and, less ostentatiously, on the cultural level 'unequal bargains' are still very much with us and, furthermore, the legacies of older 'unequal bargains' still to a large extent determine the bargaining positions of each side. The legacies of imperialist rule condition the life and prospects of many Third World peoples to no small degree. It would be a mistake, therefore, to discard lightheartedly the argument that the Third World dependency upon the industrialized nations of the world is so firmly rooted that formal imperialist control is no longer required. Social and economic structures, and the educational systems in Third World countries are — it is claimed — so firmly linked to the West that they have to conduct their affairs as if they were still subjected to formal colonial rule. This argument must be taken seriously, all the more so if we take into account the very important role which informal and indirect rule played during the age of classical imperialism, when formal imperialist rule could well be considered to be only the tip of the iceberg.

Let us briefly look into this on two levels. First, we shall consider the relevance of the *legacies* of the imperialist past for the relationship of the less developed countries to the Western countries. Secondly, we shall investigate ways in which Western predominance in the Third World survives informally, particularly on the economic plane or, in the terminology made fashionable by Paul A. Baran, whether there is a continuing, and perhaps even growing *dependency* of the countries of the Third World on the West.

One of the more important legacies of colonial rule is perhaps the modern nation-state as a coherent, political unit which is supposedly the political organization of one nation with a uniform legal order and a centralized administrative system claiming sovereignty for itself in accordance with international law. But the boundaries of these new states, drawn during the age of imperialism, usually cut right across ethnic and cultural boundaries, not to mention declared loyalties. This is particularly true of the African continent. In the Middle East historical tradition was respected to a certain degree, but only inasmuch as the European powers found it convenient to keep the decaying Ottoman Empire alive for more than a century, helping to contain and at times to suppress nationalist independence movements or, at any rate, preferring not to intervene when this happened, as in the case of the Armenians. Perhaps it could be argued that Arab national unity might have been established as early as 1838 if the European powers had not forced Muhammad Ali to respect the rule of the Sultan of Constantinople.

The emergence of the nation-state in the less developed regions of the world was stimulated by the establishment of formal colonial administrations during the last stage of imperialist rule. In many ways the indigenous governments, which took over after independence, inherited what was, at least in principle if not in fact, a Westernized governmental system. With the end of imperialist rule, however, a factor which indirectly benefited the indigenous peoples also disappeared, namely the hegemonial control which, in the British case has so aptly been called *pax Britannica* but which was to some degree effective elsewhere too. It had effectively limited internal strife amongst the indigenous peoples, by the imposition of a legal system of conflict resolution, however inadequate.

However, Albert Wirz has drawn attention to the fact that this sort of imperial legacy was not an undisguised blessing. The colonial practice of playing off different ethnic and social groups against each other in order to strengthen the core position of the colonial authority did nothing to promote a sense of unity and loyalty to a common body politic among the indigenous population; on the contrary, the strategies of imperial rule tended to fragment the indigenous communities even further. At the same time central governments far removed from the people have had little unifying effect upon the indigenous population. The practices of indirect and subsidiary rule kept alive traditional loyalties to social élites whose status was not compatible with the principle of a unified nation-state.

It is not surprising, therefore, that many of the newly created states soon experienced intense internal strife while, in other cases, the political units created during the age of imperialism broke up immediately, as was the case in India and Pakistan. Only during the course of bitter conflicts, repeatedly erupting into devastating wars, could the Third World slowly find its way towards a new, acceptable division of political power. Giovanni Arrighi arrives at essentially the same conclusion; however, he sees this as a 'positive' phenomenon reflecting the shift of power in the relationship between the Third World and the Western countries: 'the new independence of Third World countries is manifested above all in their greater promptitude and capacity to resort to war to regulate their mutual relations and consolidate their fragile national unity.'

The European powers, particularly the British, often liked to flatter themselves by thinking that they had left behind not only the idea of democratic government, but also democratic institutions. In some ways this was real: in Egypt attempts to reorganize the country according to Western constitutional ideas go back at least to Urabi. Usually governments and institutions in former colonial countries which had been granted independence were still very much dominated by those indigenous élites which had already had the say during the later stages of colonial rule, and more often than not the parliamentary institutions were seen as a guarantee of continuing informal Western influence. However, the trend is undoubtedly for Third World countries to deviate from the Western pattern of constitutional government, perhaps only temporarily. This is partly due to the rise to power of new groups which have not experienced colonial influence to the same degree. How long the Western tradition will survive the present period of internal upheaval and transition following the transfer of power is a matter for speculation.

This is even more the case with regard to the socio-economic legacy of imperialism. It has often been argued that the social structures which emerged in most Third World countries were largely determined by the way in which these regions were integrated into the economic system of the former metropolitan country. Indeed, it will be necessary to ask whether the typical social stratification in underdeveloped countries which is characterized by a gross dichotomy between a vast, almost undeveloped, traditional sector and a small Westernized modern sector almost entirely geared to export interests is rooted in the conditions of imperialist rule.

Arguments of this nature serve as a point of departure for those social scientists who emphasize the lopsided nature of the economic relationship between advanced industrial and less developed countries in the post-colonial era. They argue that during the period of classical imperialism the metropolitan societies developed bridgeheads at the periphery, in business and elsewhere, in the form of collaborationist élites who had a direct interest in serving the needs of the metropolitan country and in maintaining economic and political links with it even though these policies ran counter to the interests of the large majority of the indigenous population.

In dogmatic Marxist terms this has been described as a mere reproduction of the metropolitan capitalist system at the periphery. To express it in this way would be rather naïve. But there is much to be said for the argument that the socio-economic structures which emerged were not particularly conducive to balanced economic growth, as they favoured monocultural agrarian production (as in the case of Egypt in the later nineteenth century) or specialized export industries, very often concerned more with the extraction of raw materials than with the production of finished goods. Wherever new industries developed they were geared primarily to export markets and linked to the interests of the metropolitan countries, or otherwise tied up with external rather than internal trade. Hence they remained islands within an otherwise traditional economy, which remained based on mere self-subsistence and engendered no impulses for economic or social change.

.   .   .

It may be argued that, in one respect at least, imperialism has left behind a positive legacy, namely in the cultural and scientific fields. In terms of cultural orientation the period of imperialism was also a period of the 'acculturation' of indigenous societies to the Western rationalist tradition, though often by way of indoctrination and political pressure. Certainly, the agents of Western imperialism were convinced that their intellectual traditions would be an unmixed blessing for the indigenous peoples of the Third World; colonization was considered by many to be the bringing of civilization to heathen and backward people throughout the world. Today we are no longer so sure whether Western ideas, the Western life-style and the Western intellectual tradition, let alone Christianity, are the only ways to achieve happiness and a humane life in this world. At least to some degree, modern technology and industry cannot thrive without the rationalist ways of thought developed in the West, but in this particular respect we are perhaps also at a turning-point. The West itself is no longer so sure of the validity of the philosophy of progress which it taught to the rest of the world during the classic age of imperialism.

The value of intellectual Westernization as a secondary spin-off of colonial rule has been challenged, most radically perhaps by Frantz Fanon in his famous book *Les Damnés de la terre*. He pointed to the deep psychological split experienced by intellectuals from Third World nations who had enjoyed a European education and become used to thinking according to Western standards, only to find themselves deeply alienated from their own peoples and cut off from their own cultural heritage. Fanon went so far as to argue that the identity crisis of the Westernized élites of Third World countries could only be healed by recourse to violence against the oppressors. In his view, anti-colonial wars not only helped to create a new culture, but also restored the self-respect of the indigenous intellectual élites. It is doubtful whether this extremist recipe, which was to some extent acted upon during the North African War of Independence, was a rational way out of the dilemma in which the educated élites in many underdeveloped countries found themselves.

Indeed, if imperialism is to be condemned on cultural grounds it should be because during the colonial era too little rather than too much was done for the education of the indigenous intellectual élites. Most Western colonial regimes (perhaps with the exception of the French) were in fact reluctant to extend the benefits of higher education beyond a rather small indigenous élite, as it was feared that this would create a national-revolutionary potential. British colonial practice, in particular, was influenced by the philosophy of indirect rule which did not recommend any large-scale Westernization of the indigenous peoples (although influential men like Macaulay had argued otherwise); instead, it aimed at preserving the traditional institutions and cultures, often of a rather archaic nature, thereby minimizing administrative costs and achieving maximum submissiveness on the part of the population. All in all, with hindsight it is very much an open question whether the system of indirect rule or a policy of ruthless modernization, breaking with traditional customs and, in particular, the often rather crude legal traditions of indigenous societies, was more beneficial in the end.

Of course, in the last resort it all depends on the evaluation of the Western model of modernization. Many rulers of Third World countries ran into trouble because of an all too uncritical adherence to what, until very recent times, was considered the Western path towards modernity. The dramatic revival of Islam as a major intellectual and moral force indicates that there are alternatives which need not necessarily clash with a policy of modernization and economic and social progress according to Western standards of technology and constitutional government.

Continuities of Empire?

It remains for us to return to the question of whether the present relationship between the West and the underdeveloped world must be considered a continuation of imperialism by informal, but even more effective means. There is little doubt that in the economic sphere at least an abundance of 'unequal bargains' still exist in the dealings of the West with less developed countries. On the other hand, some of the arguments of *dependencia* theorists as to why this must be so, have worn thin with the passage of time. Johan Galtung's argument that the economic relationship between the peripheral and the metropolitan countries is necessarily always asymmetrical, if only because the terms of trade always favour the latter, can no longer be maintained as a universal law. Nor is it fully convincing any longer to argue that the collaborationist classes installed at the periphery during the age of imperialism will for ever guarantee the smooth working of the unequal trade relations with the industrialized world. For by now the 'comprador classes' have disappeared, or, at any rate, their social composition has so radically changed that the original contention, based upon the continuity of patterns of collaboration supported by joint economic interests of the metropolitan business circles and their partners in the overseas 'bridgeheads,' can no longer be sustained to the same degree as a generation ago.

.   .   .

In principle, the former imperialist powers no longer possess any legal right to force Third World countries to pursue economic policies conducive to the interests of their economies and to the economic interests of their nationals resident in those countries. In a way, the outcome of the Suez conflict in 1956 settled this once and for all. But it would be futile to deny that a considerable arsenal of indirect means still exists by which less developed countries can be pressured into adopting economic policies which are in line with the interests of the core economies. Above all, two mechanisms are available: the provision of international loans, either directly or through international organizations like the World Bank and, secondly, the granting of foreign aid. But, apart from particular instances which may operate in different ways, these mechanisms do not always provide effective leverage for a policy which could be called informal imperialism; at least, not of the variety which we associate with the classic notion of imperialist control.

Neo-Colonialism.
The Last Stage of Imperialism

⎯⎯

KWAME NKRUMAH

No problem in defining informal imperialism existed for Kwame
Nkrumah. He published several books, but is best known for his role
in Ghana's struggle for independence and as that country's first president. A spokesman for African unity, he insisted that socialism
constituted the most valid expression of the African conscience. He
denied that a state subject to neocolonialism is independent, and
argued that despite appearances it is in reality directed economically
and politically "from the outside" and that U.S. capital provided
critical support for the neocolonialist strategy. The book, the conclusion of which is presented here, attempted to document these
charges by providing detailed information on firms, consortia, and
directors, and caused Washington to turn down a three-million-
dollar loan to Ghana and send a sharp note of protest to Nkrumah.
Neo-Colonialism. The Last Stage of Imperialism is clearly modeled
on Lenin's *Imperialism. The Last Stage of Capitalism.* If it can be
criticized for being an impassioned political argument rather than a
dispassionate economic analysis, it still constitutes a powerful influence on African intellectuals. To what extent did Nkrumah, writing
twenty years before Mommsen, anticipate the latter's conclusions?

The neo-colonialism of today represents imperialism in its final and
perhaps its most dangerous stage. In the past it was possible to convert a

From Kwame Nkrumah, *Neo-Colonialism. The Last Stage of Imperialism*, New York, 1966,
pp. ix-xvi. Reprinted by permission of International Publishers Co., Inc.

country upon which a neo-colonial regime had been imposed — Egypt in the nineteenth century is an example — into a colonial territory. Today this process is no longer feasible. Old-fashioned colonialism is by no means entirely abolished. It still constitutes an African problem, but it is everywhere on the retreat. Once a territory has become nominally independent it is no longer possible, as it was in the last century, to reverse the process. Existing colonies may linger on, but no new colonies will be created. In place of colonialism as the main instrument of imperialism we have today neo-colonialism.

The essence of neo-colonialism is that the State which is subject to it is, in theory, independent and has all the outward trappings of international sovereignty. In reality its economic system and thus its political policy is directed from outside.

The methods and form of this direction can take various shapes. For example, in an extreme case the troops of the imperial power may garrison the territory of the neo-colonial State and control the government of it. More often, however, neo-colonialist control is exercised through economic or monetary means. The neo-colonial State may be obliged to take the manufactured products of the imperialist power to the exclusion of competing products from elsewhere. Control over government policy in the neo-colonial State may be secured by payments towards the cost of running the State, by the provision of civil servants in positions where they can dictate policy, and by monetary control over foreign exchange through the imposition of a banking system controlled by the imperial power.

Where neo-colonialism exists the power exercising control is often the State which formerly ruled the territory in question, but this is not necessarily so. For example, in the case of South Vietnam the former imperial power was France, but neo-colonial control of the State has now gone to the United States. It is possible that neo-colonial control may be exercised by a consortium of financial interests which are not specifically identifiable with any particular State. The control of the Congo by great international financial concerns is a case in point.

The result of neo-colonialism is that foreign capital is used for the exploitation rather than for the development of the less developed parts of the world. Investment under neo-colonialism increases rather than decreases the gap between the rich and the poor countries of the world.

The struggle against neo-colonialism is not aimed at excluding the capital of the developed world from operating in less developed countries.

It is aimed at preventing the financial power of the developed countries being used in such a way as to impoverish the less developed.

Non-alignment, as practised by Ghana and many other countries, is based on co-operation with all States whether they be capitalist, socialist or have a mixed economy. Such a policy, therefore, involves foreign investment from capitalist countries, but it must be invested in accordance with a national plan drawn up by the government of the non-aligned State with its own interests in mind. The issue is not what return the foreign investor receives on his investments. He may, in fact, do better for himself if he invests in a non-aligned country than if he invests in a neo-colonial one. The question is one of power. A State in the grip of neo-colonialism is not master of its own destiny. It is this factor which makes neo-colonialism such a serious threat to world peace. The growth of nuclear weapons has made out of date the old-fashioned balance of power which rested upon the ultimate sanction of a major war. Certainty of mutual mass destruction effectively prevents either of the great power blocs from threatening the other with the possibility of a world-wide war, and military conflict has thus become confined to 'limited wars.' For these neo-colonialism is the breeding ground.

Such wars can, of course, take place in countries which are not neo-colonialist controlled. Indeed their object may be to establish in a small but independent country a neo-colonialist regime. The evil of neo-colonialism is that it prevents the formation of those large units which would make impossible 'limited war.' To give one example: if Africa was united, no major power bloc would attempt to subdue it by limited war because from the very nature of limited war, what can be achieved by it is itself limited. It is only where small States exist that it is possible, by landing a few thousand marines or by financing a mercenary force, to secure a decisive result.

The restriction of military action of 'limited wars' is, however, no guarantee of world peace and is likely to be the factor which will ultimately involve the great power blocs in a world war, however much both are determined to avoid it.

.   .   .

Neo-colonialism is also the worst form of imperialism. For those who practise it, it means power without responsibility and for those who suffer from it, it means exploitation without redress. In the days of old-fashioned colonialism the imperial power had at least to explain and justify at home the actions it was taking abroad. In the colony those who served the ruling imperial power could at least look to its protection against any violent move by their opponents. With neo-colonialism neither is the case.

Above all, neo-colonialism, like colonialism before it, postpones the facing of the social issues which will have to be faced by the fully developed sector of the world before the danger of world war can be eliminated or the problem of world poverty resolved.

Neo-colonialism, like colonialism, is an attempt to export the social conflicts of the capitalist countries. The temporary success of this policy can be seen in the ever widening gap between the richer and the poorer nations of the world. But the internal contradictions and conflicts of neo-colonialism make it certain that it cannot endure as a permanent world policy. How it should be brought to an end is a problem that should be studied, above all, by the developed nations of the world, because it is they who will feel the full impact of the ultimate failure. The longer it continues the more certain it is that its inevitable collapse will destroy the social system of which they have made it a foundation.

The reason for its development in the post-war period can be briefly summarised. The problem which faced the wealthy nations of the world at the end of the second world war was the impossibility of returning to the pre-war situation in which there was a great gulf between the few rich and the many poor. Irrespective of what particular political party was in power, the internal pressures in the rich countries of the world were such that no post-war capitalist country could survive unless it became a 'Welfare State.' There might be differences in degree in the extent of the social benefits given to the industrial and agricultural workers, but what was everywhere impossible was a return to the mass unemployment and to the low level of living of the pre-war years.

From the end of the nineteenth century onwards, colonies had been regarded as a source of wealth which could be used to mitigate the class conflicts in the capitalist States and, as will be explained later, this policy had some success. But it failed in its ultimate object because the pre-war capitalist States were so organised internally that the bulk of the profit made from colonial possessions found its way into the pockets of the capitalist class and not into those of the workers. Far from achieving the object intended, the working-class parties at times tended to identify their interests with those of the colonial peoples and the imperialist powers found themselves engaged upon a conflict on two fronts, at home with their own workers and abroad against the growing forces of colonial liberation.

The post-war period inaugurated a very different colonial policy. A deliberate attempt was made to divert colonial earnings from the wealthy class and use them instead generally to finance the 'Welfare State.' As will be seen from the examples given later, this was the method consciously adopted even by those working-class leaders who had before the war regarded the colonial peoples as their natural allies against their capitalist enemies at home.

At first it was presumed that this object could be achieved by maintaining the pre-war colonial system. Experience soon proved that attempts to do so would be disastrous and would only provoke colonial wars, thus dissipating the anticipated gains from the continuance of the colonial regime. Britain, in particular, realised this at an early stage and the correctness of the British judgement at the time has subsequently been demonstrated by the defeat of French colonialism in the Far East and Algeria and the failure of the Dutch to retain any of their former colonial empire.

The system of neo-colonialism was therefore instituted and in the short run it has served the developed powers admirably. It is in the long run that its consequences are likely to be catastrophic for them.

Neo-colonialism is based upon the principle of breaking up former large united colonial territories into a number of small non-viable States which are incapable of independent development and must rely upon the former imperial power for defence and even internal security. Their economic and financial systems are linked, as in colonial days, with those of the former colonial ruler.

At first sight the scheme would appear to have many advantages for the developed countries of the world. All the profits of neo-colonialism can be secured if, in any given area, a reasonable proportion of the States have a neo-colonialist system. It is not necessary that they *all* should have one. Unless small States can combine they must be compelled to sell their primary products at prices dictated by the developed nations and buy their manufactured goods at the prices fixed by them. So long as neo-colonialism can prevent political and economic conditions for optimum development, the developing countries, whether they are under neo-colonialist control or not, will be unable to create a large enough market to support industrialisation. In the same way they will lack the financial strength to force the developed countries to accept their primary products at a fair price.

In the neo-colonialist territories, since the former colonial power has in theory relinquished political control, if the social conditions occasioned by neo-colonialism cause a revolt the local neo-colonialist government can be sacrificed and another equally subservient one substituted in its place. On the other hand, in any continent where neo-colonialism exists on a wide scale the same social pressures which can produce revolts in neo-colonial territories will also affect those States which have refused to accept the system and therefore neo-colonialist nations have a ready-made weapon with which they can threaten their opponents if they appear successfully to be challenging the system.

These advantages, which seem at first sight so obvious, are, however, on examination, illusory because they fail to take into consideration the facts of the world today.

The introduction of neo-colonialism increases the rivalry between the great powers which was provoked by the old-style colonialism. However little real power the government of a neo-colonialist State may possess, it must have, from the very fact of its nominal independence, a certain area of manoeuvre. It may not be able to exist without a neo-colonialist master but it may still have the ability to change masters.

The ideal neo-colonialist State would be one which was wholly subservient to neo-colonialist interests but the existence of the socialist nations makes it impossible to enforce the full rigour of the neo-colonialist system. The existence of an alternative system is itself a challenge to the neo-colonialist regime. Warnings about 'the dangers of Communist subversion' are likely to be two-edged since they bring to the notice of those living under a neo-colonialist system the possibility of a change of regime. In fact neo-colonialism is the victim of its own contradictions. In order to make it attractive to those upon whom it is practised it must be shown as capable of raising their living standards, but the economic object of neo-colonialism is to keep those standards depressed in the interest of the developed countries. It is only when this contradiction is understood that the failure of innumerable 'aid' programmes, many of them well intentioned, can be explained.

In the first place, the rulers of neo-colonial States derive their authority to govern, not from the will of the people, but from the support which they obtain from their neo-colonialist masters. They have therefore little interest in developing education, strengthening the bargaining power of their workers employed by expatriate firms, or indeed of taking any step which would challenge the colonial pattern of commerce and industry, which it is the object of neo-colonialism to preserve. 'Aid,' therefore, to a neo-colonial State is merely a revolving credit, paid by the neo-colonial master, passing through the neo-colonial State and returning to the neo-colonial master in the form of increased profits.

Secondly, it is in the field of 'aid' that the rivalry of individual developed States first manifests itself. So long as neo-colonialism persists so long will spheres of interest persist, and this makes multilateral aid — which is in fact the only effective form of aid — impossible.

Once multilateral aid begins the neo-colonialist masters are faced by the hostility of the vested interests in their own country. Their manufacturers naturally object to any attempt to raise the price of the raw materials which they obtain from the neo-colonialist territory in question, or to the establishment there of manufacturing industries which might compete directly or indirectly with their own exports to the territory. Even education is suspect as likely to produce a student movement and it is, of course, true that in many less developed countries the students have been in the vanguard of the fight against neo-colonialism.

In the end the situation arises that the only type of aid which the neo-colonialist masters consider as safe is 'military aid.'

Once a neo-colonialist territory is brought to such a state of economic chaos and misery that revolt actually breaks out then, and only then, is there no limit to the generosity of the neo-colonial overlord, provided, of course, that the funds applied are utilised exclusively for military purposes.

Military aid in fact marks the last stage of neo-colonialism and its effect is self-destructive. Sooner or later the weapons supplied pass into the hands of the opponents of the neo-colonialist regime and the war itself increases the social misery which originally provoked it.

11

THE
DISMANTLING
OF THE
WELFARE STATE

T he modern welfare state was born in Germany, with the introduction of Bismarckian social legislation, but developed chiefly in
Great Britain and Scandinavia. In the first decade of the twentieth century the governing Liberal party provided Britons with national sickness and unemployment benefits whose costs were borne by levying additional taxes on the wealthy. Greatly expanded, such national insurance
became the basis of the welfare states established in Great Britain
and in the liberated countries of Europe after the defeat of Germany
in 1945. This was part of the reconstruction effort carried out by socialist or mixed economies, invariably with state intervention in the
realm of public welfare. The welfare state was seen as a compromise between capitalism and socialism designed to abolish the inequities apparently inherent in the former without, however, unleashing social

revolution and without essentially changing the existing economic structure. The free market would be retained but modified in the interests of social justice.

The British Labour party, which swept into office in 1945, nationalized the coal, steel, and transportation industries. More basic was the provision of social services as a right rather than as a charitable meeting of needs. The National Health Service made free medical care available to all, while the social security established by the Lloyd George budget of 1911 was implemented with family assistance. Secondary education had become universally available during the war, and the government was empowered to set aside "green space" as an essential ingredient in urban planning. Costs would be met by sharp increases in income taxes and inheritance taxes.

Similarly, in France, where left-wing parties formed governing coalitions on the country's liberation, even more extensive nationalization programs, as well as economic planning, were set in motion. The modest social security system, in place before the war, grew rapidly, although rather than a national health service, national health insurance became the norm, and concern over the low birth rate prompted generous family allowances. The Scandinavian nations, having implemented their own government-sponsored public services in the 1930s, expanded these programs, and other countries, even the new Federal Republic in West Germany that was committed to maintaining as free a market as possible, also introduced various forms of welfare legislation including national health insurance, wide-ranging social security measures, and greater public investment. Hence different versions of the welfare state developed to meet economic and social needs, but all of them had in common a comprehensive education system, health care, and unemployment, retirement, and sickness benefits.

In the aftermath of the Arab oil embargo of the early and mid-1970s, however, and with the rapid economic growth and prosperity of the two-and-a-half decades since World War II now slowing down, yet with prices continuing to rise, the burden of paying for social programs produced mounting frustration. Restive taxpayers demanded reduced government expenditures, which meant reductions in social programs. This in part explained the return of conservative governments in numerous countries, whose members relished more popular support for long-standing ideological convictions. The Swedish Social Democrats, in office since 1942, were voted out in 1976 (though they returned in 1982, and other reasons, such as distrust of their pro-nuclear energy policy, had figured in the defeat). Danish conservatives, who amassed greater strength in the late 1970s, put together a new governing coalition in the early 1980s. In 1982 the more conservative Christian Democrats replaced the Social Democrats, who had governed West Germany since 1969. And perhaps most ominous for the welfare state was the ascent to office in 1979 of Margaret Thatcher's Conservative party, committed to reducing the extent of social services available in Britain, and denationalizing, or "privatizing," state-owned industries and utilities. Even though socialists won power in France in 1980 and began to implement plans for greater state involvement, more Keynesian stimulation of purchasing power, and more sweeping nationalizations and social legislation, within two years, because of shrinking economic growth occasioned by the American recession and high interest rates among other reasons, a drastic austerity program brought a halt to further change. Conservatives and Centrists won victories in the 1986 legislative elections.

Never stilled, controversy over the extent, even the legitimacy, of the welfare state emerged more forcefully than ever, and it is this controversy that is explored in the three readings that follow. Difficulty in meeting the costs of expensive social programs, particularly during a time of slowed economic growth, strengthened the criticism, but renewed concern over the "loss of incentive" allegedly following in the wake of generous social programs and over the introduction of desirable, not merely essential, services added a more far-reaching ideological and philosophical dimension to the debate. Critics recommended the substitution of cash for the granting of services in kind in cases of primary poverty, and the earmarking of purchasing power — such as vouchers in education — to promote greater freedom of choice and bring about greater decentralization and minimization of bureaucracy. Others cited the welfare state and its "extravagant" social programs as responsible for limiting Western Europe's ability — or willingness — to carry a larger share of the Western defense burden.[1] Defenders of the welfare state, many of whom recognized a need for reform, pointed to the deeply rooted concept of

---

[1] Arthur Seldon, "The Idea of the Welfare State and its Consequences," *The Welfare State and Its Aftermath*, ed. S. N. Eisenstadt and Ora Ahimeir (Totowa, New Jersey, 1985), 59–61.

welfare as a societal responsibility and were able to show basic public support for retaining essential programs. Some urged that the welfare state be preserved for the sake of social peace.[2]

Given smaller economic growth and the expanding cost of public services, the question that emerges is whether the welfare state can be saved — for some, ought to be saved — or whether it will be slowly and inexorably dismantled. While reductions in the costs of health care and social services are considered necessary, significant curtailment of government services and contraction of the public sector may have far-reaching consequences. Major cuts in long-established government spending programs and privatization of public utilities to gain short-term economic and political advantages appear tempting. Even so, inferior general education, limited health care, inadequate housing, less environmental protection, and fewer safeguards ensuring minimally acceptable working conditions can ultimately destroy the strong fabric of society that welfare state programs helped to weave.

---

[2]Eric Willenz, "Why Europe Needs the Welfare State," *Foreign Policy* 63 (Summer, 1986), 88, 106.

The Welfare State
and Its Aftermath

∿

S. W. EISENSTADT

In 1983 twenty-three scholars from ten countries participated in an international conference on "The Welfare State and its Aftermath" held in Jerusalem. Both a background paper and an opening statement was prepared by S. N. Eisenstadt, one of the members of the Jerusalem Institute for Israel Studies, which sponsored the symposium. He attempted "to assess the achievements, hopes, and criticisms of the welfare state, the calls for reevaluation of the path of democratic society, and the role of welfare services in shaping social policies in the post-welfare era." This paper and statement provided the basis for Eisenstadt's introduction to a published collection of the papers presented at the conference, and it constitutes the bulk of the reading that follows. What, in the author's view, accounts for the criticisms directed against the welfare state?

It is said that either of two disasters can befall a vision: failure or success. The welfare state has succeeded. Firmly established in some countries, evolving more slowly in others, the welfare state has become a permanent feature in most modern states. Without a doubt, it has transformed most contemporary societies, but not always according to the vision that created it. This, of course, is the nature of human history:

From S. N. Eisenstadt and Ora Ahimeir, eds., *The Welfare State and Its Aftermath*, pp. 1–6. Copyright 1985 Barnes and Noble Books. Reprinted by permission of the publisher.

transformations that occur do not always follow the original intentions, and, moreover, the very institutionalisation of such vision usually generates new social forces and problems.

The late T. H. Marshall assumed that the welfare state would be the 'apogee' of democracy. It would give citizens not only legal and political rights, but also social equality. The purpose of the welfare state, according to Marshall, was to take away the impediments that prevented full equality. This was the prime visionary impetus behind what was eventually institutionalised as the welfare state. Another very important historical element in the development of the welfare state, was the Bismarckian vision of the 'peaceful,' 'anti-socialist' incorporation of new social classes (especially the working classes) into the state, as well as the older philanthropic tradition of the social services for the 'poor.' In the contemporary world, however, it was the democratic view of the welfare state, the vision of the system as the guarantor of social equality, which became prevalent.

The creation of such conditions of social equality became a major, if not the primary, objective of the welfare state and from this goal several explicit or implicit assumptions have developed.

One such assumption stipulated that each individual is entitled to a decent standard of living, to education, housing, medical care and welfare services, as well as to relief at time of crisis. Another assumption has been that through universal services, with guaranteed standards and under governmental control, the elimination of poverty, the advancement of underprivileged groups and the narrowing gaps in income, education and employment, would be best achieved.

All of this has been regarded as an expression of justice which would have a moderating influence on social conflicts and would increase involvement of the population in matters of state and society. It was also often assumed that greater participation by larger segments of the population in the political and economic process, in close relation to Keynesian economic policies, would further economic growth and ensure the durability of a prosperous society.

The concrete developments in the welfare states have seemingly borne out these hopes. Thus, indeed, social services in the fields of employment, health, education, welfare, etc. were given an enormous boost and have greatly changed the whole contour of modern society.

The standard of living and life expectancy in the welfare state have both risen considerably. At the same time the notion of poverty has undergone a radical transformation, changing from extreme to relative distress or deprivation. The lower sectors of the society have continuously gained better living conditions, while such ills as hunger, epidemics and pauperism have been greatly reduced.

In recent years, however, it has become apparent that the measures introduced by the welfare state neither lived up to the original expectations of its creators nor have they caught up with the new problems which kept appearing, partly as a result of these very changes but primarily as a result of the institutionalisation of the welfare state, which seemingly, at least, contradicted its own major goals.

First, the emergence of a colossal bureaucracy has become a basic feature of the welfare state. While originally created to offer protection against exploitation, environmental damage, anarchy and the 'ruthlessness' of free market economy, it has often been regarded by its clients as an alien and alienating organ which cramps initiative, creates dependence and, in the end, serves only its own interests and those of its makers.

The gargantuan swelling of the bureaucratic machine has frequently resulted in a feeling of resentment against authority, a growing dependence upon the system of services and benefits offered by the state, which is now expected to solve every problem, and often a feeling of helplessness on the part of the individual client.

A second major problem is that the financing of services has become a gigantic burden. Since the cost, in relative terms, is borne more by middle and upper classes through the instrument of progressive taxation, and since these groups perceive themselves to be less in need of such services, tax evasion has proliferated and, consequently, the weaker groups have, in fact, had to shoulder more of the burden.

Of no less importance is the fact that while the standard of living in welfare states has tended to rise continuously, it has risen unequally among different sectors of the society, favouring the wealthy more than the lower strata, and thus, it seems, often widening the gap between at least some of the groups.

Some more far-reaching structural changes which have altered the whole contour of modern society have developed in close association with the combination of Keynesian and economic policies and the institutionalisation of the welfare state.

In conjunction with these trends, the development of what has often been called the model of the post-industrial society has occurred.

Its predominant characteristics include: the importance of services in relation to productive industries; a significant rise in the standard of education and economic well-being; the growing emphasis on technological and theoretical know-how; and the prominence of so-called post-bourgeois values (the quality of life and humanist ideals), in contrast to the Protestant ethics of work and morality.

The development of this model or trend became connected with far-reaching changes in the class structure of modern societies and in the modes of political participation and organisation. The old pattern of high class consciousness and political activity became weaker. Both the working class and the middle class tended to lose some of their old identity. New sectors, the middle class and white-collar workers, emerged, very often closely related to the state as part of the public sector, with more and more diversified and segmented interests. At the same time, great expectations of mobility were kindled, which the actual process of mobility from lower to middle class has often failed to meet, frequently giving rise to great frustration.

A growing shift in the modes of political organisation, participation and protest have also taken place. Political parties, the traditional instruments of political organisation and articulation of interests, have been losing their organisational strength and their ability to inspire identification. Instead, political activity has become punctuated by constant oscillations between pursuance of various discrete interests by pressure or single-issue groups, new protest groups, fighting for their aims with increasingly louder clamour, often far away from the original aims of the welfare state. Ecological pressure groups, groups demanding civil rights or those opposing nuclear armament, demanded changes of policy and a larger share in government and resources. Particularly vehement during the 1960s and 1970s were the protest movements of students, ethnic minorities and feminist groups, all demanding an end to historical injustices by means of affirmative action, injustices which they claimed had not been corrected, despite considerable effort and expense, by the welfare state.

The result of all these tendencies has been, and continues to be, rather complex. On the one hand, those demanding a say in decisions likely to affect their lives and a greater participation in various areas of policy and life, have become very local and the issue of participation has become a very central one. On the other hand, there has also developed an increasing apathy among those who desire to obtain access to the sources of power and government, but who may be deterred by the complexity of the issues and the systems in modern society in general and democratic ones in particular, and in between these forces there developed, as we have seen, continuous eruptions of single-issue groups and new protest movements.

Thus, all of these trends, in class structure and in modes of political organisation and activities, have indeed generated a new social reality which attests to the fact that most of the problems created by the welfare state were in no way dreamed of by those who were the first bearers of its vision. Neither have the problems remained constant. For example, 15 or 20 years ago, the emphasis was on the issues of efficiency; and, while they still exist, the problems of the welfare state under discussion today are primarily social, political and economic, bearing on the different aspects of the transformation of modern societies to which we have briefly alluded above and which are discussed in greater detail in the various papers in this volume.

Criticism of the Welfare State

Small wonder, then, that the welfare state has drawn widespread criticism. Critics can be divided into four major schools: the 'Conservatives,' the 'Moderates,' the 'Traditional Radicals,' and the 'New Radicals.'

The 'Conservative' criticism rests its case on the belief in initiative, decentralisation and free market economy. It maintains that the excessive interference by the welfare state jeopardises individual liberties and leads the state towards a socialist or communist regime. Too much involvement by the state undermines ambition, initiative and creativity; it runs counter to the laws of nature governing the improvement of the species through incessant struggle and adaptation. Attaining the goals of the welfare state might impoverish the country, discourage labour and curtail investment. The effective implementation of welfare state programmes tends to make citizens even more demanding, fans inflation, bloats the bureaucratic system and saps the power of the government.

The second type of criticism, the 'Moderate' school, usually comes from within social-democratic circles. It accepts the principles underlying the welfare state, but condemns their poor implementation in the distribution of resources, the abuse of services earmarked for the weaker groups by the middle class, and the burdening of the weakest segments with the brunt of financing these services. Proponents of this approach do not call for a new social order, but demand improvements in welfare plans and a redistribution of means.

The third school of 'Traditional Radical' criticism is one which is based on the Marxist tradition and accepts the basis of the welfare state, but objects to its organisational pattern, the reliance on private property and the principle of representative democracy. A just and egalitarian distribution of resources, they claim, can be achieved only through a radical reform in the procedures of economic productions, and a complete democratisation of government, through some sort of far-reaching, semi-revolutionary change.

The fourth, the 'New Radical' criticism, most fully articulated by some New Left groups, claims that the welfare state suffers from the wrong definition of its objectives. For one thing, this criticism perceives welfare as it exists as a purely material matter, but that the benefits and services are not enough and that the state should endeavour to fulfill the inner spiritual needs of the individual. Secondly, the welfare state favours a social, bureaucratic hierarchy and a conventional distribution of labour, at the expense of the community. Thirdly, the welfare state has failed to cope with the individual's sense of alienation and with the fact that work is an imposition and therefore not creative. Finally, they claim that the welfare state destroys its physical environment.

Welfare Politics
in Western Democracies

࢚࿚

SHIRLEY WILLIAMS

Shirley Williams was Minister of Health and of Labour in the Labour party governments of the 1960s. She held other ministerial posts in the following decade, and after the Conservative victory of 1979 was the opposition spokesperson on social services and on consumer affairs. She was a co-founder of the breakaway Social Democratic party in 1981, and served as its president until 1988. Williams has published several books on the subjects of unemployment and economic growth. How does she respond to the attacks launched against the welfare state? What reforms does she propose?

The welfare state of Western Europe, the most remarkable contribution to the political and social stability of these countries in the thirty years after the Second World War, is now under attack from several directions. Indeed, so fierce is the criticism in some quarters that the real achievements in terms of a better educated, healthier population, protected at least in part from the exigencies of unemployment and injury, and able to live with dignity in old age, are in danger of being forgotten.

There are two major themes of attack on the welfare state: the first is that it is too expensive, the second that it is too bureaucratic. As we shall see, there is some evidence for both charges. The 1960s and early

1970s were years of very rapid expansion in state pensions and benefits, linking them to the cost of living, so that there could be no loss of value as a result of inflation. Other countries, like the Netherlands, Sweden and, for a brief period, Britain, went further, indexing pensions to the rise in earnings also, so that pensioners would enjoy the general rise in the standard of life, while being protected against inflation. Free secondary education up to the age of sixteen or even eighteen, became universal in Western Europe, and was complemented by a doubling or trebling of higher education in many countries. Few doubted that formal education was a good of which there could not be too much. Indeed, for those of liberal and progressive views, the desirability of an increase in the quantity and quality of formal education was the ark of the covenant, the badge of being an enlightened citizen. Health care became more sophisticated as new medical techniques were tried out and then incorporated in the treatment available to all insured people, or through public health services. But the techniques were not only more sophisticated, they were notably more expensive.

By the mid-1970s, public expenditure as a share of gross national product was averaging 43.7 per cent in the OECD countries, with the Netherlands, Norway and Sweden exceeding 50 per cent. Of this total, transfer payments (pensions, benefits, etc.) accounted for about two-fifths, and the services themselves (expenditure on schools, hospitals, community services and so on) for a similar proportion. The social services were, in short, taking an ever larger share of an ever increasing gross national product. Furthermore, if the expenditure per head were to be maintained, there was no avoiding such a development. For population patterns in the 1960s and 1970s increased the ratio of dependants to those sustaining them. In most European countries birth rates rose rapidly in the late 1950s and early 1960s. The so-called bulge of children born in this period worked their way through the educational system compelling expansions at every stage, in school building programmes, teacher training and recruitment, administrative staff and so on. The dramatic decline in the death rate due to the conquest of common infectious diseases like diphtheria and tuberculosis led to a longer expectation of life. Today, the fastest-growing section of the population is the over-eighties, the very people who make the greatest demands on the medical services. Medical advances also enabled many people with serious handicaps to survive, including some severely handicapped at birth, for example with spina bifida. Their survival again carried permanent consequences for the social services, since many needed lifelong care.

The welfare state has paradoxically become the victim of its own success, creating from that success fresh demands that it cannot easily meet. But that is not the sum of the problems of financing it. The most serious problem of all is the end of the era of economic growth, combined with a growing resentment against the burden of taxation in all its forms. Against the background of constant, or even declining gross national product, the competition between private demands and public needs for each person's pocket becomes acute. People resist a fall in their material standard of life; and they become more conscious of the demands made by government through taxation. It is difficult to find any way of financing the social services that is not highly sensitive. National insurance contributions which finance a large part of Western European expenditure on pensions and on health, are now so high as to be a substantial disincentive to employing labour. It is instructive that Italy has moved in the direction of waiving insurance contributions for the first year of a new job for a young worker; the burden of this tax on labour nearly doubles the cost to the employer of each person employed. Direct taxes are no more popular. Indeed, the level of direct taxation was a significant factor in the 1976 defeat of Sweden's semi-permanent Social Democratic government. Taxes on property, known as rates in Britain, and imposed by local or state government, arouse the most resentment of all. It was skillful exploitation of this resentment that led to the passage of Proposition 13 in California in 1978. Resentment at high levels of taxation has been a major strand in the crucial shift of public sympathy away from the neo-Keynesian paternalism of the liberal and social democratic parties in the West.

But not the only one. Bureaucracy and professionalisation of the public services are the others. The welfare state has become remote from the people it serves, and heavily administered. It is staffed by professionals, whose qualifications have become more demanding, and whose pay has therefore had to be higher. The institutions themselves have become larger, more centralised and more expensive. The one- or two-teacher village school is vanishing. The big regional or district hospital with its gleaming and expensive equipment replaces the local cottage hospital, and every non-routine case is referred to a specialist. In an OECD paper, one expert on social policy, Rudolf Klein, declared that 'the implicit ideal of Welfare State services is the professionalisation of everyone' working in them. It is now rare to find non-professionals except in such lowly jobs as home-helps or unskilled hospital work, and there are occasional drives to professionalise these too. In parallel with professionalisation itself, the qualifications required to become professional have been driven up. In Britain, for example, no unqualified teacher can any longer teach in maintained schools, and the minimum length of training has risen from two years to four. Professionalisation has been accompanied by bureaucracy. The proportion of administrators to those undertaking the actual work of teaching or nursing has grown steadily in recent years. Yet neither this adoption of higher standards of qualification, nor the replacement of amateurs or the unqualified by professionals, has improved people's perception of the services. If anything, they have become more resentful of their status as 'client' or patient — passive recipients of services determined for them by others.

Professionalisation has a significance also in the wider political context. The public service has become a very large employer, and its staff is now an important pressure group. Half the members of the trade unions affiliated to the Trades Union Congress in Britain are public service workers, substantially more than all the private sector blue-collar trade union members. The horny-handed son of toil has become a teacher or a laboratory technician. Parties of the left are therefore under great pressure to sustain the welfare state as it is, and indeed to expand it, in its present, highly institutionalised form. This phenomenon is not new. For many years, teachers were a dominant force in the SFIO, forerunner to the present French socialist party. It is, however, becoming even more important.

Demography, professionalisation, the growing sophistication of equipment and technique all add to the cost of the welfare state; so, paradoxically, does unemployment. In Britain transfer payments to the unemployed have led to an increase in the share of gross national product taken by public expenditure, despite all the protestations of a determinedly monetarist government. Yet the political and public resistance to any further taxation to pay for it is now very strong. In Britain, the government has not lost much ground with public opinion in its long and bitter battle with the health service unions. The nurses alone command public sympathy.

The future of the welfare state could be one of disablement by a thousand cuts, each fought by the organisations representing staff, each diminishing the quality of the service, while those who can afford it opt out into private education or private medical treatment. Gradually, the welfare state would shrivel to what it once was, a publicly financed, low-level system used by the poor.

There is, however, an alternative future, making use of new technologies, and involving people in maintaining their own health, teaching themselves and looking after each other, an enabling state, rather than a welfare state.

The new technologies — by which I mean particular information technologies — will alter the pattern both of demand and of supply. Demand will become more flexible; for example, people will need periods of re-training and new education throughout their lives, but formal education may yield to a mixture of learning and practical experience. Some of the learning will be distance learning, using teaching machines, computers and visual display units, a further development of the ideas embodied in the Open University. In health, computerised records make it easy for people to be notified of the need for immunisation or vaccination at the appropriate age, and comparisons between large numbers of medical records will make diagnosis easier; indeed individuals will be able to feed in information to a computer and get their symptoms diagnosed. Side-effects of new drugs should be picked up more rapidly, and hospitals should save money on stocks of expensive drugs. The problem still to be resolved is, of course, that of the confidentiality of medical records.

In the personal social services too, the new technologies could revolutionise the service. Many elderly people will be able to continue to live at home, since shopping, entertainment, financial transactions and ultimately chats with friends or with a social worker will all be accessible through two-way communications systems such as teletext and citizens' band radio. Social workers will be able to monitor a group of people for whom they are responsible, visiting only those who need assistance. The pattern of supply of staff is likely to be altered too. Many older people are likely to opt for partial retirement, and will be available as volunteers or family members to undertake more personal social work. It is easy to forget that 85 per cent of the housework and shopping needed by housebound elderly people is provided by family members, friends and neighbours, as are 88 per cent of their meals. The contribution of the unofficial economy to the welfare of the elderly and the sick is still much greater than that of the statutory services.

The new technologies imply a decentralised, flexible participatory welfare state, in which the professionals are called upon where needed for advice or help, but are no longer the front line of the welfare state. In such a new structure, health maintenance and health education would take precedence over curative medicine. Greater emphasis would be placed on diet, on avoiding smoking or excessive drinking, on cutting down road accidents. Institutional care would be a last resort. Mobile crisis management teams dealing with patients suffering heart attacks who are nursed at home already show at least as good results as intensive care in hospital. And for those afflicted by chronic illness, mutual help groups of fellow-sufferers are more supportive than professionals without first-hand experience.

The prospects are exciting; but the institutions are conservative and find it hard to change. A responsive, accountable welfare state offering people choices is now feasible. If the opportunity is not grasped, the traditional welfare state will wither away, and millions of deprived people will be the losers.

The Politics of
Industrial Privatization

JOHN VICKERS AND VINCENT WRIGHT

John Vickers and Vincent Wright are fellows at Nuffield College of
Oxford University. Vickers has written on technological competition and competition policy, while Wright is joint editor of the
journal *West European Politics* and both author and editor of several
works on French and European politics and policy making. Here
they consider the varied motives — ideological, economic, political,
and financial — of the countries pursuing privatization. Is "judicious
trimming" a more desirable alternative to weakening the public
sector by radical reduction of state-owned industries?

In searching for an explanation for the boldness or timidity of the
various privatisation programmes it is clearly important to examine the
motives of those pursuing them. This is no easy task for a number of
reasons. First, there exists no systematic exposé of the reasons for privatisation: they have to be culled in ministerial speeches, in laconic election
manifestos, in parliamentary debates, in party documents, in the various
Acts which have provided for the programmes, and discerned from government policy decisions. Secondly, motives vary widely across European

From John Vickers and Vincent Wright, "The Politics of Industrial Privatisation in Western
Europe: An Overview," *West European Politics* 11 (October, 1988), pp. 4–9. Reprinted by
permission from the October 1988 issue of *West European Politics* published by Frank Cass
and Company Limited, 11 Gainsborough Road, London Ell, England. Copyright Frank
Cass & Co. Ltd.

countries — as will become clear in the following discussion — and this is scarcely surprising, since different constituencies defend privatisation for different, and often diametrically opposed, reasons. Thirdly, even within a single country, the emphasis given to different objectives changes over time. Thus, the nature of the privatisation ambitions of the Thatcher government in its second term in office (1983–87) could not have been foreseen at the time of the Conservatives' 1979 election victory. Fourthly, it is clear that the reasons for privatisations have often followed rather than preceded the various privatisation measures: 'achievable objectives became reasons to justify the programmes.' Finally, it is not always easy to distinguish unspoken motives from declared reasons, or the consequences from the wishes.

The first series of motives may be described as broadly *ideological*. For the right, especially in Britain and France, privatisation is part of the general strategy to shift the boundary between public and private in favour of the latter. It is nourished by deep-seated anti-State sentiment. In France, privatisation is clearly linked with the struggle against the long tradition of *dirigisme* or *Colbertisme*. The title of the Minister of Finance's (Edouard Balladur) defence of his programme is inelegant yet highly revealing: *Je crois en l'homme plus qu'en l'Etat.*' In the United Kingdom, privatisation has been seen as an integral part of the onslaught on Butskellism or MacWilsonism — the social-democratic, semi-collectivist consensus of the post-war era. In both countries, privatisation has been the focus of a campaign to push back the frontiers of the State — which for the right is the stultifying and inhibiting State that erodes personal responsibility and undermines individual initiative — by the creation of a proper environment for individual actors by tax incentives, the abolition of inhibitions (like exchange controls), the relaxation of planning regulations, and the weakening of market rigidities notably in the labour market. Self-help and self-reliance are the cardinal virtues, and they are seen as being undermined by collective provision. This anti-State philosophy has found some favour in right-wing circles in other European countries (notably in Greece and Portugal), but little echo in the debates in Christian Democratic circles in Italy, West Germany, Belgium and the Netherlands. It has also been singularly absent from right-wing thinking in Spain. It is instructive, too, that parts of the French right and of the British Conservative Party do not share the anti-State enthusiasm of their leaders.

A second ideological underpinning of privatisation is the belief that public industries and services limit the choice of consumers because of their monopoly positions. As Sir Geoffrey Howe, British Chancellor of the Exchequer, put it in 1981, 'The consumer is sovereign in the private sector. In the public sector he is dethroned by subsidy and monopoly.' It is further argued that public ownership deprives individuals of economic freedom by forcing them to hold 'implied shareholdings' in public sector enterprises which they might not wish to hold if given the choice. The third ideological strand in the privatisation argument is the desire to build a 'property-owning democracy': Nicholas Ridley, one of the Thatcher government's more vocal champions of privatisation, has claimed that it would lead to 'real public ownership — that is, ownership by the people.' From this motivation stems the drive to sell shares in the denationalised industries to as wide a public as possible and especially to the employees of those industries, and in practice 'popular capitalism' has been nurtured by a battery of incentives to buy and to hold those shares.

The second general argument for privatisation may be described as *economic*, and again there are several interconnected strands within the argument. In Britain and France, the economic aims are ambitious: in the former country, claims have been made that privatisation has helped to produce 'a sweeping and irreversible shift in the structure of the economy' while in France it is part of the policy to 'change the rules of the game of our economy.' The rules, it is argued, may be altered in several ways. In the first place, privatisation has been perceived as a means of furthering liberalisation. Many of the State monopolies are not natural monopolies (even in gas and electricity there may be a natural monopoly in transmission through the national grid, but not in production), and once broken up there would be greater scope for competition. It has been argued that for politically and socially-inspired loss-making services it is more efficient to provide specific subsidies to needy consumers, or to private suppliers of those services. A second economic argument has been that public sector production and services are *intrinsically* less efficient than those in the private sector. They are allegedly less efficient because they are not vulnerable to the bracing winds of market forces, and are cushioned by the statutory obligation by the State to pick up the bill for any losses made. They face no threat of bankruptcy or take-over and they have no private shareholders to satisfy. Furthermore, deprived of the possibility of direct personal financial gain, managers will wastefully pursue their own non-pecuniary goals. Moreover, when they are motivated by the need for greater efficiency and profits they are frustrated by governments pursuing their own macro-economic and income redistribution objectives. At bottom, there is a deep-seated suspicion in neo-liberal circles of politico-bureaucratic compromises which usurp the role of the market as the mechanism for allocating resources. Uninhibited, market-oriented, profit-seeking entrepreneurs are preferred to budget-maximising bureaucrats and vote-maximising politicians. Yet, it should be emphasised that this is primarily a Franco-British motivation: the managers of the major State holdings in Spain and Italy who privatised parts of their empires entertained no great belief in the intrinsic merits of market mechanisms. Nor has there been any atavistic attachment to the market evident in European Christian Democratic circles.

A third economic reason for privatisation is that it facilitates the adoption of tough labour policies, by distancing governments from unpalatable political choices. Private management, it is alleged, is more likely to tackle the unions which protect inefficient work practices and employment levels. The evidence from the European steel and coal industries, some of which carried out massive slimming-down operations under public ownership, has not dented the enthusiasm for this argument.

The need to spread 'the enterprise culture' by familiarising the public, through ownership, with the mechanisms of the market provides the fourth economic argument of the privatisers who present it as a pedagogical exercise.

The final economic argument has been that employed by the pragmatists who head the vast and rambling State holding companies in Italy and Spain. For Romano Prodi of IRI (a 'gigantic group of dwarfs'), Franco Reviglio of ENI, and for Claudio Aranzadi of the Spanish INI, privatisation has been viewed as a means of rationalising asset portfolios and reorganising investment strategies. By hiving off loss-making or marginal operations they can improve their balance-sheets, induce greater sensitivity to product specialisation, and even facilitate the process of mergers thought necessary to gain the economies of scale required by international competition and an increasingly integrated European market. The sale of the Spanish State company SEAT to Volkswagen, and of the Italian State-owned Alfa Romeo to Fiat were justified in these terms. This argument about economies of scale was also heard in France when the privatised Compagnie Générale d'Electricité (CGE), the telecommunications and heavy engineering group, merged its telecommunications assets with those of ITT in a joint venture to create the second biggest telecommunications groups after AT & T. Yet this was but another example of a disconnected objective providing an *a priori* reason: rationale and rationalisation become inextricably related.

Linked to the economic motivation for privatisation has been the *managerial* one. Privatisation is seen as a means of breaking up the vast public sector empires — each characterised by internal feuds among warring barons — and held together by statute and public subsidy. Privatisation should facilitate the hiving off of 'incoherent' parts, and the rationalisation of managerial structures. Yet the recent experience of the nationalised industries in Spain, France and Italy demonstrate that such objectives can be attained within the public sector. However, more important for the privatisers is the fact that it enables ministers to extricate themselves from time-consuming and debilitating relationships with the public sector. Ministers, it is contended, either 'go native' and espouse the cause of the industries they are supposed to control, or they interfere too much. Everywhere in Europe there have been constant confrontations between ministers and public sector managers over wage levels, investment plans, borrowing requirements, restructuring projects, and over the right to raise capital outside Ministry of Finance control. The relationship has become 'a muddle,' full of ambivalence, indecision and vacillation.' Privatisation might, therefore, ensure both autonomy and incentives.

The fourth set of seasons for privatisation have been *party political*. It has been argued that it is popular with the party faithful and is a method of soothing the right-wing radicals who are disgruntled with the timidity of policies in other areas. More significantly, it has been alleged that privatisation of the industrial public sector in some European countries is part of a strategy to create conservative voters and to undermine the unions and deprive the left of one of its traditional bastions of support. The sale of the publicly-owned housing stock at discount prices in Britain was viewed in a similar light.

Finally, a variety of *financial* reasons have been given to justify privatisation programmes. The first is specific to the United Kingdom and is linked with the so-called 'Public Sector Borrowing Requirement' (PSBR) which the government has been committed to reducing. The sales of public enterprises remove their capital investment programmes from the public sector accounts. Moreover, by a quirk of accounting convention, the proceeds from asset sales are counted as negative public expenditure (rather than the sale of a capital item). Sales of even profitable assets therefore serve to diminish the PSBR considerably, which is to say the least convenient for the government.

The second financial reason often cited is that denationalisation provides quicker and more direct access for the firms involved to international capital markets (although it is unclear why nationalised firms should be totally deprived of such a right). A third financial reason for privatisation, heard in Britain but more especially in France and Italy, is that it fosters the growth of the stock exchange: it can widen capital markets by bringing in many new investors and 'deepen' them by introducing mature companies with strong market positions. For example, the French Bourse is thought to be too small, and successive French governments, mindful of the predatory potential of London, have since the 1950s tried to enhance its place in the world's capital markets.

A fourth financial reason sometimes invoked by proponents of privatisation is that the sale of public assets reduces commercial risk for a government by diminishing the State's exposure to the vagaries of recession and the volatile exchange and business climate. It would also put an end to the immensely costly rescue operations of public enterprises (such as British Steel and British Leyland, in Britain, Renault and Usinor and Sacilor in France, and Finsider in Italy). However, it should be pointed out that such rescue operations have not been restricted to the public sector, and nationalisations have often been precisely the result of bailing out private firms in dire financial difficulty.

Finally — and here perhaps we touch upon the most important single reason for privatisation — selling State assets raises money for public sector managers (Spain, Italy and Portugal in the future) and for hardpressed governments (e.g. of Belgium) which are anxious to reduce large budget deficits, cut personal and corporate taxes and to finance public expenditure. It should be noted, however, that asset sales improve shortterm cash flow in a once-and-for-all manner: in general they do not enhance a government's long-term net worth, and may even cause it to deteriorate if profitable assets are sold off too cheaply.

It follows from this brief exploration of the reasons and motives of the privatisers that, whereas in the United Kingdom (at least since 1983) and France from 1986 to 1988 the programmes have been ideologically inspired and rooted in a wider strategy, elsewhere they are responses to more pragmatic requirements. It follows, too, that privatisation was likely to be more ambitious in scope and in nature in the first two countries than in the rest of Europe.

The Thatcher government has proved to be the most radical, since *no* nationalised enterprise is, in principle, safe in the public sector. In practice, the only condition required for a State-owned firm to become a candidate for privatisation is saleability. The Conservative government has transferred to private ownership not only firms in the competitive sector but also monopolies or quasi-monopolies such as British Gas and British Telecom (with steel, electricity and water soon to follow). No industrial sector has remained untouched, and even major strategic industries such as British Aerospace, British Petroleum and Britoil, and British Airways, the national flag-carrier, have been completely denationalised.

The ambitions of the privatisers in France were indicated in the 1986 Act, which listed 65 companies for privatisation before 1991. These comprise, with subsidiaries, a total of 1,454 firms with some 755,000 employees. The programme concerned not only those firms which were nationalised by the Socialists in 1982 but also many which were brought under State control by the Gaullist government at the time of the Liberation. The overall value of the *privatisables* has been put as high as 300 billion francs. However, the French programme, although wide-ranging and ambitious, contained no provision for the transfer of a public monopoly to the private sector: gas, electricity, and telecommunications were to remain under State ownership, and there was no question of selling Air France. Moreover, the French State still holds a majority of Elf-Aquitaine despite selling a 14 per cent stake to the private sector. Aerospace industries were also excluded from the privatisation programme in France.

Elsewhere in Europe the ambitions of the privatisers have proved modest. The CDU-CSU government in West Germany, in office since Autumn 1982, has clearly disappointed its neo-liberal supporters by the timidity of its programme. Only very few major firms are on the agenda for privatisation and, unlike France, there has been no question of transferring the publicly-owned banks (whether federally-owned or controlled by the *Länder*) to the private sector. The programme also excludes the big telecommunications and railway monopolies. Ambitions are also limited in Austria, where the programme is confined to selling minority holdings in State enterprises. Similarly, the Belgian government in August 1987 announced its intention of selling off by the end of 1988 only parts of three State-owned companies, the most important being the gas utility Distrigas, followed by the Régie des Transports Maritimes (the State shipping line) and the Office Central du Crédit Hypothécaire — the State-owned housing loan company. Again, as in West Germany, France, Italy, the Netherlands and Austria, there is no plan to dispose of the State telecommunications authority, although, as in other countries, plans have been announced to liberalise the telecommunications system.

In Italy, the major impetus for privatisation comes from the management of the State holding companies — privatisation was never part of the Craxi government's programme or his or the DC's electoral platform. The IRI, ENI, and EFIM are generally responsible for identifying the firms to be denationalised — a right recognised by Parliament. There is no desire radically to dismantle them and there is no question of losing control over the main holdings, especially those perceived as 'strategic.' Rather, the hope is to divest the holding companies of their peripheral and loss-making activities, or to raise capital by the sale of minority shareholdings. Far from weakening the public sector by radical reduction, this privatisation strategy is designed to strengthen it by judicious trimming.

THE
SINGLE MARKET
AND
EUROPEAN UNITY

S ince the fall of Rome, Europeans have dreamed of unity. Charlemagne, the Church, Napoleon, and Hitler all tried—and failed.
The latest, and most democratic, attempt is underway by the twelve
European Community (EC) countries. Determined to advance stalled
economic integration, they have pledged to unite their markets by the
end of 1992, creating the world's largest market and trading bloc and
taking a major step towards federation, that is, towards political integration. Together with NATO members' awareness that U.S. and European
nuclear arms security interests may not be identical and with the dramatic
loosening of the Soviet grip on Eastern Europe, the prospect of a "single
market" has revived the old dream of an independent, united Europe.

The chief events in the EC's early evolution are clear: emergence
from the cooperation required by the Marshall Plan; the proposals of

French Planning Commissioner Jean Monnet and French Foreign Minister Schuman to pool coal and steel resources in Western Europe; the resulting five-nation European Coal and Steel Community; the desire for more economic integration, particularly in view of the British and French failures in Suez in 1956; the 1957 Treaties of Rome establishing both the European Economic Community, or Common Market, intended to bring an end to customs barriers among its members and a common tariff for the rest of the world, and Euratom, the European Atomic Energy Commission for the peaceful development of atomic energy; French President Charles de Gaulle's 1963 veto of the British application to join (de Gaulle feared Britain's Atlantic ties and Commonwealth commitments and was reluctant to share leadership); the struggles between those who opposed the EEC's becoming a supranational organization, particularly de Gaulle, and integrationists led by Walter Hallstein, who headed the Common Market's executive Commission; the 1966 compromise that reasserted the paramouncy of national sovereignty, with the Council of Foreign Ministers exercising real authority and with each member having veto power. The impetus for a common Europe appeared to have stagnated.

Even so, in 1967 integrationists were able to blend the three European organizations, the Common Market, the Coal and Steel Community, and Euratom into a single European Community, with the right to tax (customs fees) and in some areas have Community law take precedence over national law. Most remaining customs barriers fell in 1968. Membership expanded in 1971 with the admission of Great Britain, Ireland, and Denmark. Closer ties with the Third World were made when a 1975 agreement between the Community and forty-six developing nations allowed the latter to send goods freely to EC markets while members granted greater aid and investment. In 1978 short-term efforts to stabilize currency fluctuations through a European monetary system proved successful, although this fell far short of the common currency sought by integrationists. The direct election of members of the European Parliament was established in 1979. (Previously the Parliament consisted of pro-Europeans sitting in their various national legislatures. But the Parliament, as before, could only discuss the proposals of the EC's executive Commission and pass them along to a Council of Ministers — hence the skepticism regarding integration voiced not only by participants but by social scientists as well.[1])

---

[1]Paul Taylor, *The Limits of European Integration* (New York, 1983), 299–301.

In 1981 Greece joined the Community, followed in five years by Spain and Portugal, all three nations having demonstrated their democratic credentials and having overcome fears that these southern European states, because of their lower income, would require subsidies. EC membership now comprised twelve states. By the 1970s it constituted the world's largest trading unit and was a great economic power. A decade later, its total population and gross national product equalled that of the U.S. and surpassed the output of the Soviet Union and Japan.

Serious problems, however, some new, some recurring, marked the early 1980s. Such farming countries as France continued to benefit from supports, while the British and Germans paid higher food prices as a result. The British insisted that their contribution was disproportionately high, and like de Gaulle twenty years earlier Mrs. Thatcher in 1983–84 effectively managed to block the EC from functioning until steps were taken to lower agricultural supports. Enthusiasm for the Common Market impetus once again seemed to have evaporated. Member-states knew only too well that not all customs barriers were down, that difficulties and delays in border crossings endured, and that rampant regulations in manufacturing showed no signs of easing.

Aware that the EC growth was falling behind that of the U.S. and Japan and that only the single market originally envisaged provided a solution, in 1985 the executive Commission under its new pan-European president, the Frenchman Jacques Delors, committed the EC to removing all remaining barriers to the free movement of goods, services, capital, and people among its member-states, that is, "to complete the internal market," by December 31, 1992. Three hundred areas were targeted, most importantly perhaps the elimination of all border controls, the replacement of unanimity with majority rule (no more veto power) in the Council of Ministers, more power for the European Parliament, the totally free movement of goods and services, and the harmonization of different rules and standards. To take but one dramatic example: an architect qualified to practice in Italy is to be able to practice in any of the other eleven nations. Not all approve and many are afraid: traditionalists fear the lessening of national sovereignty; smaller and less efficient firms fear extinction; internationalists fear tariff increases that might produce a "fortress Europe," that in turn might lessen U.S. commitment to defend it. Nevertheless, in a very short time we will witness one of the most dramatic episodes in the long and turbulent history of twentieth-century Europe.

Europe in the Making

∿⁄⁊

WALTER HALLSTEIN

Walter Hallstein, who presided over the Common Market's Executive Commission for the first nine years of its existence, saw the
Treaty of Rome as "the first chapter of a European constitution."[1]
Accordingly, the Market was perfectly entitled to increase its membership and functions. His successors, however, at least until 1985,
lacked his zeal for European integration. What follows is the conclusion from his book defending the need to continue on the road to
full integration. It shows the author's commitment to political as
well as economic union — and his premature assessment as to when
it would be achieved. What does Hallstein see as the relationship
between economic and political integration? How excessive was his
optimism?

We must learn from the failures and the successes of European
policy.

It has not been possible to establish unity at one stroke. The tremendous political effort needed to achieve this end could have been
generated only by the most overwhelming, immediate and compelling

[1]European Economic Community, *Bulletin*, no. 7-1967 (July, 1967), 8. Cited in Robert
Paxton, *Europe in the 20th Century* (San Diego, 1985), 630.

circumstances, such as an immense and imminent danger. The collapse of the Continent after a war that had involved unparalleled efforts was by itself not enough. For that collapse made Europeans concentrate on coping with immediate necessities: on survival, on establishing a minimum degree of order and security, on reconstruction.

But what was lacking was only the power to take a comprehensive decision — not the awareness of the need. It therefore proved right to proceed 'pragmatically,' as we have grown used to saying. We had to keep alive our great objective. But at the same time we set ourselves limited, concrete aims, which offered immediate advantages. We were successful in merging first the heavy industries and later the complete national economies of European states; we failed in merging the national armed forces. But even where we succeeded, we met obstacles. They were psychological, and therefore political. It was difficult for public opinion, and partly also for those who held positions of responsibility in the states, to grasp the full extent of the consequences involved in seeking unity. It was not easy to keep up with the various stages by which our great undertaking was carried out. The limitation of sovereignty met with strong resentment in some sections of the nation-states and was fought on emotional grounds. Since some countries — unlike Germany — had no experience and concept of what federation meant — this was where the fear arose that countries might lose their national identity. Furthermore, the willingness to co-operate with defeated Germany only developed gradually, despite some splendid exceptions.

In all these difficulties one can perceive the role that time plays in the European problem. Time 'helps' no one, neither us nor our opponents. But it is a decisive element in every political operation. One cannot turn back the clock. Consequently, it is always wrong not to take action when it is possible to do so. But, equally, time is the main factor in another respect, in getting people used to change; they can hardly be forced to accept it in their hearts and minds. When we launched our great enterprise in 1950, it seemed reasonable to assume that we would need about forty years, the space of a generation, to achieve full political union. Today, since everything has moved forward much more rapidly than expected, we are more optimistic: we could reach our goal by 1980. Time also justifies our method of seeking unity not in every sphere but, to begin with, in those spheres which stir up fewer emotions and where the practical reasons for fusion are compelling and obvious. In pursuing matters of common advantage, in fighting common dangers, in working together jointly in the political field, ideas and habits of thought and action be-come integrated 'in time.'

The Communities set up to deal with the partial and specific mat-ters of economic policy and social policy were a success. That integration can be carried out, even in very complex fields, has been fully proved. No practical problem remains insoluble. There have been no insuperable conflicts of interest. Economic union has therefore not made too heavy demands on the member-states.

To continue and complete the work of unification is therefore a question of making up one's mind, of the 'political will,' as it is often put; this, however, means nothing but being prepared to do the numerous small or great things which need to be done, the sum total of which constitutes 'political unification.'

The first task to be tackled is to complete the economic union begun long ago. We must continue to Europeanize the whole of economic policy. This involves a number of specially urgent and important politi-cal and economic matters. The climate of confidence in the Commun-ity must be strengthened; this applies above all to monetary policy and conjunctural policy. The central driving force for economic union con-tinues to be the single market, i.e. the removal of frontiers. In this sphere there has to be a concentrated effort to harmonize indirect and consumer taxes, for they represent the 'hard core' of the economic barriers that still exist. European technology policy — closely linked with European arma-ments — lags sadly behind. In this field there has not even been a general discussion of such key problems as the relationship between public au-thorities and industry; the co-ordination of procurements; the possibility of planning budgets several years ahead. The institutions, moreover, have in the last few years partly stagnated or been weakened. Yet they are the core of Europe's anatomy. Without them there is no policy. Questions in which the European Community has been denied or deprived of the necessary institutional framework do not simply drop into a kind of insti-tutional void where everything is settled of 'its own accord' on a basis of good-will; instead, other institutions — national institutions — grow up and take over. The first task here is to reassert the Treaty's intentions with regard to majority voting in the Council of Ministers and with regard to the status of the Commission, especially as regards the common policy for external trade. A further task is to strengthen the status and compe-tence of the European Parliament. On this depends the democratic legit-imacy of the Community's institutional structure, which at present is only improvised. It will be a disappointment if our British friends, with the greatest democratic traditions in the world, are unable to make this their special task. It is a task that is essential if our great enterprise is to take root in the hearts and minds of Europe's citizens. For the Community is to be a community of citizens and not merely of governments and diplomats.

These institutional problems are for several reasons no less urgent than those arising from economic technical matters.

Like all such documents, the Treaties establishing the Community were drafted in terms that were too narrow: there is a limit to human imagination, and a compromise has to be struck between the bold and the timid. Nevertheless, economic policy rapidly won the room it needed in which to operate effectively. We were successful in breathing life and dynamism into the new organism, and as a result even those sections of the Treaty which had been formulated only timidly and incompletely acquired considerable vigour. In the wake of this evolution it admittedly became the practice to create a fair number of special institutions and so provide the necessary institutional framework, but this process could not quite keep pace with developments and largely became bogged down at an early stage. There is therefore a need to redress the balance between what has been achieved in substance and the development of our institutions.

The enlargement of the Community increases this need. Naturally, the increase in the number of member-states, the growth in the differences of interest, and the fact that the new members will not be used to the ways of the Community, are factors which will make the decision-making process more difficult. This has to be offset by tightening up the Community's organization. Only if that is done will enlargement not lead to the weakening or the sterilization of the Community.

All this lies within the framework of the Treaties. But the Treaties are not just self-sufficient collections of detailed provisions, some of which remain to be defined to achieve their ultimate purpose. The Communities are also politically part of a greater whole, an intermediate objective on the road to the ultimate goal. That ultimate goal remains a European federation of states. Since Winston Churchill in 1945 (who spoke of 'a kind of United States of Europe') and Robert Schuman in 1950 (who spoke of 'federation') no one has yet come forward with a different definition. Gaullist policy has shaken this idea, but there can be no doubt about it. It is only when we have reached the final stages of our enterprise that we can be certain that it will be really permanent. Only that will justify the so-called 'sacrifices,' the political contributions of the member-states. The *sine qua non* of the admission of new members to the European Community is an unambiguous commitment to the ultimate goal.

The Community was built with this ultimate goal in view. This is apparent in the allocation of matters over which the Community was given competence: it was constructed as a political community (even though its authority was limited to economic and social policy); it is also apparent in its constitutional elements, its federalistic structure. In defending the present Community, therefore, we are safeguarding the fundamental elements of future reality.

If we look into the future in this general way, we cannot afford to ignore the experience which the European Community has taught us. To some questions, that experience provides unambiguous answers, with no alternatives. It shows that we must proceed by stages. Our method must be evolutionary: progress must be made organically on the basis of what has already been achieved. The common European interest must be embodied in a special common institution, independent of governments, in order to make possible a continuous dialogue with the representatives of partial, national interests. As long as there are several Communities, their composition must be identical. For other questions, various options are possible according to circumstances. For example, authority to deal with new problems can either be allocated to the existing Communities, or one or several new Communities can be set up for the purpose.

It has become customary to call the second part of the programme of European evolution 'Political Union.' It embraces two subjects: on the one hand, extension of Europe's as yet underdeveloped constitution into a full federation (which will then evolve as a result of combining economic and political integration); on the other hand, the inclusion of several new specific functions: foreign policy, defence, and perhaps, also, certain fundamental principles of cultural policy. There is a widespread legend that it is more difficult to integrate foreign and defence policy than economic and social policy. Even more difficult? That seems doubtful, especially if past experience is used in deciding how to proceed. Such divergences as may exist in fixing concrete objectives are limited in scope; historical rivalries, in particular, have greatly faded. All the member-states subscribe to the principles of the United Nations Charter. Peace is for all of them the guiding principle. Their geographical situation dictates the similarity of their vital interests. All have a very similar outlook. Within this broad common framework of fundamental principles they also share many individual values — although there are always different degrees of commitment, ranging from spontaneous intervention to letting things drift. There is an identity of views, for example, on security *vis-à-vis* the East; on peace in the Mediterranean and the Near East; on stabilizing conditions in Africa; and on economic aid to less-developed countries.

One of the subjects of European foreign policy is the German question, although for the Germans it is more than a question of foreign policy. Here, too, a common denominator must be found. The integration of the Federal German Republic into a united Europe is in the interest of all Europe. Like the other members of this ever more closely-knit Community, the Federal German Republic joined with all its assets and liabilities, and without any discrimination against it. The prospect of healing the division of the world which has also caused the division of Germany depends entirely on securing peace in Europe and in the world, and in winning back for Europe a share in determining world affairs. These are the political aims of European unification.

A vast potential is invested in our European policy. Our economic success has aroused the greatest interest. (Within the last twelve years, internal trade within the Community has increased by 623 per cent, its external trade by 283 per cent, its gross domestic product by 226 per cent and its industrial production by about 200 per cent). But the political investment in our great European enterprise, in terms both of the tasks undertaken and the solutions found, is more imposing still. The scope for the authorities involved has expanded beyond all expectations. This has not been painlessly achieved. This book recounts many a struggle. But struggling with the member-states is not a symptom of illness; it lies in the nature of a federal structure. A brilliant interpreter of federal constitutions, Heinrich Triepel, has said that the best attainable relationship between central and local authorities is one of 'armistice.' Wounds have been sustained, but the dynamism of the European enterprise has only been curbed, not broken. Externally, it has had world-wide repercussions. A dialogue between the continents has begun across the Atlantic, and its first result has been a world-wide liberalization of trade.

These successes have become 'vested interests' for those concerned. None of the participants could now withdraw without suffering great damage. All other European states which are free to make their own decisions would like to join us in one way or another, whatever reservations they may have had at the start.

But the edifice is not complete. And it will not grow by itself. If it is left as it is, then even the parts that are already finished will deteriorate. Whatever form life might then take in this partial construction, it would never be the full life for which the whole building is designed.

Nor does waiting improve the prospect. Already within the Community old habits have begun to reassert themselves. Already the situation in the world around has become worse. Never before have we so clearly realized that our European enterprise is of world significance, not only in its immediate effects, through the shift in the world balance of political weight brought about by the emergence of a new political continent, but also in the conditions it creates. It has generated powerful opposition in the East, opposition which stems from an expansionist policy of hegemony. We shall continue, with patience and tenacity, to work for a better understanding of what we are doing: already the integration of democratic Europe, a reliable safeguard for peace, is becoming a reality and one which is also in the interests of the East European nations. In the West we put our faith in European and Atlantic solidarity, which has been forged not merely by an arbitrary decision but by a common destiny, based on a community of spiritual and material circumstances in the present state of the world.

It is therefore high time to go further. For there is no alternative, either to our objective — unity — or to the road we set out on twenty years ago, and of which today we have covered half the distance.

William the Silent, of the House of Orange, an indomitable champion of progress and tolerance in a troubled century of Europe's history, once said: 'One does not need hope to act, or success to persevere.' How much greater, then, is our obligation to act and to persevere; for we have hope, and we have success.

The 1992 Challenge from Europe

~∥~

MICHAEL CALINGAERT

Michael Calingaert studied history, both on the undergraduate and graduate level. In the U.S. Foreign Service, where he specializes in European economic matters, he has risen through the ranks to become Deputy Assistant Secretary in the State Department's Bureau of Economic and Business Affairs. He began the study from which the following is drawn while a visiting senior fellow at the National Planning Association. The author wanted to familiarize American businessmen — and other interested parties — with what to expect from the 1992 single market and to urge them to begin preparing for the challenges presented by this new and "irreversible" force. Are the Community's plans realistic, or do the barriers pointed out by Calingaert show the limits of integration? To what extent does the 1985 White Paper fulfill Halstein's goals for European economic integration and ultimate political unification?

Despite the numerous political and economic changes that have taken place in the Community over the past 30 years — and many of these have been fundamental — the EC remains to a considerable extent a grouping of individual countries with separate economic systems. The barriers that impede the free movement of people, goods, services, and

From Michael Calingaert, *The 1992 Challenge from Europe*, pp. 20–21, 30–36, 37–38, 72–73. Copyright 1988 National Planning Association. Reprinted by permission.

capital among the member states can be divided into three categories: those representing basic historical and cultural differences; those not covered by the White Paper; and those that are the object of the measures included in the White Paper.

The first category consists of the very significant differences that reflect hundreds of years of historical development. Physical and cultural differences among the member countries are quite obvious. Differences in language, tradition and ways of thinking and acting in many respects impede the establishment of a single market, and although their effect is difficult to identify and quantify, their importance should not be underestimated. While these differences (and their significance) among EC member countries will continue to diminish, this is a very long-term process and is affected only marginally and indirectly by actions of governments and the Community (but more so by modern telecommunications and other nongovernmental factors).

The second category of barriers consists of economic factors that directly affect the operation of the market but are not included in the White Paper. Notable among these are:

- Absence of a common currency. While the EC has benefited from the considerable success of the European Monetary System in reducing the fluctuations among, and in some cases instability of, the currencies of member countries, the U.K.'s refusal to join the exchange rate mechanism of the EMS and, more particularly, the absence of a common currency in the member states increases the complexity and cost of doing business in the EC.

- Lack of coordination of macroeconomic policies. The pursuit by member governments of different macroeconomic objectives and policies, especially monetary, with no fully developed mechanism or requirement for coordination, creates obstacles to the liberalization of capital movements.

- Differences in direct taxation regimes. Although the White Paper addresses some differences in indirect taxes, it makes no reference to direct personal taxation; further, corporate taxation systems, which are characterized by disparate structures and rates — with implications for competition and decisions on investment — are covered only regarding "cooperation" between firms in different member states.

- Differences in social, environmental and consumer policies (only indirectly dealt with in the White Paper). Generally reflecting diverse philosophies and historical circumstances of the member countries, these differences have resulted in a lack of uniform treatment in regulations and laws, which inevitably affects competition and decisions on investment.

.   .   .

Responses to the Launch

By any measure, the outward manifestations of support for completion of the internal market are strong and pervasive throughout the Community. Virtually every member government has taken steps to publicize the program and to prepare its citizenry for the changes that will take place. Most visible has been France, where an extensive and comprehensive program of information has been undertaken, with the result that the level of public knowledge is probably higher there than elsewhere in the EC. Similarly, the British government launched a publicity campaign in the spring of 1988 to increase private sector awareness from around 25 percent to 90 percent by the end of the year. As part of the formation of its new government in 1988, Belgium now has a "Secretary of State Europe 1992," who is responsible for explaining to the Belgian business community and public what the internal market program means for them and how best to prepare for it.

But member governments see not only a responsibility to make their citizens aware of the forthcoming changes, but also an opportunity to bring about needed changes in their domestic economies. The Chirac government, for example, apparently hoped to use the pressures created by the 1992 program to modernize and restructure the French economy, in part by doing away with archaic laws. Such an undertaking would have been far more difficult in the absence of the EC's internal market program. Similarly, some elements in the less developed southern member states hope that the process of completing the internal market will force much needed — and potentially far-reaching — changes in the legal structure, government administration and conduct of business in their country.

The EC private sector has perhaps been even more positive in its response and has supplied much of the pressure for carrying out the program. For example, whereas French and Italian industry strongly opposed removal of the intra-EC tariffs in the 1960s out of fear they would not be able to stand up to the foreign competition, they now solidly support establishing the integrated EC market. All national industrial federations have undertaken programs to inform their members about the various proposals and their potential consequences. Individual firms are looking more and more closely at the implications of an integrated market and are acting as if this will become a reality — which in itself accelerates the process.

Business leaders are speaking out increasingly, and often in stark terms, in support of completion of the internal market. One Italian business leader asserts "a unified Europe is no longer an option . . . but a necessity," while a leading industrial association refers to 1992 as "the last chance for Europe to meet the challenge of the international market." The optimism within Community business sectors is quite remarkable. For example, a German poll in early 1988 showed that 90 percent of German firms expected the opportunities to outweigh the risks; in a 1987 survey of French business leaders, 78 percent expected completion of the internal market to benefit French industry and 65 percent expected it to benefit their own firms; and 8 out of 10 company directors polled in France, Germany and the United Kingdom considered the EC's program a positive development for their country's industry. However, these polls are hardly definitive, especially as they apparently concentrated on the upper echelons of the business community. Private sector concerns clearly exist; these are normally couched in terms not of opposition but of calls for some form of protection.

For the Community's average citizen, "1992" is becoming increasingly recognizable and is frequently being used to refer to the program to complete the internal market.

All these actions and responses have been translated into a strong political consensus in favor of completing the internal market. Indeed, the program has assumed the status of a "motherhood" issue, virtually immune from political attack. It is rare and difficult for a mainstream politician to voice doubts about the integrated market program, for it is bad politics to be seen in opposition. In fact, a number of politicians have decided that an activist, pro-1992 stance can be a good means of attracting notice and advancing their own political ambitions.

One result of this consensus is that whereas in the past at any particular moment one member government or another seemed to be facing an election, which made it difficult for it to contemplate a decision on a thorny EC issue, political parties are now more likely to stress their devotion to the internal market cause. Thus, in France's 1988 presidential election, the main candidates vied with one another in asserting their ability to lead the country to "1992"; the British Conservative Party's 1987 election manifesto boasted of its successful handling of the recent British EC presidency in making progress on the internal market; and the new Italian government introduced a program to Parliament in 1988 liberally laced with references to "1992."

However, it would be misleading to imply anything like unanimous support for the single internal market. Behind the verbiage lie differing levels and intensities of concern. These sometimes take the form of opposition to specific measures or proposals from those, as is not surprising, who fear they would be adversely affected. The national customs officials who face prospective layoffs, the telecommunication employees of the highly protected national authorities and those connected with the host of enterprises benefiting from a protected market all have reason to view 1992 with less than unbridled enthusiasm, and they can be expected to make their influence felt with the decisionmakers.

But the concerns go beyond specifically affected individuals and groups. There is a strong tradition of protection — of markets, manufacturing and service sectors and enterprises — in many EC member states. While the French proclivity for protection of domestic economic interests is well known, it is less widely recognized that German liberal trade policy is a facade behind which important segments of the economy are subject to substantial regulation and regimentation. In many respects, then, the prospect of opening up hitherto sheltered markets, as is intended by the White Paper, is cause for considerable unease in the Community.

Whatever the opposition, however, by mid-1988 the internal market program had clearly acquired momentum. Just six months earlier, observers had debated whether the program would even get off the ground. As a Commission official recently put it, "we had been pushing the ball uphill for a long time, but now it's going downhill and the only question is the angle of the slope."

Causes for Momentum

Even though the shift from uncertainty to certainty about the take-off of the internal market program was unexpectedly swift, the factors that played a role were reasonably clear. First, and of fundamental importance, was the establishment by the Single European Act of majority voting in the Council, which provided a mechanism for overcoming the obstacle to Community decision-making posed by the unanimity rule.

As discussed in Chapter 2, the new system is still in the "breaking-in stage" as the EC institutions adapt to the changes, but it will no doubt force decisions in many previously blocked areas.

Second was a resolution of the problems of budgetary shortfall, which had hung over the Community during much of the early to mid-1980s. These difficulties had served as a brake on the internal market process in two ways: they had monopolized much of the attention and energies of those involved in the operation of the EC; and they had limited the availability of resources for nonagricultural purposes. But at its February 1988 meeting in Brussels, the European Council agreed on medium-term solutions to resolve the budgetary impasse and on a doubling of "structural funds" — to about $120 billion — for the depressed EC regions in the 1989–93 period. This accord enabled Community and member government officials to turn to the longer-range objectives of the internal market and at the same time to dampen the fears of the less developed EC members that completion of the internal market would exacerbate regional disparities. The latter consideration was important in helping to ensure the consensus necessary for the success of the internal market program and in promoting the objective enshrined in the Single European Act of strengthening "economic and social cohesion" in the Community.

Third was the introduction of the concept of "mutual recognition" and its offspring "home country control." These came about as a result of recognition of the practical (and enormous) difficulties the EC had experienced earlier in attempting to legislate uniform EC-wide measures and the growing acceptance of the principle of deregulation. Indeed, one observer has asserted that the "1992 project is an adventure in deregulation."

Mutual recognition, as the name implies, means that a practice, regulation or another form of control in one member state will be recognized as valid in the other countries, even if it does not conform to such controls there. Thus, for example, the professional qualifications of an Italian architect will be automatically recognized in Germany, as will a British product manufactured in accordance with regulations imposed by the British government. The EC's role will be limited to agreeing on regulations of a general oversight nature that establish minimum conditions with which all member states must abide. The same concept applies in home country control (discussed below), whereby the supervisory or regulatory agency in the country where the enterprise is established will carry out those functions irrespective of where the enterprise actually operates in the EC. The net effect of these concepts is to reduce the area over which EC-wide agreement will be necessary and thus to enhance the prospects for movement toward 1992.

The final reason for momentum, although impossible to quantify or date, was the all-important "psychological snowball" of an idea whose time had come. The internal market increasingly became a topic of discussion, more and more people came to believe that the EC should move toward an integrated market, indeed that such action was imperative, and enterprises began to "think 1992" and to act accordingly. Thus, the process fed on itself and ultimately attained momentum.

Difficulties and Uncertainties Facing the Program

However, momentum and enthusiasm obviously will not suffice to ensure the success of the internal market program. In fact, it must be clearly recognized that serious difficulties exist, as evidenced by the significant number of proposals or issues that have been unresolved after consideration by the EC for many years predating the White Paper. The issues or measures in question are complex and difficult to resolve — to quote a German aphorism, the devil is in the detail. Almost without exception they present problems for one or another country or group within it. Often the subject of contention is linked to other issues, with a different set of problems and interests. It is rare that a country will be obdurate simply because it objects to change; far more frequently, serious issues are at stake. The scope of these issues, and the political and economic linkages, are illustrated in the following examples.

- The effort to institute approximation of coverage and rates for value-added and excise taxes runs afoul of (a) opposition by member state legislatures and governments to any impingement of one of the main forms of national sovereignty, i.e., determining taxation policy; (b) the very practical financial difficulty of offsetting any reductions in tax receipts that in many cases would result (and often would be sizable); and (c) the opposition for reasons of social policy to a reduction in "sin taxes" on cigarettes and alcoholic beverages.
- Although the issue was ultimately resolved, the Commission's efforts to obtain member states' agreement on a phased elimination of restrictions on intra-EC road transportation (such as national

quotas and limits on out-of-country trucking) met strong opposition, especially from Germany, for reasons only partly related to transportation policy. To complement its subsidization of the railroads, the German government has limited competition in road transportation through various protective devices. A politically powerful network of small transport firms has developed, benefiting from legislation on working conditions but facing a more onerous tax regime than in most other member states. Accordingly, the German government insisted that it would be unfair to expose the German trucking industry to competition from the other member states before the social legislation and tax regimes had been harmonized.

- Opening up the public procurement market to competitive forces would put at risk a number of enterprises, many possessing considerable political influence, and would affect significant levels of employment.

- Differences in climatic and health conditions, as well as in traditions, present problems in unifying animal and plant health regulations. It is no accident that the greatest backlog in internal market measures is in this area. Perhaps the most prominent difference in the health area is the absence of rabies in the British Isles, a situation the British government is firmly determined to maintain. Another example relates to plant controls, where Spain, a subtropical country more susceptible to certain diseases, finds some proposed regulations, presumably based on more temperate climates, provide insufficient protection.

In addition to clear-cut difficulties, a number of uncertainties will affect the success of the internal market effort. One is the relationship between Brussels (basically meaning the Commission) and the member states — this is the issue of national sovereignty. Over time, as the EC has moved toward an integrated market, the powers of the collectivity have increased, involving a shift in responsibilities from national governments to Brussels. To some degree, this is perceived as a threat by politicians and civil servants in national governments, as well as by part of the general public. In member states with decentralized systems of government — notably Germany — the concern presumably is compounded. As discussed in Chapter 2, this tension between Brussels and the member states is reflected in the reluctance of the Council (representing member state interests) to increase the executive powers of the Commission to the extent it desires, which has led to friction between the two and some criticism by the Commission of the Council.

Only in a limited number of areas — taxation and monetary union are notable examples — are national sovereignty concerns clearly voiced. Beyond these, such concerns have been less of an impediment to the internal market program than might have been expected; there is, in fact, little evidence of national sovereignty being an issue as such. One reason appears to be the gradualist approach employed in moving toward the integrated market so that issues are seldom posed in terms of national sovereignty. Another is that the areas of Community responsibility have largely been established by treaty. Nonetheless, the issue remains close to the surface, occasionally springing forth, particularly as differences among member states are aired about the ultimate objectives of the effort to create a single market. Prime Minister Thatcher clearly raised some fundamental, and controversial, issues in her September 1988 Bruges speech, in which she criticized the effort to "suppress nationhood and concentrate power at the center of a European conglomerate."

.   .   .

Measuring Overall Progress

Measuring progress achieved thus far and forecasting developments in the coming years is a difficult task. To the extent there is any precise measure, it is a quantitative one. As of the end of 1987, the Commission had submitted proposals for about two-thirds of the subjects included in the White Paper, and action had been completed by the Council on about one-fourth of these. The most recent tally of June 30, 1988 (the end of the German presidency of the Council) shows 211 proposals made by the Commission and 91 adopted by the Council. The Commission expects to be only slightly behind schedule, with 90 percent of its proposals submitted by the end of 1988. The Council is farther behind. On a strictly arithmetical basis, its record is not very good, with action completed on about one-third of the items at nearly the half-way point in the program. However, when compared to the timetable set out in the White Paper (which provides for more actions to be completed toward the end of the period), the numbers are less disappointing.

Although a review of the numbers provides a general idea of progress, it is more meaningful — though more difficult — to make a qualitative assessment. In doing so, it is important to recognize that "completion of the internal market" is not an all-or-nothing proposition. While the White Paper calls for completion of action on all the items (now 285) by the end of 1992 — which would enable the Community to announce that the internal market is "complete" — the program is necessarily an evolving process. As one observer put it, "1992 is a process, not an event." Action will proceed at varying paces on the different issues, depending on their intractability and the strength of the political forces involved.

Despite the exhortations and efforts of the Commission — and of the treaty obligation contained in the Single European Act — the likelihood is remote that the EC will complete action on all measures in the White Paper by the end of 1992. The process will continue beyond 1992. Indeed, it is unlikely that a specific point will be identifiable at which the internal market becomes "complete." Rather, the yardstick will be how far the Community has proceeded from its situation at the outset of the program in 1985. In any case, the EC of 1992 is likely to be considerably different from that of 1988 and certainly that of 1985.

In making a qualitative judgment on progress toward the single integrated market, assessing the relative importance of various categories of measures is essential. From the outset, the Commission has consciously avoided setting priorities, as noted above, as part of its tactic of pressing for acceptance of the entire White Paper program. However, even though all measures will contribute to the objective of completing the internal market, it is relevant to identify the key areas:

- Elimination of border controls. Apart from the not inconsiderable costs, the psychological effect of the maintenance of physical frontiers is enormous.
- Opening up of public procurement. The share of economic activity affected is massive as are the cost savings and economic transformation that could take place as a result of government action.
- Harmonization of technical regulations and standards. This is essential to the ability of companies throughout the EC to rationalize and compete internationally, especially in high technology products.
- Liberalization of capital movements and the related liberalization of financial services. Once any individual or institution can move funds anywhere inside the Community and use any financial services offered, a major step will have been taken in the establishment of an integrated market.

.   .   .

Political Implications

Although this study addresses economic and not political issues, the political implications of the program to complete the internal market cannot be ignored. While the early champions of European unification envisaged political as well as economic union, the greatest progress has occurred on the economic side. However, an important political step was taken when the Single European Act formalized the system that had developed of consultation and coordination among the member states on foreign policy issues. Beyond that, the development of the integrated market will likely provide an important impetus to increased political cooperation in two ways. First, it will require the member states to discuss and decide on issues not strictly or exclusively economic in nature, such as immigration and drug trafficking, that often involve politicians and government officials not normally concerned with issues in a Community context. Second, as the member states and their citizens increasingly interact across the range of economic issues, the pattern and practice of political interaction is bound to become more an accepted way of life.

Another aspect of the political issue is the relationship between the EC and the six nonmember European countries that comprise the European Free Trade Association (EFTA) — Austria, Finland, Iceland, Norway, Sweden, and Switzerland. These countries have benefited from free trade area agreements with the Community (i.e., tariff-free movement of goods to and from the EC), as well as a number of Europe-wide activities, notably the establishment of technical standards.

With the development of the internal market program, however, the option of membership in the Community as a way of protecting vital economic interests has become the subject of serious debate in the EFTA countries. Although each of the six countries had previously taken a decision not to seek membership — in the case of Austria, Sweden and Switzerland because of their policy of political neutrality — the perceived danger from remaining outside a truly integrated EC is causing careful rethinking. The most likely applicants appear to be Norway, which opted against membership in a close vote in 1972, and Austria, possibly with the blessings of the Soviet Union, one of the guarantors of Austrian neutrality. The economic concerns are at least as weighty in Sweden and Switzerland, but the political obstacles to membership are greater. In any event, no move toward membership will be given serious consideration by the EC in the near future. In addition to the fact that this would require the EC to deal with the possible conflict between its unification goals and EFTA neutrality (except for Norway), the Community would have to divert its attention to application negotiations while pressing forward to complete the internal market. Thus, at least in the short term, the EFTA countries will have to face the challenges of "1992" as outsiders.

The other significant political relationship between the Community and a neighboring country is that with the German Democratic Republic. During the negotiations on formation of the EC, the Federal Republic of Germany insisted on inclusion of a protocol that recognized trade between the two Germanies as constituting internal trade. Thus, an export from the GDR to the Federal Republic is not subject to tariffs or other import restrictions, whereas a GDR good entering another EC member state (directly or through the Federal Republic) is classified as an import into the EC and treated accordingly. The potential significance of this partial free trade agreement on an integrated EC market is unclear; although the risk has always existed, it could increase the possibility of "leakage" of goods into the EC, whether from Eastern Europe or elsewhere.

13

TOWARD
A NEW
EUROPEAN
ORDER?

I t is imprudent if not precipitate for studies in history to touch on contemporary developments. The risks incurred in appearing to be left behind by subsequent events are enormous. Yet no European history text that ignores the rapid and exhilarating changes that began in the late summer of 1989 can lay claim to anything resembling completeness. In the wake of Mikhail Gorbachev's twin policies of *glasnost* (opening) and *perestroika* (restructuring), the spectacle of besieged Communist party leaders in Poland, Hungary, Czechoslovakia, East Germany, and Bulgaria granting one desperate concession after another and then finally stepping aside when emboldened oppositions merely increased their demands is too astonishing not to be recounted.

Who, earlier in that year, would have predicted the fall of the Berlin Wall, the promise to rebuild multi-party democracy in Czechoslovakia, the amendment of the East German constitution giving up the Communist party's "leading right" to determine policy, the forced resignation and replacement of the discredited Bulgarian Communist chiefs and equally significant promise of wide-ranging reforms and free elections, or, before the year's end, the flight even of the hardline Romanian government after its failure to suppress with violence widespread popular protest? By early winter the Polish coalition government, which included the once-repressed trade union "Solidarity," and which was itself formed scarcely three months earlier, was so widely accepted that it ceased to make headlines. These cataclysms all followed Gorbachev's public acknowledgment that the Brezhnev Doctrine (justifying Soviet military intervention in the satellites) was dead and buried and that the Soviet Union would allow each of its Warsaw Pact partners to devise its own perestroika, the revolution from above that was being launched within the Soviet Union.

It is clear that events in East-Central Europe were not determined by leaders or committees or summit meetings. As a British columnist (Hugo Young in *The Guardian*) put it, "In Poland, in East Germany, in Czechoslovakia, extraordinary surges of popular feeling, uncontrollable by political leaders or military force, have carried all before them. Decades of oppression and brain-washing turn out not to have extinguished the capacity of these many millions of people to discern not only that communism was a grotesque failure but that they retained the power to overthrow it."

To what extent was the Soviet leader responsible? His promise not to use Soviet troops in support of the satellite regimes was no doubt crucial. Still, Poles and Czechs and East Germans and Romanians showed tenacity and it was not because of Gorbachev that their democratic instincts survived. Certainly Gorbachev, then a bureaucrat in the Brezhnev government, was not responsible for Solidarity's birth and durability. On the other hand, he perceived the necessity of reforming his own economy and recognized that the greater autonomy of his neighbors need pose no threat to Soviet security; that is, he recognized the direction in which history was taking the Soviet bloc and seemed eager to further that movement.

We may disagree over causes, but must acknowledge the consequences that have already emerged and will continue to emerge. Most historical periods are transitional, marked by slow incremental change within a seemingly immutable framework of permanence. But every now and then an upheaval takes place which shatters previously held assumptions and opens new perspectives. Nineteen eighty-nine, with the apparent end of forty-five years of cold war and the chance for a free and whole Europe, brought such an upheaval. For many, it meant the extension of free market economies; for others, it meant the opportunity to free socialism from its fatal identification with Stalinism (most conspicuously revealed by the Soviet Communist party's decisions to renounce its monopoly on power and to introduce a free market to replace the government-managed, centrally planned economy that failed to produce adequate goods); for most, it meant the extension of democratic forms. Indeed, 1989 may well be remembered, as remarked by Theo Sommer, editor of the West German newsweekly *Die Zeit*, as creating the possibility of putting three things behind us: "the bitter conflict between East and West which began when Stalin rang down the Iron Curtain . . . the horrifying prospect of World War III which has been looming on the horizon for almost two generations now; and, perhaps, even the Great Schism that rent Europe asunder in the Bolshevik Revolution of November 1917. Suddenly, a new order seems to arise out of the familiar array."

"We must now invent another phase in the history of Europe," said President François Mitterrand of France. Even so, he, like others, recognizes that these changes have given rise to a number of questions and that the responses to them vary. A reunited Germany now seems a certainty, but its spectre worries many in Europe. The future of both the Atlantic alliance and the Warsaw Pact also causes concern. What follows are three thoughtful assessments of the impact of the revolutionary changes affecting Europe at the present time. In his discussion of the demise of Western communism, Lewis Coser sees it less as the consequence of initiatives undertaken by Gorbachev than as the result of structural changes in Western European economies. Leon Aron considers the "myths" of Soviet history that *glasnost* has "destroyed." Finally, Zbigniew Brzezinski finds nationalism the chief threat to the Soviet and East European regimes in post-Communist societies.

The Death Throes
of Western Communism

ࡍࡁࡅ

LEWIS A. COSER

Lewis Coser came to the U.S. from Germany in 1941. A Guggenheim and Fulbright Fellow, he is a prolific author and editor, has
published numerous works on sociology, and has co-authored a history of the American Communist party. A founding editor of the
journal, *Dissent*, Coser speaks from the standpoint of democratic
socialism. What specific factors accounted for the demise of communism in Western Europe? How does the author appear to distinguish democratic socialism from communism?

"Since the destruction of Nazi Germany," wrote Irving Howe and I
thirty years ago in the concluding chapter of our history of the American
Communist party, "Stalinism has been the only political movement able
to seize the initiative on a world scale. . . . [I]t succeeded in appropriat-
ing most of the social dynamism of the post-war world, so that both as a
system of power and as an ideology it soon came to be a dominant problem
of our time." How times have changed! Though our characterization
seems still correct for the period in which we wrote, it is completely
inapplicable to the current scene. In fact, communism in Western Europe

From Lewis Coser, "The Death Throes of Western Communism." This article first appeared
in *Dissent* magazine, Spring 1989.

and most probably elsewhere, rather than being an inspiring messianic movement, has now become a grotesque relic. The Soviet mortgage on the political life of Western Europe has been lifted.

The near demise of communism in all of Western Europe is a historic fact that current commentators have not yet fully appreciated. It is, in my view, as significant a feature of contemporary history as the rise and fall of Nazism in the thirties and forties or the impact of the Russian Revolution in the West after 1917.

In a Europe in almost permanent crisis between the two World Wars, Stalinism provided a faith for millions not only in the traditional working class and among white collar workers but also among disaffected and alienated intellectuals. It provided a challenge to the existing state of affairs and made possible devotion to a nonreligious social ideal. Stalinism attracted not only the worst but also some of the best among the disaffected. It was a corrupt movement that also inspired actions of unquestionably heroic character. Especially those of us who, as "premature anti-Communists" fought the inroads of Stalinism in the thirties and later, must recognize that it succeeded in attracting thousands upon thousands of selfless militants who, to use Ignazio Silone's phrase, were "in search of comrades," even though it also attracted cynical manipulators, power-intoxicated bureaucrats, and manipulative and ruthless commissars.

Stalinism did not gain majorities in the European working class in the interwar years, but it succeeded — in Weimar Germany, in France, in pre-Mussolini Italy — in recruiting significant minorities among the alienated. Some of the Stalinist recruits came from marginal lumpenproletarian strata, but others came from stable trade union backgrounds or from student and intellectual strata in which idealist devotion to the image of socialism mingled in various degrees with the perverse ambition of becoming Stalin's European "engineers of the human soul."

This is not the place to go into analytical detail about the differential impact of Stalinism at various periods and in various national societies. What needs to be retained is the fact that Stalinism in those years was a corrupt and deadly movement, which, all the same, managed to infuse vast numbers of members and fellow travelers with a large measure of devotion and readiness to sacrifice. Given its strictly hierarchical structure, Stalinism could attract the brutal callousness of the commissar as well as the sincere devotion of the rank-and-filer. It was indeed a corrupt

and corrupting enterprise but — and it is absolutely indispensable to recognize this if its impact is to be assessed — it also managed to capture the
idealism of large masses of people.

.   .   .

If this in bare outline is the phenomenology of the Stalinist movement before, during, and immediately after the Second World War, what
accounts for the current disarray of Western European communism?

It would be simplistic to argue that the amazing economic recovery
and growth of post–Marshall Plan economies was the root cause of the
decline of communism in Western Europe. Economic development was a
precondition but not a direct cause. What has happened in all of Western
Europe, though in unequal degrees, is that economic prosperity has allowed the emergence of a welfare state. This new type of social order has
succeeded in creating a sense of belongingness in large strata of the
population who previously had suffered from the stigma of exclusion. It
was not only the fact that the European worker now owned an automobile, a washing machine, a refrigerator, or that he could travel previously
unheard-of distances during his (guaranteed) vacation, or that he could
be sure that his children would have access to educational channels of
mobility that had not existed before. Above all, he no longer felt de-
meaned by the solid middle-class citizens who used to dominate the social
and political scene. In the mass society of the fifties and after, most social
strata, most of the time, felt at home. When they were moved to engage
in political actions, it was not because of existential despair but in terms
of concrete grievance. To be sure, this was not the case among students
and intellectuals, at least not to the same degree. That is probably why
the appeal of Stalinism often continued longer among them than in the
working class.

Generational differences are at least as important as class differences when it comes to explaining the demise of the communist parties
of Western Europe. Older cohorts of workers there may still include some
faithful, though ineffective, Stalinist types, but the young have turned
away from the party in massive proportions. The children of the television age and the consumer society see no reason to regard the Soviet
Union as a beacon of hope. They tend to see it as a backward society in
which even rock and roll has hardly begun to make an impact. The
membership statistics of all Western European communist parties show
a uniformly constant process of aging. The party, which for decades

claimed that it spoke for the young, that it would liberate youth from the yoke of the elders, has now largely become a party of the middle-aged and the elderly. The young look upon it as a somewhat comic relic of olden days.

. . .

Yet there is one European country, Italy, which seems to contradict what I have said. While all other Western communist parties have been in decline over the last several decades, the Italian CP is still a mass party with about two million members, even though it has lost votes in recent elections. It is by no means marginalized but is solidly ensconced in the political, social, and cultural scene. It controls major municipalities, regional governments, and infrastructural bodies, especially the strongest trade union federation. It is, all in all, an integral part of the socio-political life of Italy. The party has acquired power in all national political institutions except the national government. In some cities, for example in Bologna, it has run municipal affairs ever since 1945. Given these facts, should one not revise the description I have advanced above? I think not.

The Italian party has managed to survive in body only after losing its soul. It has nowadays none of the characteristics of a Leninist vanguard party. It is, in fact, simply a more effective social-democratic party than its competitors. This is truly a case of what Max Weber meant by the routinization of revolutionary charisma. The party controls book stores and newspapers, publishing houses, seminars, and special schools. There are few cooperatives, trade union locals, or local governments in which it is not represented. This means, of course, that it has fostered the rise of a bureaucracy utterly dependent on the party. These bureaucrats are in many instances pragmatic, passionless time-servers who can be trusted to perform their duties with honesty and with only a minimum of graft or nepotism. But to suggest that they could one day lead the masses in an insurrectionary march to power is sheer fantasy.

. . .

In the rest of Europe, the communist parties are by now negligible. This is so not only in England and Germany, but also in Sweden, Norway, Denmark, Austria, Belgium, and the Netherlands. In Spain the party is split into several independent factions. The French CP has lost all influences among intellectuals, lost control of many municipalities it once dominated, and managed to get only some 10 percent of the vote in recent elections. Communists are somewhat more influential in Finland and Greece, but this is due mainly to geography.

There is one fact that has not yet been sufficiently stressed when it comes to an assessment of the impact of the communist parties of the West for some six decades: The sheer tragic waste of the lives of millions who were diverted from their idealistic and even heroic dedication by the Stalinist commissars. Several generations of militants were deceived and their energies converted into the manipulated politics of the Comintern and its successors. Nothing like this has happened on the European scene since the horrid waste and deception by which Christian crusaders in the Middle Ages were made to serve the political and commercial aims of those who made the crusades into large-scale instruments of terror, rape and conquest. If I were asked to put into a sentence my evaluation of communism in the West I would say: It destroyed the idealistic dedication of millions. At the heart of this darkness was the physical destruction of millions in the Soviet Union and the moral destruction of other millions in the European West.

Let me now turn from the inner-European factors that have led to the decline of Western European communism to those developments in the Soviet Union that once fostered but now impede the efforts of Stalin and his successors to make Moscow into a third Rome. (It is too early to assess Gorbachev's impact among the remnants of Communist cadres.)

Beginning in the middle twenties, Stalin managed to consolidate his totalitarian grip at home while still fueling the myth of revolution abroad. Even during the monstrous show trials of the thirties and the collectivization of agriculture that cost millions of lives, Stalin managed to be widely portrayed in the West as the benevolent carrier of the hopes of mankind. Thousands of intellectuals and millions of ordinary men and women persisted in believing that Stalin represented a future that worked.

It is true that the majority of those who were attracted to the Communist parties during the thirties and later soon left them. In 1939, for example, only 3 to 4 percent of the members of the French Communist party were reported to have belonged for more than six years. Most members joined and left after a relatively brief stay. But a strong inner-party cadre stayed for very long periods, often through the rest of their lives. The devotion of these true believers compensated for the skin-deep involvement of most members and fellow travelers. Those who had undergone a true conversion clung to their faith with fanatical intensity, living in a mental universe so tightly organized that in good measure they frequently lost their sense of reality.

A friend who visited the Soviet Union in the late twenties in the company of some party militants told me that they had had a violent discussion on the train to Moscow about prostitution, the communists maintaining that prostitution had long come to an end in revolutionary Russia and my friend disputing this. As the visitors came to the lobby of their hotel they were accosted by several prostitutes. My friend there indicated to the others that he had won the argument, but they insisted he was totally mistaken. These young women were only friendly comrades volunteering to be their guides through the city.

In addition to the true believers the party also managed, especially during the days of the Popular Front, to attract fellow travelers who saw it as the only bulwark against advancing fascism. But such strategies became more difficult after the defeat of Nazism and fascism. Khrushchev's and Brezhnev's humdrum politics had less of an international appeal than Stalin's. Goulash communism was not attractive in a Europe that was well fed.

The myth of the heroic revolutionary Soviet Union persisted for a long time, all evidence to the contrary notwithstanding. But the faith of the committed began to decline with the Soviet suppression of the Hungarian revolution and the revelations about the Gulag. There is no need here to mention the impact of the writings of Solzhenitsyn and other Russian adversaries of the regime of terror. Still, I do not believe that all these acts of defiance, or the Czech revolt, or the Polish resistance before and after the emergence of Solidarity, would have led to so massive a decline of Western European communism had it not been that structural changes in postwar European societies undermined receptivity to the Stalinist appeal. In this respect, I am prepared to defend the thesis that developments in the infrastructure of European societies proved more potent in destroying the Soviet myth than any superstructural development. European consumer culture, mass society, and the welfare state were more fundamental than even Khrushchev's speech or Gorbachev's revelations in killing European communism.

The demise of European communism is one of the most significant events of the second half of the twentieth century. It is also, and above all, a new opportunity for the socialist and democratic left. It may yet offer a second chance to that left, although most social movements are not granted second chances once they have muffed their original opportunities. But it is too early to tell if the European socialist left will prove capable of seizing that chance.

If the socialist parties of Europe continue on their present course, the chances of their attracting new members and voters that have now turned away from their prior communist allegiances are very small indeed. Only a renewed socialist movement that tempers realistic policies with a renewal of social idealism and utopian vision can hope to profit from the disillusionment of former CP members, followers and sympathizers.

What Glasnost Has Destroyed

ᔍℒℴ

LEON ARON

Leon Aron was born in Moscow and emigrated to the United States in 1978. He holds a doctorate in sociology from Columbia University. For the past few years he has been the resident Sovietologist at the Heritage Foundation in Washington, D.C., a conservative public policy association. It is instructive to compare his view of Lenin with that of Medvedev (in Section 4). Both Aron and Coser refer to the destruction of long-standing myths about the Soviet Union. In what respects do the two writers nevertheless differ? How does Aron's view of the Bolshevik Revolution of 1917 differ from the views of Hough and Von Laue?

Soviet society is in a state of spiritual turmoil for which there is no precedent in its entire history. A comparison with the Khrushchev years is valid but insufficient: the passion, the bluntness, the consistency, and, most importantly, the depth and the scope of the upheaval under Mikhail Gorbachev go far beyond anything that happened between 1956 and 1964. For the diagnoses being made today no longer center on "individual distortions" and "shortcomings" (no matter how repugnant) but are directed instead at virtually the entire moral universe in which Soviet society functions and from which it derives its legitimacy. Indeed, this

Reprinted from *Commentary*, November 1989, by permission; all rights reserved. Permission also granted by the author.

assault far exceeds anything said or even thought by those who for decades have been branded by Soviet propaganda as "mad anti-Communists." It is a mood strikingly similar to the one that swept the Russian intelligentsia at the turn of this century: bitter disillusion, anger, radical nihilism, and dense fire aimed at the twin pillars of the *ancien régime* — Orthodoxy and absolutism — and it could well have a revolutionary outcome of its own.

What is "Soviet humanism"? asks one of the most popular Soviet film directors, Eldar Ryazanov, and answers: "Soviet humanism" inspired Pavlik Morozov to inform on his father; "Soviet humanism" sent Soviet prisoners of war from Nazi camps directly to the gulag; "Soviet humanism" locked artists in lunatic asylums or threw them out of the country for "dissidence."

The historian Yuri Afanasiev goes still further. In the pages of the Communist party paper, *Pravda* itself, he declares: "I do not consider our society socialist, even 'deformed' socialist, [because] these 'deformations' touch upon the very foundations, the political system, the system of the relations of production, and most certainly everything else." His vision of Soviet history is "millions of *zeks*" (political prisoners); "enslaved, robbed, hapless peasants"; the long-suffering Soviet people who undertook a "great revolution" only to be "deceived" and "humiliated," only to be drowned in "sixty years of nihilism, spiritual void, and decay," only to get a "socialism without freedom and without bread and butter."

Yet it is not just the utterly unprecedented scope of these no-holds-barred philippics that sets the current muckraking apart from any similar campaign in the past. Its most original and most dangerous feature is the precision with which the heavy artillery is targeted, and the depth of shell penetration. In Gorbachev's Soviet Union, almost every major legitimizing myth is being shattered.

Take, to begin with, the myth of "social protection" (*sotzialnaya zashishennost*). According to this idea, the Soviet state, while occasionally inferior to the capitalist West in the quantity and quality of consumer goods, shields its citizens from the ills of capitalism: hunger, poverty, disease, unemployment, crime, prostitution, and, following the latest Western trends, drugs and homelessness.

The debunking of this myth began early in the *glasnost* era with the simple acknowledgment that all these evils plague Soviet society as well. Then the formerly classified data started to pour forth—even as Soviet spokesmen, including Gorbachev himself, continued to tout "social protection" in front of Western audiences. (He did so with passion, for example, in his interview with NBC before the 1987 Washington summit and repeatedly during the summit.)

Of these formerly "capitalist" evils, the newly disclosed scale and depth of Soviet poverty, food shortages, inadequate medical care, and the housing crisis have been especially shocking. With the official poverty level set at 75 rubles per person per month ($1,413 a year by the official rate of exchange and $90 by the market rate), the Soviet people have been told that 43 million of their compatriots are under the poverty level and fully 40 percent of Soviet families (about 100 million people) live on less than 100 rubles a month. Pensioners are especially hard-pressed: every third urban senior citizen and eight out of ten villagers—over fifteen million people altogether—receive less than 60 rubles a month. (In case the Soviet reader needed help in understanding what living on 60 rubles a month means, the central government newspaper *Izvestia* published a letter from an unusually affluent pensioner who complained that she and her husband were unable to spend less than 150 rubles a month on food.) The handicapped are worse off still: an invalid woman with a child was reported to be living on 31 rubles and 48 kopecks a month. Contrary to the widespread belief that "in the Soviet Union no one goes hungry," the consumption of meat and dairy products by the Soviet poor has declined by 30 percent since 1970!

But hunger in the Soviet Union results not just from poverty alone. Another, peculiarly Soviet, cause of it is rationing, a detailed description of which has also been supplied. In the Kirov region of the Russian Northwest the ration cards allot 500 grams (slightly over a pound) of cooked sausage per person per month and 400 grams (less than a pound) of butter.

.   .   .

Nothing binds the rulers and the ruled, Communists and non-Communists alike, so tightly as the tragic, heroic myths of World War II, the Great Patriotic War. For over forty years, the official catechism has been simple and dependable: the Soviet Union, confronted with the prospect of an imminent Nazi invasion and betrayed by the West, which was conniving to deflect Hitler eastward, artfully bought time in 1939 by concluding a nonaggression pact with Germany. The Soviet scheme worked: the Nazi onslaught was postponed by two years, during which time the Soviet state strengthened its defenses, trained the army, and stockpiled material. Then, after initial setbacks caused by the surprise timing of the German invasion, the Soviet army vanquished the Nazi barbarians and liberated the world from the "brown plague." What is more, the Soviet Union did it all alone, with virtually no assistance from its allies; it succeeded because of the military genius of its marshals and the skill of its rank-and-file soldiers. (As Yevgeni Yevtushenko declared in his famous poem, "Do the Russians Want War?": "Yes, we know how to fight!")

Every element of this myth is under attack today in mainstream Soviet periodicals. The nonaggression pact has been labeled "one of the most tragic and shameful pages in our history" — no clever maneuver but, as far as the Soviet Union was concerned, a genuine and inexcusable treaty of friendship. A military historian reveals how, in the spirit of this friendship, the Soviets turned over German Communist refugees to the Gestapo. And for the first time in almost fifty years the Soviet people have been reminded of the statement made by Stalin's Foreign Minister Vyacheslav Molotov a week after the signing of the pact: "It is not only senseless but even criminal to wage a war to 'destroy Hitlerism' under the false banner of a struggle for 'democracy.'"

While the very existence of secret protocols contained in the nonaggression pact was officially denied by the Soviet Union until this past August, for over a year the myth-slayers had been pointing to actions taken in the wake of the pact which confirmed Western accounts of those protocols — most notably the division of Poland between the Soviet and Nazi occupation forces. As for the adroitness of the "maneuver" itself, it is now said to have allowed Germany to concentrate all its forces in the West, to defeat France, and then to throw against the Soviet Union not only its entire military might but the newly acquired resources of a conquered Europe. Furthermore, the Soviet press has now disclosed that Soviet deliveries of "military-strategic" materials to Germany in accordance with the terms of the nonaggression pact played "a not insignificant role" in strengthening the Nazi military-industrial potential.

Soviet military strategy in World War II is undergoing a thorough critique as well. As if in answer to Yevtushenko, another popular Soviet writer, Viktor Astafiev, who, unlike Yevtushenko, is a World War II veteran, has said: "We did not know how to fight. We ended the war not knowing how to fight. We drowned the enemy in our blood, we buried him under our corpses."

Finally, in perhaps the single most dramatic achievement of *glasnost* to date, the publication of Vasily Grossman's great novel *Life and Fate* has struck at the very foundations of the war mythology by explicitly, and repeatedly, bringing up the parallels between the two savage tyrannies, Hitler's and Stalin's, and by depicting the heroic, betrayed, and martyred Soviet people as being ground between these two giant, bloodstained millstones. Said a shell-shocked participant in a readers' discussion of Grossman's book: "We used to portray the war [as] 'there are Nazis and here are we. Darkness is there, goodness is here.' Grossman changed the proportion, portraying the two systems not only in their collision but also in their eerie historical similarity."

But more than anything else, what sets *glasnost* apart from all previous "thaws" is the willingness, and the ability, of the new iconoclasts to tackle the cluster of myths surrounding the Founding Fathers of the Soviet Union. Within two years, the wave of iconoclasm reached and passed the highest points of Khrushchev's de-Stalinization, to engulf even the previously sacrosanct Lenin himself.

Unlike their counterparts in Khrushchev's time, for the current generation of myth-hunters, brought up on *samizdat* copies of Solzhenitsyn's *The Gulag Archipelago*, the issue is not the "rehabilitation" of the Bolshevik leaders killed by Stalin — Kamenev, Zinoviev, Radek, Bukharin. While welcoming such "rehabilitation," the crusading Soviet scholars and journalists of today are in no hurry to make these old Bolsheviks into new icons. They are asking, instead, "How was Stalinism born, on what soil, and why?" And they are finding complicity in Stalinism on the part of the Founding Fathers, including those who opposed Stalin on this or that point.

.   .   .

The 1917 Bolshevik coup is beginning to be portrayed precisely as that — a coup. Replacing the glorious "Great October Socialist Revolution" there is now seen to be a gang of conspirators, "taken seriously by very few people," who "did not know how to solve the complicated problems of society but offered instead a set of very simple, primitive, understandable quasi-solutions."

The myth of the October Revolution was dealt another blow by the reprinting, for the first time since 1918, of Maxim Gorky's *Untimely Thoughts*, a classic denunciation of the horrors the Revolution had already then visited upon Russia. Although the passages directly attacking Lenin were censored out, the picture that emerges is one of "thousands, yes, thousands of people — workers and peasants — starving in prisons" and of "violence which is unworthy of democracy."

As the veil of lies is lifted from the crushing of the nascent Russian democratic state by the Bolsheviks, the Constituent Assembly of 1918 is beginning to receive sympathetic coverage as Russia's last hope for a parliamentary democracy. With increasing frequency, the dissolution of the Assembly after one session on January 18, 1918 is cited today as a precedent for a crackdown that could end the current "thaw" as well.

But what is potentially most damaging to the mythology of the Founding Fathers is the attack on the old moral justification of the Bolshevik terror. This justification was supplied by Lenin himself in a passage that generations of Soviet schoolchildren have had to memorize: "Our morality is completely subordinate to the interests of the class struggle of the proletariat. . . . In the foundation of Communist morality lies the struggle for the strengthening and completion of Communism."

An oblique yet unambiguous repudiation of this doctrine was published recently by the party's main theoretical journal *Kommunist*, which compared Lenin's "class morality" to the murderous "Catechism of the Revolutionary" of the 19th-century Russian terrorist Nechaev ("Everything is moral that expedites the triumph of the revolution"). Going even further, *Kommunist* also declared: "Once everything is evaluated from the point of view of some class, then there is no moral trial and no personal ethical responsibility."

To be sure, there are still limits. When, this past April [1989], in a now-famous TV interview, the theater director Mark Zakharov suggested that Lenin's embalmed body be removed from the mausoleum in Red Square and buried, the director of the State Committee for Television and Radio was fired and the late-night program which aired the interview was "temporarily" taken off the air for "renovation of the sets." Yet despite this rearguard action, the debunking of the Lenin myth will soon reach a double crescendo. First has come the publication in *Oktyabr* of Vasily Grossman's *Forever Flowing*, a loosely-jointed narrative from which Lenin emerges both as a theoretician of totalitarianism and as its first practitioner. As a labor-camp inmate in the book puts it: "Lenin began the business of strangling Russian democracy, Stalin finished it." Then there is *Novy Mir*'s serialization of Solzhenitsyn's *The Gulag Archipelago*, the first chapter of whose second volume lays the creation of concentration camps squarely at Lenin's door.

The vengeful filling-in of the "blank spaces" in Soviet history, combined with the loss of outright denial of any moral justification for what is now revealed to have happened, has produced a predictable result: people now question the legitimacy not just of parts of the Soviet record but of the Soviet regime itself. Incredibly, the rector of the Moscow State Institute of History and Archives now feels safe in stating that the Soviet regime "was brought into being through bloodshed, with the aid of mass murder and crimes against humanity" and that "one must admit Soviet history as a whole is not fit to serve as a legal basis for Soviet power."

The fall of the Founding Fathers may mark the final destination of the Soviet crusaders, beyond which lies a gaping void. Of course, the crusaders themselves are trying to fill the void with new icons, including genuinely religious ones. Thus, in a meeting with Lithuanian intellectuals last August, Aleksandr Yakovlev, the godfather of *glasnost*, several times invoked the term "repentance," while Maya Ganina, a columnist for *Literaturnaya Gazeta*, has called for "kindness and charity for Christ's sake" and the playwright Edvard Rodzinskiy has bemoaned the loss of the Bible, "the greatest book in the world," as a weapon to combat "the deficit of morality and culture." Among political models, the czarist Prime Minister Petr Stolypin (1862–1911) is currently much in vogue for his attempt to free the Russian peasant from the shackles of the commune and make him into a private farmer; the cult of Stolypin is likely to be given a powerful boost when Solzhenitsyn's *August 1914*, of which he is a hero, is published in the Soviet Union. And following Stolypin, it is safe to predict, will be Alexander II, the czar (1855–81) who abolished serfdom and introduced political reforms that set Russia on the road to capitalism and constitutional monarchy.

As for the orthodox, they are fighting desperate rearguard battles to salvage whatever is left of the legitimizing mythology. Their spokesman, the Politburo member Yegor Ligachev, declares that "the facts of unjustified [sic] repressions" must not "overshadow the feat of the people who created the powerful socialist state." After all, Ligachev points out, in the 1930s the country became second in the world in overall industrial output, while in the much maligned 1970s "national income" increased four times and "military-strategic parity" was achieved with the U.S.

Yet all such attempts to restock the Soviet pantheon with old gods are likely to fail: once declared naked, idols are even less usable than kings. Of all the much-commented-upon contradictions embedded in Gorbachev's reforms, this is without doubt the deadliest: having set out to create a reformed one-party state socialism "with a human face," Gorbachev has unleashed forces that are methodically destroying the legitimacy of any such future arrangement. No economic reform, no amount of Western good will, even if concretized with massive transfusions of capital and technology, and no brilliant foreign-policy stratagems can hope to fill this spiritual vacuum.

And so the question is: what rough beast, its hour come round at last, slouches toward Moscow to be born?

Post-Communist Nationalism

ᘰᖾ

ZBIGNIEW BRZEZINSKI

Zbigniew Brzezinski has already been introduced as one of the authors of the readings on the Nazis. Here he discusses the threatened unraveling of such East-Central European countries as Yugoslavia and Czechoslovakia and of course the Soviet Union itself, specifically how the sight of Poles and Czechs and Hungarians going their own way could fuel separatist sentiment among Lithuanians, Georgians, and other Soviet minorities just as the dismantling of one-party states in East Germany and Hungary could encourage similar expectations in the Soviet Union — probabilities that have hardened into realities since this article appeared. What might be the consequences of the USSR becoming a "volcano" and a "battleground" of warring nationalities?

The time has come for the West to confront as a policy issue a problem that for years most Western scholars have tended to ignore and that all Western policymakers still consider to be taboo: the rising tide of nationalism in Eastern Europe and especially in the Soviet Union itself. This long-dormant issue is now becoming, in a dynamic and conflictual fashion, the central reality of the once seemingly homogeneous Soviet world. Indeed, whereas Marx once described the tsarist Russian empire as the prison of nations, and Stalin turned it into the graveyard of nations, under Gorbachev the Soviet empire is rapidly becoming the volcano of nations.

Until recently, the West preferred to downplay the reality of East European national aspirations and to downgrade the implications of non-Russian national awareness within the Soviet Union. Moreover, most Westerners perceived the Soviet Union as identical with Russia and assumed almost automatically that any Soviet citizen was a Russian. This has now changed. National conflicts have ruptured the illusion of communist brotherhood and the mirage of some sort of supra-ethnic Soviet nationhood. Henceforth, the ongoing crisis of communism within the once homogeneous Soviet bloc is likely to define itself through increased national assertiveness and even rising national turmoil. In fact, there is a high probability that the progressing self-emancipation of the East European nations and the growing sense of national distinctiveness among the non-Russian nations of the Soviet "Union" will soon make the existing Soviet bloc the arena for the globe's most acute national conflicts.

None of this should be construed as a lament for communism. Its fading is a liberation for those who have had to live under its stultifying and dehumanizing regime. Moreover, though it proclaimed itself to be a doctrine of internationalism, communism in fact intensified popular nationalist passions. It produced a political culture imbued with intolerance, self-righteousness, rejection of social compromise and a massive inclination toward self-glorifying oversimplification. On the level of belief, dogmatic communism thus fused with and even reinforced intolerant nationalism; on the level of practice, the destruction of such relatively internationalist social classes as the aristocracy or the business elite further reinforced the populist inclination toward nationalistic chauvinism. Nationalism was thereby nurtured, rather than diluted, in the communist experience.

As the communist veneer now fades and nationalism surfaces more assertively, the time is thus becoming ripe for the West to define more deliberately its interests. What sort of Eastern Europe do we wish to see emerge from Soviet domination? Is the secession of some or all non-Russian nations from the Soviet Union something that the West ought to encourage? Should we discriminate in that regard between the various Soviet nations? How should we react if the Kremlin again adopts a more repressive attitude toward non-Russians? What should be our attitude toward Great Russian nationalism, especially as it too becomes more openly assertive? What are the international strategic and economic implications of these issues? How does all this relate to our commitment to the cause of human rights?

.　　.　　.

Moreover, all these states have borders that are potentially subject to revisionist aspirations on the part of their neighbors. Poland has a lingering, though not acute, territorial grievance against Czechoslovakia, and Poland itself could be the object of German territorial revanchism. Already in the 1980s, a sharp dispute developed over the maritime border between the communist governments of Poland and the German Democratic Republic, including access to the Polish port of Szczecin. In addition, possible countervailing territorial claims exist between Poland and its currently Soviet neighbors to the east: Lithuania, Byelorussia and the Ukraine. Czechoslovakia and Hungary also harbor some resentments over the treatment of their respective national minorities living within the other's frontiers, and these could mushroom into border disputes.

Much more serious and potentially even explosive is the openly antagonistic Hungarian-Romanian dispute over Transylvania, currently a part of Romania but once part of the Austro-Hungarian Empire and inhabited by several million Hungarians who have been oppressed by the dominant Romanians. Romania, in turn, has historical claims against the Soviet Ukraine over Bessarabia and against Soviet Moldavia, and a potential one against Bulgaria over the Black Sea region of Dobruja. To complete the circle, Bulgaria nurtures national ambitions regarding Yugoslavia's Macedonia. Yugoslavia in the meantime has a rapidly growing and increasingly restless Albanian majority in the region of Kosovo, which itself could soon become the object of Albanian irredentism.

This mosaic of unsatisfied territorial desires and of national antagonisms — in itself not necessarily more complex than that of many other parts of the world, including Western Europe — is aggravated by the historical immaturity of Eastern Europe's nationalisms. While most of the region's nations are historical entities, with some legitimately boasting national histories comparable to those of any of the West European nations, Eastern Europe's nationalisms still tend to be more volatile, more emotional and more intense than those in the West. Moreover, the separate East European national states lack the tempering experience of genuine regional cooperation that in recent decades has emerged in

Western Europe, starting with the Marshall Plan, continuing with the European Coal and Steel Community and eventually maturing into the supranational European Community, with its region-wide elections to the European Parliament.

Instead, while under Soviet domination and even while their regimes proclaimed fidelity to an allegedly internationalist doctrine, the East European states developed their economies and consolidated their political systems as hermetically sealed national entities. Moscow permitted no real economic cooperation among them. Polish-Czechoslovak plans, developed during World War II, for a genuine federation between the two states were scuttled by the Kremlin, as was the postwar initiative by the communist leaders Tito and Georgi Dimitrov for a confederation between Yugoslavia and Bulgaria. Instead, all lines of cooperation ran vertically to Moscow, not horizontally among the regional states. The Warsaw Pact and the Council for Mutual Economic Assistance served essentially as instruments of Soviet control.

Otherwise, each state was strictly isolated from its neighbors. Barbed-wire fences separated communist states as much from one another as they did from the ideologically alien West. Travel was strictly controlled, and so was the flow of press and of educational exchanges. Bilateral economic cooperation was also discouraged in favor of national economic autarky, the latter only restrained by the policy of promoting some degree of economic dependence on the Soviet Union. With Moscow encouraging each state to cultivate both its official ideology and its distinctive nationalism, under Soviet domination East European nationalisms were further intensified and in some cases even warped into chauvinism.

The threat of Balkanization of the region as it emancipates itself from Soviet control is thus real. Economically retarded by the communist experiment, with narrow chauvinism intensified, Eastern Europe is faced with the prospect of internal and external strife as it gropes its way back to a closer relationship with the Western Europe it has always admired. That danger need not express itself in a replay of the old Balkan wars, but can do so through acute ethnic violence, local national clashes and even territorial collisions. The Albanian-Serb confrontations in Kosovo and the Hungarian-Romanian tensions over Transylvania could be portents of wider things to come. In brief, the de-Sovietization of Eastern Europe is not likely to be automatically tantamount to the peaceful expansion of all-European cooperation, with the European Community serving as the model.

These dangers pale in significance compared to the growing prospect of truly intense and potentially quite bloody international strife within the Soviet Union. Its various non-Russian nationalisms are less fulfilled and thus even more emotionally charged than those of Eastern Europe, in some cases with less historically defined borders and yet with even more commingling of potentially hostile peoples. Moreover, any attempt by Moscow to satisfy the desires of the historically more recognized nations — notably the Baltic ones, which have been contagiously influenced by developments in Poland — is likely to precipitate claims from newer national aspirants for equal treatment.

The scale and complexity of the Soviet national problem is striking. Of the Soviet Union's 290 million people, roughly 145 million are Great Russians. The other 145 million — who soon will outnumber the Russians because of more rapid demographic growth — are dispersed among 14 main nations with their own so-called Soviet republics, accounting for approximately 120 million of the 145 million non-Russians. Another hundred minor ethnic groupings have been organized or reorganized in a variety of autonomous republics or national regions. Complicating the picture further — and representing a potential time bomb for truly violent national feuding — is the fact that about 25 million Great Russians live scattered among the non-Russians, and more than 40 million non-Russians live outside their ethnic territories. These "outsiders," who number more than 65 million combined, represent the potential precipitating cause, as well as the likely victims, of any large-scale national strife.

Indeed, not a single non-Russian nation in the Soviet Union exists without significant intermingling of Russian or some other ethnic minority. In some, the major potential line of conflict runs vertically — against the Great Russian Kremlin and its local Russian settlers. That is the case, for example, with Estonia (with its population 25 percent Russian), Latvia (30 percent Russian), Kirghizia (also 30 percent Russian) and Kazakhstan (60 percent Russian or Ukrainian), and potentially the Ukraine (about 20 percent Russian). In others, the lines of conflict tend to be more horizontal — either against some other non-Russian minority (as with the Georgian animus toward the Abkhazians) or against a neighboring Soviet nation (as with the strife between Armenia and

Azerbaijan, each of which has significant minorities from the other). In others still, the lines of conflict are likely to be both vertical and horizontal, as is the case in central Asia, where considerable commingling exists among local ethnic groups and Slavic settlers.

Moreover, quite unintentionally, the Soviet regime has created institutional vessels that now can be easily filled with nationalist content. The Soviet political structure has consisted for decades of allegedly sovereign republics, each even enjoying the right to secede from the Soviet Union (although, under Stalin, communist non-Russian leaders were quite often shot for allegedly planning to avail themselves of this "constitutional" option). In fact, offsetting that formal structure was the real system of centralized power, located in Moscow and wielded largely by Great Russians, reinforced by a doctrine of Soviet "nationhood" based on the Russian language and history. Nonetheless, the fictional political structure of separate national republics continued throughout the Stalinist era; a political framework for the eventual expression and then assertion of ethnic aspirations was, therefore, ready and waiting for the day of national awakening.

That time arrived with Mikhail Gorbachev's *demokratizatsia* and perestroika. Gorbachev's realization that the Soviet system could not be revitalized without a significant decentralization of economic decision-making and without a broader democratization of the political system inherently meant that the national units would have to be endowed with greater authority. That automatically created an opportunity for long-suppressed national grievances to surface and for national aspirations to focus on the quest for effective control over the potentially significant local instruments of power. Hence, again quite unintentionally, Gorbachev's emphasis on greater legality — so necessary to the revival of the Soviet economy — gave the non-Russians a powerful weapon for contesting Moscow's control over their destiny.

.   .   .

Five broad stages can be discerned in the expanding process of non-Russian national awakening and growing self-assertion. In the first stage, nationalism typically has tended to focus on demands for the preservation in some significant fashion of the national language, which represent an almost instinctive desire for national self-preservation from progressive Russification. In the second stage, initial success in linguistic self-preservation then normally generates a wider insistence on the promotion of distinctive national cultural autonomy. In the third, this prompts demands for national economic self-determination. In the fourth, the foregoing combination then quite naturally fosters a struggle for national political autonomy. In the fifth, non-Russian nationalism is but a step away from openly proclaimed dreams of national sovereignty.

Generalizing boldly, the politically aroused proples in the Baltic republics, independent between the end of World War I and 1940, and in Georgia, a historical kingdom prior to the nineteenth century and briefly independent from 1918 until 1923, are now moving from the fourth to the fifth stage. The extremely important Ukraine, which numbers more than 50 million people, has at least reached the second stage, though political winds in Kiev and especially in Lvov point clearly toward the fourth and beyond. Byelorussia and Moldavia are still in the first or second stage. Most of the Soviet central Asian republics — with their Islamic self-confidence heightened by the Soviet debacle in neighboring Afghanistan — are moving from the third stage into the fourth.

In all of the non-Russian republics, however, national passions are being unleashed. Russification is being openly denounced — occasionally in turbulent demonstrations — in literally every non-Russian republic. National-minded elites who do not hide their desire for eventual sovereignty already dominate the Baltic republics politically. Most of the other republics are experiencing similar pressures from below, generated largely by their national intelligentsias. Moreover, intense interethnic violence has also broken out in hundreds of localities, with some thousands killed in communal clashes. It has been officially admitted that hundreds of thousands of refugees have fled national persecution, with, for instance, 350,000 Armenians and Azerbaijanis made homeless by national strife. In all likelihood, the problem will get worse, rather than better.

The national issue has become the central dilemma of Soviet political life, overshadowing even the economic crisis. It affects and vastly complicates almost every dimension of the political and economic perestroika. It expresses itself in a variety of ways. It manifests itself — as in the Baltic republics — in the peaceful constitutional struggle for the devolution of power from Moscow and even in unilateral legislation mandating the termination of central control over national resources. It explodes periodically — as in Kazakhstan's Alma Ata in 1986 or Georgia's Tbilisi in 1989 — into violence directed at Great Russian domination, with strong overtones of a national liberation struggle against the foreign "occupiers." It takes the form — as in Armenia, Azerbaijan, Georgia, Uzbekistan and elsewhere — of bloody interethnic pogroms, unleashing the most primitive passions. And it infects those scores of smaller peoples who do not even have their own nominal Soviet republics, prompting further demands for the national diversification of what is rapidly becoming the Soviet "Disunion."

Last but by no means least, all of the foregoing is made even more combustible by the extensive commingling of the Russians and non-Russians. With some 65 million people living outside their ethnic homelands and thus in potentially hostile environments, the grim possibility has been placed on history's agenda that Russia's empire, Marx's "prison of nations," could now spin out of control, becoming a battlefield of nations.

Such an outcome would be particularly ominous for the Great Russians. Their empire has expanded over the last several hundred years at a rate equivalent to approximately one Vermont (or Holland) per year. In the process, Russia has become the world's largest and — until now — most enduring multinational empire, controlling by far the largest piece of global real estate. Yet for the foreseeable future, the Great Russians now face the unpleasant dilemma that either a policy of repression of non-Russians or a policy of acquiescent passivity poses an acute threat to their own well-being.

To complicate matters even further, a painful nexus exists between the challenge of East European nationalism and the escalating aspirations of the Soviet non-Russians. The Kremlin would not find it easy to separate a policy of domestic repression of non-Russians from a policy of toleration for the East European nationalisms. It would be even more difficult to continue the domestic perestroika while engaging in repression of the non-Russian half of the Soviet population. Indeed, much of the recent national self-assertion within the Soviet Union was stimulated by the successful precedents set by Solidarity and the Catholic Church in Poland. Repression of non-Russian nationalism within the Soviet Union, combined with toleration of it within the Soviet sphere in Eastern Europe, would mean that the external contagion would persist, with the emboldened Poles and Hungarians publicly voicing their support for the suppressed non-Russians, and perhaps with such Soviet "allies" providing political beachheads for continued national agitation within the Soviet Union.

Thus a domestic crackdown would require some turning of the screws in Eastern Europe, even if short of direct intervention. Any such effort would entail real costs, political and economic. Moscow would have to channel its energies and resources into intimidating and bribing the East Europeans, and would have to do so without precipitating highly disruptive outbreaks in the region itself. And the last thing the Kremlin could now wish would be a conjunction of East European and internal Soviet national disorders.

The domestic consequences of the physical suppression of the non-Russians would also entail high costs. A policy of repression would have to be based on intensified Great Russian chauvinism. That, in turn, would breed even more widespread anti-Russian sentiments. Moreover, any attempt at reimposition of centralized Muscovite control would be met with political and perhaps even physical resistance. The non-Russians are no longer the pliant and illiterate people colonized by the tsars or the decapitated victims of Stalinism. They now have their own national intelligentsias and their own aroused students and, above all, their own awakened sense of national identity.

Repressive measures would require severe enforcement. That would be likely to jeopardize any serious pursuit of economic decentralization. As a practical matter, effective repression would require enhanced concentration of political power in Moscow, and that would not be compatible with continued economic decentralization. Since even the most modest scenarios of a successful perestroika hinge on enhanced economic activity, especially among the non-Russians, some of whom are the most productive contributors to the Soviet economy, it follows that domestic repression would simply kill perestroika. In effect, repression to preserve the empire would require self-abnegation by the Great Russians. They would have to forsake any dreams of greater democratization and of enhanced prosperity for themselves. The brutal fact is that their empire can be maintained only as an impoverished Great Russian national garrison state.

.   .   .

The specter that haunts the Russians in the Kremlin is that of nationalism — both within the Soviet Union and in Eastern Europe. The only constructive response to that condition is for the Russian people to be given the opportunity to shed their messianic complexes — either that of a Third Rome or of some "internationalist" Leninist mission — and to accommodate themselves to the necessity of coequal cohabitation with other nations. After three hundred years of almost continuous expansion, but now increasingly showing symptoms of imperial fatigue, the Russian people would be the principal beneficiaries of such a change in their national ethos.

The West can help especially the Russians at this crucial historical juncture by not only articulating positive visions of a confederated but nonthreatening Germany, of a regionally more cooperative Eastern Europe engaged in all-European institutions, and of a post-imperial Russia within a Soviet Confederation, but also by indicating its readiness to assist very tangibly the translation of such visions into a mutually beneficial reality. Over the years, the West has propagated pluralism, democracy and the market system as the superior social combination — while the Soviet propagandists derided these notions. Yet today these ideas dominate even the Soviet discussions of perestroika. Similarly, the West should now take the lead in advocating open and voluntary confederational arrangements as the only solution to the potentially lethal challenges of nationalism in the emerging post-communist era.